Michigan Ghost Towns

Of the Upper Peninsula

(formerly Michigan Ghost Towns, Vol. III)

Thunder Bay Press

Holt, Michigan

Michigan Ghost Towns
of the Upper Peninsula

Published by
Thunder Bay Press
Holt, Michigan 48842

Sixth Printing 1996
Seventh Printing 2002
Eighth Printing 2007

ISBN 10: 0-934884-02-1
ISBN 13: 978-0-934884-02-0

FSC
Mixed Sources
Product group from well-managed
forests and other controlled sources

Cert no. SW-COC-002283
www.fsc.org
© 1996 Forest Stewardship Council

Printed in the United States of America

About the Author

Born at Lansing, Mich., Nov. 11,1918, a descendant of Michigan pioneers, Dodge started investigating Michigan ghost towns in 1954. A member of several Michigan historical and genealogical societies, Mr. Dodge is a well-known free-lance writer and many of his articles about ghost towns and logging in Michigan have appeared in leading newspapers in the State and several magazines.

In addition to writing his family history book, published in 1967, he also authored a series about northern Michigan towns published in the Bay City Times from 1968 to 1970. This is his third book in a series about Michigan ghost towns. Volume I was published in 1970, and Volume II in 1971.

Dedication

This book is dedicated to the natives of "God's Country," Michigan's Upper Peninsula, many of them descendants of the French fur traders, *courouers de bois*, and pioneers from many nations of the world who made this beautiful peninsula truly the melting pot of all nations.

Roy L. Dodge
1972

Acknowledgments

To compile a book of this type would be impossible without the cooperation and assistance of literally hundreds of people. Most of the research for compiling the history of these former towns and places was conducted at the Michigan State Library in Lansing, the State Archives Records Depository in Lansing and from my private library of more than 100 books and booklets about Michigan and many maps dating back to the early 1800s.

I also spent several months and drove more than 6,000 miles in the Upper Peninsula, interviewing many old-time residents and local historians, visiting many of the sites described in this book, and took more than 500 photos of ghost towns, historical sites, buildings and plaques.

As in any historical work there is a margin for error. Most dates in these volumes are taken from Michigan Legislative Manuals from the years 1877 through 1970, and Michigan Gazeteer and Business Directories from various years (1872-1927). Other dates are taken from courthouse records, newspaper accounts of the period, original plat maps, historical societies of the Upper Peninsula, Centennial books, and from interviews with people who were living when the events occurred.

Although it is impossible to mention all the people interviewed and those who wrote letters giving information about local areas in response to queries, and others who provided information, I want to thank Paul Ott, Jr., of Mt. Clemens, Mich., fellow historian and mentor; Kenneth Priestly, of Vassar; Geneva Wiskemann, Dennis R. Bodem, Donald Cahput, and other good people at the State Archives in Lansing; James Borski, free-lance writer with the Menominee County Historical Museum; Paul Petosky, of Ishpeming; James E. Kent and personnel of Fayette State Park; Grace Engel, of Bark River; G. Harold Earle, of the Wisconsin Land & Lumber Co., Hermansville; Nick Illnicki, of the Marquette Historical Society; Karl Menge, of the L'Anse Sentinel; Hugh P. Beattie, of Houghton; James A. McDonald, of Calumet; G. Walton Smith, historian of Lake Linden; Victor F. Lemmer, past president of the Michigan Historical Society, Ironwood; A. L. Paulson, Calumet; The Calumet Division of Calumet & Hecla, Inc.; and hundreds of other nice people of the Upper Peninsula without whose assistance this book would have been impossible.

Others who assisted are given credit along with their contribution as it appears in the book. My humble apologies to people not mentioned, and a special thanks to the County Clerks of each Upper Peninsula county who sent maps and information for this book. Also to the editors and staff of many newspapers for their cooperation and assistance during my several trips to the Upper Peninsula.

Introduction

Very little has been written about Michigan ghost towns. This series of books is the first ever published on the subject. Ghost towns are usually thought of as being located in the far West, where actually very few ghost towns exist compared to the thousands of abandoned towns and locations that dotted Michigan maps of the late 1800s and early 1900s. Towns along the hundreds of miles of railroads and mining locations of the Upper Peninsula in 1905 appear almost as hundreds of fly specs on maps and are barely legible under a strong magnifying glass.

Upper Peninsula ghost towns differ from lower Michigan sites in that many of the abandoned houses and buildings still stand, even though many are more than 100 years old, while most lower Michigan ghost town sites are more difficult to locate and have reverted to nature. The Upper Peninsula, especially in the western and northern counties, has so far escaped the ravages of civilization common to lower Michigan, due to the remoteness of many areas. It is possible that modern-day ecologists and an ecology-minded generation may do something to preserve the beauty and natural surroundings of this last frontier of Michigan remaining in the 20th century.

It now seems impossible that the scars left on much of the country from mining will ever be erased. However, little evidence remains of the logging days when much of the peninsula was ravaged by logging the virgin timber. These scars have been healed by nature, now bearing vast stands of second-growth timber that is harvested only as it matures.

The Upper Peninsula is still an example of small-town America. People everywhere are friendly and here families still sit on their front porches on a warm evening and sleep easily at night without bolting their doors in fear of burglars ransacking their homes. It is a place where people stop to pass the time of day on the street, stand in long lines, even in the smallest communities, to attend church services on Sunday, and where fishermen, mine workers, and laborers of the woods and farms gather at the corner tavern on Saturday and discuss the week's accomplishments or failures, argue pro and con about the merits of the Conservation Department (Department of Natural Resources) and its impact on the fishing industry of the Great Lakes, regulation of deer hunting, diversion of streams for industry, etc.

Even though "Big Mack" bridged the land of the upper and lower peninsulas of Michigan, many residents, especially west of Manistique and Marquette, feel more a part of Wisconsin than of their own state. Most wholesale supplies come from Wisconsin and many people drive to its large cities, such as Green Bay, to do their shopping as these places are closer than the nearest metropolitan areas in lower Michigan.

When it was first publicized that this book was being written, many residents wrote letters saying that the people of the Upper Peninsula feel neglected as most history books give little or no recognition to their territory which is attached by land to Wisconsin and by decree to Michigan.

Although written primarily as a guide to long forgotten ghost towns, this book also relates an accurate history of hundreds of areas in the Upper Peninsula of which little or nothing has ever been written about in books.

Historians have not agreed on the definition of a "ghost town" and neither have most people. While looking for ghost towns in the Whitefish Bay area we stopped at a tavern in Paradise and the conversation went something like this:

"Do you know of any ghost towns around here?"

The bartender replied, *"No, I haven't been here long, but you might ask that man at the end of the bar. He was born here."*

After introductions, which attracted raised eyebrows and stares from the half-dozen natives present, the native said, *"No. There ain't no ghost towns around here."*

"How about Shelldrake?"

"That's no ghost town. Some guy from down below bought it and now he and his family live there."

"Wasn't a town named Emerson in this area?"

"Yeah. That was just below here next to the river, but it's no ghost town either. There ain't nothing left but a trail and a couple of flowing wells."

Webster's Dictionary defines a "ghost" as, *"A faint, shadowy semblance; inkling; slight trace."* This is the definition I have used to determine ghost towns in this book.

We hope the readers enjoy following the old railroad grades and back roads of the Upper Peninsula as much as the author has enjoyed the monumental job of compiling it and will forgive any errors that may creep in or escape the eye of the proof reader in the printing of this book.

Table of Contents

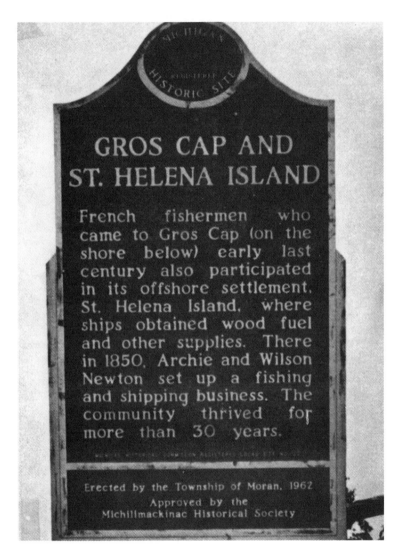

GROS CAP AND ST. HELENA ISLAND

French fishermen who came to Gros Cap (on the shore below) early last century also participated in its offshore settlement, St. Helena Island, where ships obtained wood fuel and other supplies. There in 1850, Archie and Wilson Newton set up a fishing and shipping business. The community thrived for more than 30 years.

Erected by the Township of Moran, 1962
Approved by the
Michillmackinac Historical Society

Along the shores of the Great Lakes many fishermen were early settlers and many fishing villages of early days are now ghost towns. This historical plaque is located near lake Michigan and US-2.   Photo by Roy L. Dodge (1971)

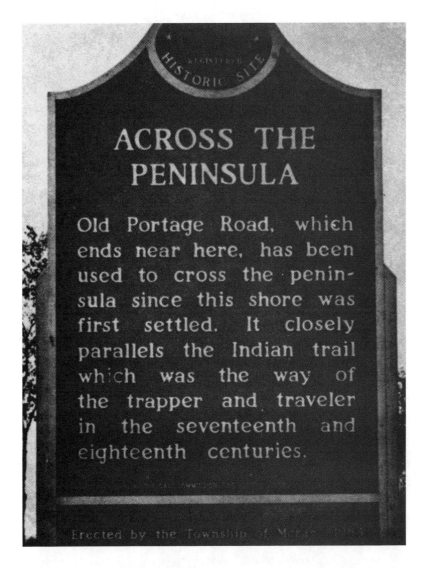

First the home of the Indian, then came the fur traders and missionaries, pioneers of the Upper Peninsula. This historical plaque is located near lake Michigan and US-2. Photo by Roy L. Dodge (1971)

Unlike lower Michigan ghost towns, many houses in Upper Peninsula ghost towns remain standing. Some of them, such as this house at Central Mine in the Keweenaw Peninsula, are 100 years old.   Photo by Roy L. Dodge (1971)

Chapter One

SETTLEMENT OF THE UPPER PENINSULA

The first permanent settlement in Michigan, of which there exists any authentic account, was at *Sault de Ste. Marie* in 1668 under the direction of Jacques Marquette, a Jesuit priest of France. *Mackinac* was settled shortly after and *Detroit* was settled in 1701.

These settlements were primarily military, supporting French claims to sovereignty. To a lesser degree they were speculative, as depots and trading posts for the fur trade carried on with Indians; and finally missionary, the points from which the Jesuit fathers extended their efforts for the conversion of the aborigines to Christianity. Agriculture was very little thought of, only by necessity.

In 1760, with the fall of *Quebec*, the Canadas (upper and lower) and all the French possessions in the Northwest fell into the hands of Great Britain by the Treaty of Paris, ratification February 10, 1763. Michigan continued under English rule until after the American Revolution. On July 1, 1796, Michigan formally passed into the possession of the United States and became a part of the Northwest Territory. At that time all Michigan from *Mackinac* to *Detroit* was an unbroken wilderness, inhabited only by Indians.

In 1800, the Northwest Territory was divided into two territories, one retaining the name "Northwest Territory," the other receiving the name "Indiana Territory." The former embraced the eastern half and the latter the western half of Michigan, the north and south dividing line passing a few miles west of *Mackinac*.

The first government land surveys were made in 1816. In 1818, by proclamation of the President, these lands were put on the market. From this event dates the permanent settlement of Michigan. In 1819 William Woodbridge became the first delegate to Congress for the Territory and held office for four years. In 1818 Illinois was admitted as a state. Wisconsin, previously part of the Illinois Territory, was annexed to Michigan.

Wayne was the only county formed from 1796 to 1817. Monroe, Macomb and Michilimackinac were organized in 1818 along with Brown and Crawford, which comprised territory now within the state of Wisconsin.

In his message to the Legislative Council in 1829 Governor Cass spoke of the Territory as being in a very prosperous condition. Immigrants to lower Michigan were pouring in freely, and eight new counties were organized in that year, all in lower Michigan.

By 1830 there were 24 counties, 15 of which had been organized. The central parts of the Territory were reached mainly by Indian trails while waterways were the only access to the Upper Peninsula. A government road had been surveyed from *Detroit* to *Chicago* and was partly cleared.

In the Upper Peninsula, settlement was discouraged in the early days by the fur trading companies as they wanted no disruption of the forests or Indian settlements, their main source of the much-valued peltries.

Immigrants were slow to penetrate the wilderness of northern Michigan and make it their home. As late as 1810 the population was estimated at only 4,783 (whites), and all commerce was confined to fur trade and to carrying a few supplies for the garrison at *Detroit.*

During the English regime, the English Lord Commissioners declared it was in the interest of those carrying freight and passengers on the Great Lakes to downgrade Michigan lands and to eulogize Illinois and Wisconsin. As late as 1859, Horace Greely, in the *New York Tribune*, spoke of the northern peninsula as *"cold and uninviting to the cultivator, diversified by vast swamps, sterile, gravelly knolls, and dense forests."*

But if the French and English had discouraged settlement, the Yankee made no effort in that direction. Instead, he put forth every effort to persuade the red men to give up their hunting grounds, as shown by various treaties with the Indians, whereby the white men soon controlled all the remaining lands in Michigan.

The War of 1812 brought a change of spirit. During the struggle, men had penetrated into the wilds of the region and come to realize the interior was not as bad as had been depicted by the fur companies and early surveyors. This change of attitude is shown in an editorial printed in the *Detroit Gazette* of January, 1822. After eulogizing the settler and stating his purpose, it continued: *"Compared with these objects, the advantages to be reaped from the fur trade dwindle to nothing. Surely, it is of more consequence to a nation that a wilderness and solitary place should be cultivated, than that it should be permitted to remain in a state of nature."*

There was one obstacle in the way of transforming this wilderness into cultivated fields, and that was the original owner, the Indian. He claimed as his property the hunting ground which the Yankee trader had almost despoiled of its wild animals. It was here that the influence of the old trader was brought into service. He was largely instrumental in inducing the Indians to cede large tracts of land to the government. In 1807, the region around *Detroit* was turned over to the United States, with the stipulation that as long as it remained government property the Indian should have the privilege of hunting and fishing there. Then followed the treaty of Sault Ste. Marie in 1820, the Chicago treaties of 1821 and 1833 and the Washington treaty in 1836. Finally by the treaty of LaPointe in 1842, the last strip of Indian land in Michigan passed into the hands of the U. S. government. Government possession meant the influx of settlers, and the influx of settlers meant the death blow to the Indian fur trade.

Immediately after the War of 1812, the American Fur Company established five fur trading posts in the Upper Peninsula, one near present day *L'Anse* on Keweenaw Bay, one near *Bay Mills* and one at *Menominee*, with headquarters at *Sault Ste. de Marie*, where John Jacob Astor placed John Johnston in charge. These could be considered the first white settlements in the peninsula, temporary as they were.

The licenses granted to traders stipulated that if any liquor was furnished to the Indian without special authority, the latter might confiscate the goods as well as any liquor kept on hand by the traders. This was a difficult rule to enforce, and if it was a problem to enforce liquor laws in the early regime, it became doubly so when the settlers' cabins began to dot the wilderness for the liquor law extended only to the red man's country and did not affect regions where the Indian's title to land had been extinguished. If the Indian could not get his drinks from the pale-face trader, he could visit the hut of the immigrant, who was bound neither by license stipulation nor by laws of the Indian country.

The decline in the fur trade was felt sooner at *Detroit* than farther inland. Already in 1827, before some of the interior trading posts had been established, Astor wrote to Crooks that he planned sending Clupp to *Detroit* to see what could be done about closing up the business at that place. This did not meet the approval of Crooks. He held that to abandon *Detroit* would leave the field open to their competitors who would lose no time in trying to hamper and annoy their northern agencies. He advised Astor to keep an agent there to at least hold the enemy in check. That was all he could do. There was no hope of making any money in the fur trade at that post much longer.

In 1854, the American Fur Company was bought out by J. B. Hubbel of *St. Paul*, Minnesota, and all its effects at *Michilimackinac* were removed. This was

3

the final blow to the Michigan fur trade. Long before this, a large number of the inland posts had been abandoned, and the men who had been prominent in this frontier commerce had either wandered westward with the Indians, died or sought other fields of labor. The removal of the company from *Michilimackinac* meant not only the destruction of his post as a great center of trade, but it meant the fall of numerous interior posts not already abandoned. It meant, for all practical purposes, Michigan's fur trading days were over. While the 1840 census reports record a sale of $54,232 worth of fur, in 1850 no sales are mentioned and only 33 men are listed as fur traders. The trading regime had passed away and the roving trader resigned himself to becoming a tiller of the soil.

By the middle of the 19th century fur trading was a thing of the past and the first era in the modern history of the Upper Peninsula had ended. The Yankee trader in his regime had pushed trade to the utmost, making no effort to preserve the furred animals for future harvest. Long before this the beaver had become scarce and many other species of wild animals followed in rapid decline.

The gay, affable, happy-go-lucky Frenchman had blazed the trail for the British and American fur traders. He was the trail blazer of the frontier; his period was the most romantic, filled with the greatest hardships. His was a regime hampered and restricted by laws and decrees, broken more often than kept, and wholly ignored by the *coureurs de bois*. He pursued the beaver hunt with might and main, until the markets were overstocked and prices fell. It was a time when the black-robed priest and trader in pelts worked side by side, shared the same camp fires and penetrated the wilds where white man had never before ventured. The influence the fur trader's career had on the life of the Indians and the service he rendered as a pathfinder, despite the evils that may be laid to him, entitles him to a unique niche in the history of Michigan and the Upper Peninsula in particular.

The Jesuit priests and missionaries left to the world a wonderful example of courageous devotion to an ideal, but their purposes were frustrated by the measures of other men, mainly the fur traders, intent on worldly ends, leaving the red man in his primitive barbarism.

Yet the fathers bequeathed to posterity a body of geographical and other knowledge which serves forever to identify them with the early history of Michigan and the Great Lakes region.

THE MINING ERA
SETTLEMENT BEGINS IN EARNEST

In 1835, a constitution for Michigan was adopted and a state government was elected which was accepted by Congress on June 15, 1836. Michigan was admitted into the union as a state upon the condition of acceding to the boundary claims of Ohio, over which an embittered controversy had arisen. This condition, at first rejected by a convention called by the legislature to consider it, was finally accepted by a second convention on December 15, 1836, and Michigan was formally declared a state by an act of Congress, January 26, 1837.

The contention between Michigan and Ohio over the exact boundary line between the two states led to what is called, by many historians, "The Toledo War," the final outcome of which has not been settled today (1972). The final decision at the time was that Michigan accept the Upper Peninsula in trade for the disputed strip of land, which was awarded to Ohio.

After several years of wrangling by members of the legislature, on March 16, 1847 the state capitol was moved from *Detroit* to what is now the city of *Lansing*, then only a clearing in the wilderness in Ingham County.

On June 3, 1850, a constitutional convention met at *Lansing* and adopted the first constitution, which was ratified by a vote of the people in November, 1851.

In 1845, the value of iron deposits in the Upper Peninsula was fully discovered, and mining operations were inaugurated the following year, although it was not until 1856 that operations were started on an extensive scale.

In 1845, the copper wealth of Lake Superior was brought to notice, and was immediately followed by a rush of speculation. It was not, however, until the completion of the Sault Canal that mining operations were conducted in an economical and systematic manner.

In 1852, Congress granted to the State 750,000 acres of land for the purpose of constructing a canal around the rapids on the St. Mary's River. A company was found willing to construct the canal in return for the lands, and after two years labor the work was completed and formally accepted by the State in May, 1855.

In the 1840s, when the first copper mines, and then iron ore mines were being opened, the Upper Peninsula was remote and isolated from the rest of the country. With the influx of immigrants to the mining areas, counties were formed, although in some cases it was many years before a government was organized for each county.

First settlers of the Upper Peninsula came from many parts of the world. French trappers and fur traders were already established and had adjusted to their environment, the rigors of the wilderness. French-Canadians came later, mostly during the lumbering boom.

As early as 1840, English miners from the Cornwall Peninsula of England settled in the mining districts. Called "Cousin Jacks," the majority settled in Houghton and Keweenaw Counties to resume their work in the mines after their worn-out copper and tin mines in England no longer produced. They were so well established in the mining districts that by 1882 nearly all the supervisors and captains were Cornish.

One of the Cornish contributions to the Upper Peninsula was the famous pastie or meat pies. Their early recipe, carried as a lunch to the mine shafts, was as follows: *"mayt"* (meat), *"turmits"* (turnips), *"tatys"* (potatoes), and *"h'onyons"* (onions), heated on their shovels held over miners' candles in the darkness of the mine pit.

Germans came to the country at an early date but settled mostly on farms or worked in log camps during the winter. Chocolay Township, near *Marquette,* was settled by German farmers, and a German family is credited with being the area's original settlers, around 1860.

During the time of the Toledo War in 1835, most people knew very little about the Upper Peninsula. A *Detroit* newspaper of the day reported the region as *"a wild, comparatively Scandinavian tract of 20,000 square miles of howling wilderness on the shores of Lake Superior."* One song that came out of the brief, bloodless battle went, *"But now the song they sing to us, is trade away that land, For that poor frozen country, Beyond Lake Michigan."*

Fifteen or 20 years later this land became the home of Finnish immigrants who arrived from the copper mining districts along Finland's northern boundary. The first group of 250 were "imported" by a mining company. Relatives wrote home to their friends and neighbors who soon followed to join the Michigan colony. An early settler of *Calumet* who came here from Norway said, *"When I come here I don't learn to speak English! I have to learn Finnish or I don't talk to nobody."* He said he spoke only Finnish until he was 16 or 17 years old.

The Finnish (Finns don't want to be referred to as such and say, "Call me a Finlander—not 'Finnish'") introduced the Finnish steam bath, or sauna, which

6

has become popular in Michigan and is especially so in the Copper Country. Later, Finlanders took to their natural work of farming and many worked in lumber camps during the logging days.

The mines also attracted many Swedes. *Ishpeming* and the mine locations around *Iron River* and *Ironwood* became major Swedish settlements. Bates Township, in Iron County, at the turn of the century was 90 per cent Swedes, and in 1885 the county was dominantly Swedish.

During the late 1800s many Swedes were hired by iron furnace companies and were brought directly from Sweden to the Upper Peninsula. Many were skilled in the smelting of ore while others worked as plant laborers or dock hands. Some of *St. Ignace's* early settlers were brought from Sweden to work in the Martel Furnace. During the lumbering era many camps were made up almost entirely of Swedes. A colony of Swedes settled the Barga County village of *Skanee*, coming directly from Sweden in the 1870s (See *Skanee*).

A colony of "Yagar," or Hungarians settled in Menominee County (see *Banat*). They were mainly farmers and laborers and experts in sugar beet raising.

Many towns and mining camps had a Chinese laundry or cook. Some early merchants were of Lebanese, Syrian or Jordanian descent. They became peddlers, storekeepers, and merchants.

Sam Jacobs, a Lebanese immigrant, was a jewelry peddler in the 1880s. Even the rugged lumberjack could not resist the glitter of a gold watch and chain. It was a mark of distinction, and even though many could not read or tell time it gave him a feeling of importance. In 1920 Sam settled down in *Iron Mountain* and opened a jewelry store.

There is scarcely an occupation which the Polish immigrants have not tried. They worked as miners in the copper and iron ranges and many deck hands aboard the lake vessels were of Polish descent.

Many Belgians settled in the iron mining districts of the U. P., particularly in the *Norway* and *Vulcan* area of Dickinson County. Several Belgian families were settlers in 1883, of Gourly Township, Menominee County.

Many Italian settlers in the U. P. lived in the mining locations and rented company houses for a small monthly payment. Because of previous mining experience in Italy, they headed for the iron mines of Dickinson, Marquette, Iron and Gogebic Counties. An early Italian missionary serving Indian tribes in the Upper Peninsula was Father Mazzuchelli of *Milan*, Italy.

It is interesting to note that Italian immigrants stayed away from the lumber camps that were so popular with the Scandinavian settlers, although many worked on railroads. Some Italians went into business and Italian names are familiar in directories of many western U. P. towns.

Ezekiel Solomon is credited with being the first Jew in the Upper Peninsula, if not in the state. He was connected with the fur trade as early as 1778. Another early Jewish fur trader and merchant was Chapman Abraham. After serving in the lakes area as a trader, he moved to *Detroit* in 1865.

John Lowe is another, who served with the English at *Mackinac*. In 1822 he was appointed as an Associate Justice by Governor Lewis Cass.

Jewish merchants were among the first store owners in the Copper Country. Only nine years after copper was discovered on the Keweenaw Peninsula, the families of Leopolds and Austrians had stores at *Eagle River, Eagle Harbor, Cliff Mine, Calumet* and *Hancock*.

J. H. Steinberg was a leading dry goods merchant in *St. Ignace* about the turn-of-the-century. He is listed in the city directory for 1895.

A few Scots became prominent in the history of fur trading and early mining days. Sandy McDonald, at one time with the American Fur Company, and later operator of a stage line, has been the subject of many stories about early days in the Upper Peninsula. Bruce Township, in Chippewa County was named by early settlers from Scotland.

Although many Welshmen settled in the mining communities, they were rapidly assimilated throughout Michigan.

Lyden, in his "Story of Grand Rapids" said, *"The Irish seemed to have followed the direction their shovels pointed with the westward tide first on the Erie Canal in 1825, and later on the railroads."* In the U. P. the Irish were railroad men, and also blacksmiths, machinists and firemen at the mine's boilers. They were also among the first to mine copper in the Keweenaw Peninsula.

Many Irishmen came from Cork County to Michigan seeking jobs in the lumber camps. Several lower Michigan counties and towns have Irish names, thanks to early Irish surveyors and their helpers. O'Toole, O'Brien and Lailey were Irish timbermen, who, on some occasions, were known to have cut "round 40s," especially if the acreage adjoined "government land."

Irish logging camp foremen were also responsible for christening many a Swede, Frenchmen, or "foreigner" who could not speak English, with a good old Irish name. When the timekeeper asked him what name to put down for a man he couldn't understand or couldn't spell the pronounced name, the foreman would say, "Just put down Sullivan," or the first Irish name that came to his mind. In this manner the name went down on the records for posterity and some of their descendants are known by these names yet today.

The Upper Peninsula was truly the "melting pot of America" in the early days. Settlers came from nearly every nation to find work and to make their homes. Among other countries represented were Montenegrins, from a small kingdom in Europe that became a part of Yugoslavia after 1918. They settled at *Wakefield*, a mining location in the western Upper Peninsula.

Slovanians, like the immigrants from Montenegro, came from Yugoslavia. They settled in *Shingleton* and in the copper country's twin cities of *Houghton-Hancock*. The Alger County town of *Traunik* was founded by Slovanians.

Croatians also settled in the Copper Country. Early Croatian settlers built the first Croatian Catholic Church in *Calumet*. "Ich" was a common Croatian name ending, such as Moravich and Ravochich.

The tiny province of Luxembourg sent several young men who became outstanding in the timber era. The Groos brothers are credited with developing timber resources in the *Escanaba* area and the settlement of *Groos* on Lake Michigan.

"Big Bill" Bonifas came to the Garden Peninsula with a bundle of clothes, $2.00, and a strong back, started cutting poles and ties, and built up a fortune estimated at between $5 and $20 million. Bonifas and his three brothers and three sisters, for whom he sent later, worked together and had soon cut a swath in the timber through half of the western section of the Upper Peninsula. They left their mark on history with at least one town named *Bonifas*. Industries developed and when Big Bill died he left most of his millions to charity in the country where he made it, unlike the "timber barons" of the pine days who "cut and got out," taking their money back East or down below and leaving the barren country behind.

Many Norwegians came here as fishermen, copper miners, and worked in the logging camps during the 1880s. One group of 589 came from *Tromoso* in the northern part of Norway and settled in Houghton-Keweenaw Counties. The Portage Lake area here has always been a center for Norwegian culture (Also see *Isle Royale*).

Little information is available regarding blacks in the Upper Peninsula. The 1880 census lists the "colored" population of each county but these were Indians, half-breeds, and other races, none listed as Negro.

Old timers of *Calumet* could only recall one black family, a man and his wife who were servants of one of the mine owners. At one time, during the 1940s, *L'Anse* had a black barber, a World War Veteran. *"He was respected and liked by everyone and when he died the American Legion conducted funeral services for him,"* Karl Menge of the *L'Anse Sentinel* said.

Other long-time residents of Alger and Schoolcraft County recalled one or two blacks who worked in the woods during the hardwood era. One later became a "jobber" and dealt in pulpwood. Only one attempt to bring blacks in as settlers is related by an old-timer of the *Iron River* area (See *Iron River* ghost towns).

FIRST TOWNS AND POST OFFICES

With the opening of the mines in the 1840s, newly arrived settlers were anxious for mail, but it was to be a number of years before any organized mail service was established. There were no railroads affording connections with the outside world and the ships, which could only operate during the navigation season, had no regular schedules. The captains of the vessels sailing from "down below," as the lower lake ports were referred to, accepted packets of mail for Lake Superior ports. Before the opening of the first ship canal at *Sault Ste. Marie* in June, 1855, the *Lake Superior Journal* was being published at the *Sault,* and for the most part only in the open season of navigation. Its columns carried many complaints about the poor mail service to the Lake Superior region.

In October of 1853, the people of *Marquette* realized, with the sailing of the last vessel of the season, that the area would not receive any mail during the long winter ahead. A mass meeting of citizens was held early in January 1854, and Peter White was selected to go to *Green Bay*, Wisconsin. He was provided with six Indians and three dog teams of three dogs each to go after the mail, taking about 1,000 letters with him to be posted.

It required a full week to get to *Cedar River* in the vicinity of *Green Bay* and much to their surprise they met five double teams with five sleigh loads of U. S. mail bound for Lake Superior places, via *Escanaba*, reaching *Marquette* on January 21 of that year. Peter White continued his journey and in *Fon du Lac*, Wisconsin, he exchanged a number of messages and letters with Senator Lewis Cass in *Washington*, with the result that the U. P. towns were promised three mail deliveries every week by team provided they could get through the snow.

At that time each and every mining and lumbering location, as it came into being, even if it had only a dozen people, had to have its own post office. This resulted in the establishment of many offices.

Before large areas of Marquette County, as well as others, were being taken to form additional counties as the iron ore and copper mines were being opened and developed, post office records show that *Crystal Falls, Iron River, Mastodon*, and *Stambaugh* were all in Marquette County, whereas they are now in

Iron County. These post offices were established between 1881 and 1884. *Floodwood*, a few miles north of *Channing*, was established as a post office in November 1887. It was the last to go to another county, Dickinson, formed in 1891, giving the Upper Peninsula its present 15 counties.

There was much confusion in the Postal Department at *Washington* and officials weren't quite sure where all the new mining towns were. Under the legislative act of March 9, 1843, Michilimackinac and Chippewa Counties were being divided to make up Marquette, Delta, Houghton, Ontonagon and Schoolcraft counties, which led to further confusion. Maps were scarce and many didn't even include the Upper Peninsula.

Early records have the *Fort Wilkins* post office, which was established in June 1845, the *Eagle River* post office, which was established in October of that year and the one at *Houghton*, established March 1846, recorded in Marquette County. When looking for the first *Carp River* post office in the Marquette iron range, established January 1847, it was recorded as in Houghton County.

Now many of the early town names are quite strange to even Upper Peninsula historians, and many of them have been forgotten. Many of these towns and post offices have come and gone and no one knows how they got their names. Perhaps the history of ghost towns in this book will shed some light on the subject. When a town name is listed with no information it is for the reason given above. All that is known is that there was a place by that name at one time. Other small stations and unimportant locations are listed to set the record straight on whether or not this was a full-fledged town. Over the years many stories have grown about the towns that were at one time *"the biggest city in the U. P., with 20,000 population,"* etc., etc. Most of these stories are told with no basis of fact and the stories grow with the telling.

As with any historical narrative there is a wide margin for error in this book but the dates and information have been checked carefully for accuracy and first hand information is from reliable sources about the area where the place is located.

Chapter Two

RAILROADS OF THE UPPER PENINSULA

In 1855, the railroad was completed between *Ishpeming* and *Marquette*, speeding the mineral output of the U. P. and open pit mining began to pay.

In 1866, the Duluth, South Shore & Atlantic was incorporated.

In 1872, the Marquette, Houghton & Ontonogan Railroad was formed. In that year the railroad from *Marquette* to *Chicago* was also completed by the Chicago & Northwestern.

October 11, 1873, the Mineral Range Railroad was opened from *Hancock* to *Calumet.*

In 1881, the Marquette & Mackinac Railroad was completed from *Marquette* to *St. Ignace* and in October, 1881, the first railroad ferry service connected the Upper and Lower Peninsulas, making the U. P. readily accessible for the first time.

In July, 1883, J. A. Hubbell, Thomas J. Brown, and a Mr. Osborn, of *Marquette*, ran a line and procured a charter for the construction of a railroad from *L'Anse* to *Houghton.* This line was later sold to the Marquette, Houghton & Ontonagon Railroad, and opened for traffic in July, 1883.

In 1887, the Duluth South Shore & Atlantic acquired the Mackinac & Marquette Railroad and the old Marquette, Houghton & Ontonogan. Inside of one year this company owned or leased 78 locomotives and 4,700 cars. In 1948, it had 26 steam and 7 diesel engines and 1,800 cars.

In 1876, an *Ontonagon* mine operator built the first telephone system in Michigan over a distance of 20 miles after seeing Bell's invention at the Philadelphia Exposition.

Hundreds of Upper Peninsula towns sprang up along the miles of railroad, and as each railroad expanded the number of towns and stations increased. As the railroads were abandoned and highways developed, many of these places became ghost towns.

12

Many towns and stations were settled along the railroads and became ghost towns when trains were discontinued, such as this section of the C. & N. W. Railroad which quit running in the 1960s. This is the way the old C. & N. W. Railroad grade appeared in 1971 when tracks were being removed. Photo by Roy L. Dodge

13

Railroad junction at *Alecto* at the junction of the Minneapolis, St. Paul & Sault Ste. Marie and the old Chicago & Northwestern Railways, near *Schaffer*. Old watchman's tower still stands. Photo taken in 1971 when the tracks of the Felch Mountain branch of the C. & N. W. were being removed.

14

During the peak of railroad building, 1850-1890, vast acreages were awarded to the railroad companies for right-of-ways and to help finance them. According to figures offered to the legislature in 1897 by Governor Hazen S. Pingree, the railroads, as of that date, owned 38 per cent of the total valuation of property in the State but under the tax then imposed, assumed only 3.5 per cent of the total tax burden.

Building the railroads required hundreds of men. Many of them were brought in by the railroad companies to do the job, some even imported from other countries, such as Sweden. This brought many new settlers into the country and more new towns and settlements were born.

The railroads put their lands up for sale and made glowing offers to settlers to purchase the land for farms. As late as 1904 the following ad appeared in the Farm & Business Directory of Houghton, Keweenaw, Baraga and Ontanagon Counties. *"The D. S. S. & A. is always glad to assist bona fide home seekers by furnishing them rates of a single fare for the round trip over its lines to enable them to examine the country; and if they buy and settle, they can have similar rates for their families, household goods and farm movables. For full particulars with regard to this north country agricultural region write to E. W. MacPherran, Land Commissioner, D. S. S. & A. Railroad, Marquette, Mich."*

Many towns, and Alger County, were named by or for railroad magnates, such as General Alger, Newberry, McMillan and others. As you read this book you will see examples of many other places named for either railroad developers or their officers.

Railroads were second only in importance to the Soo Locks and Great Lakes shipping in the development of modern day Upper Peninsula industry and the settlement of the country. (Also see *Baraga County's Ghost Railroad).*

RAILROADS, LISTING STATIONS
AND DISTANCE IN MILES BETWEEN STATIONS IN THE U. P.

CHICAGO AND NORTHWESTERN

Chicago, 0 miles; *Marinette,* Wisconsin, 262.9; *Menominee,* 264.3; *Wallace,* 279.3; *Stephenson,* 285.3; *Bagley,* 295.2; *Kloman,* 302.0; *Menominee River Junction,* 305.0; *Spalding,* 305.7; *Bark River,* 316.0; *Ford River,* 321.3; *Escanaba,* 328.0; *Mason,* 336.8; *Day's River,* 340.6; *Maple Ridge (Rock),* 352.3; *Lathrop,* 357.5; *Helena,* 362.5; *Little Lake,* 368.7; *Cheshire Junction,* 370.7; *Cascade Junction,* 382.5; *Goose Lake,* 384.6; *Negaunee,* 389.5; *Ishpeming,* 392.9; ending here.

MARQUETTE, HOUGHTON AND ONTONAGON
(Branch of the Chicago & Canada Southern)

Marquette, 0 miles; *Bancroft*, 3; *Bruce*, 6; *Morgan*, 7; *Eagle Mill*, 8; *Negaunee*, 12; *Ishpeming*, 15; *Saginaw*, 19; *Greenwood*, 21; *Clarksburg*, 25; *Humboldt*, 26; *Champion*, 31; *Michigamme*, 37; *Spurr*, 39; *Sturgeon*, 47; *Summit*, 53; *Taylor*, 56; *L'Anse*, 93.

Republic Branch

Humboldt, 0 miles; *Republic*, 11.

MINERAL RANGE
(Branch of the Michigan Central)

Hancock, 0; *Franklin*, 3; *Albany*, 4; *Boston*, 6; *Osceola*, 10; ending at *Calumet*, 12.

By 1893, more branches of the Chicago & Northwestern were built, in addition to stations listed for 1880.

IRON RIVER BRANCH
(Chicago & Northwestern)

Powers, 0 miles; *Hermansville*, 4; *Waucedah*, 12; *Vulcan*, 19; *Norway*, 22; *Quinnesec*, 25; *Iron Mountain*, 29; *Antoine*, 30; *Spread Eagle*, 36; *Commonwealth*, 41; *Florence*, 42; *Stager*, 48.

From Armstrong to Watersmeet

Armstrong, 55; *Saunders*, 61; *Stambaugh*, 67; *Iron River*, 68; *Paines*, 80; *Basswood*, 81; *Elmwood*, 86; *Tamarack*, 95; and *Watersmeet*, 103.

METROPOLITAN BRANCH
(Tracks removed in 1971)

Narenta, 0 miles; *Alecto*, 5; *Whitney*, 9; *Dryads*, 14; *Faunus*, 18; *Hulas*, 26; *Foster City*, 31; and *Metropolitan*, 35.

DULUTH, SOUTH SHORE & ATLANTIC
(From St. Ignace to Soo Junction)

St. Ignace, 0 miles; *Allenville*, 10; *Moran*, 11; *Palms*, 19; *Ozark*, 23; *Trout Lake*, 27; *Hendrie*, 36; and *Soo Junction*, 43.

FROM SAULT STE. MARIE TO NESTORIA

Sault Ste. Marie, 0 miles; *Bay Mills*, 12; *Wellsburg*, 19; *Rexford*, 25; *Eckerman*, 35; *Soo Junction*, 47; *Sage*, 49; *Newberry*, 58; *Dollarville*, 60; *McMillan*, 74; *East Branch*, 74; *Seney*, 79; *Driggs*, 88; *Creighton*, 95; *Shingleton*, 104; *Munising*, 112; *Ridge*, 119; *Au Train*, 125; *Rock River*, 129; *Onota*, 133; *Deerton*, 135; *Sand River*, 140; *Chocolay*, 150; *Marquette*, 155; *Bagdad*, 160; *Eagle Mills*, 162; *Negaunee*, 167; *Ishpeming*, 170; *Clarksburg*, 180; *Humboldt*, 181; *Champion*, 186; *Michigamme*, 193; and *Nestoria*, 201.

FROM NESTORIA TO HOUGHTON

Nestoria, 0 miles; *L'Anse*, 17; *Baraga*, 22; *Newton*, 30; *Chassell*, 41; and *Houghton*, 48.

FROM NESTORIA TO BESSEMER

Nestoria, 201; *Vermilac*, 211; *Perch* 221; *Sidnaw*, 224; *Kitchi*, 230; *Trout Creek*, 239; *Bruce's Crossing*, 250; *Ewen*, 255; *Matchwood*, 261; *Grosbeck*, 263; *Lake Gogebic*, 272; *Thomaston*, 287; *Abitosse*, 292; *Bessemer Junction*, 294; *Bessemer*, 296; ending at *Duluth*, 410.

HANCOCK & CALUMET RAILROAD

Hancock, 0 miles; *Ripley*, 2; *Clark*, 5; *Woodside*, 6; *Junction* 8; *Mills*, 9; *Grover*, 10; *Linwood*, 10; *Lake Linden*, 11.

MINERAL RANGE RAILROAD

Houghton, 0 miles; *Hancock*, 1; *Swedetown*, 4; *Franklin*, 5; *Boston*, 7; *Highway*, 10; *Osceola*, 12; *Torch Lake Junction*, 13; *Calumet*, 14; ending at *Red Jacket*, 15.

MINNEAPOLIS, ST. PAUL & SAULT STE. MARIE

Minneapolis, 0 miles; *Hermansville*, 311; *Farnham*, 318; *Eustis*, 325; *Newhall*, 33S; *North Escanaba*, 338; *Gladstone*, 343; *Masonville*, 348; *Rapid River*, 349; *Ensign*, 355; *Sturgeon River*, 363; *Isabella*, 368; *Cooks Mill*, 375; *Delta Junction*, 381; *South Manistique*, 385; *Manistique*, 387; *Whitedale*, 394; *Pike*, 411; *Corinne*, 415; *Cisco*, 417; *Engadine*, 422; *Naubinway Junction*, 429; *Gilchrist*, 432; *Hubbell Junction*, 439; *Lewis*, 442; *Trout Lake*, 450; *Alexander*, 459; *Rudyard*, 471; *Kinross*, 476; *Dafter*, 484; and *Sault Ste. Marie*, 494.

BLANEY & SOUTHERN RAILWAY (1914)

Bear Creek, 0 miles; *Blaney*, 1; *Mooreville*, 2; *Blaney Junction*, 8.

CHICAGO & NORTHWESTERN
Escanaba and Antoine (1914)

North Escanaba, 0; *Tesch*, 11; *Siding 2*, 14; *Oro*, 22; *Siding 4*, 30; *Sumac*, 37; *Sturgeon*, 38; *Appleton Mine*, 40; *Siding 5*, 42; *Loop Line Junction*, 51; *Antoine*, 53.

COPPER RANGE RAILROAD (1914)

Calumet, 0; Laurium, 3; Lake Linden, 6; Grove, 7; S. Lake Linden, 8; Hubbell, 8; Mills, 9; Mason, 11; Point Mills Junction, 12; Dollar Bay, 13; Ripley, 16; Hancock, 16; Houghton, 17; Atlantic, 22; Mill Mine Junction, 24; South Range, 25; Baltic Junction, 25; Trimountain, 27; Painesdale, 28; Ricedale, 31; Tolvola, 34; Stonington, 36; Elm River, 40; Twin Lakes, 42; Faleston, 43; Winona, 45; Seager, 49; Lake Mine, 56; Greenland Junction, 57; Adventure, 58; Greenland, 59; Greenland Junction, 57; Peppard, 58; McKeever, 59; Mass, 60.

Copper Range—Lake Shore Branch

Mill Mine Junction, 0; Obenhoff, 3; Salmon Trout, 5; Red Ridge, Junction, 7; Redridge, 8..... Stanwood, 8; Edgemere 9; Edgemere Junction, 9; Beacon Hill, 10; Freda, 11; Freda Park, 11.

KEWEENAW CENTRAL RAILROAD

Calumet, 0; S. Kearsarge, 2; Wolverine, 3; N. Kearsarge, 4; Allouez, 5; Copper City, 5; Mohawk, 7; Oiibway, 10; Cliff, 12; Crestview Junction, 14; ..... Phoenix, 14; Central, 18; Delaware, 23; Wyoming, 24; Lac La Belle Junction, 24; Mandan, 28.....Crestview Junction, 0; Phoenix Mine, 1; Crestview, 2....... Lac La Belle Junction, 0; Lac La Belle, 7.

LAKE SUPERIOR & ISHPEMING RAILROAD

Joplin, 0; North Lake, 3; Ishpeming, 7; Ishpeming Yard, 8; Negaunee, 9; Maas Mine, 10; Finnegan, 12; Eagle Mills, 15; Dead River, 18; Forestville, 22; West Yard, 25; Presque Isle, 26.

MANISTIQUE & LAKE SUPERIOR RAILROAD

Manistique, 0; Manistique River, 2; Spruceville, 6; Hargman, 7; Spur 8, 8; Hiawatha, 11; Spur 13 (Doyle), 14; Beesons, 14; Spur 15 (Camp 86), 15; Steuben, 22; Gravel Pit, 23; Spur 24, 26; Spur 25, 26; Klondike, 26; Spur 28 (Phillions), 28; Scotts, 29; Richardsons, 33; Spur 35 (Miller), 35; Shingleton, 37; Doty, 41.

HIAWATHA SPUR

Manistique, 0; *Hiawatha*, 11; *Hiawatha Mill*, 14.

McNEIL BRANCH MANISTIQUE & LAKE SUPERIOR

Manistique, 0; *Scotts*, 29; *Cooper (Camp 74)*, 34; *Maki*, 36; *Parker*, 37; *Hovey (Camp 85)*, 40.

The above list of railroads is only a partial list of railroads in the U. P. during its history. In addition to many miles of logging and mine railroads, in the early 'teens the following electric trains or interurbans were in operation:

The Houghton County Traction Company had lines from *East Houghton* to *Wolverine Mine*, 16.5 miles; *Allouez Mine* to *Mohawk Mine*, 21.5 miles; and from *Lake Linden* to *Hubbell*, about 2 miles.

The Marquette County Gas & Electric Company had a line from *Breltung Negaunee* that ran 4.5 miles to *Lake*.

The Escanaba Traction Company had a line from *Escanaba* to *Gladstone*, a distance of 10 miles.

Ed. Note: To save time and space the names of most railroads are abbreviated when used in town and station descriptions. The following is a list of most of the railroads (1910) that are abbreviated for benefit of the reader: Blaney & Southern-Chicago (B. & S. C.), Milwaukee & St. Paul (M. & S. P.), Chicago & Northwestern (C. & N. W.), Copper Range (C. R.), Duluth, South Shore & Atlantic (D. S. S. & A.), Escanaba & Lake Superior Keweenaw Central (E. & L. S. K. C), Lake Superior & Ishpeming (L. S. & I.), Manistique & Lake Superior Mineral Range (M. & L. S. M. R.), Minneapolis, St. Paul & Sault Ste. Marie (M. St. P. & S. Ste. M.), Munising, Marquette & Southeastern (M. M. & S. E.), Ontonagon, and Wisconsin & Michigan (W. & M.). R. R. means Railroad

Other railroad abbreviations may be identified by checking railroads and distances between stations.

Rock Harbor lighthouse on *Isle Royale* as it appeared in 1986. Now the "ghost county" of the Upper Peninsula, *Isle Royale* was a county from 1875 to 1891.   National Park Photograph, courtesy of Hugh P. Beattie, Park Superintendant, *Houghton*, Michigan

Chapter Three

ISLE ROYALE & UPPER PENINSULA GHOST COUNTIES

Early maps of Lake Superior showed a large island named "Minong," Indian for "great island." By 1755 it was correctly placed and marked *Isle Royale*, named by the French who took possession of the island in 1671, lured here by the fur trade.

Before any Europeans came to the island, located in Lake Superior 48 miles northwest of the tip of the Keweenaw Peninsula, it was inhabited by Indians who mined large chunks of pure copper from the terrain. Archaeologists have dated some primitive mining activities back 4,500 years.

Isle Royale became part of the United States through the efforts of Benjamin Franklin at the Treaty of Paris in 1783. At that time the island was a part of Chippewa County which included the entire Upper Peninsula. In 1847 Houghton County was formed and became part of it as "Isle Royale Township." Taxes were levied but the township never had a supervisor on the county board. In 1861 when Keweenaw County was formed, *Isle Royale* became part of it. In 1875 Isle Royale became an independent county with the county seat at *Island Mine* near Point Senter.

The island, at first all one township, was later divided into two. The east end of the island was established as Cove Township with the county seat at *Minong Mine* near *McCarg's Grove*.

County officers were elected for only one year, 1877. Officers for that year, with the county seat at *Island Mine*, were: John Fisher, Sheriff; Wm. H. Solis, County Clerk; Dewitt C. Hulett, Judge of Probate; and Jos. E. Hoppman, Register of Deeds. S. L. Chadbourne, address *Houghton*, was Prosecutor; Frank M. Hess, Treasurer; and S. L. Chadbourne, Circuit Court Commissioner. It is doubtful if any officers performed duties.

No officials were elected for 1878, and in 1879 the following were elected as Justices of the Peace: Alex McComber, *Island Mine*; James Mahon, *Island Mine*; Jos. Vivian, *Island Mine*; John Dawney, *Island Mine*; Wm. Jacka, *Minong Mine*; Thomas Davey, *Minong Mine*; M. Hanson, *Saginaw Mine*; and James Richards, *Minong*.

During its history as a county, election returns were forwarded to the state only two times; in 1876 twelve Republican votes were cast for governor and 44 Democratic votes, a total of 56 votes. In 1880, 55 votes were cast in the Presidential election.

The census of 1880 gives the population as 55; in 1890, 135. No census were recorded for other years.

Liquor taxes were paid to the state for one year during its history as a county. In 1891 three saloons or dealers were listed and paid $1,125.01 in tax according to the Michigan Legislative Manual.

In 1893, plat maps were available from the State Land Office for $1.50 each. The maps showed that 6,468 acres were state-owned and were being offered for $1.25 per acre.

In 1880, the only year taxes were paid on real estate, $127.75 was paid on an assessed valuation of $100,000.

Shortly prior to 1880 mining ceased at *Island Mine* and the county seat was moved away with records of the mining company to *Detroit* or *Cleveland*. Later the books and records of the township were recovered by the state and for a time kept in *Lansing*. After Isle Royale County had lain dormant until 1885, it was attached to Houghton County. But again, in 1897, it was attached to Keeweenaw County to which it still belongs, constituting parts of Houghton and Eagle Harbor Townships. The county government, which had never been officially organized, was disorganized in 1891.

For many years fishermen used some of the harbors and headquartered on the island, and for some years *Isle Royale* sustained a colony of Norwegian fishermen.

Lane's Geological Survey, Vol. VI, relates that in the early 1900s camping parties came here from *Duluth* and used the abandoned Rock Harbor Light house and other places. John F. Johns, before 1900, had his log hotel and a cabin built on *Johns Island* which he made available to visitors.

About the same year, 1900, the Isle Royale Land Corporation, later the Island Copper Company, had plans for establishing resorts. A site had been selected for such a development on Rock Harbor near the location of *Ransom*, but it never developed.

When the island was finally declared a national park (April 3, 1940) a campaign to preserve it was led by Albert Stoll, a newspaperman from *Detroit*. Fishermen were still living here during the fishing season, coming from Minnesota.

Towns listed during the brief history of *Isle Royale* as a county included *Minong*, settled in June, 1875, the county seat, 1877 population 350. In 1879 it was described as: *"Known as McCarg's Grove, a copper mining village of 150 population. Settled by Minong Mining Company, of Detroit, in Cove Township. Ship to Houghton, 50 miles southeast. Has a steam stamp mill. Copper is the only export. Mail weekly during the season. H. B. Hitchcock, Postmaster and mining company clerk; Dr. J. K. Gailey, physician; and Wm. Jacka, Justice of Peace."*

In 1879, *Island Mine* was described as *"An unimportant post office"*; in 1887: *"A discontinued post office on Siscowit Bay, southeast shore, 50 miles northwest of Eagle Harbor."* In 1887, *Minong* was described as: *"A deserted mining village."*

Isle Royale, in 1887, was described as the location of the copper mines of the Minong Mining Company and the Saginaw Copper Mining Company. *"Minong was the post office but has been discontinued."*

Other places were, *Tobins Harbor*, 1927, a summer resort. Mrs. E. S. Smith, hotel. Also *Singerville*, a summer resort, mail to *Duluth*.

For other towns and settlements see those listed in Keweenaw County.

Frederick Hatch, Jr., the son of a well-known Chippewa leader and legal research director for the Upper Peninsula Legal Service agency at *Sault Ste. Marie*, thinks the Chippewas of the Bad River-Red Cliff area in northern Wisconsin may still have a legitimate claim to *Isle Royale*. According to the land description in the 1842 treaty, the island lies about 20 miles north of the treaty line.

"They really goofed," Hatch said. *"The problem was that a bunch of bureaucrats were embarrassed by their oversight, so they tried to patch it up administratively themselves."*

The *Isle Royale Queen II*, recently purchased by Donald E. Kilpela, of *Livonia*, Michigan, makes trips from *Copper Harbor* to the island during summer months. Other vessels and a seaplane provide transportation to and from the island.

Rock Harbor has postal service two or three times weekly, from mid-June through Labor Day, and Rock Harbor Lodge and Windigo Inn have an emergency telegraph service.

By a recent declaration of Congress, nearly all the 134,000 acre island is now designated as a wilderness area to preserve its natural state as an *"example of a delicately balanced, pre-predator relationship in a stable ecological community."* The island has no permanent inhabitants.

Other Upper Peninsula counties that may be considered "ghost counties" are Bleeker County, 1861-63 (see Menominee County history), and the county of Washington, which was officially made a county and taken from the Ishpeming-Negaunee mining area of Marquette County for a brief time during the mining boom of the mid-1880s. Residents of Marquette County protested so loudly that the legislature backed off and rescinded the act, returning the area to its former location in Marquette County.

Chapter Four

ALGER COUNTY

Alger County was originally laid out in 1855 and was attached to Schoolcraft County until its organization as a county in 1885. It was named for the Honorable Russell A. Alger, Governor of Michigan from 1885-86.

Au Train was the first county seat and in 1887 had a population of 300. Eby M. Spencer was Postmaster; John McKinnon, Sheriff; John A. Steinlein, Prosecutor; and W. E. Jackson was publisher of the *AuTrain Alpha*, a weekly newspaper. The county seat was moved to *Munising* in 1901 or 1902.

By 1877, *Munising* had a population of 1,000. The *Michigan Gazetteer and Business Director* for that year said, *"Wild game abounds and the village is already a summer resort for tourists and invalids. It bids fair to become the 'Saratoga' of Lake Superior. The blast furnace of the Munising Iron Company produces 10,000 tons of pig iron annually."* Munising was incorporated as a village in 1897 and as a home rule city January 26, 1915.

ALGER COUNTY GHOST TOWNS

ALDER—1910, a station on the Munising, Marquette & Southern Railroad. Mail to *Carlshend*.

_____

BALDY—1910, located on the Munising, Marquette & South Eastern Railroad. Nearest post office at *Shingleton*.

_____

BAY FURNACE—See *Onota*.

_____

BEAVER—1910, send mail to *Grand Marais*. Also called *Beaver Junction*, about 11 miles south of *Grand Marais*.

_____

BENNETT—1910, mail to *Grand Marais*. Was a station on the old railroad between *Grand Marais* and *Seney*.

_____

BING—1910, a station on the M. M. & S. E. Railroad. Mail *Carlshend*.

_____

BISMARK—See *Onota*.

BLOCK—1910, a station on the M. M. & S. E. Railroad. Mail *Carlshend.*

BOUCHA—1910, a station on the M. M. & S. E. Railroad. Mail *Cusino.*

BOVEN—1910, a station on the M. M. & S. E. Railroad. Nearest post office at *Wetmore.*

BRABANT—1910, a station on the M. M. & S. E. Railroad. Mail to *Shingleton.*

BROWNESTONE—1910, a station on the Duluth, South Shore & Atlantic Railroad. Mail to *Au Train.*

BUCKEYE—1910, on the Minneapolis St. Paul & Sault Ste. Marie Railroad. Nearest post office at *Trenary.*

CHRISTMAS—See *Onota.*

CHAPMAN—1910, on the Munising, Marquette & Southeastern Railroad. Mail *Shingleton.*

COALWOOD—1910, population 100. A station on the M. St. P. & S. Ste. M. Railroad. In 1915, listed as a discontinued post office 11 miles from *Munising.* Mail *Munising.* Was in Au Train Township, near present day M-94 highway and on the present Lake Superior & Ishpeming Railroad.

DIEMLING—1910, a station the M. M. & S. E. Railroad. Mail *Carlshend.*

DIFFIN—1910, a station on the Chicago & Northwestern Railroad. Mail *Trenary.*

DIXON—Located 4 miles west of *Chatham*, on the Munising Railroad. 1910. Mail *Chatham.*

DORSEY—1910, on the M. St. P. & S. Ste. M. Railroad. Nearest post office at *Shingleton.*

DOTY—1910, on the Manistique & Lake Superior and M. M. & S. E. Railroads. Nearest post office at *Shingleton.*

ETHEL—1910, on the East Branch of the M. M. & S. E. Railroad, 16 miles east of *Stillman*. Mail to *Shingleton*.

———

EVELYN—1910, on the Duluth, South Shore & Atlantic Railroad. Mail to *Wetmore*.

———

FARM—1910, near *Grand Marais*. Send mail there.

———

FERGUSON—1910, on the M. M. & S. E. Railroad. Nearest post office at *Chatham*.

———

FINNS—1910, a station on the M. M. & S. E. Railroad. Mail to *Chatham*.

———

FISH HATCHERY—1910, on the M. M. & S. E. Railroad. Send mail to *Munising*.

———

FLOETER—Name changed to *Munising*. Not a ghost town.

———

FOREST LAKE—Post office established in 1917-19. In 1927 was described as settled in 1910. On the Munising Marquette & Southern Railroad, 13 miles southwest of *Munising*. Two busses ran daily to *Escanaba* and *Munising*. Vincent Truden, Postmaster and general store; David Makinen and A. I. Ruggles, Justices of the Peace.

———

GOGARNVILLE—In 1893 was located in Munising Township, 16 miles east of *Au Train* and 2½ from *Munising*. On the Duluth, South Shore & Atlantic Railroad, population 10. Mail, tri-weekly. Julius Gogarn, Postmaster, for whom the place was named. Fred Beland, lighthouse keeper; J. Gogarn, general store; K. Kung, lighthouse keeper; Geo. McGregor, lighthouse keeper; D. McKay, fisherman; Aaron Powell, summer resort; C. C. Powell, summer resort; and V. V. Williams, farmer.

———

GRAND ISLAND—In 1879, there was permanent population of 20 persons on the island and the settlement was known by the same name.

———

GLASIER—1910, on the M. M. & S. E. Railroad. Nearest post office at *Munising*.

———

GRAND MARAIS—The history of this harbor on Lake Superior is nearly as old as that of the Upper Peninsula, dating back to the mid-seventeenth century when Pierre Esprit Radisson first mentioned *Grand Marais* in an account of his voyage to the Great Lakes region.

First used by the Chippewa and Indian tribes as a haven, then by the voyageurs, who gave it its name, the site became a fur trading post. First settle-

Grand Marais harbor as it appeared in 1961 when Great Lakes fishing was still a main industry. Most of the old fish houses are now gone and only pleaseure craft dock in the harbor.   Michigan Conservation Department photo.

ment, or attempt to settle, occurred in 1850-51 when several parties bought up the land bordering the bay.

In his booklet, "Voyageurs' Harbor," James L. Carter states that *"On June 26, 1861, Peter B. Barbeau was issued a government patent for Lot Five on the south shore of East Bay, and late that fall, he had a trading post built on the site."* It wasn't, however, until the 1870s that the first permanent residents settled on the site. The first government lighthouse was established here in 1874 and by 1880 *Grand Marais* was a fishing village of some importance. A post office was established in 1882.

About the same time the first sawmill was erected, and for the next 30 years the village became an important logging and lumbering center. Wellington Burt, the wealthiest lumberman in *Saginaw* history, set up operations in partnership with Henry Gamble and built a 7-mile narrow-gauge railroad to haul their timber to the mill. This was one of the first logging railroads in the state and operated until nearly the turn-of-the-century when it was abandoned and the iron sold for scrap.

Evidence of the vast stands of white pine can still be seen today for miles around *Grand Marais* in the form of giant, fire-blackened stumps that dot the hills and valleys of the area.

For some time the village was divided between "East Town" and "West Town." Burt platted the village of *West Grand Marais* in 1883 and another group laid out what was called *East Town.*

Grand Marais was not listed as a village in business directories until 1885 and in 1887 was described as *"A promising village on Lake Superior, in Burt Township, Alger County, 70 miles north of Au Train, the county seat, and 25 north of Seney, the nearest railroad shipping point. Banking is done at Sault Ste. Marie. Population, 300. Semi-weekly mail stage to Seney. Walter Bell, Postmaster."* In that year the village contained two general stores, a drug and grocery store combined, three hotels, clothing store, two shingle mills, a sawmill, and two billiard halls.

In 1890, with most of the timber removed, *Grand Marais* became almost a ghost town, with less than 200 people. As the town declined the lumbering interests moved out while the new town of *Seney,* 25 miles to the south, was undergoing a boom. Lower Michigan pine timber was nearly exhausted and lumber barons were moving north, bringing the lumber camps and jacks with them. The dying village regained new strength and began another era with the coming of the logging railroad in 1893. Abandoned lumber mills were rebuilt and once more the sound of the sawmill whistles awakened residents each morning. People started moving into the village so rapidly that by midsummer a virtual tent city had grown up near the edge of town. Most of the population of the heretofore booming *Seney* moved here with the mills, some of them even bringing their own building with them on the train.

Burt's original 7-mile logging railroad, long since gone, was not replaced by miles of logging railroads entering the town from several directions. One railroad alone had 24 miles of line built exclusively to haul timber for shipment by boat to distant mills.

Within the next 20 years *Grand Marais* was destined to become one of the largest unincorporated cities in the Upper Peninsula. The peak of the boom was reached in 1910 when the *Michigan Gazetteer and Business Directory* gave the following description of the thriving town: *"The village surrounds one of the most natural and best harbors on the chain of lakes, a harbor of refuge and the only one between Sault Ste. Marie and Grand Island. The government has expended upwards of a million dollars in improving this harbor, equipping it with piers and dikes, two lighthouses and a thoroughly equipped life-saving station. This is a popular and beautiful summer resort. The temperature is at least 15 degrees cooler in summer than in the surrounding territory. The best trout and bass fishing in Michigan is in adjoining streams and lakes. Deer and partridge as well as other game abound, making an ideal place for tourists.*

"Grand Marais is lighted by electricity, has an efficient fire department, a municipal pumping station equipped with two Westinghouse pumps capable of furnishing 1,000 gallons per minute. Water pipes are laid in all the streets and water is furnished to every resident free, and no restrictions as to how much may be used or for what purpose.

"There are churches of the Catholic, Episcopal, Methodist, Presbyterian and Swedish Lutheran denominations, excellent schools, an opera house, first-class hotels, a telephone exchange, and a weekly newspaper, 'The Grand Marais Herald.' Lumber is the principal industry and fishing is extensively carried on. Miss Flora MacLachlan, Postmistress."

Grand Marais was riding high with a bustling and prosperous population of 2,500. More than 65 business places lined the streets. These included beautifully furnished hotels, several luxury saloons doing a flourishing business, a Chinese laundry, a bottling works, its own telephone company, a hospital and several fisheries lined the docks and waterfront.

The big bubble began to burst in the fall of 1910 when the Manistique Railroad discontinued their trains due to lack of business. Despite protests by the townspeople the trains were discontinued and two years later the tracks were removed. Once again *Grand Marais* was isolated from the rest of the world for all practical purposes, except by boat during the shipping season.

Most of the business places became deserted and were left standing with windows boarded while the few remaining residents hopefully awaited another big boom that would revive the town. Eventually the state built a highway, now known as M-77, along the line of the former railroad bed connecting the village with M-28 near *Seney* and for some time there were hopes of a tourist boom.

The government Coast Guard Station still operates here and a few business places remain, which include an ultra-modern motel near the Coast Guard Station, an I.G.A. store, and a gasoline station. Some of the buildings burned, others were razed, and a few remain. Today a combination grocery, dry goods, antique and gift shop operates in the old building that during the town's heyday, was appropriately called the "Grand Central Saloon" at the main corners of "East Town" overlooking the harbor and a neglected Civil War cannon. The original narrow, pineboard floors, once white from layers of sawdust used to soak up the overflow from cuspidors, are now blackened with age and creak with each step of the occasional tourist who makes the 25-mile trip over the rough blacktop and concrete highway from M-28 North to park near the harbor and see the grand view. During the few summer weekends and long holidays when a rush of tourists come from "down below" business is brisk, but most of the year the souvenir postcard rack, pop coolers, and sparsely stocked shelves of the old store gather dust.

Grand Marais still has a post office, a triangular-shaped, wood-frame building built to conform with the three-cornered intersection next to the old store. Another huge, two-story, wood-frame building that once was one of upper Michigan's largest provision and supply houses stands across the street, surrounded with weeds and brush, left to the elements. A couple of other stores, a gas station and a unique, barrel-shaped root beer stand, no longer in business, are the few business places remaining (1971). The long dreamed-of tourist boom has not yet developed and with nothing to attract tourists *Grand Marais* may well become completely deserted, as did *Fayette, Central, Allenville* and the many other ghost towns of the Upper Peninsula.

Historical marker at *Grand Marais: "Grand Marais, which is among Michigan's oldest place names, received its name from French, explorers, missionaries, and traders who passed here in the 1600s. 'Marais' was a term used by the voyageurs to designate a harbor of refuge. In the 1800s Lewis Cass, Henry Schoolcraft, and Douglass Houghton also found the sheltered harbor a welcome stopping place . . . Permanent settlement dates from the 1860s with the establishment of fishing and lumbering. At the turn-of-the-century Grand Marais was a boom town served by a railroad from the south. Its mills turned out many millions of board feet annually. Lumbering declined around 1910, and Grand Marais became almost a ghost town, but the fishing industry continued. Many shipping disasters have occurred at or near this harbor of refuge which has been served by the Coast Guard since 1899. In 1942 the first radar station in Michigan was built in Grand Marais. Fishing, lumbering, and tourism now gives Grand Marais its livelihood."* (This plaque was dedicated July, 1964 by the *Grand Marais* Chamber of Commerce). Since that date even the fishing has declined, due to controls set by the State and the decline in the fish stock of the Great Lakes.

HALLS CAMP—In 1910 a lumber camp near *Grand Marais.* Mail to *Grand Marais.*

HALLSTON—1905, a discontinued post office at the junction of the Duluth, South Shore & Atlantic Railroad and 8 miles south of *Au Train,* the county seat. Railroad name is *Munising Junction.*

This was a short-lived station and settlement that lasted from about 1890 to 1905. In 1893 population 150. F. H. Mack, Jr. Postmaster; Anna River Brick Company, brick manufacturers; John A. Charlton, brick maker; and A. P. Huchins, railroad express agent.

HANLEY—1910, a station on the M. M. & S. E. Railroad. Nearest post office at *Wetmore.*

HARTHO—1910, a station on the M. M. & S. E. Railroad. Mail to *Shingleton.*

JENKS—1910, on the M. M. & S. E. Railroad. Mail to *Chatham.*

JENNY—was a station on the M. M. & N. Railroad, 19 miles from *Munising.* Lasted until about 1920.

JUNIPER—1910, on the M. M. & S. E. Railroad. Mail to *Shingleton.*

KIVA—1915. On Whitefish River, Limestone Township, 8 miles from *Carlshend,* its shipping point. Mrs. Sigrid Kivimaki, Postmistress and grocery; William Kangas, blacksmith.

LADOGA—1910, nearest post office at *Limestone* on the M. C. & N. W. Railroad.

LEROUX—1910, on the M. M. & S. E. Railroad. Mail to *Cusino.*

LOUDS SPUR—1927, near *Eben Junction.* The location of the Loud Brewster Lumber Company. Send mail to *Eben Junction.*

LYNN—1910, send mail to *Munising.*

McVILLE—1909, a country post office, 10 miles southeast of *Rudyard.* Was not a town.

MERRIAM—In 1910 on the M. M. & S. E. Railroad, 5 miles east of *Munising.* Mail to *Wetmore.*

———————

METSER—1910, on the M. M. & S. E. Railroad. Mail to *Shingleton.*

———————

MINERS—1910, on the M. St. P. & S. Ste. M. Railroad. Mail to *Trenary.*

———————

MYRTLE—1910, on the M. M. & S. E. Railroad. Mail to *Wetmore.*

———————

NETTLES—1910, a station on the M. M. & S. E. Railroad. Send mail to *Carlshend.*

———————

OLD MUNISING—Name used for *Wetmore,* which was changed from *Old Munising* to *Wetmore.*

———————

ONOTA—This is confusing due to the fact that there were two villages by this name. Present day *Onota,* located in Rock Township, 26 miles north of *Munising,* was settled in 1880 and is a station on the Detroit Mackinac & Marquette Railroad.

1873 business directory: John S. Blackwell, Postmaster; S. L. Barney, light-house keeper for *Grand Island* harbor; Frank Blackwell, clerk for Bay Furnace Company; John C. Blackwell, County Treasurer; John Frink, Judge of Probate; H. D. Pickman, physician; Donald Rankin, coal contractor; Christian Sackrider, book-keeper for Bay Furnace Company; and William Shea, superintendent of Bay Furnace Company.

Onota, the ghost town, in 1875 was the first county seat of Schoolcraft County. This was before Alger County was organized. Described as: *"The seat of justice for Schoolcraft County, a village on Grand Island harbor on the south shore of Lake Superior, 6 miles west of Munising, and 40 miles east of Marquette.*

Population, 600. First settled in July of 1869 when a blast furnace was established, which started business the following spring. It is owned by the Bay Furnace Company and turned out in 1875 nearly 10,000 tons of pig iron since its erection the production has totaled 38,340 tons.

The country back of Onota is rolling, sandy, and heavily timbered. Stage communication with Marquette and receives daily mail. Telegraph of the Western Union.

Frank M. Blackwell, Postmaster; Edgar Adams, County Clerk; Frank M. Blackwell, store manager for Bay Furnace Company; Zephyr Boyer, blacksmith; Francis Crane, sheriff; M. H. Noble, machinist; Henry S. Pickands, agent for Bay Furnace Company; Wesley Pope, Physician; Donald Rankin, coal contractor; Maurice Ring, founder of furnace; John Scripture, carriage-maker;

Ernest Rankin, of the Marquette County Historical Society, said the location of *Bay Furnace* was originally a favorite camping place for Indians who came by trail and canoe each spring over the Whitefish and Au Train Rivers from Little Bay de Noc to spend the summer in the Grand Island area to hunt, fish and pick berries.

On June 1, 1876, fire struck the village and within two days everything had burned, never to be re-established. It later reverted to a sawmill town. The site remained vacant, except for the remains of the old furnace, and during the next half-century was overgrown with brush and weeds.

In 1938, Julius Thorson purchased 49 acres of land adjoining the site and erected a large building where he manufactured toys and wood items. As a publicity gimmick to promote the sale of his toys, Thorson called his place *Christmas*. Two years later (1940) Thorson's building burned and everything was destroyed. He then moved to Texas where he died in 1952.

On October 14, 1940, the unincorporated village of *Christmas* was platted and by the 1950s about 40 homes, a store, restaurant, motels, and about 100 people were here.

On July 8, 1966, a post office was opened to promote the tourist village. This was a gala event with the *Munising* High School Band furnishing the music. Today the tiny settlement is a tourist attraction on M-28. Each summer hundreds of tourists visit the tiny post office and gift shop that is housed in a log cabin-type building appropriately painted red and trimmed in green and white, where the spirit of Christmas exists year around. A roadside zoo and large two-story gift shop are other attractions along with an old-fashioned country-style restaurant furnished with rough-hewn tables and unfinished board interior. Delectable home cooked meals are prepared on an old iron range cook stove.

A short distance north of *Christmas* a trail leads to the bay where the old *Bay Furnace* has been restored on a site preserved by the U. S. Forest Service.

The two villages of *Onota* are very confusing to historians and the history of each is intertwined in the telling. The present village, the name which was an invention of Henry Rowe Schoolcraft, was established near Deer Lake in 1881 when the Detroit Mackinac & Marquette Railroad was built, and a charcoal kiln was built. Great forests of hardwood abounded in the area and these were used in the manufacture of charcoal for operating blast furnaces.

In 1893 the village was described as: *"A village on the D. S. S. & A. Railroad in Onota Township, 9 miles northwest of Au Train, the judicial seat. Settled in 1880. Population 200. C. H. Schaffer, Postmaster; E. P. Hoffman, railroad and express agent; John LaBree, Justice; and Onota Charcoal Manufacturing. Company, J. W. Belknap and E. P. Hoffman, proprietors."* This *Onota* is shown on today's maps and still has a post office.

This town also changed names several times. At one time it was known as *Bismark*, and another time was called *Wayne's Mill*.

PERCY—1910, on the M. M. & S. E. Railroad. Mail to *Shingleton*.

PETEREL—Located in Munising Township, on the Munising Railroad, 20 miles from *Munising*. No post office. Mail to *Shingleton*.

PETERSON—1910, on the M. M. & S. E. Railroad. Mail to *Wetmore*.

REEDSBORO—1887, was a newly-established post office and station on the Detroit Mackinac & Marquette Railroad, 17 miles southeast of *Au Train*, the county seat. Bank at *Marquette*. Population 100. Daily mail. A. Gibbs, Postmaster; A. Gibbs & Company, shingle mill. Not listed in 1893 directory.

RIDGE—1910, on the Duluth, South Shore & Atlantic Railroad. Mail to *Munising*.

ROBERTS—1910, on the M. M. & S. E. Railroad. Mail to *Carlshend*.

ROCKRIVER—In 1905 was a rural post office on the D. S. S. & A. Railroad, in Rock River Township, 16 miles west of *Munising*. Had a telephone. C. C. Brown, Postmaster; and Rock River Cedar Company, sawmill and lumber. In 1909 listed as a discontinued post office.

ROSCOE—On Munising, Marquette & Southeastern Railroad. 1910 mail *Wetmore*.

SAMSON—In 1910 on the M. M. & S. E. Railroad. Send mail to *Shingleton*.

STANDARD—1910 nearest post office at *Chatham*.

STAR SPUR—1910, a station on the D. S. S. & A. Railroad. Mail to *Shingleton*. Today a restaurant and motel is in business here on highway M-28 that parallels the railroad.

STATE ROAD—1910, send mail to *Grand Marais*.

STILLMAN—1910, a station on the M. M. & S. E. 9 miles east of *Munising*. Send mail to *Munising*.

SUMMIT—1910, nearest post office at *Grand Marais*.

TYOGA—1910, on the D. S. S. & A. Railroad. Ship via *Tyoga Junction*. Not a post office. Send mail to *Onota*.

VAN MEER—1910, on the Munising, Marquette and Southeastern railroad. Mail *Shingleton*.

VALLEY—1910, on the M. M. & S. E. Railroad 6 miles east of *Munising*. Mail to *Munising*.

WAYNE'S MILL—See *Onota*.

WEST PERCY—1910, on the M. M. & S. E. Railroad. Mail to *Shingleton*.

WHITEFISH—1910, on the D. S. S. & A. Railroad. Send mail to *Sand River*.

WINTERS—Shown on 1970 county map. Settled in 1890 and named after the first Postmaster, John D. Winters. In 1905 described as: *"A post office in Mathias Township, 11 miles from Chatham, its shipping point. Daily mail stage to Chatham. A. W. Clark, Postmaster; Rev. Wm. Brown, Methodist Episcopal; Dr. Carlson, A. W. Clark & Son, general store; J. B. Clowser, shoemaker; Edwin Davis, hardware; I. A. Davis, general store; C. Gilliland, carpenter; Joseph Heldman, saloon; Miss Lau, teacher; Lewin & Jacobs, clothing; R. C. Richey, express and telegraph agent; Y. Stevens, saloon and livery; Electra Stocking, teacher; L. W. Trenary, sawmill; R. Trenary, restaurant; and H. Winkle, meat market."*

In 1927, population 100. On the D. S. S. & A. Railway and on M-67 (same today). Bus to *Escanaba* and *Munising* daily. Telephone. Martha S. Kennta, Postmistress and general store; Brown's Theater, C. C. Brown; O. H. Snow, railroad agent; William Smith, Justice of Peace. The postoffice was discontinued in 1927.

ZERBEL—In 1910 on the M. M. & S. E. Railroad. Send mail to *Munising*.

Chapter Five

BARAGA COUNTY

Baraga County was set off and organized in 1875. The land area was formerly attached to Houghton County. The county is steeped in early history from days of the Jesuit priests, and was named for Bishop Frederic Baraga. The Lake Superior shoreline was along the main route of the early voyageurs into the heart of New France. Other famous names in its history were French Jesuit Rene Menard, Methodist Missionary Daniel Meeker Chandler, and Sir Alexander Henry who transported some of Michigan's first copper, in canoes, across the bay.

This was also the land of the Indians when the white man came. Indian burial grounds and recently discovered mounds in Baraga Township date back about 2,500 years.

A short distance above *L'Anse*, near the *Zeba* mission, a monument has been erected to mark the site of the first trading post established for the American Fur Trading Company on Lake Superior. The post was established by Peter Crebassa in 1837 and was one of five trading posts in the Upper Peninsula.

"BARAGA COUNTY'S $2,000,000 GHOST RAILROAD"

(Reprinted from the September 23, 1964 issue of the *L'Anse Sentinel* by permission.)

A few rusty nails, some old telegraph poles and a bed grown over with brush and trees in the Huron Mountain district is all that remains today of a $2,000,000 railroad which never ran a train of cars and failed to bring in a cent of revenue.

For several years men labored in the wilderness to lay 35 miles of tracks through rocky gorges and swamps from the mining town of *Champion* (now a ghost town) to *Huron Bay*. At *Huron Bay*, an immense ore dock, buildings and homes were erected in preparation for a rush of business which the promoters of the Huron Bay and Iron Range Railway thought would make them wealthy.

The Huron Mountain district has long been thought to contain great

Old Indian cemetery common to the western counties of the Upper Peninsula. This cemetery is located near *L'anse* in Baraga County. Photo by Roy L. Dodge

mineral riches. At that time it also contained much valuable timber, on parts of which loggers had already begun to work. However, it was also one of the roughest and most inaccessible portions of the peninsula.

This was in the early nineties, when fortunes were quickly and easily gained in the iron district so it seemed logical for the *Champion* mine operators to transport their ore across country to the bay, which was already known as a shipping point because of the slate quarries at *Arvon*. But in the meantime the Duluth South Shore and Atlantic Railroad extended westward from *Marquette* to *Champion*, obtaining this business. The Huron Bay and Iron Range found itself with a finished roadbed, two 100-ton locomotives and 21 flatcars on its hands, but no traffic.

Considerable space was given the project by newspapers of the Upper Peninsula. One of the contractors, Wallace Dingman, delayed the work in 1891 when he was forced to mortgage and assign his property along the road. Dingman's debts amounted to over $10,000. Time checks of laborers were bought in some communities at a 50 percent discount. Newspaper reports stated that the time checks had been outstanding for several months and *"the ragged and wretched victims watched with hungry eyes the daily train from Detroit for some relief. At Champion and Michigamme they crowded the platforms howling for the paymaster.*

"Merchants along the line, from L'Anse, Michigamme, Champion and Marquette who trusted liberally, are sorrowing over assets that have disappeared from shelves and warehouses and many of them are reduced to dire extremity by the importunities of their creditors."

The late Sam Beck of *L'Anse* was one of the few taking the one and only trip a locomotive ever made on the 35-mile line.

"The engines were unloaded at Huron Bay," Beck, a former *Champion* hotel proprietor, who worked as a railroad watchman at the time, said. *"As the last 11 miles of the road was downgrade, it was decided to make a test run."* Beck said he rode in the cab with the engineer. *"We had proceeded but a short distance up the grade when the roadbed gave way, and we went into the ditch. From that moment on, the great Huron Bay & Iron Range ceased to exist as a railroad."*

A short time after the ill-fated trip the engines were sold to the Algoma Central, and the rails, which never again heard the click of wheels, were taken to *Detroit* where they were used for the interurban service of the Detroit Urban Railroad.

"The railroad was unlucky from the beginning," Beck related. *"The slate quarries at Arvon, from which a great deal of shipping was expected, petered out in a short time (see Arvon in this book). Though the settlement at Huron Bay was maintained for a while, about all that remains today is a few pilings of the huge dock. A squaw who became angry at the storekeeper burned the rest of it down."*

The ore dock at the terminus of the railroad was an engineering feat by itself. Constructed in 1890 and 1891, the dock contained 2,000,000 feet of lumber and 3,000 piles. There was about 600 feet of pocket room. The dock was dismantled in February of 1901.

The huge rock cut where the railroad passed through is overgrown with weeds today, although Ford used portions of the grade to haul logs during his timber operations, headquartered at *Pequaming* during the 1940s. A small stream flows out of the cut now to join with others and become the Slate River.

Tons of black powder and the toil and sweat of large crews of men were required to move 40,000 cubic yards of rock in another huge cut at the summit. Remnants of wire-bound hoses found at the site indicate that steam drills were used for placing the charges. The rock is of the Canadian Shield and is the hardest of granites.

This cut cost about $500,000. It was necessary if the railroad was to follow the Slate River Valley down to Huron Bay. The hill at the summit of the divide has an altitude of 1,960 feet.

Near the cut are evidences of a large camp site with blacksmith shop and other log buildings. There are also indications that some of the workmen lived in huts constructed partially underground.

Remains of a rock fill that extended more than 500 feet over lowland beyond the cut can still be seen today. Trestle pilings made of heavy cedar and pine timbers, although partly decayed and weathered, remain where it ran for one half mile over low ground.

————

ARNHEIN—1905, population 100. On the Duluth, South Shore & Atlantic Railroad, Baraga Township, 16 miles north of *L'Anse*. Martin Erickson, Postmaster; James Byers, mayor; Moses Bishop, farmer; Martin Erickson, general store and railroad agent; J. W. Johnson, logger; Henry Key, sawmill; Martin Messner, farmer; Superior Red Sandstone Company, quarry; Union Portage Entry Quarry Company; and J. M. Wilson, logger.

By 1918 the population had dropped to less than 25 and only one general store remained, owned by Nettie Brothers.

ARVON—This village was settled in 1872 and within a year had a population of 150. A tri-weekly stage ran to *L'Anse*, 12 miles west. John Thomas was Postmaster and Morris Jones, school teacher. Stone quarries were opened on the site by the Clinton Slate Company and the Huron Bay Slate & Iron Company.

By 1887 the population had increased to 250 and the quarries were owned by the Michigan Slate Company, with a paid-up capital of one-half million dollars. The 1887 business directory lists the following: John D. Rowland, Postmaster and hotel owner; J. Andrew Anderson, shoemaker; Thomas Hooper, superintendent of slate quarries; John Lofquist, blacksmith; J. M. Turner, President of Michigan Slate Company; and James Tood, carpenter.

All that remains today is the remains of the old quarries near an abandoned railroad grade.

———

AURA—Was settled in 1914 and at that time was on the D. S. S. & A. Railroad and highway M-41, L'Anse Township, 12 miles northwest of *L'Anse*. By 1927 the population had grown to 200. A daily bus ran to *L'Anse*. There were Catholic, Lutheran, and Methodist churches and a moving picture theater, in that year Mrs. Hilda Mytty was Postmistress; Mr. Graboski ran the "New Mazda Theater"; G. G. Knepple was railroad agent; and F. J. Lyons, village president.

Aura still has a post office, located in Dan's General Store, the only business place remaining open. Across from the store is the building that once housed the "Aura Co-op Store," now empty and deserted. One church, Finnish Lutheran, freshly painted white, stands about ½ mile south of the former business section of the one-time village, and an abandoned gasoline station of 1930 vintage remains alone what may have been a main traveled road at one time. Several homes are in the vicinity.

———

BEAUFORT—1905, a station on the D. S. S. & A. Railroad, south of *L'Anse*, near *Redruth*.

———

BELLAIRE—1910, on the Mineral Range Railroad, near *Keweenaw Bay*, where mail was sent.

———

BESS—1905, a flag station on the D. S. S. & A. Railroad.

———

BRISTOL—In 1869 was the name of the new post office for the village of *Baraga*. Not a ghost town.

———

CLIFFS—1887, a station on the Marquette Houghton & Ontonogon Railroad, 18 miles east of *L'Anse*.

Main factory building of the Ford plant at *Pequaming* where wood parts were made for automobiles. With broken windows overlooking Keweenaw Bay, it is now a roosting place for sea gulls.   Photo by Roy L. Dodge (1971)

FEWSVILLE—A village, settled in 1872, in Baraga Township, 8 miles from *L'Anse*. The post office was discontinued in 1877. In 1879, described as, *"The Black Creek furnishes water power and operates a distillery and a barrel factory. A Catholic church, two schools, and a convent are located here."* The name may have been changed to *Assins*, presently a village.

GIDDINGS—Was a village in Baraga Township. Possibly incorporated with *Baraga* when it became a village.

HERMAN—1910, population 175. On the Soo Line Railroad, in L'Anse Township, 8 miles southeast of *L'Anse*. John F. Keranen, general store, Postmaster and wood; Charles Lystila, carpenter; Nels Maihanour, wood; and Margaret Shea, teacher.

In 1917, population 150. Charles T. Dante, Postmaster and general store; Farmer's Co-op Milling Company, flour and feed; and H. Kernanen, sawmill; P. L. Morrow, railroad agent. Not a complete ghost town and has a post office, store, etc. today (1971).

IRONBRIDGE—Shown on 1905 map, southeast of *L'Anse*.

KING LAKE—A station near *Nestoria*.

MURPHY—1893, on the Soo Line Railroad, 25 miles south of *L'Anse*. Daily mail. Population 12. G. H. Schonweg, Postmaster and farmer; J. T. Davis, railroad and telegraph agent.

1905, was a discontinued post office. Mail to *Sidnaw*.

NEWTONVILLE—Also known as *Newton's*, was a stone quarry and lumbering settlement 12 miles north of *L'Anse*, in Baraga Township and on Keweenaw Bay. Settled about 1880 and named for a family who settled there, named Newton.

In 1887, population 250 in the vicinity. 1893, E. D. Newton, Postmaster; Martin Messner, stone quarry; Amy Newton, telegraph agent; and E. D. Newton, sawmill. Post office discontinued about 1895.

PAPIN—1910, a station on the Mineral Range Railroad.

PERCH—1910, on the D. S. S. & A. Railroad, mail *Sidnaw*.

PEQUAMING—One of the largest ghost towns in the Upper Peninsula with buildings still standing is *Pequaming*. Located about 8 miles north of *L'Anse* the huge smokestacks and water towers are visible from the *L'Anse* waterfront

Now deserted, except for a caretaker, *Pequaming*, north of *L'Anse*, is now a ghost town. The town was purchased by Henry Ford in the 1920s and made into a model village. The old Ford water tower looms above the huge, empty hotel across the road from the deserted factory buildings.   Photo by Roy L. Dodge (1971)

where the remains of the once prosperous industrial town lies at the tip of a tree-covered peninsula jutting out into the Keweenaw Bay.

This town was founded in 1878 by Charles and Edward Hebard, who, in cooperation with H. C. Thurber, formed an incorporation with a capital stock of $2,000,000 to conduct lumbering operations in the area. The company owned more than 100,000 acres of pine land in the area. The Hebards built a large mill called the Hebard & Thurber; and by the 1890s were producing 25 million feet of lumber and 25 million shingles annually. The huge lumbering operation required nearly a thousand men, with 250 working full-time in the mills and others in the woods cutting logs.

As most towns of the day, all the buildings were built and owned by the company, including the business places. Hebard built the company houses along wide, tree-lined streets. Workers were allowed to rent the houses at a nominal sum and traded at the company store where purchases were tallied and deducted from the men's wages at the end of each month.

One of the Hebards erected his own home facing the west side of the bay, apart from the workers homes. This was built in southern plantation style—three stories high with a huge white pillared veranda extending across the front, about 30 spacious rooms, complete with servants' quarters, and furnished in elegant splendor.

By 1910 most of the virgin pine timber had been exhausted. The mill, now Charles Hebard & Son, was still in operation but its production was greatly reduced. There was only one other industry in the area at the time, the Traverse Bay Red Stone Company, which ran a quarry near *Pequaming*.

The Hebard & Thurber mill was the first large lumbering operation in the Lake Superior area and over a 20 year period was destined to boast an annual average production of 30 million feet of lumber, for a total production of 500 million feet.

About 1920, Henry Ford started a survey of the Upper Peninsula, especially around the *L'Anse* area, and announced that he was going to purchase one million acres of land. Rumors rapidly spread as to where the new Ford enterprise was going to be headquartered and Henry made personal tours of the areas. Every town and hamlet soon had stories circulating that he was going to locate in their town and things would be booming for them again.

Eventually Ford purchased the holdings of the Michigan Land and Iron Company which consisted of odd-numbered sections originally granted to the railroad along its right-of-way, in all a total of more than 400,000 acres. The purchase included the old Hebard Lumber Company and the entire village of *Pequaming* along with the Stearns & Culver Lumber Company of *L'Anse*.

In 1922 Ford had improved his holdings, expanded the *L'Anse* mill and built logging railroads to transport the hardwood timber he was going to use in his *Detroit* factories. In order to achieve complete independence in the automotive industry, Ford was convinced that he must control the sources of raw materials. To reach this goal he purchased mining properties and vast timber holdings. This also included the purchase of more forest land, docks, tugs, barges and sawmills. Ford supervised the building of the sawmills with the most modern machinery and equipment that could be purchased.

Ford paid men in the mills and woods the fabulous sum of $6.00 for an eight-hour work day and maintained the same stringent rules in camps and lumbering villages laid down for his shop workers (no drinking, saving a percentage of their wages, and a general surveillance of their homes and mode of life). The lumber camps took on a new look, much to the disgust of many old-time lumberjacks. Neat, frame buildings painted snow white; beds with springs and mattresses replaced the old-tick ridden bunks; fancy dining rooms with china plates; recreation rooms complete with radios and movies; and to top it all off each section of the camp had its own individual "house mother."

Pequaming became a model village. The old Hebard mills were remodeled and bricked, old company houses were recovered with cedar shakes to match new houses finished with the same material. Each house and building in *Pequaming* and in other camps, such as the *Ford Camp* number four near *Watton* were equipped with electricity and running water. A new water tower with "Ford" printed in the familiar script letters 10 feet high was erected, and fire hydrants placed on each of the several hundred lots in the village.

The Ford era lasted until the depression of the 1930s when production of automobiles came to a standstill. The mills ran on a part-time basis but most of the workers were laid off. Machinery laid idle until the breakout of World War II when the mills once more started humming, this time on a 24-hour, around-the-clock basis. With the end of the war, and the elimination of all wood parts in automobiles, there was no longer a demand for lumber. This, added to the nearly depleted hardwood in the Upper Peninsula, once more left the mills idle. Camp buildings were abandoned and also the entire village of *Pequaming*. The only activity in Baraga County remaining from the Ford era is the boys camp at the Ford model village of *Alberta*, a few miles south of *L'Anse*.

Pequaming was an unusual company town, due to the extensive remodeling by Ford to make it the model village, and is also an unusual ghost town. A wide, blacktop road runs along the shore of the bay north of *L'Anse* and affords a beautiful view of the town across the bay. Upon entering the main street of the village, a cemetery, also unusual due to the fact that it is triangular-shaped and surrounded by a cement retaining wall topped by an expensive wrought iron fence, lies at the entrance to the village. This is a possible three-acre plot with large, impressive tombstones and monuments and is well cared for even though the town has been all but abandoned. The entrance gate is dated 1896.

Most of the buildings, which included a huge, two-story hotel, general store that was built to serve more than 1,000 people, foreman or caretakers home, large, two-story lodge hall, and many of the 20 or more houses, are in excellent condition, although many of the streets are so grass- and weed-covered as to make them nearly impassable by automobile. Even the tiny, weathered, frame post office building remains standing near the I. O. O. F. Hall.

Many of the houses have also collapsed or been razed, and in 1971 the one remaining church was being dismantled. Except for broken windows, the huge buildings that housed the sawmills are still intact and as one stands looking out over the bay at the decayed dock pilings it almost seems that a ship will enter the harbor at any minute to take on another load of lumber.

There is a permanent caretaker living here and the lawns around the main houses are kept mowed. Keweenaw Bay is a famous fishing site and several hundred fishermen hauling their boats and fishing gear travel the main street each weekend during the summer intent on their sport. None of them seem to be aware they are visiting one of the oldest, most historic ghost towns in the state.

In addition to the caretaker, in 1971 one family occupied a house here. Four of the houses are available for rent by the week to tourists and these are rented occasionally during summer months. The old Hebard mansion, now called "the Ford Mansion," is up for sale for about one-third of the cost of replacement. Some of the furnishings could not be duplicated today and the house is in perfect condition.

Pequaming was a post office as early as 1880. In 1887 the population was 700. Daily mail, E. W. Hebard, Postmaster; Elmer E. Halse, circuit court commissioner; Wm. K. Haviland, Justice of the Peace; Charles Hebard & Son, saw and shingle mills, general store and hotel; O'Donnell, barber, and M. Wallace, meats.

In 1893, remained about the same. E. W. Hebard, Postmaster; Mrs. Josie Donlon, dressmaker; Elmer E. Halsey, lawyer; Ford W. Hebard, meat market; Samuel Latourelle, barber; John Lofquist, blacksmith; Mrs. George McKenzie, dressmaker; Wm. J. Snyder, Justice; and Miss Kate Wahl, milliner.

By 1918 the village had three churches, Catholic, Finnish Lutheran and Union Protestant. Daily stage to *L'Anse* and telephone. John A. Hickey, Postmaster; Napoleon Da'Oust, meats; Charles Hebard & Son owned the mills, store etc; and F. W. Knepple was railroad express agent.

———

REDRUTH—1887, was a newly established post office, on the Marquette Houghton & Ontonagon Railroad, between *Spur Mountain* and *L'Anse.* George McDonald, Postmaster.

1893, on the D. S. A. & A. Railroad, 21 miles southeast of *L'Anse.* Population 70. Daily mail. Peter Lofberg, justice; George McDonald, sawmill; and John Ryan, justice.

1910, a post office and flag station in Spur Township. Ole J. Lund, Postmaster; Irene Anderson, teacher; and George McDonald, justice.

1918, about the same, one addition to listing was Davis Smith, lumber. The post office was discontinued about 1930.

———

SKANEE—was named after a district in Sweden called *Skone.* A handful of remaining residents of this former village on Lake Superior, along with a hundred or more visitors, celebrated Arvon Township's first 100 years in mid-July of 1971. Highlights of the two-day celebration and parade included Milford Nelson leading the last milk cow remaining in the area, a soap box derby in which one lad was injured, and a bicycle built for two traveling down the graveled main street. Some of the old-timers talked over the "good old days" and speculated on the future when the neighboring Huron Mountains may reveal some of their long-hidden treasure in the form of gold, silver or uranium, all of which have been discovered at one time or another during past years. Sometime around 1941 national news was made when uranium was discovered here.

One of Michigan's most famous lumberjacks, John Driscoll, was christened "Silver Jack" after his excursions to a stream in the Huron Mountains during the logging days of the area when he returned to camp with a pocketful of silver nuggets. Driscoll never revealed the location of the place where these were supposedly found, but only said when his logging days were over he was going to stake out his claim and make a fortune from the silver mine.

Unfortunately he met an untimely death at a boarding house in *L'Anse* without divulging his secret or having had an opportunity to develop his claim. Silver Jack died there on April Fools Day, 1895, after returning from the spring log drive on the Yellow Dog River where he had caught cold after several weeks of working in the ice cold waters.

Driscoll died at the Ballenger Hotel in *L'Anse* which, along with the entire business block, was destroyed by fire the following year, 1896. His only living relative, a brother, who was a bartender in a *Saginaw* saloon, was notified and came here to give him a decent Catholic burial. Silver Jack was laid to rest with proper last rites in an unused section of the "Old L'Anse Cemetery" and his brother started the return trip by train back to *Saginaw*, intending to arrange for a headstone for his famous brother's grave. Somewhere along the line on his return to *Saginaw*, according to old-timers in the *L'Anse* area, the sole remaining Driscoll changed his mind and ended it all by committing suicide. Attempts to locate Silver Jack's exact burial spot to erect a marker or some type of memorial to the "King of the Lumberjacks" have been unsuccessful and here lies the secret of the location where silver nuggets lay in abundance; somewhere in the foot-hills of the Huron Mountains.

The *Skanee* reunion and celebration brought back to many some of the great glory that was once *Arvon's*, the days of the slate quarries, the O'Neil gold legends, the days of the two-million-dollar railway pioneering into the *Skanee* region, along with other memories of the founding of the village.

Regarding the centennial, the *L'Anse Sentinel* said in part, *"Skanee people were proud of their two days. They rest content that they have a church or two in the region, that they still have a schoolhouse (and town hall), and that nature continues to smile on the region. Truly Skanee is happy!"*

Skanee was first listed in business directories in 1877 and described as, *"A settlement of 110 persons on Huron Bay, 18 miles north of L'Anse. Settled in 1871, has a Lutheran church and ships timber and farm produce. Mail weekly. Walfred Been, Postmaster. (Been was the first settler and encouraged settlers from his native land of Sweden to settle here and form a model village for farming and fishing). Walfred Been, general store; Peter Hawkenson, saloon; and Reverend Oscar Zelien, Reformed Lutheran. The post office was estab-lished in 1876."*

During the next decade there was little change in the town, a carriage maker and a couple of other businesses had been added and the population increased by about 50. By 1890 the population had increased to 225.

Skanee reached its peak in 1910 when it boasted a population of 500. In that year O. W. Been was Postmaster; Gustav Dahlberg, dry goods; N. M. DeHaas, sawmill; Axel Erickson, hardware; Charles Hartvigh, grocery; August Paulson, justice; Peter Shifferman, physician; Peter G. Westrom, machinist; Adolph Wicks, carpenter; and John Zillen, physician.

Arnold Tapio, now of *Dearborn*, said he worked in a lumber camp near *Skanee* in the early 1920s for a man named Bill Johnson and drove a bay horse named "Blind Tom" one summer on the skidway. *"We were cutting hardwood, maple, etc., and some yellow birch for veneering,"* Tapio said. *"Any pine that*

50

wasn't cut was burned in a big fire that went through there years before."

Tapio said "Billy The Finn" bought the only tavern in *Skanee*. When he died his wife took over and is there today.

About all that remains in *Skanee* is a grocery store and the tavern.

———

ZEBA—This was at one time an Indian mission, with 300 or more Indians living in the area. The name *Zeba* is Indian for *Little River*. Father Baraga had a mission here for a short time in 1831 but later moved across the bay to *Assinins*.

One year later, 1832, the first Indian church to be erected on Lake Superior was erected here as a Methodist mission. In 1835 the church was rebuilt. In 1848 it was rebuilt again, whether the other buildings were destroyed by fire or frame buildings built in place of log isn't known. The present church standing on the same site was built in 1888. This neat, tiny church with its pointed steeple is painted yellow and overlooks the bay from the high hill on which it stands. Several homes surround the street that leads to the church.

In 1927 *Zeba* was described in the Michigan Gazetteer and Business Directory as *"A rural post office on US-41, 4½ miles north of L'Anse. Mail daily. William Tellefson, grocery and meats."* There is no business here today.

A short distance from *Zeba* south towards *L'Anse*, is Curwood Park, a county campgrounds. Overlooking the bay at this point is a stone monument 10 or 12 feet high with a bronze plaque that reads *"This monument is on the site of the first trading post established by the American Fur Trading Company by Peter Crebassa in 1837."* Presented by L'Anse Township Schools, National Youth Administration, 1938. The plaque also bears a picture of an Indian head.

OTHER STATIONS AND SETTLEMENTS

The following places are designated on 1905 maps: *Hibbard, Leo, Perch, Pope, Taylor Junction, Tioga, Treadeau, Tunis, Rhode, Robinson, Summit, Sturgeon* and *Vermilac.*

These locations were mostly spurs or sidings along the railroads of the county, with little or no population. Possibly a few of these places were at one time logging centers of little importance, such as *Sturgeon*, located about 1 mile above *Nestoria*. Most of the other places were flag stops along the railroad between *Nestoria* and *Sidnaw*.

51

Chapter Six

CHIPPEWA COUNTY

Chippewa County was set off in 1826 with land area taken from Mackinac (first called Michilmackinac) County. *Sault Ste. Marie* is the county seat. Called "The Soo" by many people, the city was once called by Henry Clay *"the remotest settlement in the United States, if not the moon."* It was the first permanent settlement in Michigan and is the third oldest remaining town in the United States. Etienne Brule landed on its present site in 1618, and named it Sault de Gaston, in honor of Louis XII, the King of France. In 1668, the Jesuits built a mission here, and the site became a center for missionary work under Father Jacques Marquette.

The Soo was under French domination until 1762, when the English took possession. After the Revolutionary War, the Treaty of Paris in 1783 ceded all lands south of the Great Lakes to the U. S., but the British refused to surrender the region around the Soo or their holdings in the upper Great Lakes region. The American Army built Fort Brady in 1823, thus ending the French and English reign in the Soo.

In 1855, the State of Michigan, financed by a land grant from Congress, built a canal and lock at the Soo to replace an old lock destroyed by American troops in 1814.

The Weitzel Lock was finished in 1881 and was taken over by the Federal Government in that year. Fifteen years later the Poe Lock was added to meet demands of increased navigation. The double battery of locks aided migration and was a major factor in the development of the territory, following the discovery of mineral deposits in the Lake Superior region.

The headquarters of the American Fur Company, founded by John Jacob Astor, was also located at the Soo and Governor Lewis Cass signed the Fort Brady treaty with the Indians here.

John Johnston, pioneer fur trader, had a home built here in 1795, and located at 413 Water Street.

Henry R. Schoolcraft, first official Indian agent at the Soo, built a house here in 1826-27 and using this as his headquarters wrote some of the books that later served as a basis for Longfellow's "The Song of Hiawatha."

———

ALBERTA—See *FIBRE.*

ALGONQUIN—1910, mail *Sault Ste. Marie.*

BARBEAU—In 1887 it was a trading post 18 miles south of *Sault Ste. Marie* and 4 miles west of the St. Mary's River. No post office. In 1893, John Sheeran was Postmaster. 1909 A. Hunter, Postmaster; W. B. Garden, blacksmith; and A. Hunter, grocery.

1915, RFD *McCarron.* Shown on 1971 highway maps. Named for Honorable Peter Barbeau, first president of *Sault Ste. Marie* village.

BAIS DE WASAI—Was first settled in 1915 and at that time was RFD *Sault Ste. Marie.* By 1927 the population had increased to 220. Located in Sugar Island Township, 6 miles south of *Sault Ste. Marie.* Ambrose E. Thibert, Postmaster, general store, soft drinks and billiards; Emil Hytinen, poultry and justice; John Williams, justice of peace. Not shown on 1971 highway map.

BAY MILLS—Named for the plants of the Hall and Munson Company. For many years this was a trading post and the area was inhabited by Indians. A post office was established here in 1879 and lasted until 1909. The first permanent settlement was in 1882 when a sawmill was built here. In 1890 a sash-and-door factory was doing a flourishing business and lasted about 15 years. In 1904 the factory burned down and a few years later the sawmill ran out of timber and quit business. At one time the village had a population of 1,900 but after the factory burned most of the population moved away.

In 1893, *Bay Mills* was described as: *"On the shore of Lake Superior, and on the D. S. S. & A. Railroad, Superior Township, 12 miles west of Sault Ste. Marie. Contains Methodist, Indian Mission and Episcopal churches, two saw-mills, a sash and blind factory, planing mill, a box factory and pulp mill. Mail twice daily. W. K. Parsille, Postmaster; John Allport, machinist; Dr. Thomas L. Armitage, druggist; W. J. Bell, photographer; Henry J. Curry, stage line and ferry; Leon Daust, meat market; Stephen DeWitt, carpenter; David Dibb, carpenter; R. F. Francis, telegraph agent; A. B. Gill, millwright; Thomas W. Gilpin, lumber inspector; Hall & Buell, lumber manufacturers; the Hall & Munson Company, sash door and lumber manufacturers; James E. Hicks, barber; Rev. F. L. Leonard, Methodist; W. K. Parsille, general store; John McGregor, Congregational; Niagra Paper Company, pulp manufacturers; Amos Scanlan, hotel; Dennis Shannahan, blacksmith; and Charles VanHorn, saw filer."*

By 1909 the population diminished to less than 75 people and by 1918 the post office had been discontinued and mail was delivered by RFD from *Brimley.* Only one general store was doing business, operated by M. Sugar.

In 1940 only vestiges of the stone and concrete foundations remained. The red bricks embedded deeply into the hard-packed road were once the paving of the main street of town.

BRASSAR—Not a ghost town, in fact was never a town but a rural post office, 6 miles east of *Sault Ste. Marie*. 1927 population 72. Mail tri-weekly. Urban Nightingale, Postmaster and grocer.

BRIMLEY—See *Superior*.

BURSAW—Not a ghost town. A post office by this name was established in April, 1896 but was discontinued in August of the same year.

CANAL—Not a ghost town but in 1927 was a branch of the *Sault Ste. Marie* post office.

COTTAGE PARK SPUR—1910, on the Minneapolis St. Paul & Sault Ste. Marie Railroad. Mail *Sault Ste. Marie*.

CRAWLEY—May have been a village or settlement. A post office by this name was established in 1890 and discontinued in 1895.

DAFTER—See *Stevensburgh. Dafter* is a post office in 1971. Probably named after an early settler but stories conflict on the origin.

DELL—Was a post office from about 1910 to 1915 and was named for the first Postmaster, John Dell. In 1918 population 100. On the M. St. P. & S. Ste. M. Railroad, 35 miles southwest of *Sault Ste. Marie*. W. Hayward, general store. Send mail to *Dick*.

DICK—Was a lumbering settlement during the hardwood lumbering era of the early 1900s on the M. St. P. & S. Ste. M. Railroad, in Trout Lake Township, 39 miles west of *Sault Ste. Marie*. Had a post office for a short time until 1916, when it was served by RFD *Trout Lake*.

1915 population 60. Had a telephone. F. M. Wheeler, Postmaster, general store and lumber. Nothing remains of the village today except perhaps a few summer homes built in the area after the village ceased to exist. Remains of some of the old buildings still evident.

DONALDSON—This village was once a booming lumbering center. A post office was established in 1881 and lasted until 1931. Located 13 miles south of *Sault Ste. Marie*, in Bruce Township, on what is now highway M-129. In 1877 it contained several saw and shingle mills, boarding houses, a general store, blacksmith shop, and three churches. In that year David Lyall was Postmaster.

The business directory of 1893 listed Rev. W. E. Brown, Methodist; Mrs. John Cummings, music teacher; George Freeborn, shoemaker; David Lyall, general store and Postmaster; Wm. Lynch, carpenter; Homer McGinnis, saw and shingle mill; Robert McKee, saw and shingle mill; Roderick McKenzie, justice; Rev. P. T. Rowe, Episcopal; Ryerson Rutledge, justice; and Alonzo Williams, blacksmith.

Still shown on 1972 highway maps.

DORGANS—Was a station or siding on D. S. S. & A. Railroad between *Brimley* and *Raco*.

DRYBURG—Named by local residents who determined that no strong drinks would be sold here. Was a post office and flag station on the M. St. P. & S. Ste. M. Railroad, in Rudyard Township, 4 miles from *Rudyard*. In 1915 Wm. S. Leonard was Postmaster; J. Davis, express agent; and N. L. Field, general store. J. F. Sanderson was Postmaster in 1918. By 1927 only 12 people were living here. There was a Presbyterian Church; J. F. Sanderson, Postmaster and general store; N. L. Field, general store; Raoul Gervals, blacksmith; and Louis Pointer, railroad and express agent.

Dryburg is not shown on 1970 highway map.

EDWARDS—See *Shelldrake*.

EMERSON—Named after Chris Emerson, *Saginaw* millionaire lumberman and considered by some an eccentric. Thousands of tourists travel highway M-123 between *Eckerman* and *Paradise* each summer and visit the Tahquamenon Falls area, unaware that they pass near the site of this one-time lumbering and fishing village at the mouth of the Tahquamenon River where it empties into Lake Superior. What was once a road to the site is now a marsh and weed-grown trail almost impassable by automobile. A spring flowing from a weed-covered mound is about all that remains where the town once was.

Founded in 1882 by the Cheesebrough Lumber Company, as late as 1939 twenty-five people, all fishermen and their families, lived in the tiny village and engaged in commercial fishing. About 1940 an unnamed citizen deeded 2,000 acres at the mouth of the river to the state and today this area is designated as a State Campground.

In 1890 the village was described as: *"Located 13 miles north of Eckerman. A regular boat runs weekly to the Sault during navigation season. Settled 1882. Population 109. F. B. Cheesebrough, Postmaster. Cheesebrough Brothers, sawmill; F. B. Cheesebrough and August Johnson, justices; and Rev. Peter Rhynard, Baptist."*

Over the next quarter of a century various lumbering companies set up mills at *Emerson*, including Corky Culchane and Moore, Parke and Sharpe.

After the logging was finished only a few fishing families remained on the site. In 1914 the post office was discontinued and with the coming of World War II the village ceased to exist.

The Chesbrough mill at *Emerson* as it appeared in the 1880s. *Emerson* was a village and post office from 1884 to 1914, located a few miles south of *Paradise* on Whitefish Bay. Nothing remains today. Photo courtesy of Paul E. Petosky, *Ishpeming*, Michigan.

ENCAMPMENT—1910, Mail *Donaldson*.

FIBRE—Not really a ghost town but declined from the days when it was a busy logging center on the M. St. P. & S. Ste. M. Railroad. Located in Rudyard Township, *Fibre* still has a post office and is designated on 1972 road maps. *Fibre* was settled in 1890 and for one year (1895) was named *Alberta*. In 1896 the name was changed to *Fibre* and has remained. Name taken from pulp wood and shingle bolts (wood fibre), the only products shipped at that time.

The business listings in 1927 were Albyn E. Doud, Postmaster and general store, sawmill and barber. The Doud's were early settlers. Thomas Askwith, carpenter; Wm. Borranger, well driller; Vern Haskins, apiarist; and Andrew Hoverson, mason. Bus daily to *Sault Ste. Marie* and *Trout Lake*. Had a Presbyterian Church and telephone service.

Leonard Spencer, former resident, said most of the buildings were razed by fire several times. Today Charles Doud operates the store here.

FREEMAN—At one time was a post office.

GATESVILLE—First called *Goetzville* after Joseph Goetz who settled here in 1882. Was a post office from 1882 to 1917. In 1893 tri-weekly stage to *Raber, Detour, Pickford* and *Sault Ste. Marie*. Two churches. Some of the businesses were Alois Goetz, general store, feed and grain; George Goetz, carpenter; Alvis Huss, meat market; Phillip Huss, tailor; M. C. Butler, meats; Joseph Oberle, blacksmith; and George Winling, brewer and cooper (barrel maker).

GOODWIN—Was a small mill town near *Trout Lake*. A huge clubhouse, built during the lumbering days for big shots and their visitors, remains standing and is used for a resort hotel.

HENDRIE—In 1893 was a small station on the D. S. S. & A. Railroad. Lasted until about 1910. Send mail to *Trout Lake*. Not a post office.

HIGHBANKS—For many years this was a banking grounds for timber during the logging days. Located on the shore of Whitefish Bay, 40 miles northeast of *Newberry*, the settlement was first known as *Highbanks* until 1947, when the post office was established, and someone decided on the name of *Paradise*.

Land patents were granted by the Federal Government in the 1870s to individuals in Pennsylvania, New York and New Jersey. In 1899, the Calumet and Hecla Mining Company purchased much of the land in this region and sold it to lumbering companies. After the pine timber was cut a man named Edmund LeDuc bought the cut-over land and liked the surroundings so well that he is said to have called it *Paradise*. Another version is that it was named by Leon McGregor of *Bay City*, a resort promoter.

The tiny village is 5 miles north of the mouth of the Tahquamenon River, former site of *Emerson*, and 11 miles from the Lower Tahquamenon Falls and the Upper Falls, which attract nearly one-half million visitors annually.

The present village has a high school, three churches, four gasoline stations, three general stores, two taverns, four restaurants, several motels, etc. The post office, which was established in 1947, handles from 300 to 600 postcards a day during the months of July and August each year during the tourist rush.

HULBERT—Named for the Hulbert family, pioneer landowners. In 1893, on the D. S. S. & A. Railroad, 17 miles east of *Newberry*. Population 25. Daily mail. W. H. Townsend, general store. Was first called *Taquamenon*.

In 1917, a discontinued post office. Send mail to *Eckerman*. In 1922-23 the post office was reactivated and is still operating (1972). By 1939 the population had once more increased to about 300 and *Hulbert* became famous for its winter deer yards. Feeding of the deer was begun by S. R. Freeman, the village barber. As a result of his efforts, other experimental feeding stations were established in the area by the State Conservation Department.

HUNTERS MILL—Seven and one-half miles north of *Soo Junction*, on a branch of the Tahquamenon River, is the site of an abandoned lumber camp. Probably most of the ruins have been eradicated by the elements.

IROQUOIS—Was a village and post office from 1882 to 1905. In 1893 described as located in Superior Township, 25 miles west of *Sault Ste. Marie* and 7 from *Wellsburgh*, on the D. S. S. & A. Railroad. Mail semi-weekly. Hector Mackay, Postmaster; Edward Guck, railroad and telegraph agent; Simon Johnston, fish dealer; Mackay and Sons, saw and shingle mill; Alexander Mulligan, teacher; Simon C. Teeple, justice; Calvin Vanluben, carpenter; Ransom Vanluben, blacksmith; and Alfred Vidden, justice.

In 1905, the last year of the post office, a tri-weekly mail stage ran to *Wellsburg*. Henry Mills was Postmaster; Joseph Blass, constable; F. F. Evans, justice; L. J. Fohey, school teacher; Hector MacKay, sawmill; and Charles Reid, general store.

JOHNSONBURG—A siding and station on D. S. S. & A. Railroad between *Brimley* and *Raco*. A post office was established at this location, Scammons Cove on Drummond Island, in 1905 and at that time the village was named *Kreetan*. In 1914 the name was changed to *Johns Wood*, perhaps by the Postmaster whose name was H. C. Johnson. Johnson also ran a sawmill and general store. In that year, population 300. W. I. Buddington, physician; E. O. Coy, general store; T. A. Lindsay, hotel; and George Smith, electrical engineer.

The remains of this one-time village and that of the old fort, now on private property, are excellent sites for anyone interested in artifacts. They are both located on the south side of the island at the end of one of the roads shown on maps.

KELDEN—Was a post office and settlement a few miles south of *Rabar* in Pickford Township. In 1905, Walter Todd was Postmaster. Margaret Brennan was a school teacher; and C. H. Avery, general store and notary.

In 1915, C. H. Avery was Postmaster, general store and notary and there were two lumber mills run by C. Desorneaux and Frank Payment, who also was a boat builder.

KREETAN—name changed to *Johns Wood*. See *Johnsonburg*.

LARCH—1905, a country post office, 4¼ miles from *Dafter*. James H. Guest, Postmaster. 1915, a discontinued post office. Mail RFD *Dafter*. This place was not on a railroad and was not a village.

LARAMIE—1927, discontinued post office in Sugar Island Township. RFD *Willwalk.*

LIME ISLAND—Was a post office from 1891 to 1892, then reactivated from 1914 until about 1940 when it was again discontinued. Never was an established village but at one time had a population of about 100. Located on the St. Mary's River, in Raber Township, it was a fueldock for the Pittsburgh Coal Company and located 3 miles from *Rober.* In 1927, Alfred E. Newton was Postmaster and R. F. Folkner, manager of the docks.

McVILLE—1905, a country post office in Rudyard Township, 8 miles from *Rudyard*, its shipping point. Daily mail. Robert Anderson, Postmaster.

MAXTON—Was a short-lived sawmill settlement and post office founded in 1904, a few miles northeast of *Drummond*, on Drummond Island, and on Potagannissing Bay. From 1904 until 1930 there were two or three sawmills operating on the site. In 1905 William A. Cloudman was Postmaster. In 1915 W. W. Dunham ran a general store and sawmill here. As late as 1927 there was a post office with tri-weekly stage to *Johns Wood* and *Drummond.* W. A. Cloudman, Postmaster; Art Sahwl and Company, fish and groceries.

OAK RIDGE—Not really a ghost town but was a settlement on Neebish Island, in Soo Township, descriptive of the high land of Neebish Island and the growth of trees. Settled in 1890. Was a post office in 1915. John R. Berry, Postmaster and general store.

In 1927, population 200. Daily bus to *Sault Ste. Marie.* Marie Thibert, Postmistress and Henry A. Thibert, general store.

MUNUSKONG—See *Thorice.* "Munuscong"—where Indians made large mats (*Bay of the Rushes*).

PAYMENT—Was a post office and lumbering settlement in Sugar Island Township, 12 miles east of *Sault Ste. Marie*, on the St. Mary's River. Was a post office in 1899 and had a business section with a meat market, saloon, etc.

In 1909 daily mail. Angus McCoy, Postmaster; William Caughlin, Wagonmaker; John M. Dow, blacksmith; C. H. Foster, justice; King Brothers & Company, liquor dealer; Daniel McCoy, carpenter; Alma Spalding, teacher; Sugar Island Lumber Company, sawmill; and D. C. Wilson, boat building.

By 1915, and the advent of World War I, only Angus McCoy, Postmaster and general store, and Caughlin, the wagonmaker, remained in the village.

In 1927, contained a Catholic Church; A. McCoy was still Postmaster and general store; and Daniel Edwards had converted the old saloon into a billiard hall. The post office was discontinued about 1942-45.

PINE RIVER—First name chosen for *Rudyard*, but was name of post office in lower Michigan, so had to choose a different name.

POINT AUFRENE—Not a ghost town. Name changed to *Raber*.

RACO—Another name formed by combining of Richard and Avery Company (R. A. C. O.), founders of the village. In 1914 was a recently established post office, on the D. S. S. & A. Railroad, 8 miles west of *Brimley*.

1917, population 200. J. A. Lillie, Postmaster, and Richardson & Avery, lumber manfacturers. Was at one time a banking and loading ground for logs and had a peak population of 350.

The first observation tower for spotting fires in Michigan was located near *Raco* atop a high pine tree adjacent to the main road. The tree was standing until about 1928 when M-28 was widened and paved and the tree had to be removed. The first fire observer used spikes on his boots, similar to those used by utility workers now, to reach his platform. This led to wood and steel fire towers, for many years a familiar site in northern sections of Michigan. Today they have been replaced by planes and the towers have been abandoned or torn down.

The post office at *Raco* is still active, 1970.

RIFLE RANGE—On D. S. S. & A. Railroad, 1910. Mail *Strongs*.

ROCK VIEW—1927, was a village on US-2 in Pickford Township, 5 miles from *Pickford* and 6 miles from *Cedarville*.

SCAMMON—Was a post office established in 1882 on the south coast of Drummond Island. 1887 population 150. Mail stage from *Detour* semi-weekly. C. A. Watson, Postmaster; Island Cedar Company, saw and shingle mills, C. A. Watson, superintendent.

SCHLESSER—Settled about 1890. In 1893, a post office and settlement 10½ miles from *Detour*, population 50. Semi-weekly mail. John Schlesser, Postmaster, for whom the town was named. Other business listings for 1893 were John Cameron, meat market; George W. Cooper, agent; Hugh Manghar, cooper (barrel maker); John Schlesser, general store; and James Whaelan, Justice of the Peace; Phillip Quantz, carpenter; Benjamin Robinson, general store.

In 1905 a discontinued post office. Send mail to *Gatesville*.

Main Street of *Shelldrake* as it looks today. Only one-half dozen of the original houses remain and are privately owned.   Photo by Roy L. Dodge (1971)

This is the site of the *Shelldrake* mill as it looks today. Some of the rotted pilings of the wharfs remain out in the harbor, a faint reminder of the one-time booming lumber town.   Photo by Roy L. Dodge (1971)

The day the lumber mills burned at *Shelldrake*. Wharf with railroad tracks extended out into the harbor for loading lumber onto Great Lakes ships. This fire occurred in 1910. Only a few houses remain today. Photo courtesy of Paul E. Petosky, *Ishpeming*, Michigan

SEEWHY—Was a station on the D. S. S. & A. Railroad, between *Hulbert* and *Eckerman.* Contained a general store and sawmill. Post office established about 1915. In that year received daily mail. C. Y. Bennett, who named the station from his initials "C. Y.," Postmaster, general merchandise, lumber, lath, shingles, posts and ties.

In 1927, post office discontinued, send mail to *Eckerman.*

SHELLDRAKE—The rooftops of a few scattered buildings covered with weathered shingles, now worn and warped from age, can be seen along highway M-123 between *Paradise* and *Whitefish Point.* What was once a wagon road, with grass grown up between the tracks, leads from the paved road through a low marshy spot to the buildings and remains of the one-time lumbering and fishing village of *Shelldrake*, first called *Edwards* after the first resident living on the site when the village was founded in the late 1890s.

The village is located between two branches of the Betsy River on White-fish Bay. At this point the waters of Lake Superior are usually calm and placid. The now rotted and blackened pilings still jut up from the water where the docks and railroad extended out into the bay during the days when *Shelldrake* was a model lumbering village for its day. In addition to the sawmill, there were houses for the workers, a hospital, school house, and an icehouse in which enough meat could be stored to last the population of sometimes 1,000 through the winter months when the town was isolated. A long boardwalk extended the length of the main street in front of the business buildings and the dwellings were equipped with bathrooms, all the buildings were plastered and piped for hot water supplied by the sawdust burner. Some of the fire hydrants can still be seen lining the main street and at the far end of town, where some of the remaining houses and vacant lots have been purchased as summer vacation homes, pieces of water pipe stick up from the ground where they have been dug up by bulldozers clearing the ground.

In the 1930s some of the houses were occupied by Indians, a general store operated during the summer months, and one of the old hotels was open year around and used as a clubhouse by deer hunters during the season. The burner was standing, and remains of the powerhouse were visible.

Mrs. Hazel Petosky, a former resident, recalls the village about the turn of the century. *"The town was named 'Shelldrake' after Shelldrake or Merganser ducks which at that time were numerous in the area. Shelldrake was first named 'Edwards' after the first people who lived there. The first lumbering company was Moore, Parke and Sharpe and they brought their machinery and equipment by scow across the Bay Mills, where they had a lumbering operation."*

Moore-Parke & Sharpe built a mill at *Shelldrake* to take out pine timber from the huge forest that surrounded the area. Chemicals and hardwood timber were also available in the area, which is located between *Whitefish Point* and *Highbanks*, now known as *Paradise*.

For several years the *Shelldrake* mills were supplied by 12 lumber camps. The logs were first hauled from the forest by big wheels. Later, other companies came in and built a railroad, then the logs were hauled by train. The first company to build a railroad was Corklane who came from *Port Austin*, Michigan. He was later killed by his own train.

Soon after the first mill was built a boarding house was erected, called a "Bay City House," to room all the men. At one time there were nearly 500 men working in the area.

At one time *Shelldrake* was one of the richest lumbering towns in the area. It had a general store that carried groceries, dry goods, grain and feed, supplies, etc. Mail came in by foot or dog teams to the post office during the first year and later by horse and wagon. Mail came from *Eckerman*, 35 miles distance, and also served *Emerson* from the same route.

Logs for the mill were dumped into the Betsy River before being sawed into lumber. As each succeeding lumber company came and went they took out their particular kind of timber, such as pine, hemlock, spruce, ironwood (used for chemical) and other hardwood.

Mrs. Petosky said there were many logging companies in the town over the years including the Bartlett Lumber Company that logged 12 years. *"There was a tramway and a large dock built out into the bay from which steamers unloaded supplies and took lumber out to distant ports,"* she said.

Just before fire destroyed the mills in 1910, the village was described as: *"Population 350. On Whitefish Bay in Whitefish Township, 26 miles north of Eckerman. Stage daily to Eckerman. Calumet & Hecla, sawmill; J.H. Cox, physician; W. O. Grace, blacksmith; Moore, Park & Sharp, logging contractors; Harry Park, general store; Peninsular Bark & Lumber Company, loggers; T. A. Russell, hotel; and Mae Skelton, teacher."*

In 1915, Lena M. O'Brien was Postmistress. Other business listings for that year were Bartlett Lumber Company, sawmill, loggers and general store; A. B. Cooke, physician; John Jokum, hotel; J. L. Lynch, lumber dealer; J. H. Moher, meats; Patrick O'Brien, logger; R. A. Santimo, hotel; and the Shelldrake General Hospital.

For a time during the 1920s and 1930s the town was owned by a *Detroit* company, headed by Duncan McCrea, former Wayne County Prosecutor. Finally it came into the hands of a Mr. Irwin and In 1968 was sold to 35-year-old Brent Biehl, a *Mt. Clemens* businessman, who moved there in 1970 and plans eventually to restore the town. Biehl purchased 175 acres, which includes most of the remaining houses and two or three former business buildings. There were originally between 40 and 50 houses and the main street extended for half a mile along the bay.

The post office here lasted from 1905 until 1922 when it was discontinued. After the town was deserted ships put in at *Whitefish Point* to take on timber.

———

SPUR 59—Many lumbering settlements and sawmill towns located along the railroads in the Upper Peninsula were called "Spurs." Spur 59, 97, etc. designated the number of miles the particular siding was located from *Sault Ste. Marie* on the track.

———

STEVENSBURGH—in Bruce Township. Post office established in 1879. In 1887 described as: *"A settlement 10 miles south of Sault Ste. Marie. Has daily mail. Richard Welch, Postmaster; Joseph W. Hembroff, general store; Robert McKee, sawmill; Issac Shaw, blacksmith; Daniel Young, builder; and Gregg Young, mason."*

In 1893, 1½ miles from *Dafter*, a station on the M. St. P. & S. Ste. M. Railroad. Daily mail. Edward Pearce, carpenter; Henry Robertson, sawmill; other business listings same as 1887. In that same year (1893) the name was changed to *Dafter* and remains a post office today (1971).

———

STRONGS—Named after an early storekeeper and mill operator. In 1905, population 150. On D. S. S. & A. Railroad, in Superior Township, 24 miles west of *Newberry* (near *Eckerman*). C. L. Clark, Postmaster and railroad agent; Hackley, Phelps & Burrell Lumber Company, sawmill; Daniel McIntyre, hotel; D. D. Martin, saloon; E. Durner, general store and shingle mill.

Was settled in 1899 by 15 families who came to work in the woods cutting shingle bolts. The shingle mill employed several workers and within a few years became an established village.

Post office still active (1971).

———

STRONGVILLE—Named after an early pioneer settler. In 1887, *"A recently established post office in Pickford Township, 32 miles from Sault Ste. Marie. Daily stage to the Soo and St. lgnace. Judson D. Smith, Postmaster."* The settlement contained one sawmill and a blacksmith shop. About 50 farmers lived in the area.

In 1909, located 6 miles from *Rudyard*. Daily mail stage to *Rudyard*. T. A. Baker, Postmaster and township clerk; Haywood and Loomis, lumbermen; A. G. Hull, painter; John Oga, carpenter; George Potts, justice; Mrs. G. A. Potts, music teacher; R. A. Sanderson, dairy; Mrs. Leoline Sprague, school principal and W. J. Wallis, lumberman.

The post office was discontinued in 1913.

———

SUPERIOR—This village, 12 miles southwest of *Sault Ste. Marie* and on the D. S. S. & A. Railroad, was platted in 1887. The following year, 1888, a post office was established.

Within a short time the population reached about 100 and in 1893 was described as: *"A village on the Waska River, one-half mile from Whitefish Bay, and on the D. S. S. & A. Railway, in Superior Township. Stages four times daily to Bay Mills. W. L. Scribner, Postmaster and general store; Mrs. F. Belanger, restaurant; Rev. Brown, Methodist; A. Couthart, Cooper (barrel maker); Henry Curry, livery; Edward Dupree barber; John Fenwick, hotel; R. F. Francis, telegraph and railway agent; Joseph Geering, painter; C. Kilbourn, general store; Joseph Larone, hotel; Rev. John McGregor, Congregational; E. Minard, carpenter; T. V. Quackenbush, justice; Josia D. Scribner, mason; J. A. Scribner, builder; J. G. Scribner, hunter; W. L. Scribner, general store; Mrs. Sordan, dressmaker; and K. Sugar, general store."*

When the D. S. S. & A. Railroad reached the terminus in Minnesota, the station at this point was known as Superior, so the railroad company requested that the name be changed. According to old residents, the choice was left with the Postal Department in Washington, and an official named *Brimley* was honored when the name *Brimley* was made official in 1896.

In 1940 the population was 430. Today only one store, a gasoline station, a fish market, operated by an Indian who sells smoked fish, and two taverns remain in the business section.

———

TAHQUAMENON—Name changed to *Hulbert*. See *Hulbert*.

———

THORICE—This name is a combination of names of two promoters, C. J. Thorensen and Fred Price—"Thor" and "Ice." The township name, Bruce, was chosen by early Scotch-Irish settlers after a county in Ontario, Canada, from which they came. *Neebish* comes from Aneebish or "place of the leaf." *Munuscong*, "the bay of the rushes," where Indians made mats from the reeds.

In 1910, population 200. Also known as *West Neebish*. Is in Bruce Township, 18 miles southeast of *Sault Ste. Marie*. Daily mail. F. W. Roach, Postmaster; Dan McIntyre, hotel and saloon; The Road Company, general store.

66

By 1915, the Chicago Mill & Lumber Company had set up a mill in the settlement, and in that year C. J. Hallmann was Postmaster. By 1917, the population had dropped to 50 and Willis B. King was Postmaster.

Sometime between 1927 and 1932, the name of the village was changed to *Munoscong*.

––––––––

TONE—1905, a country post office, 22 miles south of *Sault Ste. Marie* and 4½ from *Pickford*. Daily mail. Name commemorates Wolfe Tone, an Irish patriot admired by the Scotch-Irish settlers of the area.

––––––––

TROMBLEY—In 1917, was a small lumbering settlement located on Munoscong Bay, 22 miles southeast of *Sault Ste. Marie*. B. A. Griffin, Postmaster; Chicago Mill & Lumber Company, sawmill and box factory; Dr. Deo, physician; A. Fairchilds, machinist; George E. Griffin, general store; Howard Johnson, hotel; and H. A. Perry, boat builder. In 1927, only one store remained operated by Mrs. G. E. Griffin and mail received from *Sault Ste. Marie*.

––––––––

VERMILLION—Named from the deposits of red ochre near the Lake Superior shore. Was originally a station of the U. S. Life-Saving Service and was designated as Lake Superior Station No. 9. In 1883, the following message, addressed to *Vermillion Point*, Michigan, was received from *Washington, D.C.*— *"On and after June 1, 1883, the stations of the life-saving service will be designated and known as exhibited in the following table. The present designation by numbers will be abandoned. Officers and employees of the lifesaving service will, in all correspondence, and upon all official forms, observe the changes within."*

The Vermillion life-saving station was located 10 miles west of *Whitefish Point* and was thereafter known as *Vermillion*.

Paul P. Petosky, of *Ishpeming*, was born here while his father, Frank F. Petosky was Officer in Charge after the station was designated as a Coast Guard Station.

Petosky said the old life-saving station was washed out into Lake Superior during a storm and in 1938 and 1939 a new Coast Guard Station was erected. The station was abandoned in 1943, and is no longer in use.

The station was then sold to a party in Ohio for $20,000 and at that time there were plans to retain the buildings as a tourist attraction. For some reason the plans fell through and within a few years the building was nearly destroyed by vandals and the elements. Petosky said he returned to the station and retrieved some of the old records and correspondence. Copies of some of these are reproduced in this book.

Coast Guard Station at *Vermillion* on Lake Superior in 1940. Left abandoned in 1943 and sold to a private party, it has suffered vandalism by thoughtless people and not much remains today. This picture was taken in winter while mail was being delivered by dog sled. Dog and sled (dot on left) were owned by Truman McLean, mail carrier from *Whitefish Point* who owned three sled dogs. Photo courtesy of Paul E. Petosky, of *Ishpeming*, Michigan

Life was hard in these stations and during the winter months the families living here were isolated from the outside world. Mail was delivered once a week, or when the mail carrier could get through with his dog team and sled. *Vermillion* life-saving station was described in 1905 as: *"Population 25, in Whitefish Township, 60 miles northwest of Sault Ste. Marie. Kate Carpenter, Postmaster; J. A. Carpenter, keeper of the U. S. Life Saving Station; John Clarke and Fred Weatherhog, cranberry growers; W. H. Clarke, mason; Philip Eby, Taxidermist; A. Laford, barber; and C. Shipley, painter."*

Within the next few years the population increased by two people when A. H. Lamitzke moved in and started another barber shop, probably in his own home. W. H. Clarke was promoted to a Surfman for the U. S. Life Saving Station and was also Postmaster in 1909.

Things changed a little within the next five years, although the population remained the same. W. J. McGaw was Postmaster and barber; John Anderson, boat builder; J. A. Carpenter, photographer; Ocha Albert and James Scott, boat builders; and John Clark and Fred Weatherhog, cranberry growers.

A trail through the windblown Lake Superior sand and pine stumps left from the logging days leads from *Whitefish Point* to the former site of the old station. A small lake near the site is named "Weatherhog Lake" but only hollows in the ground remain to show that anyone ever lived at *Vermillion*.

Life-Saving Service,

Office of Superintendent, Tenth District,

Sand Beach, Mich., **August 9th 1892.**

Keeper,

Vermillion Point Life-Saving Station,

Sir:

In accordance with the instructions contained in paragraph 180 Revised Regulations 1884,authority is hereby given you to hire a team at an expense not to exceed $25 to haul one-years supply of of wood for your station. When the labor has been performed,you may submit bill on forms herewith.

Respectfully yours,

Jerome G. Kiah

Superintendent.

(1892 letter to station keeper) Courtesy of Paul E. Petosky, of *Ishpeming*, Michigan, who was born at the *Vermillion* Coast Guard Station where his father was a keeper.

WARRENVILLE—In 1848, the name of present day *De Tour* (not a ghost town). Much of the mail was wrongly forwarded to *Warren*, near *Detroit*, so in 1915 the Postmaster, Roderick Munro, asked for the name to be changed to the French "De Tour"—to go around.

WELLSBURG—Was a station on the D. S. S. & A. Railroad. In 1893 daily mail. E. J. Guck, Postmaster.

By the turn-of-the-century the population had increased to 75. In 1905, George W. Disberry, logs, ties and poles; C. W. Erickson, wood; Ewald & Reese, fruit crates; E. J. Guck, station agent; Thomas McBride, lumber; John O'Brien, carpenter; Wm. Raynard, wood; and M. E. Steele, hair jewelry maker.

Mr. Guck stayed on as Postmaster until the post office was discontinued about 1909, then RFD *Brimley*.

In 1919 the postal name was *Raco*. See *Raco*.

_____

WEST NEEBISH—See *Thorice*.

_____

WHITEFISH POINT—The first lighthouse, a brick tower, was erected here in 1849. About 1900 a steel lighthouse replaced the old one and a lifeguard station was built.

Although inhabited by Indians and known to voyageurs for many years, *Whitefish Point* isn't listed in business directories until 1879. In that year: *"A supply landing for lumber camps in that section, and noted for its fisheries and advantages for a summer resort. In Sault Ste. Marie Township. Its exports are fresh and salt fish. Population 59. Mail, tri-weekly. S. P. Mason, Postmaster. E. M. Baker, general store; Alex Barclay, cranberry grower; Wm. Branding, fisherman; George Brown, furs and game; John Clark, cranberry grower; Chas. Endres & Son, fishermen; Nicholas Gangrew, assistant lighthouse keeper; Albt. James, cooper; Chas. J. Linke, lighthouse keeper; S. P. Mason, hotel and dealer in pine lands; Post-Jones & Company, fish dealers; and S. G. Teeple, fisherman.*

For many years cranberries were a cash crop and a dozen or more cranberry growers were listed in directories for the area. In 1893, John Clarke, Postmaster; Charles Endress & Son, general store; Charles Kimball, lighthouse keeper; and Rev. C. F. Chambon, Catholic.

The village reached its peak population in the early 1900s and the Life Guard Station was changed to a Coast Guard Station. 1905 population 200. John M. Greig, Postmaster; daily stage to *Eckerman*, 30 miles south. Alex Barkley, cranberries; A. Booth & Company, fish; F. X. Brassette, express agent; Robert Carlson, lighthouse keeper; James Clarke and John Clarke, cranberries; also John Greig, Wm. H. Clarke, Wm. Hawkins, and Frank House.

The paved road north from *Eckerman* and M-28 ends at *Whitefish Point*

Fish nets spread out to dry at the only remaining fishery at *Whitefish Point* on Lake Superior.   Photo by Roy L. Dodge (1971)

———

where a complex of houses and the Coast Guard Station is located. A gravel road with a turn-around crosses some wharves and ends at the beach where the point juts out into Lake Superior. Between *Whitefish Point* proper and the station there are several houses. A man named Tom Brown collects old bottles and has them for sale at one of the homes.

An old, abandoned schoolhouse, setting on blocks over a large hole hollowed beneath, from the blowing wind, stands beside the road near the station. Another old, two-story frame house that appears to have been moved here recently stands near the school site.

Once an important fishing point, with the decline in Great Lakes fishing and due to the limitation of the lakes fishing, only one fishery was in operation here in 1971. The huge complex of buildings, piles of boxes used to store fish, and nets stretched out to dry, is owned by Brown's Fisheries.

All that remains of *Whitefish* village is one house and a combination grocery store and post office. A lone street light hangs over the pavement at this point on the road.

This combination store and post office is all that remains of the one-time village of *Whitefish Point*, a few miles north of *Paradise* in Chippewa County. Photo by Roy L. Dodge (1971)

Natives of the area say there is a log house on the bay that is one of many houses that dotted the area. Only the mournful sound of the warning signal from the Coast Guard Station and an occasional auto breaks the silence near the one-time village of *Whitefish Point.*

WILLWALK—located in Sugar Island Township, 10 miles southeast of *Sault Ste. Marie.* Settled in 1912, a post office was established in 1917. William Walker was Postmaster and pioneer merchant. When the post office was established, Walker submitted several names to the Postal Department but all were refused. Walker finally submitted the name "will walk," taken from his name and this was accepted.

The 1927 directory listed Frank Aaltonen, lands and timber; Thomas Ford, express agent; W. G. Miller, station agent; and William Walker, Postmaster, general store, livestock, timber lands and notary. The post office discontinued in 1929.

Chapter Seven

DELTA COUNTY

Delta County was set off in 1843, and was formerly a part of Mackinac County. The county government was organized in 1861. When the county was plotted in 1843, it also included present day Menominee County and parts of Dickinson, Iron and Marquette Counties. The territory resembled the shape of a triangle or the Greek letter "Delta," from which it received its name.

It is said that in 1619, Etienne Brule visited the area on his way westward. The county was first inhabited by Indians called the "Nokay Indians," or "Nocquet" by the French.

Flat Rock, on the Escanaba river, is said to have been the first settlement. The first settlers were L. A. Roberts, a fur trader, and his wife who was said to be an Indian.

Masonville, in 1847 called *Geneva* was the county seat from 1860 to 1864, when it was moved to *Escanaba*.

In 1864 the Peninsula Railroad was completed and the first iron ore shipped from *Negaunee* to *Escanaba*. Another railroad, the Escanaba and Lake Superior, was begun in 1881 and completed the following year.

DELTA COUNTY GHOST TOWNS

ALECTO—1910, on the Minneapolis St. Paul & Sault Ste. Marie Railroad at the junction of the Chicago & Northwestern, just below *Schaffer*. Some of the old houses remain near the tracks and in 1971 the signalman's lookout tower was still standing.

The C. & N. W. Railroad tracks from *Felch* to this point south had been removed and workers were tearing up the rest of the tracks and ties between *Alecto* and *Escanaba*.

BARKVILLE—Not a complete ghost town. Located on US-2, 12 miles west of *Escanaba*, settled in 1871 when the C. & N. W. Railroad starting construction on the connecting link between *Menominee* and *Escanaba*.

From the time of its settlement until 1900, the village was called *Barkville*. Bark River residents celebrated their area centennial in 1971.

When the last C. & N. W. passenger train ran in 1965 the depot was closed and an obituary posted on the door: *"The Chicago & Northwestern Railway died here on September 2, 1965. Age, 83 years."*

The town was settled to harvest hardwood in the area and large charcoal kilns were built to process the wood. It is said the name was derived from the abundance of bark found in the river.

Today the population is only one third of its 750 population in 1910.

BAY de NOQUET—Post office established November, 1878. In 1887, described as: *"A small settlement, sometimes called 'Whitefish,' at the head of Little Bay De Noc, Masonville Township, 12 miles northeast of Escanaba, and 7 east of Brampton."* R. Peacock, Postmaster and sawmill. Not listed after 1877.

BAY SIDING—1879, on the C. & N. W. Railroad, 5 miles north of *Escanaba*.

BEAVER—1893, on the C. & N. W. Railroad, 17 miles north of *Escanaba*. Not a post office.

BICHLER—1910, mail to *Groos*.

BIG RIVER—Was located in Nahama Township, 18 miles northeast of *Escanaba* and 8 from *Sturgeon River*, nearest shipping point, in 1887. Population 100. Daily mail. Peter Jordan, Postmaster, general store, ties and posts; Ferdinand Cardinal, carpenter; John Cornell, cooper (barrel maker); Ramile Marsier, blacksmith; Louis Pillow, saloon; Andrew Welberg, contractor; and George Williams, ties and posts.

BURNT BLUFF POINT—Or *Burnt Bluff*, after the name of the peninsula upon which it is located in Green Bay. In Fairbanks Township, 6 miles south of *Fayette*. 1877, had a store and a fishery operated by D. A. Wells.

There is a legend about the town (later called *Sac Bay*) regarding a Frenchman who ran a saloon and bawdy house here in the 1870s. Workers at the Jackson Iron Company furnaces were paid each month in gold pieces and saloons were barred from the town of *Fayette*. Workers took the narrow gauge railroad south to *Sac Bay* and other saloons along the route to spend their money. During the purge of *Fayette* by a group of vigilantes (see *Fayette* history) it is said that the Frenchman at *Sac Bay* also became one of their victims. He escaped the mob by rowing a boat across the bay to *Escanaba* after burying his money, which was all gold coins, beneath a large beech tree. His despised place of business was burned to the ground, it is said, and from there the story became embellished with each telling until it isn't known what became of the buried gold.

Some say the man returned later and dug it up, others tell the story of the dying man drawing a map which fell into other hands, etc., etc.

Today the area is becoming a tourist area due to its proximity to *Fayette* and the State Park located there.

————

CAMPBELL—1879, a station 19 miles above *Escanaba*. See *Defiance*.

————

CENTERVILLE—See *Lathrop*.

————

CHAISON—1910, on the C. & N. W. Railroad. Mail to *Brampton*.

————

CHANDLER—Also called *Chandler Falls*. 1910, on the Escanaba & Lake Superior Railroad. Mail to *Cornell*.

————

CORNELL—See *Kingsley*.

————

DAYS RIVER STATION—1879, 13 miles above *Escanaba*, on the C. & N. W. Railroad. Postal name *Brampton*. Not a ghost town.

————

DEBEQUE—Was a post office in 1877. The post office at *Maple Ridge*. See *Maple Ridge*, also *Rock*.

————

DEFIANCE—The post office for *Campbell*. In 1893, the name of the post office, and a station on the C. & N. W. Railroad, in Maple Ridge Township, 22 miles north of *Escanaba*. Population 125. Daily mail. Joseph Lusardi, Postmaster; Samuel Bisson, sawmills; Christiansen Delarlais, fresh and salted game; August Doucette, ties; John Lusardi, shoemaker; Joseph Lusardi, general store and blacksmith. Four companies were shipping ties, posts and poles.

In 1905, the town was christened for the third time in its history and was known also as *Trombely Station*. Population 100. Joseph Lusardi, Postmaster.

Within the next few years the town grew rapidly and in 1909, the population was 250. Five men were listed as loggers; W. A. Cross, lath mill; S. L. Hall & Company, sawmill; Thomas LaBranch, cattle; John Lusardi, meat market; Louis Tondolo, saloon; and Albert Wellette, teacher, in addition to other businesses.

1917, C. F. Worch, Postmaster.

Today a town in the same location is designated on county maps as *Trombly*.

————

DOUCETTES—1910, a station on the M. St. P. & S. Ste. M. Railroad, mail *Winters*.

————

ENSIGN—In 1893, was a post office and station on the M. St. P. & S. Ste. M. Railroad, 22 miles northeast of *Escanaba*. A. W. Wolfe ran a sawmill near the tracks.

A few years later the post office was discontinued until 1914. By this time a village was established and in 1917, the population was 450. Some listings for that year were; Fred C. Gorhan, Postmaster; Stone Anderson, lumber; Andrew Barbeau, timber and land; Paul Burczikowski, wood; August Froberg, lumber; Pulius Gagnon, general store; Glennwood Dairy Farm; R. E. Gorham & Son, general store, dry goods, groceries, flour, feed, hardware, wagons and harness, timber, real estate, and auto livery; Herick Brothers, fish; Gus Lamberg, timber; Magnusson Brothers, timber; and Ramie Mercie, fish.

Ensign remained a post office until 1967-68, when it was once more discontinued. Today the siding is used to load pulp wood, the only business on the site.

FARRELL SPUR—1910, on the M. St. P. & S. Ste. M. Railroad. Mail to *Cooks*.

FAYETTE—This village, located on the Garden Peninsula bordering Big Bay de Noc, is Michigan's only restored ghost town and is rapidly becoming a tourist attraction. Still under development by the Michigan Department of Natural Resources, thousands of visitors come here each week during summer months and tour the old buildings that are open to the public and walk past the old homes of former Jackson Iron Company workers of the 1800s.

The town boomed through the 1870s and 1880s. The village consisted of a store, office building, superintendent's house, machine shop, barns, nine frame homes, hotel, opera house, and 40 log houses. Approximately 500 people lived here at the peak of its existence.

From the first year's production of 4,546 tons of pig iron in 1869, the output increased to 14,075 tons in 1875 and went to nearly 20,000 tons annually before the decline began.

The hardwood forests were denuded in the area and it became necessary to transport wood from more distant points. This increase in the cost of charcoal to operate the ovens made the operation of the furnaces less profitable.

On May 12, 1883, fire destroyed the furnaces. The damage was repaired and production continued until about 1891 on a reduced basis.

Cleveland Cliffs acquired the Jackson Iron Company holdings in 1905.

The history of *Fayette* and the early days is probably best told by Ms. Adele Elliott, one of three sisters who lived in the old "Elliot Mansion" near *Fayette* all their lives and donated much of the period furnishings and artifacts to the state for use in restoring the village. Much of the following is taken from the "History of Fayette and Fairbanks Township" by Adele Elliott.

76

Blast furnaces at *Fayette* about 1870. Note old hotel and livery barns in background. Michigan's only restored ghost town. Photo courtesy of James E. Kent, Fayette State Park Supervisor.

Crew at one of *Fayette* furnaces when the town was booming in the 1870s. Lack of hardwood for fuel for the furnaces forced their closing in 1892 and *Fayette* became another ghost town. Photo courtesy of James E. Kent, Fayette State Park Supervisor.

The post office at *Fayette* was established October 3, 1870, with William Pinchin as postmaster. During the early years mail was brought from *Escanaba* over the ice in winter and by boat in summer. The nearest point at which mail could be taken from the train was *Brampton* and the trip overland was long and hard.

Prior to the founding of *Fayette* the tiny, sheltered bay was called "Snail Shell Harbor" due to its shape, and was well known to Great Lakes sailors. Hiram G. D. Squires was the first known owner. After the coming of the Jackson Iron Company the name of its general agent, Fayette Brown, was given to the furnace location.

The Jackson Iron Company was the first iron company to begin operations in the Upper Peninsula, having been founded on July 6, 1848. The company was about 18 years old when Snail Shell Harbor was purchased from Mr. Squires along with 16,000 acres of heavily-timbered land.

In May, 1867, construction of the first furnace was commenced with Jos. H. Harris as manager. On Christmas day of that year the first iron was run. By 1875 more than 70,000 tons of iron had been produced. In 1880 the population was 378, so there were at least 200 men employed.

The company owned sets of huge, beehive-shaped brick charcoal kilns, familiar to the Upper Peninsula. These held from 30 to 40 cords of wood each. There were kilns at Puffy Creek, one at South River, one at *Fayette*, on Section 5. One set down on Section 9, one set on Section 17 near Mud Lake, one set at Centre Kilns, Sect. 29 and one set known as the Summer Island kilns on Sect. 5, T37, R19W. In addition to those listed in *Sac Bay* and Fairbanks Townships there were also sets at Garden Bay and at Kates Bay.

On Section 23, T38, R19W, Aime Rochefort burned and sold charcoal to the company. The furnaces closed before his timber had all been converted into coal and he suffered a loss of the remainder through forest fires.

The furnace, large general store and machine shop were built of local limestone. Other buildings were of frame construction (many still standing) and consisted of the large hotel, houses and apartments, blacksmith and carpenter shops and a drug store with a meat market at the rear. Upstairs in the same building was a large hall with a stage. On the docks which lined the south and west side of the harbor were warehouses, a hoisting house and a sawmill. A large barn and livery stable cared for the many teams of horses.

In 1871, Charles L. Rhodes came to *Fayette* and replaced M. H. Brown as agent. In that year a wooden track railway was completed and the first locomotive built at the new shops of Porter, Bell & Company, of *Buffalo*, N. Y., was shipped to the Jackson Iron Company for use at *Fayette*. This wooden railroad track was taken up in November of 1871 and replaced with 28 lb. iron rails. A second locomotive was ordered for the line. The two locomotives, one 10-ton and the other 12 ton, soon were named the *A. W. White* and the *J. W. Hicks*. Rolling stock for the railroad consisted of 10 coal cars, 10 wood cars, and three flat cars.

A narrow-gauge railway was built from *Fayette* south through the various kilns to the Summer Island kilns near *Fairport*. Residents of the peninsula were very proud of having a railroad years before the Soo Line went through to the north. Horses and a few donkeys were kept for transporting wood, coal and iron. At each set of kilns a boardinghouse, a group of log cabins and adequate barns were provided for the workers. Sets of large scales were also installed.

The harbor must have been a busy place during the short navigation season. In May, 1887, the *Delta News* stated, *"Some 2,700 tons of pig iron have been shipped from here during the past week. The Danforth alone carried 1,300 tons. The Ada Medora and the Havana are now loading for their second trip this season to Chicago."*

Some of the boats owned by the company were the *Joseph Harris, J. B. Kitchen* and the *Fayette Brown*. There were probably others as well. The *Lady Washington* was the daily passenger boat for some time. This boat belonged to the Delta Transportation Company, with Harry G. Merry as officer.

Midway up the furnace hill a road led off to the right and continued up the hill. On this high ground a racetrack was laid out to the joy of lovers of fine horses. This was also the picnic grounds and baseball field.

No saloon was permitted in town other than the bar which was maintained in the hotel. However, after a loyal worker, Fred Hink (known as "Pig Iron Fred"), became disabled in a plant accident, he was allowed to open a tavern about a mile from the village on the Garden Road.

By 1877, a stage line from *Fayette* to *Garden Bay* and *Manistique* ran four times a week. This line was owned by Peter Plant who guaranteed "full satisfaction and good accommodations." Captain Sandy McDonald operated a stage line during the winter across the ice to *Escanaba* and furnished transportation there by sail boat in the summer.

By 1879 *Fayette* was an established furnace town, complete in every detail and well under way to becoming one of the major cities of the Upper Peninsula.

Daily communication was established between *Escanaba* and *Fayette* by January of 1880. The town continued to thrive. The company carried on the monthly payroll the names of over 300 workers and paid out between $5,000 and $6,000 in gold every month.

With the exception of two or three fires that caused extensive damage to the furnaces, life in *Fayette* was calm and serene. Even though saloons were not allowed within the village proper there never was a place in history without entertainment, and *Fayette* was no exception. The workers made good money and were paid in gold each month. They had money to pay for drinks and favors and some silly company rule wasn't going to deny them the chance for a little fun on Saturday night. Company rules also could not deter men who were willing to furnish the need of the workers from setting up bistros on private property in the area. By 1880 these needs became very apparent to several enterprising businessmen, and, by george, what *Fayette's* male population wanted they were going to get!

Within a year or two, saloons and houses of ill-fame sprung up around the village much to the consternation of the law-abiding citizens and eight or ten justices of the peace who had been sworn into office. All the good people were determined to put a stop to the lawlessness that accompanied the arrival of "dens of evil." Many workers with wives and children were squandering their hard earned cash on liquor, women and song and the numbers of men getting "rolled" for their money increased.

The final spark that roused the citizens to arms occurred in August of 1880, when a girl escaped from the "stockade" of a saloon and house operated by a man named Jim Summers. The place was located about 1 mile south of town and was surrounded by a high wooden fence to keep the curious from peering in and to keep the girls from leaving without permission, which was seldom given because many of the girls did not arrive of their own free will.

One day in August a girl did escape and made her way to *Fayette* after two days wandering through the woods. The frightened girl found her way to the home of the deputy sheriff, assuming that he would protect her from her pursuers. Instead of affording her protection he turned her over again to Summers, who by that time was waiting outside in a buggy.

When the citizens discovered that they could not depend on their officers, a public meeting was called and it was decided to rescue the girl. Other bullies from the Summers Gang were whooping it up in a saloon operated by "Pig Iron Fred" about a mile east of town. Hinks was the only one allowed by the company to operate a saloon in the area.

The vigilante mob made its way to Pig Iron's and in a short time disposed of the Summer Gang there with mops, sticks, clubs and any weapon at their disposal. They then proceeded to Summer's Stockade, rescued the girls from their

81

"jail" and put the torch to the buildings. Within a few hours all that remained of the infamous resort were piles of smoking ashes. Summers, too, was apprehended in the unexpected raid. He was badly beaten and his clothes torn to shreds. The vigilantes left him bleeding and battered on the beach to die. The following morning some of his friends returned with the intention of giving him a decent burial, but his body had disappeared.

On Saturday, May 12, 1883, a fire destroyed the furnaces. Villagers, including women and children, fought the blaze along with help from the steamer *Lady Washington*, and the village fire engine was pressed into use but the blaze soon spread to the warehouse next to the harbor and this too went up in flames.

This was thought to be the end of *Fayette*. The loss was about $40,000. Harry Merry, of *Negaunee*, was sent here by the Jackson Iron Company and after examination of the ruins he found the damage not as great as reported. The company decided to rebuild at once with the expectation of producing iron again within three months. The first cast was made in September of 1883 as planned and the furnaces were enlarged.

By June of 1885, due to a slump in the iron market, it was decided to idle the furnaces for an indefinite period. Although the company had a large stock of pig iron on hand it could see no reason for adding to it with the prospect of the iron trade. In hopes of starting the furnace early in the spring of 1886, a large supply of raw ore was brought in before the shipping season closed in the fall of 1885.

Fayette never returned to fame as a furnace town. Sporadically it returned to blast between 1886 and 1890, but each time it was only a glow in the dying embers of a great blaze of glory. In the early 1890s the machinery was disassembled, the population scattered, and obscurity descended on this monument to man's ingenuity. After less than 25 years of operation the plant was abandoned.

About 1892, John DeVet, a former employee of the iron company, moved his family from their home near the Catholic church down into the furnace location and became overseer for all the company's property. DeVet opened a small general store in the old opera house. *Fayette* became a shipping point for hay and grain raised by neighboring farmers. DeVet died in 1907, two years after the company sold out to the Cleveland Cliff Iron Company. Mrs. DeVet continued to run the store for a few years.

About 1900, Andres Peterson of *Sac Bay* moved in. Peterson refurnished the hotel and kept it open for several years. Peterson was succeeded by Charles Arnold who kept the hotel going from 1912-14.

Anderson Brothers, of *Washington Island*, rented the big store during the years and went into business. They were followed by Mr. Nygaard (1914) of

Escanaba. In 1916, Frank D'Hooge, mayor of *Ashland*, Wisconsin, paid a visit to *Fayette* where he had lived as a boy. He decided to buy the remainder of the village. Once valued at $300,000 the entire site was purchased for a few thousand dollars. Once more the big store was restocked and many repairs made to other buildings. Fred Van Remortel, brother-in-law of D'Hooge, was placed in charge. The blacksmith shop where J. Hynes had shod the teams of all the area for so many years was again opened and a new blacksmith, Robert Clinch, took over. Many of the houses were rented for cottages, fully furnished.

D'Hooge advertised *Fayette* as a summer resort and much effort was expended to attract summer visitors. The hotel was kept open summers for several years. This venture failed to pay off and in 1923 the big store burned with all its stock and contents.

During the ensuing years the grocery store changed hands several times and the post office was continued as a "country post office" until the state purchased the old furnace location and the remainder of the village along with 171 acres of land.

At the time of acquisition by the state, only 12 of 32 houses were standing, three commercial buildings, only one of eight factory buildings, along with the ruins of the furnace complex, namely charcoal and lime kilns. None of the log cabins or frame houses which had been located along the road to *Fairport* were standing.

From 1900 and into the 1950s *Fayette* had been a fishing village, a resort town, and finally a ghost town of unoccupied, weathered, windowless ruins. Time had restored foliage to the town and the 100 foot limestone bluff on the east side of the harbor was covered with trees. *Fayette* had once more become one of the most beautiful spots in the area.

Although the state purchased the town in 1950, restoration wasn't started until 1967-68. Even then the project went very slowly. A state park and camping grounds was established here under the supervision of the very capable James E. Kent, who was also put in charge of restoring the ghost town. Due to lack of funds and also because such a job is very painstaking, progress was very slow. Some of the buildings are open to the public but it will be some time before the town will be completely restored, Kent said. Some of the restored buildings have been closed to the public due to vandalism and stealing by unsupervised visitors. With only a few workers to manage both the park and the village, Kent said it is impossible to properly police the area so visitors are allowed to only peer through the windows of some of the restored houses.

––––––––

FERRY—1879, a station on the C. & N. W. Railroad, 8 miles west of *Escanaba*. Not listed after 1879.

FLAT ROCK—Was the first permanent settlement in Delta County and the site of the first sawmill in the county, if not in the entire Upper Peninsula. The sawmill was erected here on the river in 1836.

1879, population 50. Four miles north of *Escanaba*. The N. Ludington Company operated a general store and water-powered sawmill here.

―――――――

FRIDAY—1910, on the C. & N. W. Railroad. Mail *Perkins*.

―――――――

GARTH—1910, in Masonville Township, 16 miles from *Escanaba* and 5½ from *Rapid River* on the M. St. P. & S. Ste. M. Railroad. Mail to *Rapid River*. Garth Lumber & Shingle Company, saw, shingle, lath and planing mills and after whom the town took its name.

―――――――

GENA—The first lumber mill was built here in 1847. Name changed to *Masonville*. Was the county seat of Delta County from 1860 to 1864.

―――――――

GROOS—Was settled by natives of Luxemborg. 1905, a post office on the Escanaba & Lake Superior Railroad, in Wells Township, 5 miles north of *Escanaba*. Telephone. Named for Jacob A. Groos, Postmaster, live stock and justice; John Groos, physician; C. Stephenson, flour mill; and W. E. Wells, railroad agent.

In 1915, the post office was discontinued and mail sent to *Wells*. Escanaba Pulp & Paper Company, pulp mill; and Jacob Groos were the only business listings.

1917, John Bichler, stone quarry; and Jacob Groos, farm implements.

―――――――

HALES BAY—Not a ghost town. Was the postal name for *Garden*.

―――――――

HOOP SPUR—1910, mail *Winters*.

―――――――

HYDE—1910, the station for *Ford River*, 6 miles south. Railroad name *Ford River Junction*. Never was a village, only a country post office. 1905, T. Derouin, Postmaster and general store. The old general store remains standing and is used as a dwelling and antique store. Many nice homes have been built in the immediate vicinity. A weathered sign near the railroad crossing reads *Ford River*.

―――――――

ISABELLA—It is difficult to find the remains of this now long-gone village that one time had a population of several hundred people and a prosperous business section. One bar or tavern and a deserted townhall are located on US-2, about 20 miles west of *Manistique*.

Isabella was settled in 1868, to supply charcoal to the furnace at *Fayette*. Originally located on the shore of Big Bay De Noq, in Nahma Township. In 1893, on the Soo Line, population 200. R. W. McClellan, Postmaster, general store, lumber and charcoal; Chas. Bennett, general store; Rev. O. J. Goodman, Universalist; Jos. Heldmann, saloon; J. Hines, blacksmith; Jos. Kohiman, contractor; Jacob Landis, mason; E. G. McClellahan, lawyer; Peter Mailmann, justice; and O. H. Snow, shingle and sawmill.

By the early 1900s, two hotels were added. Geo. H. Tousignant, Postmaster; Peter Foy and John Larsen, hotels; Gibbs & Tousignant, general store; A. Schroer, railroad agent; and O. H. Snow, flour mill.

During the late 1880s Robert McClellan operated kilns at *Isabella* and sold his output to the iron company at *Fayette*.

Nothing remains today. About a mile south from US-2 is an old log house, empty and forlorn, standing some distance back from a gravel road. A good size orchard remains on the site and the front yard is lined with 100 year old poplar trees towering skyward.

Other old farm buildings stand in the vicinity. The remains of old farm buildings, surrounded by clusters of worn-out lilac bushes faces the bay on the south side of a blacktop road.

Isabella, proudly named in honor of the former queen of Castile, is no more.

————

KINGSLEY—This was the railroad name and *Campbell* was the postal name of the town. 1905 population 200. On the E. & L. S. Railroad, Baldwin Township, 15 miles northeast of *Escanaba*. Geo. M. Mashek, Postmaster; Stephen Charlebois, Saloon; John D. Colburn, shingle mill; Marial LeFlure, saloon; and Geo. Mashek, general store and sawmill.

1917, population 100. A. Lundgaard, Postmaster and store manager for Geo. Mashek; Cheereman Land & Lumber Company; G. E. Lemire, express agent; George Mashek, general store, etc.; and Anton Verdo, hotel.

————

LARCH—1910, at the junction of the Chicago & Northwestern and Soo Line Railroads. Mail *Escanaba*. Not a village.

————

LATHROP—Was one of the first settlements in the county, settled in 1865. In 1879, described as, *"Better known as Centerville, a village on the C. & N. W. Railroad in Maple Ridge Township. Hay and potatoes exported. Daily mail. Azel Lathrop, Postmaster, boarding house, justice and town clerk (probably for whom it was named); John McHale, farmer; Timothy Mahan, justice; and Ambrose Phelps; boardinghouse."*

In 1887, Azel Lathrop, general store and other enterprises; C. E. Haven, telegraph agent; Herman Johnson, Hugh McFarland, and Chas. Habler were all justices.

Things remained about the same in the embryo village until the turn of the century when it became a center for logging. Business listings for 1905 included, Adolph E. Haberman, Postmaster and telegraph agent; H. Bittner & Son, general store; John and Peter Britz Brothers, lumbermen; Nicholas Britz, ties, posts etc.; Nels Isaacson, saloon; William B. Malloy, timber; West Miller, saloon; Ralph Rheaume, ties and posts; Wm. Rich, blacksmith; and Wright Brothers, saw and shingle mill.

1927, Mrs. E. B. Fosterling, hotel.

After reaching a population of about 100, by 1910 there were 127 residents. Over the years a Catholic and Methodist Episcopal church was built and Rev. Hocking was minister. Other early 1900 business men were C. A. Cully, physician; Michael Eagle, blacksmith; Frank Johann, saloon; Mrs. Wm. Lampson, dressmaker; Miss McNaughten, teacher; and O. L. Malloy, manager Michigan State Telephone Company.

The post office was discontinued about 1950 and Lathrop ceased to be a village. One old, empty former hotel still stands today and the siding is used for shipping occasional loads of pulpwood. The few residents probably do not consider it a ghost town.

_____

LEMAY—1910, a station on the Escanaba & Lake Superior Railroad, mail *Cornell.*

_____

McDONALD— 1872, a newly established post office.

_____

MALTON— Listed as a post office in 1881 Michigan Manual.

_____

MAPLE RIDGE—This village, as did many U. P. towns, had several names. In 1879 the postal name was *de Beque.* In 1887, listed as a station on the C. & N. W. Railroad, 24 miles north of *Escanaba.*

1893, postal name changed to *Rock,* which it remains today. In that year was a post office, railroad name *Maple Ridge.* Population 50. Daily mail. Michael Kerby, general store and saloon; Andrew Kleiber, justice.

By 1905 had two general stores, one operated by Mrs. O. Kleiber and the other run by Larson Brothers; R. L. Bridges, saloon; and Joseph E. Sayer, lumber; John Larson, Postmaster.

Within the next 10 years the village boomed and in 1915 had a population of

350. Some business listings for that year included August Larson, Postmaster; Comines Brothers, general store; N. DeBeck, hotel; Albert Larson, lumber; Larson Brothers, general store and lumber; Adolph Neveu, livery; Maple Ridge C.O.O.P. store; Oskosh Excelsior Manufacturing Company; and Jos. E. Sayen, sawmill.

Although *Rock*, located today on M-35, has a small population most of the old stores and former factory stand empty and deserted. The badly weathered old depot bearing a faded sign, *ROCK*, has been deserted for years. Across the road from the depot stands the foundations and concrete walls of what probably at one time was a sawmill or factory. One real estate company is in business and is widely advertised. Otherwise the village is almost a ghost town of deserted buildings.

NAHMA—Fourteen miles east of *Rapid River* and about 5 miles south of US-2 is the village of *Nahma*. Once the location of one of Michigan's largest lumber mills, most of the 102 company houses and business buildings remain standing on this small peninsula jutting out into Big Bay DeNoc. The area is now owned by the American Playground Equipment Company of Indiana. *Nahma* isn't a total ghost town but with about 50 residents compared to the 1,000 workers and their families who once lived here, it is only a ghost of the town it once was.

This fire-blackened sawdust burner at the mouth of Sturgeon River ovelooks Big Bay De Noc at *Nahma*, former lumbering town of the late 1800s.   Photo by Roy L. Dodge (1971)

Nahma, which means "sturgeon" in Indian, was established by the Big Bay DeNoquette Lumber Company of *O'Coneto*, Wisconsin in 1881 as headquarters for their lumbering operations in the Upper Peninsula. Within a few years their extensive sawmills were the largest in the state and employed more than 1,000 men.

The Nahma and Northern Railroad constructed 51 miles of railroad north from the bay to carry supplies to lumber camps located along the line and hauled millions of feet of logs back to the mills.

Joe Sefik, age 61 in 1971, a native who started working in the company store at the age of 14 years said, *"I used to work two days a week loading box cars with supplies for delivery to lumber camps. We started work at 4 a.m. and didn't finish loading until 10 o'clock at night."*

Rows of empty company owned houses remain in *Nahma*. After part of the town was destroyed by fire, fire hydrants were installed in each block and ladders placed along the streets. These houses are similar to many company houses in Upper Peninsula ghost towns.   Photo by Roy L. Dodge (1971)

Sefik said the Bay DeNoquette Lumber Company built 102 houses (most of them still standing), for workers and their families, a hospital, community building, school house to seat 300 to 400 students, a company store and post office, in addition to the mills and a roundhouse for four steam engines and repair shops for railroad cars.

"In 1921, fire struck the town and destroyed 19 buildings, including the store and post office," Sefik said. The stores and buildings were rebuilt and measures were taken to prevent such a re-occurrence. Fire hydrants were installed in each block of the 50 square block village and racks were built holding two ladders long enough to reach the roofs of the houses. No serious fires

occurred again until 1931, when lightning struck the company store and burned it to the ground. *"That happened in May of 1931, and we were back in business that August,"* Sefik recalled. The present store and post office is the one erected in that year after the fire and is built on the same foundation and is of the same construction as the original building.

The last log was sawed in the *Nahma* mills in July of 1951, and the entire town was put up for sale. *"There were two stipulations in the sales agreement,"* Sefik said. *"One was that it could not be sold to anyone unless they established an industry to keep the town going. The other was that no houses could be sold to individuals until the town was paid for."*

In 1952, the present owners bought the village and used some of the former factory buildings to manufacture playground equipment. Sefik was kept on as store manager, and although many of the shelves and showcases are now empty, a stock of groceries and meats, along with some housewares, dry goods items and clothing are kept for the few local residents and occasional tourists.

Streets of the village are lined with rows of neatly painted former company houses built by the Bay DeNoquette company. The 100 foot long community building stands vacant along with the former "Nahma House" hotel. The school was put up for sale in 1970, after consolidation with three other townships. Students now attend the new Garden School, 10 miles distance.

Roland Bramer, age 47, has been Postmaster since 1959. Bramer said the post office was established February 20, 1882, with James McGee as Postmaster.

Today the *Nahma* post office serves 180 patrons, most of them on the one rural route in operation.

At one time the village was served by two churches, one Catholic and one Protestant Episcopal. Services are still held at the Catholic church on the west edge of the village but in 1971 the other church was being razed.

For a few years during the 1890s, *Nahma* had a small newspaper called "Short Stories." It was published for the Bay DeNoquette Company by a patent medicine firm who filled most of the pages with their advertising, interspersed with brief news items of *Nahma* residents and display ads of local merchants. Sefik still has copies of some of the old, yellowed newspapers. He also has many of the old company records. In 1935 local beef was purchased for 4 cents per pound. The store also purchased cattle and other hides for the same price. Pork sold for 15 cents per pound; pigs feet 19 cents per pound and prime beef 16½ cents per pound retail.

Sefik said his father started working for the company in the 1880s and was a

Old Engine No. 5 at *Nahma*, one of four locomotives owned by the lumber company built in 1905. When the logging days were over the rails were removed and this engine was left near the station as a reminder of *Nahma's* lumbering days.   Photo by Roy L. Dodge (1971)

night watchman at the mills. He and his brother, Frank Sefik, who is superintendent of the American Playground Equipment Company, were born in *Nahma*.

Before the fire of 1921, the village had a three-story, 100-bed transient house for single workers and a hospital with a good doctor in charge to take care of the workers' ills and injuries. There was also a community building with a bowling alley, soda fountain (no liquor), men's lounge and reading room, and an auditorium.

When the company folded in 1951, the railroad tracks to *Nahma Junction*, several miles north, were removed. Today one old, rusted train engine stands, a silent sentinel to the days when *Nahma* was booming. The engine is located at the end of the wide boulevard main street that is lined with towering poplar trees.

Sefik said the engine is one of four owned by the lumber company. It was built in 1905, and has a wooden cow-catcher. The locomotives probably cost as much when new as the town sold for. The other engines, along with the "Russell" log cars and other rolling stock, were sold to the Antrim Iron Works and went into the scrap piles for resmelting.

Sefik said some of the houses have been sold for summer homes, after provisions of the original purchase agreement had been fulfilled.

An old steel, silo-type sawdust burner towers skyward next to the bay at the mouth of the Sturgeon river. An Indian legend tells of the time before the whiteman's arrival that sturgeon filled the stream each year at spawning time and make a solid bridge across the river where the Indians walked across on top of the backs of the fish.

According to the *Michigan Gazetteer & Business Directory*, the village was settled in 1850, and was formerly an Indian village. In 1940, about 100 of these Indians, formerly of the Chippewa, Ottawa and Potawatomi tribes, lived across the river from *Nahma* in what was called the *Nahma Indian Settlement*. The land was owned by the Bay de Nocquette Company, which also hired many of the Indians in their mills. The families paid $1 per year rent to keep them from declaring squatter's rights to the land.

In 1848, George Richards and S. H. Kerfoot, of *Chicago*, built a sawmill on the Sturgeon river near *Nahma*.

In 1872 *Nahma* was described as a lumbering village at the mouth of the Sturgeon River, near the head of Big Bay du Noquet. *"There is only one mill here owned by McDonalds & Beardsley, who are also proprietors of the village and the only parties doing business here. The only communication with Nahma is by water. It is 30 miles northeast of Escanaba, from whence it gets its mail. E. D. Beardley, Postmaster."*

The original lumbering operations apparently did not last long. In 1879 *Nahma* was described as *"An unimportant point in the southeastern part of Escanaba County (sic) on Big Bay de Noquette."*

Sometime in the intervening years (1872-1882) the post office was discontinued but reactivated in 1882. Business listings for 1887 included James McGee, Postmaster; D. J. Budd, physician; Walter J. Ellis, justice; A. Gammon, hotel; Robert McClellan, coal; Peter Millman, justice; Frank Marcia, blacksmith; Jos. St. Peter, livery; Walter Stratton, hotel; and Peter Washoo, justice.

1893, four miles from Sturgeon River (later *Nahma Junction*). Population 350. Henry M. Martin, Postmaster; A. Calhoun and Samuel Gray, barbers; Joseph Jolly, confectioner; John Levillra, stage and livery; W. R. Powers, insurance; Dr. Alfred J. Scott; Geo. B. Sporer, fish; and Reverend George W. Stillwell, Congregational.

Other listings in the early 1900s were: W. E. Barlow, Postmaster, County Clerk, Deputy Sheriff and manager of the Bay De Noquette general store and sawmill; Decor Blaise, barber; Alex Buetcher, insurance; J. P. Cameron, meats; J. C. Conrad, boarding house; F. B. Davis, insurance; George Duncan, blacksmith; G. J. Farnsworth, insurance; W. C. Gerow, railroad agent; Archie Johnston, constable; Ruth Lagerquick, teacher; Dr. W. J. Laird; R. J. McMillen, hotel; Tillie Starrine, teacher; and Nelson Venet, livery and mail carrier.

As late as 1940, *Nahma* had a population of 700 and the mills had a capacity of turning out 40,000 feet of hardwood lumber or 60,000 feet of soft wood lumber per day. After the mills closed down in 1951, most of the people moved away and today the village is nearly deserted.

————

NEW MINNEAPOLIS—This was a town that remained for the most part on paper and in the mind of Henry J. Bebeau. He purchased land in Section 34, T-39, north of *Garden* bordering Valentine Creek and started to build his own town.

Bebeau started on his project in earnest by erecting a group of buildings that included his own modern house, a store building, and a large community hall, along with barns, sheds and other buildings. This town was started during the time the Jackson Iron Company was operating its blast furnaces at *Fayette* in the 1880s. The company was extending narrow-gauge railroads from their factory to other areas to haul cordwood for charcoal and sand used for making molds. They were also improving most roads in the area and Bebeau probably was depending on an influx of settlers moving into the area as the cleared timberland was being opened up to farming to support his enterprise.

Within a few years the project was abandoned and the property was eventually purchased by N. L. Neveaus. Later Charles Clifton rented the land and combined it with another 160 acre farm nearby. Clifton started a livestock farm which was maintained until 1908. There isn't a building remaining today. Some of them were destroyed by fire and the remainder was moved away.

————

ROCKY POINT—See *Sander's Fishery*.

————

SAC BAY—In 1879, located on *Burnt Bluff Point* peninsula in Fairbanks Township, 25 miles southeast of *Escanaba*. A hamlet without postal facilities (also known as *Burnt Bluff Point*).

————

SALVA—1910, a station on the Escanaba & Lake Superior Railroad 1 mile north of *Cornell*. Mail to *Cornell*.

————

SANDER'S FISHERY—1877, an extensive fishery and small settlement on Green Bay, 3½ miles below *Escanaba*, which is the trading point and post office. John Sanders, fishery and boarding house.

Two years later a post office had been established and a population of 20 was given. The 1879 business directory listed E. P. Royce, Postmaster and lawyer, along with John Sanders, fishery.

By 1887, the place was also known as *Rocky Point*, in Ford River Township, daily stage to *Ford River*. Population about 25.

Not listed in directories after 1887.

___

SANDERS POINT—Name changed to *Gladstone*, after the British statesman, Wm. Ewart Gladstone. Not a ghost town.

___

SCHAFFER—Residents of this one-time village, probably numbering less than 100, celebrated their centennial in conjunction with *Bark River* this year (1972) and not one of them considers it a ghost town, although it is pictured as such in their section of the *Bark River* Centennial book. A listing of business places about 1900 describes charcoal kilns, Coburn's store; a cheese factory, depot, livery, stable, garage, blacksmith shop; Gravelle's Saloon; Dr. Chollette's office; LeClaire's Saloon; a second garage with a barber shop attached; another cheese factory; pool hall; Provost's Store; Dubois Saloon; butcher shop; a third store; in addition, a church and school.

All that remains today of the once thriving village of more than 300 population are a large, brick, Catholic church building, one store and a tavern.

Schaffer was settled in late 1872, on the proposed line of the C. & N. W. Railway that was later to be called "the Felch Branch," extending from *Narenta* to *Metropolitan*. First settlers were French-Canadians and included businessmen, lumberjacks, and many farmers.

The embryo village was named after Charles H. Schaffer who was born at *Waterloo*, Ontario, Canada, in 1846. He lived to be nearly 100 years old (having died in 1945). Schaffer purchased 8 acres next to the railroad tracks in the village in 1887. He built a battery of half a dozen or more charcoal kilns on the property and the rail stop was known as *Shaffer*. In 1893, he sold out to his brother-in-law, Louis Coburn, who built the first store.

By 1910, the population had reached more than 300 and the predominance of the first French Canadian settlers can be seen in the names of businessmen for that year.

A description of the village from "The Square Deal," reprinted in the centennial book is worth repeating because it is typical of most villages of that era and the news style of the day. Headlined *"Schaffer A Good Town—One of the Live Villages in Delta County, Michigan"* it reads as follows: *"One of the best little villages in Delta County is Schaffer, with a population of 300, on the Metropolitan Branch of the C. & N. W. Railway. It is 12 miles from Escanaba, the judicial seat . . . There is one church here, Catholic. Schaffer is a good location for factories of most any kind, and the citizens are noted for their hospitality.*

"Thomas Provost is Postmaster. He has been engaged in business in Schaffer for three years. He carries a large assortment of everything in the general store line and makes every effort to please the public by giving every one a square deal. All subscriptions or news items left with Mr. Provost will be forwarded to Square Deal, Escanaba.

"Phillas Desormeau and Frank Gosselin are proprietors of the Farmers' Hotel. They have a livery barn in connection, also a neat bar stocked with the best of wines, liquors and cigars. Fine free lunch every Saturday night. Desormeau & Gosselin took charge of Gravell's Saloon and Hotel on May 1 last. Both are Escanaba men and are making a big success of their new place. Old Escanaba beer on tap as well as Menominee River brew. Everybody is treated courteously. Call and see them when in Schaffer. They will treat you right.

"J. P. Cholette has been engaged in business in Schaffer for about six years. He carries a nice line of jewelry, confectionery, some groceries and novelties. He appreciates all trade given him.

"A. Leclaire has been engaged in the saloon business for eight years in his present stand. He carries a full line of wines, liquors and cigars and appreciates the trade given him. Hotel in connection, run by Baptiste Dute, who also has a livery barn.

"Theophile Duford has just opened a fine general store, and will carry in stock a complete line of everything in general merchandise. He will do his best to please his customers by giving good value for everything he sells.

"J. D. Shakelford has been engaged in the general merchandise business for about three years. He carries a complete stock of dry goods, millinery, clothing, groceries, etc., and makes every effort to please the public by giving every one a square deal. Mr. Shakelford also handles timber and buys and sells horses. He has worked up a nice business by courteous treatment to all."

For many years the C. & N. W. Railroad furnished employment for many workers of the community. Railroad service was discontinued in 1970 and the tracks and rails removed the following year.

The centennial book describes the *Schaffer* of 1972 as: *"A settlement which experienced a boom, bustled with business, then gradually phased out to a type of village, whereby its occupants depend on employment in outlying areas, business activity is limited, and the population increases at a very slow pace, and most everyday needs are purchased outside of the community."*

This is a very good description but with the decline in Upper Peninsula population and lack of industry during the last quarter of a century, it is very unlikely that the population will increase at even "a very slow pace." Born with the railroad, this village died with the railroad, just as thousands of other Michigan towns have done.

ST. JAQUES—This place was first settled as *Sturgeon River*. In 1893, on the Soo Line Railroad, Nahma Township, population 6. C. E. Bersee, Postmaster, railroad and express agent.

By 1905, the population was 65 and the name had been changed to *St. Jaques*, in Bay de Noquet Township. A. Schorer, Postmaster and express agent; Publius Gagnon, general store and charcoal kilns; and R. C. Willie, lumber.

During the next 10 years the village grew to 200. In 1914, P. Gagnon, Postmaster; L. P. Coolaw, hotel; W. C. Gerow, express agent; and Gagnon General Store, bark, ties, cedar, etc..

In 1927, had a Catholic church and one store. Send mail to *Nahma*.

Today a half-dozen houses and a gasoline station remain along US-2, all that's left of the one-time village.

STONINGTON—This once prosperous village in Bay de Noc Township, on Little Bay de Noc across from *Escanaba*, reached its peak about 1927 of 750. It was settled in 1897.

1910, described as: *"Population 400. Daily mail. Hans H. Bonefield, Postmaster and school director; Peter Anderson, carpenter; Christ Bonefield, blacksmith; Selma Carlson, teacher; John Champ, meats; John Christensen, livery; George Cook, constable; Hilda Engberg, teacher; John Engberg, carpenter; Ole Ericksen, farm machinery; Peter Honborg, fish; Alma Johnson, teacher; Jacob Larsen, justice; Elias Larsen, justice; Mayme Leahey, teacher; John Nystrom, justice; Andrew Skaug, cedar jobber; Skaug Brothers, general store; and Thorsen & Pederson, sawmill."*

In 1927, had Danish-Norwegian and Swedish Lutheran churches. Daily mail. Hans Lorenson, Postmaster; Andres Hansen, Jr., justice; Otto W. Johnson, barber; Skaug Brothers, general store and sawmill; Smith Brothers, sawmill; Thorsen Brothers, garage; Semer Thorsen, blacksmith.

The post office was discontinued about 1957-58, and today the only business in the village is a small combination store and gasoline station. One of the old general store buildings stands vacant. The Community Hall is in use but only the rotted pilings of the former shipping docks remain and the fisheries are gone.

TESCH—May also have been called *Alecto*. This settlement, at the junction of the C. & N. W. and the Soo Line Railroads, was never a village and did not have a post office. Located only a mile south of *Schaffer*, the residents received mail from there. For many years this was a busy junction and the old wood frame watch tower, with faded signs designating the station as *TESCH* on all four sides of the building, still stands, silent sentinel overlooking the piles of ties and sections of iron rails plied alongside the grade of the abandoned branch of the C. & N. W. Railroad.

Several weatherbeaten frame houses, most of them lived in, remain along the street facing the railroad that was once *Tesch*.

TROMBLY—1940 population 50. See *Defiance* for history.

UNO—Was a post office and resort village in the northeast part of Delta County. In 1910, located in Garden Township, 12 miles from *Stuben* (in Schoolcraft County), the nearest rail approach. A. H. Dickinson, Postmaster and summer resort.

1915, population 30. O. O. Dickinson, Postmaster; James B. Buckley, stage line; Dickinson Brothers, hardwood timber and lumber; Lakeside Summer Resort and Lumber, O. O. Dickinson, manager.

Uno is still designated on county maps, although the post office was discontinued in 1921. Is still a resort area.

VAN'S HARBOR—This was an early settlement on Big Bay de Noc, in Garden Township on the Garden Peninsula. The area was once inhabited by Indians and most of the entire peninsula was farmed by Indians, hence its name.

After the furnaces closed at *Fayette* this settlement became one of the important harbors along the bay with boats making daily round trips from *Escanaba* during the navigation season. Names of some of the boats were Captain John Coffey's tug, *Anabel*, and steamers *Welcome*, *Duluth*, *City of New Baltimore*, *Saugatuck* and later, the *Maywood* with Capt. Charles McGauley in charge.

In 1893, *Van's Harbor* had a population of nearly 1,000 and was described as 12 miles south of *Van Winkle*, on the Soo Line railroad. Daily mail. L. Van Winkle, Postmaster; E. L. Foot, doctor and dentist; James Freeman, saloon; James Gibbs & Sons, hotel; David W. Kee, physician; Lewis VanWinkle, justice; Ulysses VanWinkle, transportation agent; VanWinkle & Montague, general store, lumber, shingle and picket manufacturers.

By 1910, the population had dropped to 200. Described as 13 miles south of *Cooks*. Stage daily to *Cooks*, fare $1. Daily mail. E. L. Neman, Postmaster. Felix Prassed, livery; Bert Campbell, dock agent; Leo Cousino, saloon; H. Gardner, hotel; Robert Knox, manager of Van's Harbor Land & Lumber Company; Alexander McPhee, notary; Patrick McPhee, land looker; Edward L. Neman, manager of company store; Evelyn Rosseau, dressmaker; Nelson Rousseau, saloon; Van's Harbor Land & Lumber Co, mill and general store, Perley Lowe, president; and Ward Brothers and Wm. Winters, fishermen.

In 1915 or 1916, the LaFollette Seaman's Law went into effect, requiring that a double crew be carried on runs such as that between *Van's Harbor* and *Escanaba*. Business did not warrant the extra expense, it was said, and the shipping route was abandoned. The village became all but abandoned within a short time, and in 1927, mail was sent to *Garden*. The only business remaining was Patrick McPhee, grocery and a few fishermen.

———————

VAN WINKLE—in 1893, a post office and station on the Soo Line, 17 miles west of *Manistique*. Daily mail.

———————

1905, a discontinued post office. Send mail to *Isabella*.

———————

WINDE—1910, listed as a station on the C. & N. W. Railroad. Mail to *Perkins*.

Chapter Eight

DICKINSON COUNTY

Dickinson County was the last county in the Upper Peninsula to be organized, in 1891. The land area was taken from Marquette, Iron, and Menominee Counties. *Iron Mountain* is the county seat.

Although noted for its many iron mines, Dickinson County (as were most Upper Peninsula counties) was also an important lumbering district for many years. Both lumbering and mining are still carried on today. The standing timber in the county in 1927 was estimated to be 610,250,000 board feet, making it the 14th county in the amount of timber left standing. The county was named for the Honorable Don M. Dickinson, Postmaster General under President Grover Cleveland.

DICKINSON COUNTY GHOST TOWNS

ALFRED—1905, population 100. On the Ford River and on the Chicago, Minneapolis, and St. Paul Railroad, Breen Township, 30 miles northeast of *Iron Mountain*. Telephone. A. Kemmeter, Postmaster, and C. H. Woodford, railroad agent.

1909, population 35. H. A. Bauman, Postmaster, general store, ties, posts and forest product; and Andrew Phillips, saloon.

Post office discontinued in 1910, mail received by RFD *Northland*. Note: Chicago, Minneapolis & St. P. Railroad was changed to Escanaba & Lake Superior at a later date. *Alfred* was located on this railroad and on the east Dickinson County line.

ANTOINE—Was a mine settlement, called a "location," known as *Traders Mine* and also *Trader Junction* on railroad maps. On the C. & N. W. Railroad near the north *Iron Mountain* city limits. 1910, Mail *Iron Mountain*.

APPLETON—or *Appleton Mine* was another location on the C. & N. W. Railroad between *Waucedah* and *Vulcan*. Remains still visible.

ARAGON MINE—A location on the Wisconsin & Michigan Railroad. 1910, mail *Vulcan*.

98

1) Bad Water Lake (now part of the flowage at Twin Falls Plant of Wisconsin-Michigan Power Company). Former site of thriving Indian Village, mentioned in diaries and notes of early explorersand survey teams.

2) & 3) Abandoned Mines (and usually included settlements, called "locations") in the Iron Mountain Area: Trader's Mine, Cornell Mine, Cuff Mine, Globe Mine, Pewabic Mine, Pewabic Pit, Walpole Mine, Millie Mine, Keel Ridge Mine (site of a cave in where several miners' bodies were never recovered), and the Chapin Mines, now marked by a flooded pit at the north side of *Iron Mountain*. Also in this area is the perserved Cornish Pump.

4) Indiana Mine, open pit, flooded, with remains of fine stone and brick foundation.

5) Quinnesec Mine, Cundy Mine. A few original buildings remain in what was the early "rail head" town during the Menominee Range Development. Most of the community was destroyed by fire in 1906 and partially rebuilt.

6) Big and Littel Quinnesec Falls, noted on earliest maps of the area. Translated, the name means Smoking Waters.

(Map of Dickinson County) Information by Dean Turner of *Ironwood*, Michigan.

(7) *Norway* area mines: Aragon, Cyclops, Perkins, Norway—one shaft house still standing. Also Strawberry Lake, flooded cave in what was once the center of the city. The entire town was moved because of the caving. Parts of "Old Town" remain north of the area.

(8) Abandoned mines in *Vulcan* area: Brier Hill Mine, West Vulcan, Central Vulcan, East Vulcan, Verona. A few mine buildings remain; also foundations of other buildings (made of rough native red sandstone), and two shaft houses. Some houses built in the early 1870s remain and the oldest frame building on the Range, a mining company office and company store built in 1873.

(9) The *New York Farm*, established in 1866 as a supply farm for logging camps in the area and along the Menominee River.

(10) *O'Callaghan's Mills*, or *Sturgeon Mill.*

(11) Abandoned mines in the *Loretto* area: The Loretto, Appleton, where an engineering feat diverted the Sturgeon River to avert flooding the Loretto Mine. Some houses remain and are occupied, also mine building traces.

(12) Abandoned mines in the *Waucedah* area: Breen, Emmett, The Breen mine was the first mine on the Range, opened in 1866. About five houses and a "Grange Hall" in run down condition are all that remain. The abandoned cemetery north of the village contains tombstones bearing a likeness to early New England stones, crude carving, ornate lettering, poetic sentiments. The area is overgrown and difficult to locate.

(13) Site of *Hamlin*, early logging camp; few traces remain.

(14) Site of *Holmes' Farm*, logging camp supply farm. One of the original squared log buildings is preserved in *Norway* and used as a private museum by Jake Menghini, who has a collection of local logging and mining artifacts.

(15) Site of the Flannigan Lodge on Brown's Lake, burned in the 1940s. This elaborate lodge was built by the first mayor of *Norway*, later Chief Justice of the Michigan Supreme Court, Richard Flannigan.

(16) Abandoned mines: Metropolitan and Calumet. The road north from *Vulcan* was the first "ore road" on the Range. Some traces of the orginial 1873-74 road can still be found in existing truck roads.

(17) Ardis Furnace ruins near Lake Antoine.

(18) Abandoned railroad depot sites in *Channing, Randville, Iron Mountain, Quinnesec, Norway, Vulca, Loretto* and *Waucedah*. Most have disappeared. Two have been converted to residences, one in *Iron Mountain* (elaborate 1880 brick) is now a sports shop.

Information by Dean Turner, Assoc. Inc., real estate, *Iron Mountain.*

BERGAM—1910, on the Wisconsin & Michigan Railroad. Mail *Loretto*.

BJORKMAN—1910, on the C. M. & St. P. Railroad. Mail *Iron Mountain*.

BRYDEN—See *Ralph*.

CALLAN—1910, on the Wisconsin & Michigan Railroad, mail *Vulcan*.

CALUMET MINE—1910, on C. & N. W. Railroad, mail *Quinnesec*.

CAREYS—1910, on C. M. & St. P. Railroad, mail *Randville*.

CI ANO—1910, on Wisconsin & Michigan Railroad, mail *Vulcan*.

EAST NORWAY—Was a location and station on the Wisconsin & Michigan Railroad, mail to *Norway*.

East Norway was one of the mining locations so numerous in the *Vulcan-Norway* area. *Norway* proper at one time reached a population of more then 5,000, when the mines were active. The first pitting occurred in 1877 and *Norway* was founded on the Vulcan hematite vein at its richest point. The Menominee Range produced millions of tons of iron ore. The mines in the area were so close together that the underground tunnels ran beneath the town site and the village caved in. Stores, houses and buildings started sinking into the ground and the entire town was moved to its present location. This mine, as did all the others, became inactive and several of them flooded. *East Norway* is no more.

FELCH—Located on present day County Road 569, 12 miles east of *Randville* on M-95, is rapidly becoming a ghost town. Until a few years ago the county road was M-69, a main route for traffic going east to *Escanaba* and even today the population remains about the same as in 1927, when it dropped from more than 500 people to less than 200.

Settled in 1882, on the C. & N. W. Railway, Felch Township, 25 miles north of *Iron Mountain*, in 1917. Reached a population of 600. At one time the village contained several grocery and general stores, saloons, blacksmith shop, etc. Some of the business listings for 1909 were, Andrew Rian, Postmaster; H. R. Burkardt, railroad and express agent; Carl Carlson, township treasurer; Carlson & Edburg, loggers; Miss Donahue, teacher; Charles Forell, supervisor; Henry Hellman, saloon; Wm. Naslund, saloon; John Ovist, general store; Andrew Rian, general store and blacksmith; Martin Rian, painter; Olaf Rian, township clerk; A. J. Scott, superintendent of Calumet mine; Ward Solberg, cigars and confectioner; and Glenn Stratton, teacher.

1915, had Swedish Baptist and Swedish Lutheran churches. Andrew Rian, Postmaster; general store etc.; Felch Creamery Company; L. W. LaLonde, express and telegraph agent. Other businesses remained about the same as 1910.

The old Felch General Store stands near the terminus of th C. & N. W. Railroad tracks in *Felch*. Both the store and railroad are now abandoned. *Felch* at one time had a population of 600 and was a booming village during the logging days.
Photo by Roy L. Dodge (1971)

In 1917, the population had dropped to 150. Minnie Rian was acting Postmaster. Business listings were Advance Industry, quarry; Felch Township Telephone Company; Andrew Rian, real estate and boarding house; Charles J. Salberg, billiards; E. J. Johnson, general store; John Sundstrom, auto repair, implements, etc.

In 1971, the tracks of the old C. & N. W. Railroad had been removed at this point and came to a dead end near the end of the former Main street where a tavern now occupies one of the original buildings, across from the vacant, old Felch Supply Company general store. A grocery store remains in business on this street and on County Road 569 is a hardware store, road commission building, and someone recently re-opened a gasoline station and was putting up new signs. A Department of Natural Resources office is also located here and a township fire department building. One church remains and a large school, now consolidated with a new district that apparently is intended to serve several counties. Once a going town, today is only a shadow of its former self.

———

FEW MINE—1910, on the Wisconsin & Michigan Railroad, mail *Quinnesec.*

———

FLOODWOOD—In 1893, described as *"A post office and lumbering village on the Milwaukee and Northern Railroad, Sagola Township, 32 miles north of Iron Mountain. Population 200. Edward Johnson, Postmaster, and railroad agent; Joseph Baril, hotel; L. J. Evans & Company, shingle mill; Kirby, Carpenter & Company, general store and sawmill; N. Ludington Company, general store and sawmill; Ludington, Wells & Van Schaack Company, general store and lumber manufacturers; James McNally, hotel; A. Porterfield, lumber; and Sawyer & Goodman, general store and saw mills."*

In 1905, a discontinued post office. Send mail to *Channing.*

In 1910, the settlement still had a population of nearly 100 people and at that time was on the C. M. & St. P. Railroad.

The remains of the one-time village are now located on M-95, about 10 miles north of *Channing.*

———

FOSTER CITY—Only a store and one gasoline station, along with perhaps a dozen homes remain in the one-time thriving logging village of *Foster City.* Founded in 1886, and named after A. L. Foster, the first Postmaster who was superintendent for the A. M. Harmon Lumber Company. This company built a dam on the Sturgeon River and set up their mills and lumbering operations.

In 1887, described as: *"A recently established post office in Breen Township* (at that time in Menominee County, Dickinson County wasn't organized until 1891). *It is a station on the Felch Mountain branch of the C. & N. W. Railroad. Population 75. A. L. Foster, Postmaster."*

Business listings for that year were A. L. Foster, lumber and timber; A. M. Harmon, Lumber Company; Daniel Kisor, justice; and F. L. McGillan, railroad and express agent.

1893, population 350. A. L. Foster, Postmaster etc.; N. H. Allen, blacksmith; P. G. Anderson, justice; J. B. Gaston, physician; Wm. Greenwood, justice; A. M. Harmon, Lumber Company, sawmill; T. A. Peets, express agent; George Potter and E. B. Richardson, music teachers; and W. A. Rideout, log contractor.

Although area historians, including present old-time natives, give credit to the Morgan Lumber & Cedar Company as founders of the one-time village, the Morgan Company didn't arrive here until about 1900, and apparently bought out the interests of the original A. M. Harmon Lumber Company.

In 1905, only a few business listings are given, including R. W. Pierce, Jr., Postmaster; Gust Johnson, logger; the Morgan Company; W. Paul, lumber inspector; O. Pegg, railroad agent; and S. (Swan) J. Peterson, logger.

Mrs. Ellen Haiderson, 73, (in 1971) the daughter of Swan Peterson, still lives in a neat, white frame house which stands next to the present grocery and post office combination on County Rd. 569 in *Foster City*. Twenty two years a widow, Mrs. Haiderson was Postmistress of the village for many years.

The story of Swan Peterson reads like a Horatio Alger story of an immigrant who, with nothing but his bare hands and who could speak only his native tongue, worked his way up from nothing until, in 1925, he had saved enough money to buy the town of *Foster City*.

Peterson was born in Sweden in 1869, came to the United States and the Upper Peninsula at age 21 and found work in the mines. In 1898, he decided to try his hand at lumbering, an occupation he was familiar with in his native land. He purchased a small acreage near *Foster City* in 1898, cleared the land and built a log cabin for his family, which included five children. In addition to clearing his land and planting crops to last through the winter, Peterson walked 21 miles to *Randville* where he took a train from there to *Floodwood* and started in as a jobber cutting cedar posts and ties. Within four years he was hiring 60 men and had 21 of his own horses working in the woods.

This rusty railroad switch and former station (background) are all that remains of old *Foster City*, one-time busy lumbering town on the C. & N. W. Railroad. Photo by Roy L. Dodge (1971)

Within a few years Peterson, along with the other settlers, who were all Swedish, built their own church. Mrs. Halderson said for many years only Swedish was spoken in the church and school.

Peterson took some of the money he had made logging and purchased a general store in *Hardwood*, just below *Foster City* on the C. & N. W. Railroad and was in business there until 1925 when he heard the Morgan Lumber & Cedar Company was moving out and their holdings were for sale. This included nearly the entire village of *Foster City*, which was located along the C. & N. W. Railroad and along the river. Mrs. Haiderson said there was no M-69 highway until 1927.

Peterson's purchase included nine company houses, the former home of the company superintendent, a large, three-story mansion painted snow white and located on a high bank overlooking the village, a 32-room hotel, the mills and dam, company barns, store and all other buildings.

At one time there were 200 men working in the mills, Mrs. Halderson said. Peterson paid $30,000 for the town and continued to operate the mills until the start of World War II. By this time Peterson owned a large dairy herd and continued in the dairy business. The old mill buildings were beginning to deteriorate so they were torn down. About the same time, one of the tall chimneys of the hotel was toppled in a windstorm and caved in a large section of the roof. Peterson removed the top story of the building but its·days as a hotel were numbered.

This combination grocery and post office, a gasoline station and a few houses now stand along County Road 569 near *Foster City* in Dickinson County. Photo by Roy L. Dodge (1971)

A series of misfortunes occurred about this time. A spring flood took the dam out, draining the former mill pond that covered many acres of low land along the river, and in 1946, at the age of 78 years, Swan Peterson was killed in an automobile accident.

In 1927, *Foster City* had a population of 250. In addition to the Swedish Mission church there was also a Catholic Church. Ellen A. Peterson (Mrs. Halderson), Postmaster; S. H. Bridges, logger; Ed Carlson, apiarist; J. E.

Eckstrom, apiarist and Pastor of Swedish Mission; Swan J. Peterson, proprietor of the Foster City Hotel; Lawrence LaLonde, railroad agent; Charles G. Pearson, justice; Stanley E. Peterson, gasoline station; Harry J. Peterson, justice; T. S. Peterson & Company; Swan Peterson, president, general store, meats, real estate, logger and dairy; and Magnuson Swanson, livestock.

Mrs. Blanch Milligan, Postmistress for 30 years, is the present Postmistress and is about to retire. Part of the original postal equipment was still in use (1971) in a corner of the present grocery store operated by Pat Milligan, Jr. and his wife. Pat Milligan is a disabled Army Veteran of World War II, having lost his right leg above the knee on Iwo Jima.

The former company house and hotel still overlook the remains of the village and the former freight office is located beside the grade of the old C. & N. W. Railroad, which was abandoned several years ago. Today the post office at *Foster City* has 56 patrons, which includes all the residents of Breen Township. One of the Peterson's huge barns still stands across the river near what was at one time the main road leading into the village.

Mrs. Halderson said the township residents are trying to encourage the Department of Natural Resources to rebuild the dam and flood the old millpond for a fishing and boating site, hoping it will encourage tourists and perhaps revive the town again. With the growth of tourism in the Upper Peninsula since the building of the Mackinac Bridge it is possible that someday the village may become a resort town.

GOLDEN—1910, on the Escanaba & Lake Superior Railroad, mail to *Channing*.

———

GRANITE BLUFF—In 1893, population 50. T. H. Strup, Postmaster and contractor; Vivan C. Cheliew, sawmill; F. Z. Franer, railroad and express agent.

1905, on the Chicago, Milwaukee & St. Paul Railroad, Breitung Township, 4 miles from *Randville*. J. J. Collins, Postmaster; Frank Forgetto, cordwood; Louis Lansing, contractor; National Hardwood Company, lumber and sawmill; and Alex Swansen, wood.

This location never developed into a village of any size and was mainly a siding and flag station along the line.

In 1916, things remained about the same. J. J. Collins, Postmaster, dealer in ties, posts and poles. Another wood contractor was listed, F. Tunney. In that year (1916) the post office was discontinued. In 1971, one gas station and two or three rundown houses are all that remain.

GRATTON—1910, on the Chicago, Millwaukee & St. Paul Railroad, mail *Channing*.

———————

HARDWOOD—1893, population 100. 1905, about the same. On the C. & N. W. Railroad and the east branch of Sturgeon River, Breen Township. This village was less than 5 miles east of *Foster City* at a crossing on what is now County Road 569.

Some 1905 business listings were, Peter J. Anderson, Postmaster, general store and timber; Ina Arms, teacher; Henry Chalebois, saloon; Martin Coonen, hotel; Andrew Engequist, blacksmith; A. P. Farrell, lumberman and land looker; Mrs. O'Connor, teacher; and Spies Lumber & Cedar Company, capital $50,000, A. Spies, president.

Things remained about the same in 1910, except for a few business changes. Ed Bushane was blacksmith; Alex Beachthel, saloon; A. P. Farrell, hotel; Jos. Felardeau, hotel; Fred LaDuke, hotel and saloon; Larsen, railroad agent; and Clara Moore, teacher.

In 1915, Peter J. Anderson estate is listed as operating the general store and timber business. In that year only one hotel remained in business. After Swan Anderson sold out and moved up-river to *Foster City*, *Hardwood* faded out and *Foster City* became the main village of the area.

Today, *Hardwood* is merely a crossing along the grade of the C. & N. W. Railroad with one tavern and gasoline station. The remains of one old log cabin stands near the railroad and one building still bears the faint letters of "——————————— French-Blacksmith" near what was the original main street facing the railroad.

———————

HENDERSON—1910 on the Escanaba & Lake Superior Railroad, mail *Ralph*.

———————

HYLAS—1910, on the C. & N. W. Railroad, mail *Foster City*.

———————

KEEL RIDGE—Generally associated with a mining disaster, only the county mine inspectors and possibly a few pioneers know the exact location of the site, which for more than 80 years has been the tomb of eight men.

The old Keel Ridge Mine is located about two blocks north of U.S. Highway 2 and 141, approximately ¼ mile east of the *Iron Mountain* city limits.

Some signs of mining activity are still visible—an old railroad bed, remains of stone foundations, piles of ore, a cave opening to what was once a shaft, and several deep holes. Cliff-like sides of the larger of these suggest that earth and rocks caved straight down about 100 feet to the water below. Somewhere under that water (a mining publication of the time says it's 100 feet deep) are the bodies of eight miners entombed by the cave-in, on April 10, 1883, one of the two worst mining disasters in Dickinson Company history.

Probably the only known unregistered grave in the county, a part of Menominee Company at that time, the official report and the names of the men who were buried there, mistakenly listed as victims of the "Red Ridge" mine accident, can be found at the courthouse in *Menominee*, Michigan.

Keel Ridge Mine, opening in 1880, produced 53,445 tons of iron ore to the spring of 1883. With the ore body depleted and obvious signs of sinking throughout the area, pumps and machinery were removed prior to the abandonment. All men were on the surface on the 10th of April when a rumbling was heard and the ground began giving away. Thinking the shaft was about to collapse, they ran to a supposed place of safety. Only one, feeling that the fall might extend to the surface, continued his flight and escaped. The mine did cave from the surface and literally swallowed up the miners, burying them 200 feet below.

A futile attempt was made to recover the bodies but the depth made this impossible and the mine became the tomb of its victims.

KELVIN—1920, on the Wisconsin & Michigan Railroad, mail *Vulcan*.

KING—1910, on the C. & N. W. Railroad, mail *Quinnesec*.

LINDSLEY—1910, on the Escanaba & Lake Superior Railroad, mail to *Ralph*.

LORETTO—Not much remains of this former mining town between *Waucedah* and *Vulcan* on US-2. The town was named after the Loretto mine and at one time was served by two railroads, the now extinct Wisconsin & Michigan (nicknamed the "Wisky Mich") and the Chicago & Northwestern. Tracks of the old Wisky-Mich were being removed in 1971. Some of the original buildings remain in the one-time village and a few families live here.

After the mines closed down the village remained active for some time and had a population of 500 as late as 1940.

At one time there was a C. & N. W. depot, located more than a mile from the village.

In 1905, described as population 500. Waucedah Township, 5 miles from *Norway*. Henry Truscott, Postmaster, justice and superintendent of the Loretto

Iron Companry; Ole Anderson, saloon; Daniel Andrews, carpenter; John Champion, machinist; Wm. Champion, bandmaster; Charles Chellew, blacksmith; T. Donovan, township clerk; E. G. Fuller, school principal; E. Hansen, railroad agent; Etta Johnson, teacher; A. Jolotti, saloon; Dr. E. O. Lockart; Loretto Cornet Band; Lynch & Roach, general store; Meyer-Ruwitch, general store; Miss Spalding, teacher; E. Stevens, physician; Vincent Brothers, saloon; Thomas Vowler, hotel; G. M. Warner, express agent; A. Welin, livery; and P. L. Williams, hotel.

1927, population 300. Mrs. Joseph Walsh, Postmaster; Alphonse Bergen, soft drinks; C. H. Baxter, superintendent for Loretto Iron Company; A. Massa, machinist; A. Scafasci, general store; and Marcott Brothers, auto repairs.

McRAE—1910, on the Escanaba & Lake Superior Railroad, mail *Northland.*

MERRIMAN—1905, a station on the Superior Division of Chicago, Minneapolis & St. Paul Railroad, 7 miles north of *Iron Mountain.* Mail *Iron Mountain.*

METROPOLITAN—Also known as *Felch Mountain*, was named after the mine at this location which was founded about the same time as the *Vulcan* mine discovery. Settled in 1878, the village was founded in 1880. In 1887, population 400. At the terminus of the Felch Mountain branch of the C. & N. W. Railroad. At that time located in Iron County. L. A. Friederichs, Postmaster, physician and druggist; Swan Anderson, saloon and livery. Other business listings for 1887 were, A. M. Burns, shoemaker; P. J. Carey, saloon; H. A. Carlson, Metropolitan Hotel; Marmaduke Harper, justice; M. Hourigan, saloon; C. Kasper, grocery and meats; M. Kurll, meat market; Barney McLaughlin, justice; T. Mahon, railroad agent; Metropolitan Iron & Land Company, sawmill; Fredeick Parry, general store; and White & Triant Lumber Company.

By 1905, although several hundred mine workers continued living near the mine, the business section of the town had dwindled. Only three or four saloons and two general stores remained, while *Felch*, a short distance from *Metropolitan*, was growing rapidly. In that year, John J. Ovist was Postmaster and had a general store; Chas. Brondstram, saloon; A. W. Dunlap, railroad agent; Andrew Rian, general store; Chas. Salberg, saloon; and Wm. West, saloon.

By 1915, the village was mostly a lumbering town. Alfred Anderson, Postmaster and general store; John and Matthew Blomquist, ties, posts etc.; Carl Carlson, ties and posts; and J. J. Ovist and Andrew Rian had general stores and timber.

110

In 1927 there were two churches, Baptist and Lutheran. Postmaster Anderson had added a gas station to his store. Jack Blomquist, confectionery; Matthew Blomquist, road contractor; Jack Felander, blacksmith; Matt Johnson, justice; Geo. Nygard, clothing and barber; Geo. Omar, blacksmith and barber; John Omar, carpenter; and Roger Vanhow, railroad agent.

Today the mine is closed and the area is sparsely populated.

———

MULLIN'S TRADING POST—See *New York Farms.*

———

NEW YORK FARMS— (As told by Dean Turner of *Iron Mountain*)

The *New York Farm* was established in 1866, as a supply farm for logging camps in the area and north along the Menominee River. The original property covered several thousand acres and was part of a land grant to Jesse Spalding. The grant was signed by Abraham Lincoln. The farm has now been divided into five or six farms, small tract resort properties, etc. Two of the original barns remain standing along with the stone foundations of the original "big house."

Across the river from the farm stood the Mullin's Trading Post, among the earliest of the Indian trading posts in the area. This site is now inundated by the flowage from a downstream power plant.

The *New York Farm* was connected with the city of *Menominee* by a log tote road in the 1860s. First ore shipments from the Menominee Range were transported over this road by wagons and teams. The road was extended to *Vulcan* after the "iron ore strike" of 1871. This road, much of which is now County Road 577, is still barely traceable for most of its length. (See map of locations.)

———

O'CALLAHAN—Also called *O'Callahan's Mill* and known as *Sturgeon Mill*, was once the site of a thriving community built around one of the early lumber mills in the *Norway* area. Dean Turner of *Iron Mountain* said almost no traces of the original buildings remain on the site, except for a few outlines of foundations. Of the several streets lined with houses, mills, office and stores and a school, none remain. Turner said several of the houses were moved to neighboring communities or farms after the site was abandoned and can still be identified. Footings of the old mill dam are still visible.

The O'Callahan brothers, George and James, built their first mill here about 1878-79. The late Victorian style mansions they built still stand in *Norway's* "Ole Town" section, he said. The O'Callahan family and *Sturgeon Mill* are the subject of several chapters in a book titled "Klondike Mike." Mike Mahoney was a strapping nephew of the O'Callahans, logging camp champion wrestler, and later one of the fortunate few who made a strike in the Alaskan Klondike.

Calvin Ries, of *Norway*, said there were no saloons in the village of *Sturgeon Mills*. Some of the company houses were removed to *Vulcan* and still lived in, he said. The O'Callahan mansions stand on Norway Hill and have 12 foot ceilings and doorways four feet wide with solid oak doors and trim, Ries said.

The C. & N. W. Railroad ran right through the center of *Sturgeon*, splitting it in half. There was a spur line to the lumber mill. George Kroehnke was the C. & N. W. railway and telegraph agent at *Vulcan* but lived in *Sturgeon*. Kroehnke was the last person to remain living in the town and stayed until the last house was gone. There was no post office and mail was received RFD *Vulcan*.

Ries said some of the stories told by old-timers around *Norway* of knifings and shootings in saloons of the area are hair-raising.

One time during the history of *Sturgeon* was born the legend of a "lost payroll" from one of the camps that totaled more than $100,000. Some people say it was found and descendants of the family are wealthy and still live in the area. As with most stories, the tales grow in the telling and it is possible that the money was never recovered.

A historical plaque has been erected along US-2 near *Norway*, dedicated to a flowing well or spring. Tourists stop to fill their thermos bottles with the clear, sparkling water yet today at the small roadside park where it is located. The plaque reads: *"Norway Spring. In 1878 a sawmill was built near here as the first industry in the Norway-Vulcan area by John O'Callaghan* (sic) *which ran until 1902. A 1,094 foot deep hole was drilled in 1903 by the Oliver Mining Company on a slope north of here are the leavings of the Few and Munro Mines, which operated from 1903 to 1922. These are now owned by the Ford Motor Company"*

ORNUM— 1910, on the Wisconsin & Michigan Railroad, mail *Norway*.

RALPH—Formerly known as *Bryden*, in 1905, population 200. Located on the Escanaba & Lake Superior Railroad, Felch Township. Hugh A. Campbell, Postmaster and Railroad agent; Pittsburgh & Lake Superior Iron Company, loggers. Other firms doing logging in the area were the Isaac Stephenson Company; Two Rivers Manufacturing Company; Wolverine Cedar Company; followed a few years later by the West Branch Cedar Company; and the Wolverine Cedar Company.

1910, population 100. Located in West Branch Township.

1915, population 75. Hugh Campbell, Postmaster, dry goods, groceries etc.; Allan Wells, railroad agent.

By 1927, *Ralph* was well established as a farming village and resort area. It had an Episcopal church and in that year Mrs. Campbell was Postmistress and trained nurse; L. P. Giffany, garage; Otto Hintz, general store; Louis Kikbush, justice; Al Klotz and Robert Nelson, trappers; Frank Paulie, dairy farm; Quinn Brothers, livestock; the Ralph Fish & Gun Club; Vina Salsbury, dressmaker; Harvey Staines, justice; Allan A. Wells, railroad agent; and the Stephenson Company, loggers.

The *Ralph* post office was operating in 1970 and is designated on present day road maps.

———

RANDVILLE—Was located on the Chicago, Milwaukee & St. Paul Railroad between *Iron Mountain* and *Sagola* on what is now M-95. A gasoline station operating on a part-time basis and a few houses remain in the area. A faded cross buck sign along the railroad track reads *Randville*. When we pulled up to the intersection we met several young people walking along the road and asked the oldest, a girl about 15, if she could direct us to *Randville. "You are right in the middle of it,"* she replied. This is an apt description of the former village.

In 1893, a post office and station on the M. & N. Railroad, 13 miles north of *Iron Mountain*. Daily mail.

The hamlet reached a population of about 50 at the turn-of-the-century. In 1910, B. A. Wilbur, Postmaster; E. H. Hassman, railroad agent; Fred Johnson, lumber; Fisher Negaunee, drayage; Ed Ryan, saloon; and B. A. Wilbur, hotel.

In 1915, one general store remained, operated by B. A. Wilbur who was also Postmaster. P. Maloney, express agent.

Sometime between 1927 and 1930 the post office was discontinued and *Randville* ceased to be a village.

———

RICHARDSBURG—In 1927, listed post office as discontinued, 4 miles east of *Iron Mountain*. Mail to *Iron Mountain*.

———

RIVER SIDING—1910, on the C. & N. W. Railroad, mail *Iron Mountain*.

———

RUPERCHTS—Was the name of the location at the original exploration drift near *Vulcan* to locate the ore. There are now eight homes in this area of *East Vulcan*, C. J. Ries of *Norway* said, and the now famous *Iron Mountain* iron mine is in this section. It is now a tourist attraction.

———

RUSSELL—1910, on the E. & L. S. Railroad, mail *Ralph*.

SOUTH NORWAY—1910, a station on the W. & M. Railroad, mail *Vulcan*.

_____

STURGEON—1910, the postal name for *Loretto*. See *O'Callahans Mill*.

_____

SUMAC—1910, on the C. & N. W. Railroad. Mail *Iron Mountain*.

_____

SUMMIT—1910, on the C. & N. W. Railroad. Mail *Waucedah*.

_____

TOLLENS SPUR—1910, on the C. M. & St. P. Railroad, mail *Channing*.

_____

TRADERS JUNCTION—See *Antoine*.

_____

TURNER—Or *Turners Junction*, in 1910, a spur and station on the E. & L. S. Railroad, mail *Channing*.

_____

WANN—1910, a station on the Wisc. & Mich. Railroad, Mail *Vulcan*.

_____

WARD—1910, on the E. & L. S. Railroad, mail *Ralph*.

_____

YOUNGS—In 1927, listed as a discontinued post office, send mail to *Granite Bluff*.

Chapter Nine

GOGEBIC COUNTY and the HERMIT OF GOGEBIC

Gogebic County bounds the state of Wisconsin for 80 miles. A long legal dispute was waged between Michigan and Wisconsin regarding the southern and western boundaries of the county when it was set off in 1887. It was the 20th century before the dispute was finally resolved by the U. S. Supreme Court.

The name was taken for the Gogebic iron district, which had been known for several decades but was not exploited until a railroad reached the area. Gogebic probably means "rock" and is taken after the name of the lake.

The Gogebic Range prospered in the 1890s when the swift expansion of railroads created a wide market for *Bessemer* steel rails. The city of *Bessemer* and adjacent camps grew into cities in a single season. Many of the rough and tough miners had little regard for law and order and *Bessemer* became the scene of many fights between rival camp crews. Citizens were about to take things into their own hands when the city council drew up stringent ordinances. Some of the violations and fines included: *"Vagrancy and street walking"* with a penalty of $25 fine imposed. *"Driving or riding a horse, and running a train or bicycle faster than 10 miles per hour,"* drew a like fine, and a $50 fine was imposed for such crimes as *"improper diversions and false fire alarms,"* or *"street and alley rioting."* Anyone found guilty of delivering a cord of wood measuring less then 28 cubic feet was liable to a $100 fine, and the same applied to any person smoking on a dynamite wagon.

The county reached a peak population of 33,225 in 1920. Since then the population has decreased each year, and in 1970 was 20,676.

A historical marker in the state park just east of *Bessemer* gives a brief history of Gogebic: *"The Gogebic was the last of the three great iron ore fields opened in the U. P. and northern Wisconsin. Beginning in 1848, with Dr. A. Randall, federal and state geologists had mapped the ore formations almost perfectly long before any ore was mined. One geologist, Raphel Pumpelly, on the basis of his studies in 1871, picked out lands for purchase which years later became the site of the New Port and Geneva mines. The first mine to go into production was the Colby. In 1884, it shipped 1,022 tons of iron ore in railroad flat cars to Milwaukee. By 1890, more than 30 mines had shipped ore from this range. Many quickly ran out of good ore and had to be closed. Others took their places as richer ore bodies were found. Virtually all mining here has been underground as attested by many shafts and "cave-ins." The soft hematite ores common to this range usually have been sent in ore cars to Ashland and*

Escanaba, there to be loaded into ore boats and taken to American's steel mills." Dedicated in 1958.

Victor F. Lemmer, in his story "Ghost Mines of the Gogebic Range," tells the story of the "Hermit of the Gogebic."

"*The Names of two men are linked with the discovery of the Colby, the first successful iron ore mine on the range; Richard "Dick" Langford and Capt. Nat Moore.*

Langford came to the U. S. from Ireland in 1847 and moved to the Upper Peninsula five years later. A prospector at heart, within a few years Langford became known as 'the hermit of the Gogebic.'

"*While others were accumulating wealth, I spent my time and what money I could get hold of in prospecting the minerals of this locality,*" Langford said *shortly before death in 1909. Blind and penniless, Langford spent his last days in the Ontonagon County infirmary.*

"*My labors have brought wealth to others and me to the poorhouse,*" he said. '*I could have established my right to a one quarter interest in the Colby mine, but I did not care to take such a step. I have never had a lawsuit, been*

Dick Langford, called the Hermit of Gogebic, spent most of his life prospecting and wandering the mineral ranges of Gogebic. He lived in this miner's shack until he went blind and died in the county infirmary at age 83. Photo courtesy of Victor F. Lemmer, *Ironwood*, Michigan

arrested, served as a witness or juryman. In fact I have never been put under oath.'"

Langford was one of the first prospectors in the Gogebic area. In 1868 he sunk a test pit some distance to the east of where the Colby mine later was located, but did not go down deep enough to strike the ore body.

In 1872 or 1873, Langford said, he discovered the Colby ore body, but did nothing about it.

Some 10 years later he showed some iron ore samples to A. Lanfear Norrie, of *New York* and *London*, who had come to prospect the Gogebic area. Mr. Norrie wasn't interested in the samples, but Captain Nat Moore, an unemployed mining captain, was.

Langford is said to have taken Captain Moore to the spot where he pointed out the deposit. Langford said he was supposed to have a one-fourth interest in the mine, but didn't get it.

Captain Moore denied Langford's story and said he found the Colby deposit beneath the roots of a birch tree that had been blown over by the wind.

The mine was opened during 1884, and 1,022 tons of ore were dug out, hauled to the railroad where it was loaded on flat cars to be shipped to *Erie*, Pennsylvania, via *Milwaukee*.

With the Colby opened and the ore body proven, one of the greatest land rushes of the North Country began. Within a year seven mines were in operation and scores of other sites under option. Two thousand miners were employed between Sunday Lake and the Montreal River.

Lemmer said mining camps and towns sprang up almost overnight. Typical frontier mining towns with wooden buildings, wood sidewalks, streets of slush and mud in winter and blowing dust in summer. Each town was well-supplied with saloons, gambling halls and other places of pleasure for prospectors, lumberjacks and miners. Among some of the towns were *Hurley*, Wisconsin, and *Ironwood, Bessemer* and *Wakefield*, Michigan, which survive yet today but are only shadows of the towns they were during the mad rush of the mining days.

Although *Hurley* is over the line in Wisconsin, it is a next-door neighbor to *Ironwood* and when citizens on the Michigan side got tough on the lawless element of the mining camps, *Hurley* stayed wide open and soon had the reputation of the toughest town in the north. Two fires destroyed much of *Hurley*, but each time the destroyed part was rebuilt. By 1890, it had 58 saloons, 20 hotels, four oyster houses, three groceries, two druggists and a Presbyterian minister who soon left for a more promising field, Lemmer said. As late as World War II the main street, lined with saloons and brothels, was in the spotlight when a national magazine featured the town as "America's Sin City" in full color photo pages.

Ironwood's business district also was swept by flames, but the town was rebuilt on higher ground, bigger and better than ever. It had 55 saloons, 16 hotels, 15 boarding houses and a Chinese laundryman.

There are many stories of tent towns that became thriving communities as ore mines were opened. Stories of gold discoveries brought an influx of prospectors and speculators who sold mining stock, much of it worthless, that floated throughout the country. Many of these town have been lost to history and the few that lasted long enough to become listed in directories or designated on maps appear in the following chapters.

Langford withdrew from the mobs of prospectors and lived out most of his 83 years in isolation roaming the remote areas of the Gogebic Range alone.

GOGEBIC COUNTY GHOST TOWNS

ABITOSSE—1910, on the Duluth, South Shore & Atlantic Railroad. Send mail to *Bessemer*. A station located 4 miles from *Thomaston*. Not a post office.

_____

ANVIL LOCATION—Post office established February 18, 1918. Daniel F. Shea, first Postmaster. The post office was discontinued in 1968-69.

In 1927, population 1,000. Settled in 1920. A mining settlement, on the Chicago & Northwestern and Soo Line Railroads, Bessemer Township, 11½ miles west of *Bessemer*. Hourly bus to *Ramsay* and *Bessemer*. Daily mail. James S. Morrison, Postmaster; Chas. E. Anderson, director of the Anvil Amusement Hall; Max Sternel, prop. of amusement hall, pool, bowling alley, confection and movies; Anvil Hospital; Parco Destasio, barber; Gustav Lintelman, express agent; James Morrison, Postmaster; Matt Murrasich, confection; Parent-Teachers Club, Fannie Lyle, president, Mrs. Eunice Becker, secretary; Youngston Steel & Tube Company, J. S. Morrison, manager.

The mine was part of the Anvil-Paims-Keweenaw mines, opened in 1886. Its last skip of ore was hoisted on January 31, 1957.

_____

BESSEMER JUNCTION—1910, on the D. S. S. & A. Railroad.

_____

BLEMERS—1910, on the C. & N. W. Railroad, 7 miles west of *Watersmeet*. Mail *Watersmeet*.

_____

BLUEBILL—Didn't last long enough to have a business listing. Post office established March 4, 1914. Discontinued July 31, 1917. Paul V. Rowlands was first and only Postmaster. Located 13 miles north of *Boulder Junction*, Wisconsin, mail to *Boulder*.

BONIFAS—Named in honor of William Bonifas, millionaire lumberman who left his fortune to his widow, Catherine, who became a well-known philanthropist in the Upper Peninsula.

Post office established July 6,1910. Edward L. Neman, first Postmaster. Discontinued July 15, 1930. After that, mail to *Watersmeet*.

1915, population 150, 3 miles from *Watersmeet*. Daily mail. Bonifas Lumber Company, general store and lumber; and H. M. Weed, physician.

In 1927, just before the post office was discontinued, it remained about the same. On the C. & N. W. Railway, E. L. Neman, Postmaster; Wm. Bonifas Lumber Company; F. J. Sensenbrenner, of *Neenah*, Wisconsin, president; J. C. Kimberly, *Neenah*, Wisconsin, secretary treasurer, general store and lumber.

———————

CAMP FRANCES—1910, on the Soo Line Railroad, mail *Tula*.

———————

CARLSON—A country post office established January 29, 1921 and discontinued September 30, 1924. Jos. J. Benik, first Postmaster. In 1927, a discontinued post office, on the C. & N. W. Railroad, Carlson Township. Telephone. P. C. Fuller, general store.

———————

CISCO LAKE—Near the Wisconsin-Michigan State line, 5 miles south of *Turtle*.

———————

CROZIER'S MILL—1905 and 1927, on the Ontonagon River and a branch of the C. & N. W. Railroad, 4 miles from *Watersmeet*, its post office.

———————

DEFER—1910, on the Soo Line Railroad, mail *Montreal*.

———————

DUKE—Post office established April 14, 1901. Andrew Emerson, Postmaster. 1905, on the Soo Line, Wakefield Township, 16 miles northeast of *Bessemer*. Andrew Emerson, Postmaster, logs, ties and poles; Blanchard & Rogers, sawmill.

Post office discontinued October 31, 1906. Send mail to *Ballentine*.

———————

DUNHAM—On the C. & N. W. Railroad, Bessemer Township, 17 miles southeast of *Bessemer*. Post office established October 6, 1902. Frank Scott first Postmaster.

1905, population 200. Frank Scott, manager of Ashland Iron & Steel Company, general store, wood and logs; Elizabeth Keough, teacher; Henry Meyer, blacksmith.

1910, about the same. John McNicolas, Postmaster; A. Emerson, poles, posts and general store; Ed Graham, general store; Maud Hollinger, teacher; and Lake Superior Iron & Chemical Company, general store.

On June 15, 1911, *Dunham* folded up and the post office was discontinued. Only a few people remained and in 1914, the population was 30. Send mail to *Marenisco*.

———

GOGEBIC STATION—Was established in Ontonagon County before Gogebic County was formed, on February 7, 1887. The post office was established June 4, 1886, Frank Crowe, first Postmaster. On May 25, 1894 the name was changed to *Gogebic*.

———

HARTLEYS—Shown on 1929 maps on the C. & N. W. Railroad, between *Wakefield* and *Dunham*.

———

HOLMESVILLE—Although a post office by this name was designated on November 20, 1888, it never became a town. Jerry Holland was appointed Postmaster. Post office discontinued March 31, 1890.

———

IRONDALE—First settled in 1885 and on November 24, 1886, a post office established. Marshall Hubard, first Postmaster. On June 29, 1888, the name was changed to *Ramsay*. (Not a ghost town).

In 1892, a settlement on Black river and on the M. L. S. & W. Railroad, Bessemer Township, 2½ miles east of *Bessemer*. Population 300. Irving Lucia, Postmaster; J. P. Butler, Union Hotel; J. W. Chamberlain, teacher; Belona Norman, Proprietor Commercial Hotel; Daniel Coughlin, saloon; Mitchell Dorsey, justice; East Dangler Mining Company, iron ore; M. P. O'Brien, superintendent Mikado Mining Co; and A. Weed & Company, sawmill.

———

JESSIEVILLE—Post office established January 26, 1887, Mary L. Downs, first Postmistress. Discontinued June 12, 1891. Listed in 1910, mail *Ironwood*.

———

KILTON—Listed as a post office in 1927.

———

MARSHONA—Post office established May 21, 1917, Joshua D. Veale, Postmaster. Not a town and probably never operated as a post office.

———

MONTREAL—Post office established August 4, 1903, Ella Stage first Postmistress.

1905, a farmer's post office on the Soo Line Railroad, Ironwood Township, 8 miles north west of *Bessemer*, and 4 miles from *Ironwood*.

On November 15, 1913, the post office was discontinued.

120

1927, H. B. Snell, grocer; and John Stool, grocer. Mail to *Ironwood*.

_____

PLANTERS—Was either the former name of *Bessemer*, or combined with *Bessemer* when the *Bessemer* post office was established.

_____

PURITAN—A mining location in Bessemer Township, 3½ miles southeast of *Bessemer*. The post office was established on May 7, 1910. Richard Harris, first Postmaster.

1915, population 300. Connected to *Bessemer* and *Ironwood* by streetcar. R. J. Harris, Postmaster, general store, etc.; the Oliver Mining Company was operating here.

1927, Lillian Thebert, Postmistress and confectionery; C. M. Anderson, Puritan General Store and meat market.

Apparently mining operations ceased and the post office was discontinued on August 15, 1953.

_____

RAMSAY—See *Irondale*. 1910, population 134; 1960, population 1,158. Not a ghost town.

_____

ROSS—1910, a station on the C. & N. W. Railroad. Mail *Wakefield*.

_____

SIEMENS—1910, on the C. & N. W. and Minneapolis St. Paul & Sault Ste. Marie Railroads. Mail *Bessemer*.

_____

STATE LINE—1910, a station on the C. & N. W. Railroad. Mail to *Donaldson*, Wisconsin.

_____

STROM—A post office was established by this name on September 25, 1918, and operated until February 28, 1921. Hilda Krutarl, first Postmistress. After 1921, mail to *Marenisco*.

_____

TAMARACK—1910, a station on the C. & N. W. Railroad. Mail to *Watersmeet*.

_____

THAYER—1910, a station on the C. & N. W. Railroad, mail to *Watersmeet*. About 5 miles southeast of *Gogebic*.

_____

THOMASTON—On the Soo Line Railroad, in Wakefield Township, 8 miles from *Bessemer*, first settled about 1890. The post office was established on November 7, 1891.

1893, population 150. L. W. Dodendorf, Postmaster; Mrs. W. A. Carpenter, restaurant; L. W. Dodendorf, railroad agent; and E. C. Walker, restaurant.

Business listings for 1905 were, F. W. Knepple, Postmaster and railroad agent; J. Bertrand, machinist; Eric Carlson, teacher; Mrs. W. K. Conoley, hotel; J. Harrington, machinist; A. Hoard, hotel; John Larson, and P. McManus, machinists.

1910, C. M. Garmon, Postmaster and railroad agent. Population remained about the same at about 100. Miss C. Ayotte was teacher in 1910. J. G. Shefchik, hotel; and A. Kronberg, contractor. Five machinists were listed.

The post office was discontinued in July, 1923 and reestablished December 31, 1924, with Susie Laberdine as Postmistress. Discontinued again on August 14, 1926.

In 1927, population 100, 4 miles from *Wakefield*. Mail to *Wakefield*. Listings for that year were, Mrs. N. F. Laberdie, restaurant; Mrs. Andrew Kronberg, grocery; Black River Lumber Company; Grace Snell, hotel and restaurant; and Mrs. Andrew Mamberg, grocery.

TULA—Post office established here on February 5, 1907. Josiah Lane first Postmaster. In 1915, population 100. On the Soo Line Railroad, Wakefield Township, 9 miles from *Wakefield*. A. J. DeVries, Postmaster and manager of the Tula Lumber Company

The post office was discontinued on December 16, 1916 and *Tula* became a rural route of *Thomaston*.

TURTLE—1910, a station on the C. & N. W. Railroad.

TWECOMA—1910, on the C. & N. W. Railroad, mail *Watersmeet*. Post office established August 12, 1918, Samuel Hill first Postmaster. Discontinued May 31, 1926.

VERONA—Was a mining location and settlement on the C. & N. W. Railroad, Wakefield Township, 4 miles east of *Bessemer*. 1910, population 50. A. Burdeau, Postmaster; Genevieve Davies, teacher; Margaret McCracken, teacher; and Verona Mining Company (Mikado Mine), W. J. Davies, superintendent.

1917, population 300. I. A. Burdeau, Postmaster and general store; W. S. Peters, general contractor; Plymouth Mine (Coates & Tweed); and the Verona Mining Company.

The post office was established June 7, 1906, with Isaac A. Burdeau first Postmaster. Discontinued December 31, 1953, send mail to *Wakefield*.

WELLINGTON—1910, a station on the C. & N. W. Railroad, mail *Marenisco*, 5 miles northwest.

Chapter Ten

HOUGHTON COUNTY

Houghton County embraces the lower half of the Keweenaw Peninsula and much of the adjacent mainland, measuring 60 miles from north to south. It was organized in 1846 and reorganized in 1848. It was named for Professor Douglass Houghton, the father of Michigan's geological department. *Hancock* and *Houghton*, located on the banks of Portage River and Lake, are in the center of what is known as the "Copper Country."

Over 400 years ago, Jacques Cartier at *Montreal* learned of the Upper Michigan copper deposits, modern development of which did not begin until the 1840s.

Unfortunately, Douglass Houghton met an untimely death and did not live to see the remarkable growth of the copper industry that one time made Michigan the world's greatest producer of this product. On May 15, 1856, the *Democratic Free Press* of *Detroit* carried the following notice: *The Wisconsin came into port on yesterday from the upper lakes, with her flags at half mast, bearing the body of Dr. Douglass Houghton, State Geologist of this state, who was drowned in Lake Superior last fall. . . But few men in life had more sincere and devoted friends and fewer still died more universally lamented. He did more to develop the resources of this state than any other man. . .*

The governor, state officials, and leading citizens of *Detroit* turned out to pay their last respects to the "Little Doctor." He was buried in Elmwood Cemetery in that city and his widow placed a seven-foot monument on his grave.

In 1969, the monument was still standing, although forgotten by most. The lot was classified as "abandoned." The inscription of his name on the monument is almost illegible, wiped away by time and the elements. He was 36 years old at the time of his death.

During an expedition to the Great Lakes, preparing to locate the source of the upper Mississippi and to study smallpox among the Chippewa Indians, he routinely reported the location of copper-bearing rock in the Keweenaw Peninsula. This report led to the early mining boom that helped open northern Michigan to settlement.

Late in the fall of 1845, while working along Lake Superior, Houghton's boat capsized and his body wasn't located until the following spring. Helen Wallin, formerly with the Information and Education Division of the Michigan Department of Natural Resources, said his body was identified by the initials "D-H" marked in hobnails on his boots. He was taken to *Detroit* for burial. A bronze plaque on a stone monument at *Eagle River* in the Keweenaw Peninsula stands near the location where Houghton drowned in 1845.

With the decline in copper mining after World War II, the population of Houghton County has continued to decrease each year. Peak population was reached in 1910, with 88,098. By 1970 the population had decreased to 34,653.

A newspaper article of September 12, 1971, depicts the death toll for the end of the great copper mining era of Michigan that lasted for more than a century. *"Houghton—Salvagers have started to remove the rails of the Calumet Hecla Mining Company's industrial railway, which once carried millions of tons of copper ore in Michigan's Upper Peninsula.*

The line, with branches and spurs, is 45 miles in length and stretches from Tamarack Mills to Lake Linden and then northerly to Seneca in Keweenaw County.

Removal of the line was caused by a strike which took effect August 21, 1968, against the Universal Oil Products Company, the parent corporation.

The railway at one time carried ore between the mines at Calumet and the mills and smelters on Torch Lake in Houghton County.

Also being removed are the rails of the Copper Range branch line between Mill Mine Junction and Freda, a milling town.

Freda once was the location of the Champion Copper Mill which crushed all Champion Mine rock for more than half a century.

The Copper Range Railroad is a subsidiary of the Copper Range Company, which owns the White Pine Mines in Ontonagon County."

The old Copper Range Railroad, which once collected over $1 million per year chugging miners and freight through the Copper Country, was established October 15, 1888, and saw its million dollar heydays during the busy copper mining days from 1918 to 1920. (*Bay City Times*—March 31, 1972)

HOUGHTON COUNTY GHOST TOWNS

ALBION—Probably a mine location. 1910, mail *Calumet*.

ALSTON—Formerly *Laird*. (See *Laird*, also). Settled about 1895. In 1905, population 25. Jos. W. Alston, Postmaster and for who the name was taken. J. W. Alston, real estate and lumber; Silas Dunlap, livery; Leonard Gillespie, farm machinery; Theodore Grinier, portable shingle mill; Alex Henderson, general store; Lavac & Lamont, saloon; D. J. Lewis, railroad agent; Wm. McKernuro, blacksmith; Leonard Thompson, saw and shingle mill; and John Willette, hotel and saloon.

1910, population 50. Leonard Thompson, Postmaster, saw and shingle mill and supervisor; Melena Bertrand, teacher; Edward Fox, carpenter; A. LaMont, saloon; W. H. Oakley, general store; Bridget Powers, Mary Schneck, Nellie Scott, Anna Sullivan and Margaret Sullivan, teachers; and John Willette, hotel and saloon.

1915, population 60. On the Mineral Range Railroad. Had a Methodist Episcopal church. Chas. F. Cayanus, Postmaster; W. H. Boylan, railroad agent; A. L. Ely, real estate; Chas. Heikkinen, farm machinery; Heikkinen & Cayanus, general store; Thompson & Gillespie, saw and shingle mill; and Mrs. John Willette, hotel.

Olaf Olson, who cooked in *Alston* area lumber camps, said he worked during the winter of 1915-16 in a camp owned by John Messner, owner of "Messner's College," a *Calumet* saloon.

"We had Frenchmen, Indians, Swedes, Irish and men of all nationalities working in the camps," he said. *"We were working there when prohibition came in 1916 (local option) and about 100 men left camp and went into town. They drank all the liquor they could hold then brought what was left from every saloon in town. They came back to camp yelling and singing. Several men pulled a 'pung' (sled) with barrels of beer and whiskey piled on them and went on a drunk that lasted for a week or 10 days,"* Olson said. *"There was no work done in that camp for a long time!"*

After the lumbering was finished, a company built a large fertilizer factory near *Alston* to process muck and convert it to fertilizer. The surrounding area for miles around was swamp and cranberry marshes, Olson said. A short time after the factory was built it sank into the ground and had to be abandoned.

In 1918, *Alston* remained about the same. Population 50. Finnish Lutheran and Methodist churches. In that year, Chas. F. Cayanus, Postmaster; A. L. Ely, real estate; W. H. Boylan, express agent; Gillespie & Son, sawmill; and Mrs. John Willette ran the hotel, which was minus a saloon.

1927, on the Mineral Range Railroad. Alston Store Company, general store; Christansen Lumber Company, sawmill; Floyd Drew and Fred Freitag, justices; Edward Mill, grocery; and John Willette, hotel.

ANTHONY—1910, a station on the Soo Line Railroad. Mail to *Sidnaw*.

ARCADIAN MINE—1905, a post office on Portage Lake, Franklin Township. F. H. Rogers, Postmaster.

About 1909, the name was changed to *Franklin Mine*. (See *Franklin Mine*.)

———

ASKEL—1910, a village in Portage Township, 20 miles south of *Houghton* and 3½ from *Arnheim*. Daily Mail. Leonard Karky, Postmaster and Minnie C. Ala, teacher.

1915, Jacob Tauriainen, Postmaster; Andrew Heikkenen, blacksmith; Leonard Korky, flour mill; Otter Lake Threshing & Milling Company, John Naaske, manager C.O.O.P. store; Jacob Saari, fruit grower.

1927, population 25. Settled in 1890. On the Soo Line Railroad. Tri-weekly mail. Mrs. Ida Saari, Postmaster.

———

ATLANTIC—1910, mail to *Atlantic Mine*.

———

ATLANTIC MINE—Settled in 1865. Described as a post office and mining village, chiefly miners. Population 1,600. In Adams Township and on the Copper Range Railroad, 3½ miles south of *Houghton*. Contains Methodist and Catholic churches and the stamping and hoisting works of the Atlantic Copper Mining Company. Daily mail. Thomas H. Terrill, Postmaster; Thomas Bennett, machinist; David Cavan, township clerk; James Collins; A. David, physician; F. J. Douglass, express agent; Wm. J. Evans, superintendent of stamp mill; Peter Floyd, mine captain; Elizabeth George, saloon; John Gray, blacksmith; Patrick Hanley, saloon; Wm. Harris, engineer; John Hosking, engineer; Herman Kehl, meats; F. Mullen, school principal; Wm. Piper, mine captain; Richard Polglaise, mine captain; Jos. Richards, blacksmith; Harry Rickard, mine clerk; Samuel Shepherd, shoemaker; Peter Thomas, engineer; Wm. Tonkin, mine agent; Wm. Toy, blacksmith; Sam Trembath, machinist; H. A. VanTassel, mine clerk; and John Vial, blacksmith.

1893, population same, A. D. Edwards, Postmaster; Atlantic Copper Mining Company, mine, stamp mill and general store, David Caven, manager; John Clegg, Deputy Postmaster; Cornet Band, Wm. H. Toy, leader; Alfred David, physician; A. D. Edwards, Township Clerk; R. T. Farrand, physician; Patrick Hanley, saloon; Nathan Hocking, saloon; Fred Jeffers, school principal; Kehl Brothers, meats; Karl Keiski, shoemaker; James Trigenze, blacksmith; and Rev. J. L. Walker, Methodist.

The 1905 population was pegged at 2,500. Catholic, Methodist, and two Finnish churches. An opera house; Jerome Bezotte, hotel; Patrick Hanley, Michael Hessler, John Hocking, Jacob R. Messner, and Niva & Pekkala, all saloon operators; John Moore, physician; Edward Pokinghorner, music teacher; J. B. Quick, physician; John Jolly, livery; Rev. A. Schneider, Catholic; and Ben Tamblyn, meats.

1915, two miles from *South Range*. Chas. M. Cole, Postmaster; opera house; Atlantic Mining Company, general supply store etc., Joseph Paul, store manager; Jacob Holmlund, undertaker; Jerome Bezotte, hotel; Frank Maki, general store; John W. Moore, doctor; Alfred Mills, meats; and DeForest A. Stratton Company, handle and turning factory.

1927, population 1,860.

In 1940, population 1,100. *"A former mining village, once the site of a moderately profitable mine that paid nearly $1 million in dividends."*

Shown on 1972 maps, but no population given.

_____

BALTIC—1905, population 1,200. On the Copper Range Railroad, Adams Township, 6 miles southwest of *Houghton*. John B. Dee, Postmaster and manager of South Range Mercantile Company general store; F. W. Denton, superintendent of Baltic Mining Company; C. S. Norton, physician; N. M. Page, railroad agent.

1918, population 3,000. Wm. Maynard, Postmaster; Edward Blenert, railroad agent; R. W. Hodges, physician; Otto Olsen, manager South Range general store.

_____

BEACON HILL—1905, population 260. On Copper Range Railroad, Stanton Township, 16 miles northwest of *Houghton*. John R. Bennetts, Postmaster and general store; N. H. Burkman, deputy sheriff; L. S. Burnham, justice; and W. J. Uren, superintendent of the Tri-Mountain Mining Company copper mine.

1910, about the same. Geo. Osborn, justice; and Edward Koepel, mine superintendent

1915, Edward F. Winkelmeyer, Postmaster and manager of Beacon Hill Store; Edw. Koepel, mine superintendent and stamp mill.

_____

BOSTON—In 1893, on the Mineral Range Railroad, 7 miles north of *Houghton*.

1905, Ida M. Hosking, Postmaster; James Inch, band leader; Dr. Maas; J. H. Seager, general store; and Mr. Webb, railroad agent.

In 1909, the name was changed to *Demmon*. (See *Demmon*)

Big Louie Moilanen was born at the ghost town of *Boston* and grew to be the biggest man in the world. Moilanen was 8 feet, 4 inches tall and weighed 450 pounds. Photo courtesy of A. L. Paulson, *Calumet*, Michigan.

Old maps of the early 1900s show *Boston*, or *Boston Location*, located about ½ mile north of *Demmon*, which no longer appears on Michigan maps, while a *Boston* is designated on 1972 maps. Neither *Demmon* or *Boston* were listed as post offices in 1970.

In 1966, Department of Natural Resources Forest Fire Officer, Sulo Levanen, of *Houghton*, mentioned in a fire report that many old mining excavations were bypassed. A nearby resident said that at one time a small community existed there and was the home of Louis Milanen, called "Big Louie." At that time he was believed to be the nation's tallest man. He measured 8'4" tall and weighed 440 pounds.

A. L. Paulson, who operates a museum at *Calumet*, said Big Louie was born in *Boston* about 1900. *"His parents were normal size people,"* Paulson said. Big Louie worked in the local mines as a boy and later took a job as bartender in a *Hancock* saloon. By this time word had traveled about his enormous size and he was contacted by an agent from the Barnum & Bailey Circus. Big Louie took the job and traveled with the show for some time.

Although billed as "The Biggest Man on Earth," the medical phenomenon that gave him his size was also the cause of his death. Big Louie passed away in 1926 at the age of 26 years. He was buried in a specially built coffin in the Wasa Cemetery near *Hancock*. Paulson still has one of Big Loule's suits of clothes on display in his museum.

————

BRITTON SPUR—Railroad name for *Plato*. See *Plato*.

————

BROTHERTON—A station on the Milwaukee & Northern Railroad. 1893, 12 miles from *Kitchi*. Daily mail. F. N. Monroe, assistant Postmaster; C. F. Monroe & Company (Chas. F. and Frank Monroe) general store.

Was a post office from December, 1890, until 1894-95.

————

CENTENNIAL—or *Centennial Heights*. Mine locations.

————

COBURNTOWN—Named for August Coburn, mining promoter in the county during the early days. Coburn died in 1863.

1927, population 150. On the Mineral Range Railroad, 1½ miles from *Hancock*. Mail to *Hancock*. Koski Brothers, grocery; John Paggeoni, soft drinks. Not listed as a post office.

Arnold Tapio, former *Houghton* resident, said the place wasn't a town but had a store and town hall. Tapio said he and other natives and Finlanders took turns going from one town hall to another in the early 1920s, going to dances on

Saturday nights. Tapio said they called *Coburntown* "Helltown" because so many fights were staged there. *"That is the main reason people went there, to get into a fight,"* he said.

Nothing remains today.

———

CORKTOWN—In the 1860s and 1870s was the name of a section of *Houghton* near the St. Ignatius Church. Apparently not a separate village.

———

CRAIG—1893, also known as *Portage Entry*, located on the shore of Keweenaw Bay at the mouth of Portage river and on the Soo Line Railroad in Schoolcraft and Portage Townships, 13 miles southeast of *Houghton*. Settled in 1883.

1887, mail semi-weekly. John Hall, Postmaster; Geo. Craig, light keeper of Portage Entry; Francis Jacker, artist and etcher on fungi; Jacobs-Wolf & Company, stone quarry; John Peterson, fish dealer; Samuel Quinn, keeper Portage River range light.

1893, population 200. Daily mail. John Hall, Postmaster and Samuel Quinn, general store.

1905, listed as a discontinued post office. Send mail to *Jacobsville*.

———

CRYSTAL LAKE—1893, on the Soo Line Railroad, 35 miles southwest of *Houghton*. Population, 50. Michael Ryan, saloon; and Thomas Shaw, sawmill. Not listed after 1893.

———

DEMMON—(also see *Boston*). 1909, population 100. Settled in 1896. Formerly known as *Boston*, Frankin Township, 4 miles north of *Houghton*. Grace McKay, Postmaster and music teacher; Co-Op Flour Mill; Geo. Emery, railroad agent; Franklin Mining Company, copper; Kemppainen Brothers, general store; Louis Pykonen, general store; J. H. Seager & Company, general store; and Gus Waarala, confectionery.

1915, population 600. Business listings remained the same, except H. B. Roger, Jr., Postmaster; and Frank Bastian, express agent.

In 1917, the town was booming. A few business places had been added to the directory for that year. They included Enoch Henerson, mine superintendent; John and Paul Gaspardo, dairies; Wm. Hawke, hotel; Dr. Clarence Hawkins; the Johnson Estate, dairy; John Karvonen, gardner; R. J. Maas, physician; Jacob Manley, dairy; and E. F. Niemi, express agent.

The *Demmon* (former *Boston*) post office was discontinued in 1934 or 1935 and is no more.

DONKEN—Spelled several ways, *Donkyn* and *Donkeyn,* in some publications. 1927, population 100. On the Copper Range Railroad, Elm River Township, 20 miles south of *Houghton.* Daily bus to *Houghton.* E. J. Case, Postmaster; Case Lumber Company, lumber and general store; John Fewless, meats and hotel; Steve Winowiski, barber; and Emil Muenzel, justice.

Donken was a post office in 1920, until about 1935, and perhaps reactivated in later years. In 1968 it was said there were five postal boxes in use in the former village.
———
EDGEMERE—1910, a station on the Copper Range Railroad, mail to *Tri Mountain.*
———
ELM RIVER—1905, on the Copper Range Railroad, in Elm River Township, 22 miles southwest of *Houghton.* About 3 miles southwest of *Stonington* and near *Beaver Dam.* Thomas H. Eddy, Postmaster and manager of the Elm River Copper Company, general store; and J. E. Godejahn, railroad agent. 1910, mail to *Tri Mountain.* 1927, mail to *Stonington.*
———
ELO—Settled in 1906. 1927, population 75. A village in Portage Township, 4 miles from *Pelkie.* Bus daily to *Pelkie* and *Hancock.* Daily mail. Aroo Pesola, grocery and Postmaster.

Post office discontinued in 1957 or 1958.
———
FARNHAM—1893, name changed to *Withey.* See *Withey.*
———
FRANKLIN JUNCTION—1910, on the Mineral Range Railroad.
———
FRANKLIN MINE—Formerly the *Arcadian Mine.* 1910, population 500. On the Mineral Range Railroad, Franklin Township, 3 miles above *Houghton* and 2 miles north of *Hancock.* Connected with *Houghton* by electric railway. F. H. Rogers, Postmaster; Mortimer Brown, barber; Wm. Flynn, saloon; Franklin Mining Company, copper; R. J. Maas, physician; and James H. Seager & Company, general store.

1915, population the same. New listings were Frank Gemingini, confection; Houghton County Detention Hospital.

1917, population 100. No post office. D. Helliksen, baker and Wm. J. Hodges, meats were added to business listings.

Was a post office in 1927. Population 2,000. Settled in 1852. Electric railway to *Houghton.* Dolph Gemingini, shoe repair; Frank Gemingini, confection; D. Hellikson and Wm. Hodges, meats; Ernest Matteuce, soft drinks; Fred Pantera, confection; and Herman Eonen. The Franklin Mine post office was discontinued in 1956 or 1957.

———

FRAST JUNCTION—1893, on the Chicago Minneapolis & St. Paul Railroad, 2½ miles from *Withey*. See *Withey*.

———

FREDA—1910, population 500. On the Copper Range Railroad, Stanton Township, 17 miles west of *Houghton*. Had Congregational church and a stamp mill. Bienard F. Burckman, Postmaster; Champion Copper Company, stamp mill; Arthur Dingle, leader of Champion Mill "Lake Shore Band"; Harry Jolie, barber; Wm. E. McNamara, physician; Napoleon Mercier, saloon; and Richard Stodden, hotel.

1915, population 500. A Catholic church had been added. Nathaniel West, Postmaster; Geo. Fraser, hotel; Napoleon Mercier, hotel; and L. Stevens, railroad agent.

1917, things remained the same with the addition of E. Winkelmeyer, movie theater.

In 1971 the rails of the Copper Range Railroad were removed and the copper mill, which crushed all Champion Mine rock for more than half a century, was closed down several years before leaving *Freda* a ghost town.

———

FREDA PARK—1910, mail *Freda*.

———

FROST—Shown on 1905 railroad maps. 1910, mail *Kenton*.

———

GREGORYVILLE—Located in Schoolcraft Township, opposite from *Lake Linden*, on Torch lake, was founded by Joseph Gregory (Gregoire) in 1867.

Gregoire operated a sawmill on the site from 1867 to 1872 under the name of Joseph Gregory & Company, in partnership with Lewis Deschamp and a Mr. Normandin. In 1872, Gregoire bought out his partners and made improvements on the mill. He also built a large door, sash and blind factory. The new industry thrived until August 27, 1876, when fire destroyed the mills at a loss of $20,000, which was only partially insured.

Gregory built a temporary mill and operated it with power from the engine of the sash and door factory and built a large double rotary mill, with a capacity of cutting 40,000 feet of lumber per day. Gregory furnished all the lumber and sawed timber used by the Calumet & Hecla and other mining companies in the area from his temporary mill until it was rebuilt.

Gregory owned 25,000 acres of pine lands and 40,000 acres of hardwood timber. He also owned a steam tug, the *Mentor*, which operated on Torch and

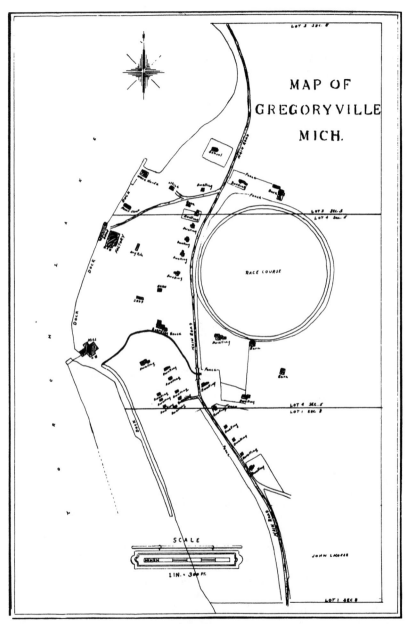

Map of *Gregoryville*   Photo courtesy of G. Walton Smith, *Lake Linden*, Michigan.

Portage Lakes. He also owned several other tugs and barges to transport his products to market.

The settlement encouraged the immigration of many French Canadians as workers in his mills and lumber camps. Gregoire became known as the "Father of the French Canadians" of the township.

In addition to the many houses, stores and the Jos. Gregoire mansion that grew around *Gregoryville*, in 1882, a race track was built at a cost of $4,000. From the Schoolcraft Township centennial book of 1966, *"the print of the racetrack at Gregoryville and the picture of the 1880s and 1890s are proof of the sport of horse racing. This track was one-half mile, outlines of it could be seen until a few years ago when it was plowed over for a potato field."*

Among the owners of horses that raced in those days were Joseph Omsby, Sr., whose son, Wallace, was the driver of "Farmer"; Champ Keough, a former tavern owner of *Hancock*; Charles Beauchene; Jim Byers, of *Baraga*; and William Parks and Alec Horton.

GOORSE POINT—See *Point Mills.*

GROVERTON—1887, a newly established post office in Fortis Lake Township, 9 miles from *Houghton*. Martin Dee, Postmaster; August Allbrook, wagonmaker; Edward Banaker, saloon; John Leary, saloon; Wm. Mellon, constable; Dr. W. Gore Orr; and Henry Smith, hotel.

1893, name changed to *South Lake Linden.* (See *S. L. Linden*)

HAZEL—1910, a station on the Mineral Range Railroad. Mail to *Alston.*

HECLA—see *Calumet.* Olaf Olson, former resident of *Calumet*, said there were 64,000 company houses owned by the Hecla & Calumet Mining Company in 1910-14. These houses were spread out around the city of *Calumet* for several miles and each section was named, such as "Yellow Jacket," "Bluejacket" or the name of the mine in which the residents worked. *Hecla* was probably one of these sections of town. After World War I, Olson said, these houses were up for sale from $5 to $12 each and many were purchased and moved or torn down for lumber.

HIGHWAY—1893, a small settlement, 6 miles south of *Calumet.*

1910, on the Mineral Range Railroad. Mail *Hancock.*

HUBBELL MILLS—See *Rubicon.*

Stone quarry at *Jacobsviile*. Photo courtesy of G. Walton Smith, *Lake Linden*, Michigan.

HURON—1877, a mining village, three-quarters of a mile south of *Houghton*, near which are located the Houghton (formerly Huron) and the Isle Royale copper mines. Its post office is *Houghton*. This location is listed for each year through 1927.

———

INCLINE—This settlement was located a short distance north of *Lake Linden*, along the highway that leads to *Calumet*, near the top of a high hill, hence its name. First settled in the 1870s, 15 or 20 log and frame houses were built. A few were two-family houses. A school, sandstone quarry, a smelter and railroad terminal gave employment.

The sandstone quarry at the hamlet provided rock for foundations of buildings and machinery. With the advent of portland cement and better grades of sandstone, the quarry was closed and made into a dam for fire protection, The dam was 85 feet wide and 250 feet long, with a 300 foot drop to the town. The place is also known as "the old swimming hole" and is about 30 feet deep at its deepest point.

The school at the southeast of the dam (which remains today) was a country school with one teacher. The building was torn down and is now a summer cottage on Portage Lake.

All the houses, school and other buildings are gone and only a few fruit trees and some rose bushes are left to remind us that here at one time people lived, raised families and enjoyed life at the little village of *Incline*.

———

JACOBSVILLE—(information by G. Walton Smith, *Lake Linden* historian)

A post office was established here, at the mouth of Portage River, on a point extending into Keweenaw Bay, on November 29, 1887.

Although there had been fishermen in the area for some time, it wasn't until 1880 that permanent settlement was made. In that year Furst and Jacobs opened a sandstone quarry on the site. The business venture became an overnight success. The village was platted and named *Jacobsville* after one of the partners operating the quarry. By the turn-of-the-century the population grew to 800.

In 1905, quarrying and fishing were the chief industries. Business listings included Geo. Pfifer, Postmaster; Portage Entry Redstone Company, J. R. Jackson, chairman; E. D. Edwards, sec., Z. W. Wright, treasurer. and Burt Froney, superintendent. Other listings were Agnes Beaudette, teacher; Mrs. K. E. Carlson, boarding house; Matt Hautala, saloon; Daniel Leary, quarry; Abraham Narra, fisherman; Nara Brothers & Pfeifer, general store; Chas. Nara, deputy sheriff; Frank Witz, lighthouse keeper; Cora Wyckoff, teacher; and J. W. Wykoff, superintendent of Portage Entry Quarry Company.

Smith said in the early days there were two churches, Finnish Lutheran and Congregational, and in later years an Apostolic Lutheran church. L. H. Hennes & Company had a store in the 1880s and later Chas. Marsy and Cecil Tomlinson.

There was an eight-grade school and a high school. After the quarry closed it became a one-room school with only eight grades. Later the children were bussed to the Lake Linden-Hubbell school.

The post office continued until 1964, Smith said, and a light house was in operation for many years until a new cement pier was built in the 1920s.

For many years a voting precinct operated, but the few residents now vote at the Bootjack precinct.

At one time the A. O. U. W. had a large lodge building called the "Redstone Lodge 176."

———————

KENTON—The few remaining residents of *Kenton* probably do not consider their town a ghost town. The American Legion Post is very active and a ranger station of the National Forest Service is located here. Only one or two stores along the main street were open for business in 1971, and other buildings in the one-time boom town are vacant and deserted.

Kenton grew from a small station on the railroad, with less than 75 residents in 1890, to a good size lumbering town of more than 500 population. Today the population is less than 100.

Earl DeMolen, of *Kingsford*, said his family moved here about 1895. *"Houses were so scarce that we had to live in an old lumber camp for a few weeks,"* DeMolen said. The mill was on the East Branch of the Ontonagon River and was owned by the Sparrow & Kroll Lumber Company Mr. Kroll had moved here several years before and taken up homesteads for himself, his wife, and three children, Lottie, Arthur and Charlie.

"The white pine timber on those homesteads was really something to see!" he said. *"Many of the trees were five feet through at the stump and straight as a die."*

Within a few years Kroll went into the real estate business and owned extensive timber lands. He went in partnership with a man named Sparrow and for the next 35 or 40 years this company ran the biggest timber operation in the district.

Albert DeMolen worked for the company driving a tram pony hauling lumber from the mill. Earl and his four brothers each went to work in the mills as they became old enough, which at that time depended on size and ability, not age.

137

Main street of *Kenton*, on M-28 highway in Houghton County. Although this is not a complete ghost town, *Kenton* is typical of many Upper Peninsula towns that once had a large population during the mining and logging days and now are all but deserted. Photo by Roy L. Dodge (1971)

138

Earl said his education was limited to a few winters in the one-room school where one teacher taught eight grades.

It was in the Sparrow & Kroll mill where John Bergerson, who in later years ran a livery, lost a leg in a mill accident. *"Artificial limbs were not available so someone whittled out a peg for John and he wore it until his death, about 12 years ago (1959-60),"* DeMolen said.

Heino Anderson died about 1968, and William Shingler was killed by a train while returning home from his store. Heino Anderson was Postmaster in 1915.

Listings for various years were Dr. C. F. Moll. 1905, Wm. Kroll, Postmaster and Rev. Cleaver, Congregational; Isreal Dion, Kenton Hotel prop.; Ted Farrel, general store; Kenton Lumber Company; Andrew J. Kimes, hotel; Frank Lewis, meats; Miss Minnie Robinson, teacher; Louis Sandon, doctor; and Mr. Morford, railroad agent.

––––––––

KITCHI—About 3 miles east of *Kenton*, on the Soo Line Railroad. The small village of *Kitchi* sprang up around the logging camps in the early 1890s.

1893, located in Duncan Township. Population 100. J. W. Griffiths, Postmaster; Griffiths & Daugherty, general store; Hanlin & Son, hardware; Neff & Company, sawmill; Patterson & McAlpin, saloon and hotel; J. D. F. Pierson, general store; Taylor & Anthony, lumber; and Chas. Thompson, railroad agent.

Earl DeMolen, of *Kingsford*, who was born in 1888, said his father, Albert, followed the lumber camps as a teamster most of his life in the Upper Peninsula. When DeMolen was a small boy he rode with him in various camps and started working in lumber mills at age 12 or 14 years.

The DeMolen's lived in *Kitchi* for a time around 1890. There was a big hotel, extensive sawmills, and several saloons, De Molen recalled.

"While we lived at Kitchi one of my brothers died at age six years and my 16 year old sister," he said. *"Dr. Hope, from Kenton, did everything he could to save them but they both died."* At that time there was a cemetery at *Kitchi* and they were buried there. A few years later the town was abandoned and the bodies of the children were reinterred at the new cemetery in *Kenton*. DeMolen said he returned a few years ago but there was no trace of the cemetery at *Kitchi*.

In 1905, *Kitchi* is listed as a discontinued post office.

––––––––

LAIRD—1893, a country post office in Laird Township, 14 miles west of *Baraga*, from which it receives a tri-weekly mail. Wm. M. Peterson, justice and

Postmaster; Thomas J. Chappel, justice; Wm. Cruze, justice; Jay T. Drew, J. C. Dunstan, and James P. Edwards, justices. Edwards was also a surveyor and Byron Leigh, justice. Sometime, around the turn of the century, the name *Laird* was changed to *Alston*. See *Alston*.

————

LINWOOD—1910, on The Mineral Range Railroad, mail *Lake Linden*.

————

MASON—1910, on the Copper Range and Mineral Range Railroads, mail *Dollar Bay*.

————

MESSNER—1910, on the Copper Range Railroads, mail *Tri Mountain*.

————

MESSNARD—1927 reads "see *Hancock*."

————

MIDWAY—1910, on the Mineral Range Railroad, mail *Osceola*.

————

MILL MINE JUNCTION—1910, on the Copper Range Railroad, mail to *Atlantic Mine*.

————

MILLS—1910, on Copper Range and Mineral Range Railroads. Mail to *Lake Linden*.

————

NEW HOME—1893, on the M. & N. Railroad, 45 miles southwest of *Houghton*. Population 70. W. F. Berney, acting Postmaster and general store; Miller & Thompson, sawmill. The following were listed as farmers: John Clark, W. H. Cole; Hans Hanson; D. C. Hoffman; J. Lennenthal; J. O. Luslow; Lee McKenney; August Beebe; and Arvilia Swift. Not listed in 1905.

————

NISULA—1905, a post office on the M. C. Railroad, 40 miles south of *Houghton*.

1909, population 225. In Laird Township (west of *Alston*), and 16 miles from *Mass City*. August Nisula, Postmaster and for whom the town was named. Other listings were, Donal Drant, justice; Fred Hiltunen, blacksmith; Rev. Daniel Lewis, Methodist; J. D. Lewis, railroad agent; Peter Maronen, blacksmith; Martin Matero, general store; Abram Maula, general store; Nisula & Company, farm machinery; Bridget Powers, teacher; and Mr. Willet, saloon.

1915, population about 150. Mrs. Abram Maula, Postmistress; W. H. Boylan, railroad agent; Fred Nelson, general store; Laird Milling Company, feed and grain; Abram Maula, general store; and Rubicon Lumber Company, sawmill.

1927, population 200. Settled in 1900. On the Mineral Range Railroad and M-35 highway, Laird Township. Daily bus to *Hancock*. Lutheran church. Abram Maula, Postmaster and general store; Farmer's Co-Op Store Company, general store; Kokila & Ryan, confection; Matt Milli and Tovio Saari, justices. Nisula had a post office in 1969, and is shown on 1972 highway maps.

OBENHOFF—1910, on the Copper Range Railroad. Mail to *Tri Mountain*.

ONELLA—In 1915, a rural post office in Stanton Township, 5 miles from *Houghton*. Arthur Lampinen, Postmaster; Henry Lampinen, flour, feed and saw-mill.

1927, a settlement in Stanton Township.

OPEECHEE—This town was known in 1877 as *Osceola* and was a mining village 1 mile south of *Calumet*. Population 600. Not a post office. The name *Osceola* stuck until the 1880s and in 1887 was again *Opeechee*, on the Mineral Range Railroad, in Osceola Township. Population 1,400. Had a Methodist church. Vivian Johnson, Jr., Postmaster; Thomas Harris, job printer; W. M. Harris, news agency; Kohlahass & Ward, meat market; A. J. Lawbaugh, physician; Osceola Consolidated Mining Company, John Daniell, superintendent; Vivian Johnson, Jr. & Company, general store.

1893, the post office at *Osceola Station* in the new township of Osceola. Population 1,600. Vivian Johnson, Jr., Postmaster and general store; E. Bollman, contractor; Thomas Crago, barber; F. A. Kohihasse, meats; Dr. A. I. Lawbaugh; Rev. J. S. Mitchell, Methodist; Osceola Mining Company; and Tecumseh Copper Mining Company.

1905, population 1,900. Names added or changed in that year were, Rev. David Cosier, Methodist; Solomon S. Lee, physician; Chas. Sandry, barber; Thomas Sweeney, railroad agent; James Watson, dentist; and B. J. Willeson, express agent. Others remained about the same.

New listings in 1910 were John Condon, constable; Rev. Healy, Methodist; Wm. Hoar, boarding house; and Alfred Nicholls, school principal.

Within the next few years the name was officially changed to *Osceola*. In 1915, Thomas Sweeney, Postmaster. Population declined to about 1,000. Other listings were, Dr. J. R. W. Kirton; Errico Taddeucci, confectionery; Johnson Vivian, general store.

Only two additions were made in 1917, Jacob Paulson, confection; and the La Salle Copper Company.

In 1927, on U. S. 41, Calumet & Hecla Copper Company, James McNaughton, general manager; Tim Harrington, justice; A. L. Paulson, general store; Jacob Paulson, confectionery; Ruohonen & Vsitalls, blacksmiths and auto repair; and Errico Taddeucci, confection.

The post office was discontinued about 1924-25. *Osceola* is shown on 1972 Michigan State Highway maps but only the empty mine shafts remain of the once booming copper industry located here.

OSCEOLA—See *Opeechee* for history.

OSKAR—Also spelled *Oscar*. In 1893 *Oskar*, in Hancock Township, 6½ miles northwest of *Houghton*. Mall tri-weekly. Oscar Elliason, Postmaster and for whom the location was named. Nels Buakman, wood, charcoal and ties; and O. Elliason, cordwood, timber etc.

1905, *Oskar*, population 250. On Portage Lake, Stanton Township. Daily mail. Pauline Burkman, Postmaster; Noah Bennetts, lighthouse keeper; Nels Burkman, general store; John Carvna, blacksmith; H. Hermanson, shoes; August Laiana, wood; North Canal Brick Company, kilns; Gust Olson, general store; Miss Peck and Miss Sewart, teachers; Fred Satio, shoemaker; and John Schabach, farmer.

1909, a few changes were Genevieve Bogan and Edna O. Burkman, teachers and John Schabach, superintendent of Poor Farm.

1915, population given as 368 but only two listings. John Koller, Postmaster, and Herman Hermanson, general store.

1917, population given at 417.

1927, population 50. Herman Hanson, general store; Meriam Koller, confectionery and notions; Hemaer Kury, garage; and Alex O. Olson, grocery and auto tires.

Post office discontinued in 1927-28.

OTTER—1910, on the Mineral Range Railroad. Mail to *Ashton*.

OTTER LAKE—See *Tapiola*.

PAAVOLA—1915, also known as *Concord City*. Population 400. In Franklin

Township, 2 miles from *Hancock*. Helen L. Michaelson, Postmaster and confectionery; Louis Pykkonen, general store.

1917, population 600. Hilda Nayh, Postmistress; Matt Nayh, general store; C. F. Asiala, general store; and A. K. Thompson, general store.

1927, Apostolic Lutheran and Evangelical Lutheran churches. Wm. Thompson, Postmaster and general store; Henry Lampella, general store; and the Paavola Dance Hall.

PERKINSVILLE—Seven miles from *Hancock*, mail there.

PILGRIM—1910, on the Soo Line Railroad. Mail *Houghton*.

PLATO—Is another town which had several names. In 1910, the postal name was *Plato* and the railroad name *Pori*. In 1927, was called *Plato*, and the railroad name was *Britton Spur*.

Listed in 1893 as *Pori*. On the M. & N. Railroad, 40 miles southwest of *Houghton*. Population, 150. C. P. Anderson, Postmaster and general store; Patrick Horn, hotel; A. B. LaVeque, general store; Roncan & Marceau, saloon; Benze Rosted, general store; and R. S. Trask, physician.

1927, on the C. M. & St. P. Railroad, Laird Township, 9 miles from *Greenland*. Clarence C. Audree, Postmaster; Von Platen-Fox Lumber Company, loggers; J. W. Wells Lumber Company, loggers.

Post office went out about 1929 or 1930.

POINT MILLS—1905, population 300. In Torch Lake Township, 7 miles east of *Houghton* and 3¼ from *Dollar Bay*. Daily mail. Joseph Gibson, Postmaster; Arcadian & Franklin Stamp Mills and Mining Companies; Wm. Bennett, boardinghouse; Jos. Besson, constable; John Brey, saloon; Oliver Fountain, livery; Jos. Gibson, general store; C. W. McCallum, teacher, and Maud Menzie and Eleanore Nelson, teachers; Ernest Thiebeault, general store; Didace Vinette, hotel; and Martin Yauch, saloon.

G. Walton Smith said the two mills were built here in 1899. The Arcadian, on 406 acres of land, had three stamps and a capacity of 1,500 tons per day. The pump house had a capacity of 15 million gallons every 24 hours. Had a dock 675 feet long. Other buildings included shops, warehouses, stables, coal handling apparatus to be built in 1901. A townsite was laid out and dwellings etc. erected for employees.

The Arcadian Mining Company was organized June 28, 1898 and today the Arcadian shaft house at Ripley is a tourist attraction. The rail connection with the mine was the Mineral Range Railroad.

The Franklin Mill, built in 1899, had 200 acres. It had four stamp heads capable of treating 1,500 tons of ore each day. Dwellings and a boarding house were built for employees. The company was organized April 3, 1857.

Calumet & Hecla also had a drydock here for their dredge from *Lake Linden*. It was a natural gorge, two large gates at the opening on Portage Lake were closed and covered by Andrew Nelson and Lawrence Michael. On the first trip from *Lake Linden* to *Point Mills* the dredge was towed by the tug *Hebard* from *Pequaming*. Later the C. & H. tug took over the job. This was done every five or six years from 1915 on. Both of the mills were closed in 1918. A post office was established here on March 14, 1899, and discontinued October 15, 1919.

A school was built here for eight grades. Students are now bussed to *Dollar Bay*.

Point Mills' first Postmaster was James O. Baudin, in 1899.

1909, population 400. Calumet & Hecla Mining Company; H. C. Compson, railroad agent; Mrs. L. E. Dean, teacher; Oliver Fountain, livery; Haun & Schotle, general store; Wm. Ivey, constable; Mary Nelson and Miss Peterson, teachers, and Jessie Priest, teacher, in addition to 1905 listings.

1915, Laura A. Gibson, Postmaster. 1917, population 800. Milton J. Gibson, Postmaster; Dr. C. T. Abrams; Joseph Gibson & Son, general store; Toledo Asphalt Block and Pavement Company; and Robert Warne, railroad agent.

PORI—See *Plato*.

PORTAGE ENTRY—See *Craig*.

QUINCY—1910, near *Hancock*. Mail *Hancock*.

RED JACKET—Adjacent to *Calumet*. According to the Calumet Centennial Book the *Red Jacket* and *Calumet* post offices were combined and named *Calumet* in 1929. 1910, population listed for *Red Jacket* at 4,211. The 1893 Michigan Gazetteer & Business Directory states that the post offices were combined in 1891-92.

RED RIDGE—1905, population 450. On Lake Superior and the Copper Range Railroad, in Stanton Township, 13 miles west of *Houghton*. Albert Everett, Postmaster and manager of the Atlantic Mining Company general store and stamp mill; C. H. Cole, doctor; Rev. C. H. Horger, Congregational; Thomas Kneebone, blacksmith; and S. N. Lanctor, hotel.

1910, population 500. J. W. Squire, Postmaster; Atlantic Mining Company and Atlantic & Baltic, stamp mills; W. C. Barry, carpenter; Rev. Fred Dighton, Congregational; A. G. Erickson, school principal; Albert Gabe, carpenter; Fred Hellinbolt, hotel; Miss McClosky, teacher; W. E. McNamara, doctor; Fred Mehrig, carpenter; Wm. Polkingham, justice; Miss Ragan and Rosella Ryan, teachers; Red Ridge Band; Wm. Treuelia, mason; and Miss Wright, teacher.

1915, Francis J. Bartlett, Postmaster and company store manager; the only other listings are the stamp mills; Henry Dullinger, hotel; and Dr. Grooms, physician.

By 1917, *Red Ridge* had a moving picture theater; F. J. Bartlett, Postmaster; and Oliver Sylvestre, hotel.

The Copper Range Railroad served the village and hauled ore and copper to and from the stamp mills for 50 years. In 1971, the rails were removed along with the only industry.

———

RED ROCK—1905, a discontinued post office. Send mail to *Jacobsville*. This was a short-lived settlement. Probably the site of a stone quarry and named after the color of the red stone product.

———

RICEDALE—Shown on 1910 maps, near *Tri Mountain*. 1910, on the Copper Range Railroad, mail *Tri Mountain*.

———

RIDGE—1910, mail *Allouez*.

———

ROBINSON—1887, a station on the Marquette, Houghton & Ontonagon Railroad, 7 miles south of *Houghton*, nearest post office.

———

RUBICON—Had two names. Postal name was *Rubicon*, railroad name *Hubbells Mill*. Shown on 1905 maps.

———

SALMON TROUT—1910, on the Copper Range Railroad, mail *Red Ridge*.

———

SENTER—1915, population 40. On the Copper Range Railroad, Portage Township. James P. Hanley, Postmaster, and the Atlas Powder Company.

———

SHORELINE—1910, on the Soo Line and Mineral Range, mail *Hancock*.

———

SILVER—Was never a village. From about 1900 to 1930s was a farmer's post office, in Laird Township, 5½ miles from *Alston*. Donald Grant was the first Postmaster and in 1927.

SOUTH LAKE LINDEN—1910, on the Copper Range Railroad, mail to *Hubbell*. Formerly *Groverton*. In 1893 changed to *South Lake Linden*. In that year, *"A village on the west bank of Torch Lake, and the Hecla & Calumet Railroad, Schoolcraft Township, 1 mile southeast of Lake Linden. Post office established here in January, 1887. It is the site of the Calumet and Hecla furnaces, which are connected with the mines some six miles distance by the H. & T. L. Railroad. The works gives employment to some 300 men and smelts about 180 tons of mineral per day.*

"The village has good hotel accommodations and possesses some large stores. The Bell Telephone Company connects with Lake Linden. . . Population 1,200. Daily mail. Modest Manseau, Postmaster."

Sometime between 1893 and 1905, the name was changed again to *Hubbell*, which is a town today.
————

ST. MARY'S JUNCTION—1910, on the Soo Line and Mineral Range Railroads, mail *Demmon*.
————

STACKPOLE—1910, mail *Winona*.
————

STANTONS—1910, mail *Kenton*.

Many of these abandoned mine shafts still stand in many areas of the Copper Country from the days when Michigan's Upper Peninsula led the nation in copper production. Picture taken about 1900. Photo from the Roy L. Dodge collection.

STANWOOD—1910, on the Copper Range Railroad, mail *Tri Mountain*.

STONINGTON—1910, on the Copper Range Railroad, mail *Winona*.

SWEDETOWN—1910, on the Soo Line and Mineral Range Railroads. Mail *Hancock*.

1893, a small station on the Mineral Range Railroad, 4 miles north of *Houghton*, its post office.

TAMARACK—A mine location. 1910, mail *Calumet*.

TAPIOLA—A Finnish name, also known as *Otter Lake*. 1905, in Portage Township, 23 miles south of *Houghton*, Maria Nelson, Postmistress.

1910 additions, Flora E. Kangas, Minnie C. Ala, and Phoebe Parks, teachers; Tobias Peterson, contractor; and Henry Nelson, general store.

1915, Oscar A. Peterson, Postmaster; John Maliniemi, general store; Wm. Michaelson, sawmill; Henry Nelson, general store; Otter Lake Agricultural School; T. Peterson, land agent; Fred Savela, general store; A. K. Thompson, general store; and the Worcester Lumber Company.

The only change in 1917 was Frank Fosman, grocer. No postmaster listed for 1917.

1927, a discontinued post office. Send mail to *Chassell*. Isaac Lassila, general store; and Fred Savela, general store.

TOIVOLA—In 1909, population 25. On the Copper Range Railroad, in Adams Township, 16 miles southwest of *Houghton*, and 12 from *South Range*. E. A. Lange, postmaster, and James Boughner, sawmill and lumber.

Olaf Olson, of *Harrison*, said he worked as second cook in lumber camps three miles north of *Toivola* in 1914-15. There was a small barrel stave factory near the village, he said. Most of the timber cutting was tamarack, used for shoring in mines, and hard wood for barrel staves at that time.

"All that's left of the old Copper Range Railroad is the grade," Larson said. It was a wide-gauge track.

The only business listing in 1915 was G. Salmi, general store.

1917, population 50. Edson Mack, Postmaster and railroad agent; and John G. Salmi, general store.

147

Pronounced "Toy-vo-la," the name is Finnish, meaning the place of Toivo. By 1940, the hamlet had become the center of a Finnish agricultural community, with 450 population.

———————

TORCH LAKE CITY—The name for *Lake Linden* when it was first settled.

———————

TWIN LAKES—1910, on the Copper Range Railroad. Mail *Winona*.

———————

WITHEY—1893, described as formerly known as *Farnham*. In Duncan Township, 50 miles south of *Houghton*. It is connected with Frast Junction, 2½ miles distance, on the Chicago Minneapolis & St. Paul Railway, by a branch built by the Frast Shingle Company. Population 100. Daily mail. George B. Daniels, Postmaster; Frast Shingle Company, shingle mill; and John Marsden, saw and planing mills.

This was a short-lasted settlement, probably from about 1890 to the turn-of-the-century. As with most mill towns, when the timber was removed in the area the mills moved out and the town folded up and disappeared.

———————

WOLVERINE—1910, mail *Allouez*. Was located near the Houghton-Keweenaw County line in the extreme north part of the county.

———————

WOODSIDE—1910, on the Copper Range and Mineral Range Railroads. Mail to *Hancock*.

Chapter Eleven

IRON COUNTY

Iron County was set off and organized in 1885 from Marquette and Menominee Counties. The iron ore deposits of the county had been but recently explored, and the opening of numerous iron mines suggested the county name. Paint and Michigamme Rivers, with their tributaries, drain most of the county. Iron mining is the leading industry. *Crystal Falls* is the county seat.

Iron County reached its peak population in 1920, with 22,107 and within the next few years started to decline until, in 1970, it reached a low of 13,813.

An historical plaque in front of the Iron County Courthouse at *Crystal Falls* tells some of the county history: *"This county was set off in 1885 from Marquette and Menominee counties. Iron ore deposits which gave the new county its name were the first on the Menominee Iron Range to be discovered. Shipping of ores began in 1882 when the railroad reached Iron River. Iron River was the first county seat, but in 1889, after a celebrated struggle, the government was shifted to Crystal Falls. Logging, which began in 1875, had been second only to mining in Iron County's economy."* The courthouse was built in 1890.

An historic marker is located at a roadside park on US-2 highway, between *Crystal Falls* and *Iron Mountain,* designating this as the first roadside park and picnic tables established in the state. The plaque is interesting due to the fact that another site in southern Michigan has been also designated as the first roadside table site.

The plaque reads, *"In 1918 the Iron County Board of Supervisors approved the recommendation of the Road Commission, through its manager, Herbert F. Larson, to purchase this 320-acre tract of roadside virgin timber and dedicate it as a forest preserve. The following year Iron County established Michigan's first roadside park and picnic tables. This was quite likely America's first such facility. Since then similar parks have been provided by most states for the comfort and enjoyment of the traveling motorist."*

At the intersection of M-141 and US-2, a short distance west of *Crystal Falls,* stands an eight-foot-high, cone shaped monument dedicated to Finnish Pioneers. The monument stands on a triangular patch of ground between the two highways, near a township hall. The engraving reads, *"Dedicated to the Finnish Pioneers of 1850, erected 1958."* Also, *"To Trail Blazers, by the Finnish Historical Society of Hiawathaland,"* On one side of the plaque is engraved a picture of a log cabin and a farmer plowing a field with a team of oxen.

Iron County Courthouse at *Crystal Falls* built in 1890. After a long drawn out controversy, the county seat was moved from *Iron River* to *Crystal Falls*.
Photo by Roy L. Dodge (1971)

This monument, dedicated to the Finnish Pioneers of Iron County, stands at the intersection of US-2 and M-141 highways about 4 miles west of *Crystal Falls*. Photo by Roy L. Dodge (1971)

IRON COUNTY GHOST TOWNS

AMASA—Located on M-141, 12 miles above *Crystal Falls*. The 200 or 300 residents of this once booming town probably do not consider it a ghost town but compared to days gone by it is today only a shadow of its former self.

1893, population 600. In Hematite Township, on the Chicago & Northwestern Railroad. Theodore B. Breck, Postmaster, doctor and druggist; Fred Curra, constable; James George, livery; M. E. Gleason, general store; F. H. Hawery, blacksmith; Hemlock River Mining Company, Chas. E. Lawrence, superintendent of iron miners; Wm. Leary, saloon; Maud Mathison, teacher; Gordon Murray, miner; J. H. Parks, logging contr.; James Podgett, justice; and Nicholas Wieyr, constable.

1905, population 800. Carrie Extrum, Postmistress. Other listings were, John Wormwood, railroad agent; Amasa House Hotel, Frank Steddick, proprietor; Rev. Bateman, Methodist; Father Becker, Catholic; Rev. Hoikka, Finnish; Albert Drake, Township Clerk; Thobert Bigson, supervisor; James Edwards, mine captain; Finnish Band; Hemlock Mining Company, a game warden, half a dozen saloons, Christenson & Company, general store, and many other business places.

1909, population 850. Settled in 1888. Abram Gill, Postmaster; Anna LaLaux, Jane LaLond, J. W. Langdon, and Mrs. J. W. Langdon, Jean McKay and Laura VanVoorhees were all school teachers.

1915, Catholic, Lutheran and Methodist Churches. The population had dropped to 500 and only a few business places were listed. Oscar Brusseau, confections; I. E. Crow, express agent; Hematite Mercantile Company, general store; Hemlock River Mining Company, iron miners; Peter McMurchie, physician; Louis Marks, general store; Geo. Primeau, hotel; and John Wormwood, railroad agent.

Another boom occurred in the late 1920s and lasted until the depression of the 1930s. 1927, population 1,200. Methodist, Swedish, Finnish, and Catholic churches and a picture theater. Had a modern $300,000 school, two iron mines, the Porter and the Warner, and a 10,000 acre cattle ranch raising purebred Hereford stock.

1927 business listings included, John H. Nowell, Postmaster; Amasa Co-Op Store; John Holmes, manager; Wm. Hermansen, the Amasa House Hotel; Amasa Moter Company, garage; Chanberg Company, movies; Hematite Mercantile Company, C. W. Hughes, president, department store; Dr. R. E. Hillmer; Iron County Lumber & Fuel Company, Axel Axelson; Hanery Levine, general store; E. Rentola, autos; Wm. Paulukuhn, general store; Ralph Remo, barber; The Triangle Ranch, Chas. H. Shutz, manager; Henry Vivian, justice; John Winquist, village supervisor; and Ward Wormwood, Township Treasurer.

Amasa has three fine churches today and a small business district, but the industry of yore is gone, all gone. One restaurant is open on the main corners, called "Somewhere Else," with large letters "EAT" printed above the sign. This makes the sign read *"Eat Somewhere Else."* Rueben Hansen is the owner.

Many of apparent original main store buildings along the main street are vacant, but as in the old days when she was booming, *Amasa* has an ample supply of bars and taverns. Hansen said there are seven taverns doing a bang-up business most Saturday nights.

People queue up in long lines waiting to get into church services each Sunday, even though the town's population has shrunk to less than one-third of the number in the 1920s.

ARMSTRONG—1893, on the C. & N. W. Railroad, 13 miles southeast of *Iron River*. No post office. From 1905 to 1927, listed as *"Post office at Saunders, 5 miles west."*

ATKINSON—1893, was a recently established post office 26 miles north-west of *Crystal Falls*, and 7¾ miles from *Beechwood*. Mail by special delivery.

"Mail by special delivery," was one way of stating that any mail delivered here was purely coincidental. When a farmer or logging teamster from the *Atkinson* area came to town for supplies, or the mill boss came to *Beechwood* for a few rounds with the boys, they picked up any mail going in their direction.

Sometime around the turn-of-the-century the sawmill at *Atkinson* closed and a few years later another town was founded near the site, called *Gibbs City*. See *Gibbs City*.

BALASAM—1905, on the Chicago Minneapolis & St. Paul and the Chicago & Northwestern Railroads, depots adjacent, 4 miles southeast of *Amasa*, its post office.

Listed as a station with two depots in 1927. Nothing remains today except the rusted railroad spur.

BASSWOOD—1910, on the C. & N. W. Railroad, between *Beechwood* and *Elmwood*, about 5 miles north of *Beechwood*. No post office.

During the logging days a few lumber jacks built rough shacks here while cutting logs. Archie McKrause homesteaded the area. Nothing remains today.

BEECHWOOD—Was the postal name for *Hazel*, on the C. & N. W. Rail-road, about 7 miles northwest of *Iron River*. It now has reverted to about the same as it was 90 years ago.

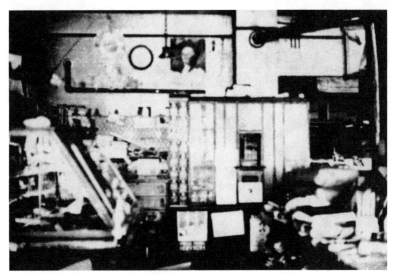

The old *Beechwood* general store and post office is all that remains of *Beechwood*, a one-time logging village in Iron County. This is typical of the turn-of-the-centruy stares located in the thousands of towns and villages of the U. P. during the boom days of logging and mining.　　　　Photo by Roy L. Dodge (1971)

1893, described as, *"A country post office on the C. & N. W. Railroad . . . Daily mail. Population 10. J. J. Larson, Postmaster and hotel."* The chief difference today is that there is no longer a hotel, only the old general store with the original postal boxes partition in a section of the store in the rear.

1905, in Atkinson Township. Jens J. Larsen, Postmaster and hotel. All other listings were farmers, Ole Alnas, Lars Anderson, C. Halways, A. Johnson, C. Johnson, Gustav Lindahl, M. McGuire, James McRae, and Edward Nordstrom.

Sometime between 1910 and 1915, the general store was built. 1915, Jens Larsen was still Postmaster. Sandgren & Anderson, general store. Population, 32.

From 1917 through the 1920s *Beechwood* experienced a boom and became the center of a large area being timbered off. 1917, population 350. Settled in 1887. On the C. & N. W. Railroad and on highway US-2. (Old US-2, now a mile or more north of US-2) Bus twice daily to *Iron River* and *Ironwood*. Finnish and Bethany Lutheran and Swedish Mission churches.

Telegraph and express. Mamie Anderson, Postmistress; A. J. T. Anderson, general store; Andrew Antio, lumberman and contractor; Beechwood Mercantile Company, general store, implements, automobiles, accessories, and garage; Art C. Gould, livestock; Matt E. Kosky, logger; Lindahl Brothers, loggers; Gust Markula, poultry; Gust Nilson, sawmill; and Nels Peterson, livestock.

Mrs. Anderson was Postmistress until 1943, when Louis Hendrickson purchased the store and took over as Postmaster. He died in 1950 and his wife, Mildred Hendrickson, has been acting Postmistress since 1950.

The *Beechwood* store is typical of a 1920s general store. The fixtures and display racks are of early vintage and many items of the old general store days, such as lanterns and kerosene lamp shades, are stocked. Only one or two customers visit the store and post office during a day. There is some activity on the railroad siding when pulpwood is cut and shipped.

The hotels with their saloons, visited by the lumberjacks during the logging days, are gone and only two or three houses remain.

BURNT BLUFF—In 1885, (at that time located in Menominee County), was a station on the northwest terminus of the Felch Mountain branch of the C. & N. W. Railroad, 4 miles from *Metropolitan*, its nearest post office.

CLINCH—1917, a discontinued post office. Mail *Crystal Falls*.

DIANA—On the Chicago, Milwaukee & St. Paul Railroad on 1905 maps, about 8 miles north of *Amasa*.

DUNN—Or *Dunn Mine*, 1910, mail *Crystal Falls*. Located one mile north of *Mastadon*. Dan Fitspatrick, of *Stambaugh*, said the mine has been closed for many years. *"It had a store and a boarding house for miners."*

ELMWOOD—1893, a station on the C. & N. W. Railroad. Postal name is *Paint River*. Lasted until about 1912. In 1910, was a busy railroad center on the C. & N. W. and had a depot and station agent.

Elmwood played a unique role in Upper Peninsula history when an area native enticed several Negro families to move in as settlers on cleared land left from the logging. The entrepreneur had a plan to raise hundreds of acres of potatoes and would pay the blacks to work the fields and harvest the crop. The plan failed, natives of the area say, when the blacks refused to remain during the long, cold winters and returned to whence they came.

Today the Consolidated Paper Company has a pulp office here and there is a pulp wood siding. The post office was discontinued around the turn of the century. 1910, mail to *Beechwood*.

FORTUNE LAKE—Designated on 1920 maps, a short distance northwest of *Alpha*, near a lake of that name.

155

GIBBS CITY—Once called *Atkinson*, back in the 1890s a sawmill was erected on the Paint River and operated for a few years. This, along with the settlement around it, disappeared. Part of the old *Atkinson* dam is evident, about one half mile north of the site of *Gibbs City*, 9 miles northwest of *Iron River*.

In 1915, R. F. Gibbs of *Pentoga* started another sawmill and *Gibbs City* grew up around it. It became quite a town, with running water to all the homes, a railroad station, company stores and the works. When the mill closed in 1921, due to lack of timber, *Gibbs City* became a ghost town of deserted houses.

1927, population 100. Settled in 1914. On the C. & N. W. Railroad, Iron River Township. Bus to *Iron River* daily. Telephone. Geo. W. Esbrook, Postmaster, groceries, meats etc.; The Chicagoan Lake Resort Amusement Company, general store and supper club; Gibbs City Mercantile Company, groceries and meats.

During the depression years a C. C. C. Camp was located near the site. In 1948, an attempt was made to revive the ghost town. This short-lived enterprise, called the "Comfort Club" was an attempt to make a resort center of the place and rent some of the vacant houses to tourists and hunters. The rusty old neon sign still hangs precariously from a rusted pole near the road where the tavern once did business, but *Gibbs City* finally went up in smoke. The story is best told by Grace Engel, free lance writer and historian of *Bark River* who wrote the following story for the *Menominee Herald-Leader* of April 13, 1966.

"It took just four hours to burn an entire city last night. The logging community of Gibbs City, just north of Iron River, was put to fire while hundreds of persons watched.

"The town was considered a hazard to the safety of tourists and sightseers, and was demolished by a crew headed by Wayne Ross, a logging contractor, and George Pond, relative of the original builders of Gibbs City.

"Removal of the old store safe was one of the first projects for the wreckers. A cable was tied to a bulldozer and attached to the safe, still inside the building. With a mighty pull, the heavy safe was pulled through the wall of the store, to land about 10 feet from the building. Most of the homes had already been stripped of salvageable material.

"These homes, which had withstood the elements for years, quickly succumbed to the fire. Tongues of flame ate through tarred paper roofs and siding paper. Etched against an early, spring evening sky, each board and rafter glowed fiercely. When weakened timbers caused the walls and roofs to cave in, sparks shot high into the air rivaling any fireworks display. The heat could be felt many yards away, and fire control men constantly warned viewers to move away.

Dan Fitzpatrick, of *Stambaugh*, Michigan, looks over the remains of the loading docks at *Gibbs City* on the old C. & N. W. Railroad grade.   Photo by Roy L. Dodge (1971)

"When flames gutted the interior of the store building, loud explosions from paint cans were heard, plus the sharper report of glass bottles and old light bulbs.

"Smaller homes were burned first, then the two-story home of R. F. Gibbs and finally the huge store connection buildings. A parade of fire marched from one end of the avenue to the other, climaxing in a roar of smoke and noise as the last building collapsed.

"Considered one of the most active communities in the U. P. until the lumber mill burned in 1921, Gibbs City today is a pile of blackened boards, broken glass and heat cracked stones.

"Footprints in the snow and mud testify to the great number of onlookers.

"Dozens of curiosity seekers had prowled the buildings for anything that would remind them of the occasion, bits of wood, newspapers, postcards, even part of the ornate post office fixtures.

"Traffic was tied up for blocks. About 600 cars lined the forest highway and side roads near Gibbs City. As one state trooper said, 'This is the first time Gibbs City needed a traffic patrolman in 50 years!'

"Many walked a mile or so from parking places to view the destruction. Visitors came from several Michigan and Wisconsin counties.

"Some of the people in the crowd had lived in the lumber town or nearby in the years past. To some it was a sad occasion. They had seen the town born, now they were watching it die. Within four short hours of black smoke and orange flame. . . and colorful memories rising over Gibbs City the town was gone."

Fifty thousand feet of lumber in the form of railroad ties came through the R. F. Gibbs mill each day. In 1915, twenty men worked in the mill and five active logging camps were operating during the fall and winter.

The Gibbs Company issued its own coin and script, redeemable at the company store, which provided such necessities as coal oil, groceries, candies and clothing, also luxuries that included tobacco and "snoose" (snuff).

Disaster struck in 1921, when a flywheel broke on the steam engine and flew into the boiler, causing an explosion and the death of one man. The entire mill was destroyed by fire.

All that remains today are pieces of the boiler along the banks of the river. Nature has already covered much of the ravages of fire and the elements. Tall

The R. F. Gibbs saw mill at *Gibbs City* taken during the boom days before the boiler exploded and destroyed the mill. One man was killed in the explosion.
Photo courtesy of Grace M. Engel, *Bark River*, Michigan

159

General store and post office, with living quarters above, at *Gibbs City*, one-time booming village in Iron County. Store, houses and buildings were burned by D. N. R. in 1965.   Photo courtesy of Grace M. Engel, *Bark River*, Michigan

160

grass, nearly waist high, has grown up in the still visible grade of the railroad. Sturdy pilings of the old loading docks still cling in position with the tenacity of old pine stumps that still dot the surrounding countryside. With a little searching, tops of fire hydrants and pieces of water pipe can be located. The entire area is rapidly becoming overgrown and within a few years will revert to the earth.

During the boom times, *Gibbs City* had a dance hall that rang with fiddle music, square dance calls and laughter, a pool room, and in later years, a theater featuring silent films operated on a mercury tube, hand-cranked projector.

The general store, owned and operated by members of the Gibbs family, was also the post office and was built at the turn-of-the-century.

Until 1962, this store was operated by George and Carol Pond, descendants of the original owner. After that date the building was used for storage of old furniture and momentos of the logging era.

Until it was burned, "Old Camp," a man in his 80s, who was still active in the woods, served as unofficial caretaker of the store and buildings.

The ghost town of *Gibbs City* contained memories for old-timers, some of them still living, and also for thousands of vacationers who, through the years, visited the town, poking around the old buildings and taking pictures.

───────

GREAT WESTERN—1910, on the C. & N. W. Railroad, mail *Crystal Falls*. Was a siding or spur during logging days. Nothing left.

───────

HAZEL—Railroad name for *Beechwood*.

───────

HOLLISTER—1910, on the C. & N. W. Railroad. Mail *Crystal Falls*.

───────

KELSO—1910, on Chicago, Milwaukee & St. Paul Railroad. Mail *Crystal Falls*. Near *Mastadon Mine*.

───────

MANSFIELD—Or *Mansfield Mine*, in 1893, a post office in Iron County, 7 miles east of *Crystal Falls*. Daily mail. Herman Rau, general store.

1905, on the Michigamme River, Mansfield Township. Mail stage daily to *Crystal Falls*. Mary Mellon, Postmistress; Mansfield Mill Company, shingle mill; Morrison, teacher; and Pearce, teacher; Chas. Peterson, grocer.

During its heyday as a mining town there were several boarding houses, a company store, and at least one saloon. On September 28, 1893, the Michigamme River overflowed its banks and flooded the mine where 27 miners lost their lives. The mine was sealed off and never reopened.

This plaque is located at the scene of a mine disaster near *Mansfield Mine*, another ghost town several miles northwest of *Crystal Falls* in Iron County.   Photo by Roy L. Dodge (1971)

A few people hung on though, and in 1910, a branch of the C. & N. W. ran to the site. There were 50 residents. John Anesi and Samuel Jacobs each ran saloons and Chas. Peterson had the store. The place was all but abandoned by 1915 and mail was sent to *Crystal Falls*.

What apparently was once the old railroad grade has been widened and leads north from US-2 through the site of *Mansfield* and ends at the Way Dam. A rough wood plaque has been erected at the point where the road crosses the Michigamme River relating the mining accident of 1893. Just north of the river are some old concrete foundations, remnants of machinery, and along this road are several log cabins and sheds sinking into the ground. A few houses are occupied in the area but only one or two year-round residents live here.

MAPLETON—1915, in Bates Township, 4 miles east of *Iron River*. RFD from *Iron River*. Adolf Forsberg, general store.

1917, Peter F. Lardie, general store.

Today, there is a motel, tavern and township hall, located on US-2 between *Iron River* and *Crystal Falls* near the former site.

MASTADON—1893, on the C. & N. W. Railroad, Mastadon Township, 8 miles south of *Crystal Falls*. Post office discontinued. Send mail to *Mastadon Mine*. Was station for the mine.

MASTADON MINE—1893, 7 miles south of *Crystal Falls*, and 3½ from *Mastadon*, on the C. & N. W. Railway, its station. Iron is mined and shipped. Population 500. Daily mail. E. S. Roberts, Postmaster and mine superintendent; Edward Blake, agent for the South Mastadon Iron Company; P. C. Butt, physician; Delphic Iron Mining Company, Whittlesy Brothers & Company, lessees; P. E. Roberts, general store; Samuel Speare, justice.

By 1905, *Mastadon Mine*, too, had folded and the post office discontinued. Send mail to *Crystal Falls*.

———

MAYWOOD—1910, mail to *Channing*.

———

MINERAL HILLS—Is considered a village (see *Palatka*), and was incorporated in 1919. 1927, population 400. Iron River Township, 2½ miles north of *Iron River*. Cleveland Cliff Iron Company; Wm. J. Collins, village clerk; John Connibear, village treasurer; Davidson Ore Mining Company; Rudolph Ericson, village president; M. A. Hanna Company, James Mining Company, Jones & Laughlin Ore Company; Mineral Mining Company; Albert B. Pearce, village assessor.

In 1940, population 344, 1950 population 333, and 1960 population 311. The village government was disorganized about 1969-70, population 234.

Only a residential district remains of this one-time village. The surrounding area was at one time built up with company houses of the various mining companies where mine workers and their families lived. Vacant fields with fire hydrants standing next to weed-choked concrete sidewalks, and old foundations surround the area. In 1971, one mine was operating.

Minerals Hills is typical of many abandoned, or partially abandoned mining villages of the Upper Peninsula.

———

NANAUNO—Name changed to *Iron River*. In 1887, *Iron River* is described as: *"A mining settlement, formerly known as Nanauno, in Iron River Township, Iron County, of which it is the county seat and a station on the P. Division of the C. & N. W. Railway... It is exclusively devoted to iron mining, and has a population of 2,200. Has a Presbyterian church. Daily mail. F. L. Bond, Postmaster, etc.*

———

NAULTS—1910, on the C. & N. W. Railroad. Mail *Pentoga*.

———

NET RIVER—1910, on Chicago, Milwaukee & St. Paul Railroad. Mail to *Amasa*.

———

PAINT RIVER—See *Elmwood*. Name changed to *Elmwood* in 1893.

PALATKA—Dan Fitzpatrick, of *Stambaugh*, said this was once a big iron ore mining area. Today all the mines have been closed. The first money order was written in 1908.

Name changed to *Caspian*. It now has an historical museum that is a tourist attraction.

A newspaper article of March 31, 1971, stated that a public hearing was scheduled to consider a consolidation plan for the five communities of *Iron River, Stambaugh, Caspian, Gaastra,* and *Mineral Hills. "If the proposal is approved by a majority of voters. . . a second election will be scheduled to select city commissioners who will write a charter for the new city to be submitted to the voters for ratification,"* the article said in part.

"Backers of the consolidation plan see the proposed new town as the best way to promote economic growth in western Iron County. . . According to the study, the new town could offer better governmental service at less cost.

"Iron County, which lost nearly one-fifth of its population during the 1960s, is considered one of the most economically depressed areas of Michigan."

The article, from United Press International, datelined *Lansing*, went on to say, *"Under the merger plan, the new Iron County city would have a population of about 6,000 and would be the 8th largest home rule city in the Upper Peninsula."*

Some of the iron mines here were the Berkshire Mine; Spring Valley Mining Company; and the Verona Mining Company which included the Baltic, Bengal, Caspian and Fogarty Mines. The Verona Mining Company was the largest in the area.

Today (1971), the mines are barricaded to prevent people from accidently falling down the shafts and most of the area is covered with mountains of slag and debris from years of active mining. Former streets, once lined with company houses, are now grown to weeds and brush and it is difficult to imagine that several thousand people once lived in the area.

PANOLA—1910, on the C. & N. W. Railroad, mail *Crystal Falls*. Fitzpatrick said there is nothing left of the one-time station and siding. Known today as *The Panola Plains*.

———

PAVOLA—1910, on the C. & N. W. Railroad. Mail *Crystal Falls*.

———

PARKS SIDING—1910, on the C. M. & St. P. Railroad. Mail to *Amasa*. About 10 miles north of *Amasa*, on the Deer River, a branch of the Michigamme. Nothing remains.

———

PENTOGA—1905, population 250. On the C. & N. W. Railroad, Stambaugh Township, 15 miles southwest of *Crystal Falls*. Francis Hood, Postmaster; Brule River House (hotel), John Withy, prop.; Milford Dubois, general store; Mrs. Chas. W. Gibbs, teacher; R. F. Gibbs, livery; R. F. Gibbs & Son, general store; Willard Goodhall, barber; Louis Green, justice; Geo. W. Hamilton, school principal; F. G. Hood & Company, sawmill; Pentoga Hotel, Chas. Mekash prop.; LaRock Brothers, carpenters; Dr. Herbert A. Owen; Wm. Pantze, constable.

Only a few changes in 1910, Chas. W. Gibbs, Postmaster and general store; H. Cox, constable; Walter Hartho, railroad agent; Thomas Mononbo, hotel; S. Hayes, hotel; and John Withey, saloon.

1915, population 300. A. E. Huebel (Archie), Postmaster; Iron Range Lumber & Cedar Company, sawmill etc.; Montambo Brothers, general store.

By 1927, *Pentoga* was nearly a ghost town. Only a few places were listed, J. H. Hanarahn, Postmaster and store; W. Hartho, express agent; Willard Kinney, livestock; and Daniel J. Montambo, justice.

Fitzpatrick said *Pentoga* was settled in 1900 and was on the Brule River, which is the dividing line between Michigan and Wisconsin. *"There are few old buildings still standing and a few people live in the area,"* he said. *"In 1920 a big fire swept the village and destroyed the business district."*

———

PONCA—1910, on the C. M. & St. P. Railroad. Mail *Crystal Falls*.

———

SAUNDERS—1893, population 100. On the C. & N. W. Railroad and on the Brule River, Stambaugh Township, 21 miles southwest of *Crystal Falls*. Lumber is shipped. J. F. Bronoel, Postmaster; M. E. Gahey, poultry; Menominee

Bay Shore Lumber Company, sawmill etc.; Oconto Lumber Company; C. T. Pendelton & Son, lumber; Sawyer-Goodman Company, lumber; Antone Swartz, hotel; and Whitney, Stinchfield & Brown, lumber manufacturers. By 1905, most of the lumbering was completed. R. Craven, Postmaster and general store; G. W. Marlin, veneer manufacturer; Northwestern Lumber Company, shingle mill; and C. W. Plant, railroad agent.

1910, population 40. E. R. Smith, Postmaster and store; C. W. Plant, railroad agent; and Hulda Nelson, teacher.

1915, population 100. E. R. Smith, Postmaster and store; Wm. R. Damitz, railroad agent; Marcoff & Oberg, sawmill.

1927, located 4 miles from *Caspian*. Bemis Brothers, general store; and Otto G. Damitz, dairy.

Nothing remains today except a few old houses and a few families live here.

STAGER—Was about one mile south of *Mastadon*, on the C. & N. W. Railroad, near the Wisconsin line. Fitzpatrick said it is now a resort area on Stager Lake. *"It had a depot, not operated today, but was not a town or post office or town,"* he said.

SPRING VALLEY—Was an old mining settlement and name of a mine near *Old Caspian*. The former town site can be reached by going south from *Stambaugh* and is near the village limits. Only old poplar trees, abandoned mine shafts, and foundations of company houses, now overgrown with grass, weeds and brush remain on the site.

UNION MINE—1910, on the C. & N. W. Railroad. Mail *Crystal Falls*.

YOUNGSTOWN MINE—Listed in 1910. No information.

Chapter Twelve

KEWEENAW COUNTY

Michigan's northernmost county, Keweenaw, lies closer to the North Pole than the city of *Quebec*, Canada. The name is Indian, translated by some as meaning "portage" or "place where portage is made." Keweenaw appears on the earliest French maps of the Great Lakes region. The county was set off and organized in 1861 and was originally part of Houghton County. *Eagle River*, with less than 100 residents is the least populous county seat in Michigan, and the county has the smallest population of any in the state, gradually declining from the turn-of-the-century from 7,156 in 1910 to 2,417 in 1970.

Keweenaw is in "Copper Country," the name applied to the counties lying in the copper area which extends for 150 miles from the tip of Keweenaw point to Iron County on the south. Out of a stretch of less than two miles along this line, the Calumet & Hecla Company, by 1927, had paid over $150 million in dividends. Normal production was at the rate of 200 million pounds per year and provided normal employment to 20,000 men with an average payroll of more than a million per month. For many years Michigan was the largest producer of copper in the U. S. and the United States produced 60 per cent of the world's copper.

Strikes in the mines and the high cost of production has caused a decline in the industry in recent years and is the reason for the drop in population of this county. The area is steeped in history and today tourism is becoming the chief industry.

Although Keweenaw is the smallest county in Upper Michigan, it has the longest shoreline—84 miles of rugged beauty and sandy beaches. In its 587 square miles it has numerous inland lakes and 271 miles of streams.

With an annual average snowfall of 265 inches (the winter of 1964-65 set an all time record of 294.5 inches) the county is popular for skiing, skating and winter sports.

Evidence of the copper industry can be seen almost anyplace one looks in the form of ghost towns that were once the sites of prosperous mines. Over 10 billion pounds of copper had been shipped from the Copper Country by 1966, and the former Calumet Division of Calumet & Hecla, Inc. produced more than one half of this amount. The industry also left behind more than 10,000 miles of tunnels beneath the scenic lakes and forests that now cover much of the county.

Perhaps, sometime in the future, new methods will be discovered to once again mine the copper that remains. Experiments are being constantly conducted with new pumping methods and chemical means of treating ore, etc. to once more develop the industry

This historical plaque is located at a roadside park on M-41 north of *Calumet.*
Photo by Roy L. Dodge (1971)

KEWEENAW COUNTY GHOST TOWNS

ARNOLD MINE—Is typical of many abandoned copper mine sites in the county, a short distance south of *Copper Falls*. The *Arnold* was founded in 1864, had its stock listed on the Boston Stock Exchange and had capitalization of $2.5 million. It absorbed the *Copper Falls Mine*, once an important red metal property, in 1898.

The *Falls* mine had worked from 1850 to 1893 and had produced some 25 million pounds of copper. The product came mainly from the *Owl Creek* fissure and before the mine closed it had paid $100,000 in dividends.

In the early days the *Arnold* property had a 2.5 mile narrow-gauge railroad which was called the "Arnold & Eagle Harbor Railroad." When the mine closed the rolling stock of the line was sold. This included one Baldwin locomotive plus other rolling stock.

G. Walton Smith, copper country historian said, *"As far as can be recalled the Arnold operated during the period 1899 to 1911 and produced some 2 million pounds of fine copper."*

When the mining firm viewed further operations as hopeless, it was moved, in 1926, to dispose of the property. The former Calumet & Hecla later took over much of the track.

A recent flooding of Jacobs Creek (1971) brought the old mine to light, revealing the workings of the mine and rock dump piles long hidden from view.

The site can be seen in a somewhat picturesque view by traveling here on the regular US-41 highway between *Phoenix* and *Eagle Harbor.*

———

BETE GRIESE—Located at the end of an 8-mile-long, winding black top road east off US-41 that follows for some distance along the beaches of Lake Superior, lies the harbor at *Bete Griese* (French for "grey beast"). The road ends at a channel leading to the harbor of refuge and from a small tract of towering, virgin pines can be seen the lighthouse and many pleasure craft at dock along the shore of the one-time important village of mining days. In 1940, the buildings were abandoned and there were ten residents. Today it appears to be a small resort center but the old clapboard buildings remain much the same as they were many years ago.

At intervals along the road plaques designating former mining sites can be seen, such as "Mendota Mining Company-1885," etc. The steep hills, around through which the roadway winds, are now covered with heavy second growth timber. Frequent signs warning of rock slides are posted along the route, making

About 8 miles east of US-41 lies the harbor at *Bete Griese*, one-time an important village in the mining days. This is what the remains of the village look like today. Photo by Roy L. Dodge (1971)

it difficult to look for possible former mining sites or activities while driving. Some of the scenery along the route is breath-taking. If you plan to take this tour be sure to carry a lunch as restaurants up in this country are as scarce as buffalo or wild Indians.

CENTRAL MINE—In 1872, described as, *"A village at the location of the Central mine, in Sherman Township. It lies 7 miles back from Eagle River, the county seat, and 5 from Eagle Harbor. The place was first settled about 1857, and now numbers a population of 1,000. Copper mining is the leading industry of the place. The A. M. U. Express and Mineral Range telegraph companies have offices here. The country around is slightly broken and heavily timbered. Hay and potatoes are the chief agricultural products. Copper alone is shipped. The production of the Central mine for 1871 was 905 tons and was surpassed . . . only by the Calumet and Hecla and the Quincy mines. It divided that year $50,000. Total dividends paid by it have reached $410,000 on an original investment of $100,000."*

The 1873 business directory listed H. C. Burns, Postmaster; Narcis Bulley, blacksmith; Central Mining Company, merchants; Jos. Dreher, builder; James Dunstan, mining captain; T. B. Dunstan, lawyer; Harlow Everett, hotel; James Hancock, blacksmith; Henry Kierchoff, shoemaker; Chas. Kingston, contractor; Nick Merrigan, builder; Frank Ottis, hotel; C. B. Petrie, agent; John Roberts, blacksmith; Geo. H. Satterlee, clerk; Casimer Spaum, shoemaker; and Dr. S. H. Whittlesay.

In 1875, 1,100 tons of copper was shipped. Mail received weekly. T. B. Dunstan, Postmaster.

1887, population 1,300, chiefly miners. Stage to *Phoenix, Copper Falls* and *Delaware Mine*. Daily mail. H. C. Burns, Postmaster; Central Mining Company; Albert Cruse, justice; James C. Dunston, justice; John W. Kingston and John F. Robert, justices.

1893, population 1,000. H. C. Burns, Postmaster; Jane Bryant, milliner; Central Mining Company, mine and general store; Rev. Wm. Edmunds, Methodist; Chas. Kingston, meat market; and the following were justices—Wm. Rickard; John Roberts; and John Trevorrow.

1905, population 100. Telephone. Daily mail. F. M. Bradshaw, Postmaster, teacher and Township Clerk; John R. Adams, justice; Rev. E. O. Hammond, Methodist; and J. W. R. Kirton, physician.

1909, a discontinued post office. Send mail to *Phoenix*.

The mining village hung on until the turn of the century and within a few years all but two or three people gave up the ghost and left. A wood sign along paved US-41 tells the story: *"Central Mine—In 1854 heavy masses of native copper were discovered in the bottom of an ancient pit dug by prehistoric miners. In November of that year the Central Mining Company was organized. A rich ore body was soon opened which had produced a total of $9,770,528 by July, 1898, when the property was finally abandoned.*

"Until the Kearsarge lode was discovered in the '90s, the Central Mine was the biggest and most profitable producer in the Keweenaw district. At one time the population reached a total of approximately 1,250 people and reunions of former residents are held here annually. Keweenaw County Road Commission."

A few old houses, some of them more than 100 years old, remain scattered over the site of the one-time town. Foundations and remains of mining operations are visible at the end of what was the main street. The old church, built in the late 1880s, still stands and is the only painted building remaining. This is where the annual reunions are held.

Two or three of the houses were rented out for summer cabins in 1971. One of the houses is rented by John G. Phillips, of *Ahmeek*, 25 miles south. *"When we moved here most of the furniture was here and we found many old mementoes in the house,"* Phillips said. Among some of the things were several cases of bottles from the long extinct Knively Brewery Company at *Eagle River*. A grocery order book listing items delivered to the store from 1888 to 1889 was in a kitchen cabinet drawer.

Phillips said Anton Sibilsley owned the store at that time. He also found records showing Englehart Bammert as first owner of the house, in 1888. Floors

This church and a few houses remain on one of the streets of *Central*, once a booming mining village in Copper Country. Former residents and their descendants meet for a reunion here each year.   Photo by Roy L. Dodge (1971)

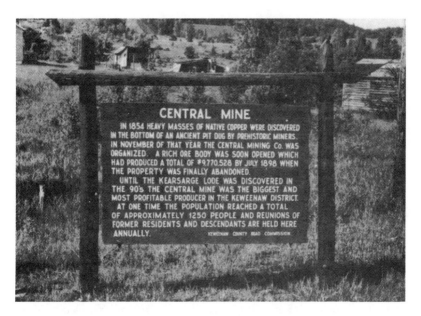

This plaque tells the history of the ghost town of *Central*, located on US-41 in Keweenaw County. Photo by Roy L. Dodge (1971)

of the house are made from native white pine and are from 18 inches to 28 inches wide and run the full length of the house. The houses are owned by the Calumet and Hecla Company, he said, and may be up for sale within a short time.

CLIFF—See Clifton.

CLIFTON—1872, *"a post office at the location of Cliff mine, some years ago one of the most productive mines in the Upper Peninsula. The production in 1871, however, was only 91 tons making it rank 13th in the list of Lake Superior mines for production.*

"Clifton is 4 miles back from Eagle River, in Clifton Township. It was settled about 1844, and now has (1872) 400 inhabitants....... Copper is the only shipment. D. D. Brockway, Postmaster; D. D. Brockway & Son, general store; O. A. Farwell, superintendent Cliff mine; and Paull & Gottstein, miners."

By 1877, the population had increased to 700. *"It is the location of the once famous Cliff mine, now thrown completely into the shade by the wonderful Calumet and Hecla. The mine is 1,080 feet deep, and produced in 1875, 825 tons of copper."*

In 1877, had two churches, Methodist and Catholic. Daily stage to *Calumet*, 12 miles distance. Frank Simon, Postmaster; O. A. Farell, mine superintendent; Rev. A. S. Fair, Methodist; Frank & Friend, general store; Dr. James M. Mead; Rev. Lucas Mozina, Catholic; and James Sowden, captain of Cliff mine.

In 1879, the population had dropped to 250 and a graded school had been built. Daily mail stage to *Eagle River*. J. C. Trenbath, Postmaster; A. J. Lawbaugh,physician; and Rev. Isaac Wilcox, Methodist. Otherwise remained the same as 1877.

1887, post office discontinued. Send mail to *Phoenix.*

COPPER FALLS MINE—The Michigan Gazetteer for 1872 described it as: *"At the location of the Copper Falls Mine, in Eagle Harbor Township, has sprung up a village of about 400 inhabitants, and for their convenience a post office has been established bearing the name of the mine . . . The place was settled about 1845 or 1846. The county is broken, being a succession of high bluffs and deep ravines, and is heavily timbered . . . Copper is the only article of shipment."* In 1871, 400 tons of copper was produced, making it 6th in production. In that year it paid $20,000 dividends. Total capital invested at that date was $510,000. Dividends totaled $100,000.

1872, Austrian & Hart, general store; Thomas Bradford, physician; Leo Leichner, bootmaker; James Rosewarne, hotel; and William Webb, Postmaster.

1877, population 500, chiefly miners. Wm. Webb, postmaster; John Clemo, barber; Hart & Gutman, general store; Hatfield & Company, general store; I. Leichner, shoemaker; and Christian Messner, photographer.

Only one change was made in the 1879 directory, with C. C. Berry added as "notions."

A few changes were made in 1887. Daily mail. E. M. Manford, Postmaster; B. F. Emerson, superintendent of mine; Hickey Brothers, teaming contractors; and John Renfrey, saloon.

1893, population 400. J. H. Moyle, Postmaster and mine superintendent; Bradfield & Hatfield, general store; Wesley Clark, justice; J. B. Hottenhoff, mason; Jacob Jurmen, carpenter; Nels Lind, boarding house; D. K. MacQueen, physician; S. Pellon, blacksmith; and Andrew Schafer, carpenter.

Only three or four houses remain in the one-time village of *Delaware*, another mining ghost town of the Copper Country located along US-41 highway between *Calumet* and *Copper Harbor*.   Photo by Roy L. Dodge (1971)

1910, population 30. Daily stage to *Phoenix, Eagle Harbor*, and *Eagle River*. Telephone. Wesley Clark, Postmaster.

By 1927, eight people lived here. The last deposits of copper were found, and the last firm to work the lode quit the place in 1898. After that many of the houses, including the school house, were razed by people from *Eagle Harbor*, who used the material for their use. Some cabins were built along Copper Falls Creek by summer residents.

CREST VIEW—1910, also a *Crest View Junction* shown on 1920 maps, the *Junction* was between *Cliff* and *Phoenix*. *Crest View* was between *Phoenix* and *Eagle River*.

DELAWARE—The remains of this one-time mining town can be seen on the east side of US-41 highway, about 10 miles north of *Central*. A few old houses remain along the highway, one of them bearing a handmade sign advertising rocks. The others appear to be uninhabited. Evidence of mining can be seen near the area and the mills were located near *Lac La Belle*.

In 1877, *"settled in 1846.... Eagle Harbor is its shipping point by vessel, but on completion of the railroad to Lac La Belle, 6¾ miles distant, will be its shipping point."*

175

In that year, population 1,150, chiefly miners. Daily mail. Jeremiah Hanley, Postmaster; H. Holcomb, justice; Philip Manger, shoemaker; Chas. H. Palmer, Jr., superintendent Conglomerated Mining Company; and William. R. Vivian, justice.

By 1893, the population had dropped to only 25. Daily mail. A. P. Thomas, Postmaster; Patrick Byrnes, Jos. Chapman, and John H. Gatiss, Jr., were justices of the peace. Wm. Gattiss, and the Lac La Belle Mining Company, copper miners, were also listed.

In 1905, called a mining camp of 30 people. Daily stage to Calumet. Wm. R. Vivian, Postmaster; H. Turenne, justice; and Wm. Vivian, agent for Lac La Belle Mining Company

1910, described as a mining camp on the Keweenaw-Central Railroad, Grant Township. W. J. Penhallegon, superintendent of the Manitou Mining Company; A. H. Sawyer, chief engineer of Keweenaw Copper Company; George H. Noteware, teacher; and C. J. Woolway, physician.

By 1915, the post office had been discontinued. Send mail to *Mandan.* Population about 50, Charles Brown, hotel.

FULTON—1910, send mail to *Allouez.*

GAY—1905, a village in Sherman Township, on the shore of Lake Superior, 20 miles from *Calumet. "The stamping mills of the Mohawk and Wolverine copper mines are located here. B. S. Shearer, Postmaster and superintendent for Mohawk Mining Company; J. P. & G. H. Peterman, general store; and the Wolverine Copper Mining Company, business listings."*

1909, population 550. John H. Jackson, Postmaster and manager of the J. P. & G. H. Peterman General Store; J. E. Rowe, express agent; J. M. Walsh, physician; and David L. Vinton, superintendent for the Wolverine Mining Company.

In 1915, population 800. Additions to business listings for that year were, Jos. E. Gay, leader of the band and railroad agent; and N. N. Wallentine, physician.

1927, population 600. Settled in 1904. On the Copper Range Railroad, Sherman Township, 11 miles from *Mohawk.* Has Catholic church. J. H. Jackson, Postmaster and manager. Petermann Stores Company; C. F. Brewington, physician; Fred Kline, railroad agent; C. L. Adams, mine superintendent; Jos. Ricard, confection.

Today *Gay* is only "a shadow" of the one-time booming village of the copper mining days.

HEBARD—1910, a station on the Mineral Range Railroad, northwest of *Traverse*. Mail *Mohawk*.

———

JOHNS—1910, located on *Isle Royal*, at that time a part of Keweenaw County. Mail to *Duluth*, Minnesota.

———

LAC LA BELLE—*Haven Falls* is located near this present day summer resort, named after Doc. Haven, who was head of the local government division of the Michigan Highway Department, who was mainly responsible for its name.

Lac La Belle was located near the premises of the one-time active *Delaware* copper mill, and was part of the mining enterprise which crushed the rock which was then dispatched to smelters for refining. A smelter was built here but it never melted a pound of red metal.

The little creek which results in the impressive falls originates in the *Delaware* area. This was the mining firm which bore several names, such as the Conglomerate and the Oneida.

It was to this site that the earliest beginnings of the Keweenaw Central Railroad eventually terminated. The railroad was built in 1907, and lasted until 1918. It serviced mainly the mines of the Copper Country, *Phoenix*, *Keweenaw* and related properties. Almost all signs of the railroad are extinct in the *Delaware-Lac La Belle* area.

Driving on US-41 between *Delaware* and *Copper Harbor* is almost like going through a tunnel made of trees. This sign marks a trail leading about one-half mile east of US-41 to the ghost town of *Mandan*.   Photo by Roy L. Dodge (1971)

At one time *Lac La Belle* was an important shipping point and used as a port of refuge by Great Lakes ships caught in storms. By 1910, the post office was discontinued, mail to *Mandan*.

———————

MANDAN—Driving US-41 highway between *Delaware* and *Copper Harbor* is like driving through a dark tunnel made by overlapping branches of thick forests along the crooked, meandering, narrow two-lane pavement. About 4 miles north of *Delaware* is a neat, rustic road sign that reads *Mandan*. These signs, designating former towns, were erected by the County Road Commission in 1970-71 and are very attractive. Turn right at the sign down a trail through the woods and about one-half mile the road appears to end at a six-foot-high concrete foundation of what may have been a store at one time. Several other remains of foundations are in the immediate vicinity. By following the trail around this foundation, and making another right turn south, some of the former houses of this one-time village appear. Most are in a run-down condition with broken windows, weathered siding, and leaky roofs, typical of many north Michigan ghost towns. Two or three of the houses apparently are rented by summer tourists and have crude signs designating the owners.

Next to one of the eight or 10 houses is another foundation and pile of debris marking the spot of another fallen house. Beyond this row of houses, at the junction with another trail, are several more concrete foundations, overgrown with weeds and brush and surrounded by trees, making them a little difficult to locate. Other trails branch off from the main trail in this area, indicating that more evidence of habitation may be located here also.

In 1910, *Mandan* was a busy place, with 300 population and located on the Keweenaw-Central Railroad, Grant Township, near *Clear Lake*. Business listings included, A. H. Sawyer, Postmaster and superintendent for Keweenaw Copper Company; Olive M. Blight, teacher; Cora A. Davis, teacher; M. D. Ferris, express agent; C. G. Hall, justice; J. P. Petermann, general store (this was a chain of stores) ; and C. J. Woolway, physician. (Note: names of doctors, preachers, etc. may appear in business listings of several area settlements. They operated as more or less "circuit riding" doctors, preachers, etc.)

In 1915, population 26. Adam J. Bessolo, Postmaster, railroad, express and telegraph agent; and "old alphabet" J. R. W. Kirton, physician.

1927, population 40. *"On US-41, Grant Township, daily bus to Eagle Harbor, Phoenix, and Ahmeek . . . No business listings."*

The "Michigan Writer's Project," of 1941, described the site as: *"A closed mine and deserted company village, where a score of empty houses are guarded by a caretaker."* The only caretaker in June of 1971 were the black flies and mosquitoes that have no rivals when it comes to keeping "nosey people" from

One of a dozen or more houses and foundations remaining on the site of the one-time village of *Mandan*. One of many ghost towns in the Copper Country of the Upper Peninsula.   Photo by Roy L. Dodge (1971)

———

taking pictures and just looking around. Probably the elements and mother nature are the reason for the preservation of many other ghost towns of the Upper Peninsula. Many old houses, more than 100 years old, have withstood the fierce gales of Lake Superior, record snow falls of 294 inches in one winter, summer storms and winter blizzards, and but for these conditions may not have survived the vandalism and "don't give a damn" attitude of thousands of tourists.

———

NORTH KEARSARGE—1910, a station on the Keweenaw-Central railroad. Mail to *Mandan*.

———

OJIBWAY-1910, a station on the K.-C. Railroad. 1927, on the Keweenaw Central and on the Gratiot River, Allouez Township, 3 miles from *Mohawk* and 7 miles from *Eagle River*. Mail to *Mohawk*.

———

PENN MINE—Listed in 1872 as a post office. 1879, listed as a discontinued post office, 5 miles east of *Eagle Harbor* and 13 miles southwest of *Copper Harbor*.

———

PHILLIPSVILLE—1927 directory, see *Kearsarge*. Abandoned mine locations and empty business buildings stretch for several miles along US-41, between *Mohawk* and *Calumet*. Near an old, insulbrick-covered, two-story building housing an antique shop and bearing 3-foot-high letters reading "THE LAST PLACE ON EARTH," is another sign that reads "Phillipsville." This is located about one-half mile north of *Kearsarge*. There is also an abandoned gas station with a sign that reads "Phillipsville."

PHOENIX—Name taken from Egyptian mythology. Described in 1872, as: *"A village of about 500 souls, in Houghton Township, 1½ miles back from Eagle River, at the location of the Phoenix mine. This mine is owned and worked by the Phoenix Copper Company, of Boston, Mass. The capital invested amounts to $820,000. It was not hitherto a dividend-paying mine, though now producing largely. Its product for the past two years has been, 1871 . . . 879 tons, 1872 . . . 477 tons. Hon. Frank G. White is agent for the mine. Settled in 1845."* The directory listed John Francis, boots and shoemaker; S. H. Frank, deputy Postmaster; M. Freud & Son, general store; Alex Givson, shoemaker, and John Wissnett, tailor.

1877, population 1,000. Has a Methodist church and exports copper and potatoes. Mineral Range Telegraph. Daily stage to *Calumet.* Briggs & Sutter, general store; Kate Brockie, assistant school principal; Wm. Cronins, express agent; Alfred Cruse, hotel; M. A. Delano, agent Phoenix Copper Company; Rev. A. S. Fair, Methodist; A. J. Lawbaugh, physician; E. B. Wood, school principal; and Wm. Zassenhouse, justice.

In 1879, described as: *"60 miles north of L'Anse, the nearest railroad. Eagle Harbor is its shipping point by water (2 miles). The location of the mines and stamping works of the Phoenix Mining Company, the 1877 product which amounted to 1,342,385 pounds of copper. Stage to Calumet daily."* D. W. Sutter, Postmaster; A. Albrecht, wagonmaker; Chas. Briggs and Dominick W. Sutter, general store; Emanuel Broad, saloon; Danile D. and Albert A. Brockway, general store; Wm. Cronins, express agent; Alfred Cruse, hotel and meats; Moses A. Delano, agent for copper company; Nicholas Gassmann, saloon; John Hermann, jeweler; W. G. Kellog, justice; Mrs. W. G. Kellog, teacher; Albert I. Lawbaugh, physician; John Messner, saloon; James Prideau, grocery; E. B. Truesdell, school principal; and Rev. Isaac Wilcox, Methodist.

1887, Daily stage to *Calumet, Copper Falls, Eagle River, Delaware Mine,* etc.. Population 1,000. New additions to the business directory were, Geo. Bottomly, justice; J. F. Schroeder, Prop. Commercial House (hotel); James Prideau, grocer; and Louis Rader and Geo. Wilson, justices.

By 1893, there was a slump in the copper market and the population of *Phoenix* dropped to about 100, Business listings, (mostly farmers were listed in that year) were, Daniel Sullivan, Postmaster and hotel; E. Broad, saloon; E. Bruneau, lumberman; Wm. Chapman, supervisor; and James Flinn, lumberman.

At the turn-of-the-century things picked up again and in 1905 the population was 350. Fred Bond, Postmaster; Ed Barber, hotel and saloon; Blight & Sons, fuse managers.; Amos Bommert, blacksmith; Jos. Brunette, hotel; Frank Fecteau, hotel and saloon; Dr. J. R. W. Kirton; J. P. Peterman, general store; N. J. Tinnant, teacher; Chas. Trudell, hotel and saloon; and Lynn Young, teacher.

180

In 1910, the population dropped to a low of 46. Only one hotel and a saloon were listed, operated by Frank Fecteau; Rev. H. Eplett, Methodist. Same teachers, blacksmith, doctor, postmaster, etc.

1915, Henry Petermann, Postmaster; Mary Barett, hotel; A. N. Chattel, doctor; C. W. Dean, express agent; and Frank Fecteau, hotel. Population remained about the same.

1927, population 70. On the Eagle River and US-41 highway. Seven miles from *Mohawk* and 2½ miles south of *Eagle River*. Daily bus to *Mohawk*. Catholic and Methodist churches; Chas. Bryant, Postmaster; Amos Baumert, blacksmith; Petermann Stores, Inc., Charles Bryant, manager general store.

In 1971, four or five old buildings remained along US-41 highway, one contained a liquor store.

_____

ROCK HARBOR—1910, a summer post office on *Isle Royal.*

_____

SNOSHOE—1910, a station on the Keweenaw-Central Railroad. Mail Mohawk. Located between *Traverse* and *Gay.*

_____

SOUTH KEARSARGE—1910, on the K.-C. Railroad. Mail *Kearsarge.* "Kearsarge" was named for the U. S. S. Kearsarge by a former naval officer who became an employee of the Calumet & Hecla Company. The old Calumet Mining Company saw its stock rise from $1 a share to $75 a share in 1865-66. After the consolidation of mine interests under the Calumet & Hecla name in 1871, the company paid more than $160 million in dividends up to 1940. The *Kearsarge* mine was closed in 1930, having been opened since 1882.

_____

TOBINS HARBOR—1910, located on *Isle Royal.*

_____

TRAVERSE—1910, a station on the Mineral Range Railroad, between *Hebards* and *Snoshoe*, northwest of *Gay*. Mail *Mohawk.*

_____

TRAVERSE BAY JUNCTION—1910, a station on the M.-R. Railroad, mail *Gay.*

_____

WYOMING—A blacktop road leads from US-41 to *Lac La Belle*, just below *Mandan* and about 1½ miles west is another County Road Commission sign that reads *Wyoming*, pointing south on a good dirt road. About a mile down this road, at a dead end, is the site of the one-time village of *Wyoming*. Either the settlement was too small to list in business directories or book agents were afraid to solicit business here when told that it was known widely in the Copper County as "Hell Town" due to its rough reputation.

Located on the banks of the Montreal River, just below *Mandan*, in the 1870s it was the site of a stamping mill and the old Wyoming Mine. With four saloons running wide open the town was the hang-out for miners from area locations and became known for miles around as "Hell Town."

There are perhaps two small cabins and one or two house trailers near the clearing. Only the hollows of basements where homes and stores once stood remain on the 10 acre field now grown waist high to quack grass, weeds and brush. The trail leading down to the river was fenced with barbed wire in 1971. Perhaps more remains are located near the river.

Many areas of the peninsula are a veritable paradise for rock hounds. At *Agate Harbor*, near M-26 west of *Copper Harbor*, the beaches and cliffs are scattered with glazed, multi-colored agate stones.

Stories of silver and gold discoveries have been told many times. Throughout the various lodes numerous bulks of native silver were uncovered in the early days. The largest of the silver nuggets (troy weight, 8¾ pounds) was shipped to the Philadelphia Mint, where it was put on exhibition.

Don Clarke, of *Bay City,* Michigan, who claims to be an expert on Copper Country history and has studied the country for many years, has a photo of a fleet of about fifty 1927 Chrysler autos that he said were salvaged when a train carrying a load of new cars was wrecked near a town around *Copper Harbor* in February of that year during one of the huge snowfalls. Some of these cars (confiscated by area natives), are said to still be in the area.

The site of another Copper Country ghost town, *Wyoming* or *Hell Town*, is at the end of a gravel road near *Lac La Belle*. Nothing remains on the site to show a town ever existed.

Photo by Roy L. Dodge (1971)

Chapter Thirteen

LUCE COUNTY

Luce County was organized in 1887, and named for Governor Cyrus G. Luce, Governor of Michigan from 1887-1890. The chief product of the county has always been lumber, and in recent years depended mainly on tourism as an economic base. The Tahquamenon Falls, on the river of the same name, near *Newberry*, draws millions of tourists annually.

Luce County is the second smallest of Upper Peninsula counties. In 1910, the population was 4,004, reached a peak of 7,406 in 1940, and 7,827 in 1960. The population has since declined and in 1972, has 6,789.

During the years, Luce County had products other than lumber, but apparently the industries failed. In 1887, the Vulcan Furnace Company operated here and pig iron, along with lumber was shipped.

In 1893, the qualities of "Newberry Celery" was being expounded, a product foreign to upper Michigan. Called the Newberry Celery and Improvment Company, Limited, officers were H. L. Harris; M. W. O'Brien; F. F. Palms and was a subsidiary of the Peninsula Land Company.

Also, in 1893, the Burrell Chemical Company manufactured wood alcohol, a by-product of charcoal manufacturing. The Newberry Furnace Company also manufactured pig iron. In that year the Burrell Company hired 50 employees and the blast furnace employed 200 workers.

Descriptive literature claimed, *"The Newberry Celery and Improvement Company have the largest celery gardens in Michigan and are shipping celery to all parts of the Northwest."*

Although the celery enterprise failed the Peninsula Land Company continued to take an active part in the progress of the county. In 1894, the company donated 560 acres of their land holdings at *Newberry* for construction of The Upper Peninsula Hospital for the Insane. Erection of the buildings was begun in 1894, and it opened in November 1895. Within a few years there were 500 inmates and 80 employees. The hospital is still in operation.

LUCE COUNTY GHOST TOWNS

DANAHER—1910, a station on the Soo Line, mail *McMillan*. Named for the Danaher Lumber Company which was active in this area at the turn of the century.

———————

DEER PARK—1893, a post office in McMillan Township, 28 miles north of *Newberry*. Population 300. E. E. Bradley, Postmaster; Bradley & Hurst, sawmill; J. H. Fraham, notary; W. Green, hotel; and O. Randolph, meat market.

Deer Park was platted as a village August 1, 1902, but was abandoned before it officially became a village. In 1905, three years later, listed as a discontinued post office. Send mail to *Newberry*.

———————

DOLLARVILLE—This village received its name from Robert Dollar who started as a "cookee" in a logging camp and rose to be the owner of the world famous Dollar Lines shipping company. Never became the successful logging village it could have been due to restrictions in land sales, but did reach a population of 600 or more. At one time a group of investors from Scotland built a mill on the river here but neglected to buy timber rights and were unable to operate.

A short time later the Peninsula Land Company took over the mill only to discover their charter prohibited cutting timber on the Tahquamenon river and without timber the mill was useless.

Finally, the Dollarville Lumber Company, headed by Robert Dollar, took over. Dollar couldn't buy timber close enough to the mill to be hauled in by team so he leased a tug to haul rafts of logs to the mill. In order to do so he had to buck the current of the river and the project proved unprofitable. Dollar was determined to recoup his loss by using the tug and in this way he started on a career which eventually made him a chief figure as a shipping magnate on the Great Lakes.

NOTE: In 1887, three Dollars were listed as lumbermen, Robert, Joseph, and William Dollar.

In 1887, Dollarville was described: *"In the southwestern part of McMillan Township, (Chippewa County), a station on the D. M. & M. Railroad. Has a Methodist church. Population, 350. James Stitt, Postmaster; J. H. Carey, railroad and express agent; Land Department Lumber Company; Alexander*

Little, meat market; David McGrath, Justice of Peace and saloon; Robert Reed, hotel; and J. C. Stitt, general store."

1893, population 400. Luce County had been formed and was located 1¾ miles west of *Newberry*, the new county seat. A station on the Soo Line Railroad. A. McArthur, Postmaster; F. W. Brock, railroad agent; Dollarville Lumber Company, W. L. Ducey manager, saw and planning mills; Bettes-Darcy & Company (A. Bettes, Wm. D'Arcy and Wm. D'Arcy Jr.) general store, lumberman's supplies etc.; C. H. Fanjoy, photographer; W. M. Gibson, lumber inspector; Geo. Himelspach, hotel; D. E. Lockwood, justice; E. McDonald, vet surgeon; John McMillan, blacksmith; M. Mahoney, constables. Minthorn, lumber inspector; W. J. Pentiand,saloon; A. A. Salmon, hotel; and W. T. Wells, school principal.

Dollarville reached its peak in 1905, with 600 residents. Business listings included, Peter Garrick, Postmaster and railroad agent; Danaher Hardwood Lumber Company (Ray E. Danaher, and James Danaher, Jr.) lumber manufacturings and general store; Anna Grant, teacher; Maude Grant, school principal; Wm. Hughes, blacksmith; H. M. Keal, teacher; Archie S. Love, saloon; Geo. McDonald, livery; Mrs. Neil McIntyre, boarding house; R. E. Danaher, manager telephone Company; Samuel Minthorn, lumber inspector; Bert Nelson, lumber inspector; Wm. Palmer, barber; Mrs. M. Roch, hotel; and Martin Rody, boarding house.

Population dropped in 1910, to 400. Peter Garrick, Postmaster; Albert Conkey, grocery; Danaher Lumber Company; Harry English, confection; Allen D. Ford, school principal; Christina Graham, teacher; Anna Grant, teacher; Mrs. McIntyre, boarding; Alex Pentland, saloon; and Mrs. Schufofski, boarding house.

The 1915 population was 300. J. L. Minard, acting Postmaster; W. H. Krempel, grocery; Chas. Smith, hotel; and the South Shore Cedar Company. By this time the big lumbering days were over. After the hardwood was depleted all that remained were posts and shingle bolts, and enough eight and 10 foot lengths for railroad ties. Dollarville was on its last legs as a lumbering town.

During the following years nature took over and second growth trees started covering the scars of the logging days. The few remaining residents prepared for a new industry soon to be labeled "tourism."

By the late teens an occasional chug-chug of a Model T-Ford could be heard and the first tourists began to arrive, mostly in the form of deer hunters who waited in long lines at the straits to cross on the auto ferry. When the new highway came, *Dollarville* would be booming once more.

As the population dwindled, and with the expansion of Rural Free Delivery, the town lost its post office and mail was delivered from nearby *Newberry*. By 1927, most signs of the logging days were over. Harvey Nelson installed a gasoline pump in front of his billiard hall, and Royal Saunders opened a gasoline station. The new paved highway, M-28, however, bypassed the town isolating it from the main stream of traffic and the tourist boom never materialized.

By 1940, the population was about 100 and 30 years later only about 200 live in the area. A newspaper item of April 11, 1971, tells of attempts of the residents to restore the old logging dam, built during the days of Robert Dollar, to put the town back on the map as a tourist center. The new dam was completed in the spring of 1972 at a cost of one quarter million dollars. According to an economic survey which paved the way for the dam, the restoration project should double tourist expenditures in Luce County to about $6 million a year.

In addition, according to the survey, the dam will increase the county's tax base by 60 per cent and its per capita income, now one of the lowest in the state, by 50 per cent.

Most of the restoration cost is being financed by the U. S. Department of Interior and the Upper Great Lakes Regional Commission, the article said. The remaining $50,000 was to be allocated by the Legislature.

A small group of people, not more than a dozen, turned out for the dedication of the new dam, and maybe—with the 1970s saturation of tourists in Michigan—maybe, *Dollarville* will once more become a town.

EAST BRANCH—1887 and 1893, located on the D. S. S. & A. Railroad, 69½ miles northwest of *St. Ignace*.

HUNTERS MILL—Not a village or post office but at one time was the site of extensive lumber camps. Located about 7½ miles north of *Soo Junction*, on the Tahquamenon River, which was also called "dark river" or "golden river" by the Indians. This was the original home of the legendary Hiawatha of Longfellow fame.

Millions of feet of lumber was floated down the river during the logging days to be shipped by rail.

———————

McMILLAN—The *McMillan* of today is only a ghost of the booming logging town of the early 1900s. The village reached a population of more than 300 in 1910.

1887, located in Chippewa County, near the Mackinac and Chippewa County line, and on the Soo Line Railroad.

Population 40. Daily mail. W. S. Locke, Postmaster; Other listings were, J. K. Anderson, hotel; D. M. Campbell, teamster; and D. L. West, general store. Several justices of the peace and one farmer was also listed.

Additional listings in 1893 were, D. M. Campbell, veterinary; John Foster, teacher; Chas. Fuller, trapper and hunter; D. H. Gallighar, shoemaker; M. Neazer, boarding house; Elmer Nichols, railroad agent.

By the turn-of-the-century the population was 100, and in 1905, Mrs. Nettie Morgan, Postmaster; Ethel Barbour, teacher; Danaher Lumber Company, loggers; O. W., Hatch, Township Treasurer; Duffy Jumice, mail carrier; W. S. Locke, shoemaker, and Township Clerk; Mrs. Morgan, general store; W. F. Morgan, railroad agent; Northern Cooperage and Lumber Company, sawmill; and John Tait, supervisor and notary.

1910, population 300. Only a few changes for that year. H. J. Skinner, Postmaster; Caplan & Block, general store; H. E. Gailighar named his hotel "The Columbia"; Jim Foster, general store; Jos. Grondier, saloon and livery; Bert Koontz, saloon; Geo. Koontz, barber and Township Clerk; Northern Cooperage Company, sawmill; and L. M. Prentice, druggist.

By 1915, the saloons were out and one lumber company stayed on. H. J. Skinner was Postmaster and ran a general store. Other business listings were, A. M. Caplan, general store; Northern Cooperage & Lumber Company, sawmill; and John Waltz, livery.

Second growths of timber started coming on in the 1920s and although the big timber was over lumbering continued on a limited scale. In 1927, the population was about 200 and *McMillan* was now located on highway M-28, Columbus Township, 13 miles west of *Newberry*. Methodist church. H. J. Skinner, Postmaster and general store; William Bonifas Lumber Company, Mrs. H. E. Gallaher, hotel; E. N. Hammond, grocery and sporting goods; Robert Bryers, County Road Commissioner; and Wm. McGarey, restaurant, billiards soft drinks, etc.

Today the population of the entire county has decreased. It is doubtful if the population of *McMillan* exceeds 100. It still has a post office, one of two in the county, and the industry is the tourist trade brought by the highway. The business district is made up of two taverns, one or two stores and the post office. The old Lincoln School is closed and about 50 houses remain in the village.

————

McPHEE—1910, a station on the Soo Line Railroad, mail to *Newberry*.

————

MURNER—1910, mail to *Dollarville*.

————

PERIOD—1910, a station on the Soo Line Railroad, mail *Newberry*.

————

SAGE—1910, between *Soo Junction* and *Newberry*, on the Soo Line railroad, mail *Newberry*.

————

SOO JUNCTION—In 1893, on the D. S. S. & A. Railroad, 12 miles from *Newberry*. Population 25. F. D. Griffin, Postmaster, railroad and telegraph agent.

1905, J. H. Everett, Jr., Postmaster. Everett also added a boarding house to the settlement. G. F. Willman, railroad and express agent.

Within the next few years *Soo Junction* added a saloon and hotel, in addition to Everett's boarding house, operated by John H. Johnson. In 1909, C. L. Clark was Postmaster and railroad agent.

By World War I, saloons were outlawed, but Johnson continued to operate his hotel. Clark was still Postmaster and Everetts had gone out of business. In 1917, Mrs. L. A. Clark took over the boarding house and converted it to a grocery store and restaurant.

Chapter Fourteen

MACKINAC COUNTY

Mackinac County was first laid out as Michilimackinac by a proclamation of Governor Lewis Cass, on October 26, 1818, and the government was organized in 1849. *Mackinac* was designated as the county seat until 1885 when it was moved to *St. Ignace.*

The name was taken from the Indian *Michinimackinong*, the place of Giant Fairies, or Great Turtle place.

Bordering on Lake Huron and Lake Michigan, the county area includes many islands lying offshore, including historic *Mackinac Island*, one of the oldest settlements in the state, first settled about 1840.

The census of 1880 listed the population of the county at 2,202 an increase of about 500 over 1870. In 1960, the population was 10,853. Mackinac County is one of 11 Upper Peninsula counties that showed a decline in population from 1960 to 1970, with a loss of 1,193 people.

MACKINAC STRAITS

Nicolet passed through the Straits in 1634 seeking a route to the Orient. Soon it became a crossroads where Indian, missionary, trapper, and soldier met. From the 1600's through the War of 1812 first Frenchman and Englishman, then Briton and American fought to control this strategic waterway. In 1679 the *Griffin* was the first sailing vessel to ply these waters. The railroad reached the Straits in 1882. Until the Mackinac Bridge was opened in 1957 ferries linked the north and south.

This historical plaque is located at the rest area on the north side of the Mackinac Bridge.   Photo by Roy L. Dodge (1971)

Mackinac County is also the site of the famous Mackinac Bridge, or "Big Mack," an engineering marvel designated as one of the seven man-made wonders of the world by the American Institute of Architects. The bridge was the final realization of man's dream to connect the two Michigan peninsulas over the Straits of Mackinac. The famous bridge was opened to traffic in 1957 after four years of construction requiring the work and talent of more than 10,000 men. The Mackinac Bridge has a total length of more than 5 miles. Its center span of 3,800 feet is the third longest in the world, and the 8,614 feet between anchorages is the longest of any bridge. The two main towers rise 552 feet above the waters' surface. The tower moorings go down another 210 feet below the water's surface.

The history of Mackinac County, especially that of *Mackinac Island*, has been well documented over the years, and so many books, memoirs, etc. have been published about the area that space limits lengthy details in this book.

The present county seat, *St. Ignace*, is one of the oldest settlements in Michigan, and was established and abandoned several times during its long history. Known as *Point St. Ignace*, in 1876, population 300. Had a Catholic church, two or three sawmills, two hotels and two stores. Mail delivery daily by boat during the navigation season, and tri-weekly in winter.

St. Ignace began its growth as a city when it became designated the county seat, about 1885, and a new court house costing $18,000 was erected. An ore dock was built at a cost of $300,000, and an iron furnace hired 150 men. In 1886, the population had increased to 3,000, about the same as 1970.

MACKINAC COUNTY GHOST TOWNS

ALLENVILLE—During the lumbering days this village, about one-half mile east off Highway 123, and 12 miles northwest of *St. Ignace*, was first known as "First Kiln Stop" along the railroad. Charcoal kilns were being operated along the railroad by the Marcel Furnace of *St. Ignace*.

In 1905, described as: *population 100. On the Soo Line Railroad, Brevoort Township, 10 miles north of St. Ignace. Albert Eckers, Postmaster and general store; J. D. Erskine, general store; Wm. Luepuitz, mason; E. E. Nichols, express agent; John N. Roggenbuck, grocery; Stephen Sckeraszy, flour and sawmill; Herman Shimmelpenny, general store; and George Appleford, hay presser.*

A few years later, 1909, the population was given as 400. *"Has German Lutheran, Catholic, and Presbyterian churches."* Albert Eckert, Postmaster and general store; S. Christman, grocery. Other changes, in addition to 1905, were: Bertha Gibbs, teacher; Miss Lennon, teacher: Wm. Massey, Jr., hotel; Muskegon Paper Company, sawmill; Charles Sockwech, general store; and Joseph Sveltner, sawmill. Other listings remained the same.

By 1917, the population had dropped again to 100. In that year James Erskine was Postmaster; Appleford Brothers, sawmill; J. D. Erskine, general store; F. W. Litzner, general store; Wm. Massey, hotel and general store; and W. E. Tangstaff, hay presser.

1927, population 150. On Soo Line Railroad and Highway US-2, daily bus to *Sault Ste. Marie, Manistique,* and *Escanaba.*

Lutheran and Congregational churches. James Erskine, Postmaster; J. D. Erskine, general store and railroad agent; August Kaminski, general store; W. E. Langstaff, hay presser; Mackinac County Fair Assn., Robert Sekeresy, Secretary; and Wm. Massey, Jr., hotel and general store.

Post office discontinued August 31, 1958. James G. Erskine, Postmaster.

Several of the former business buildings remain today. One, apparently the hotel and grocery, still has equipment and shelving, racks, etc., but has been vacant for years. Other buildings look as though they would fall down in a hard wind. There are no signs of the former depot and other buildings. Perhaps one or two families live there. One old church is still in use.

BOVEE—1905, a discontinued post office. Mail to *Gould City.*

BREVORT—Was known in the 1880s as "The Warehouse," because of a large storage building used by a steamship line that traveled between *St. Ignace* and *Manistique.* The settlement was named for Judge Brevort, an early surveyor. The first Postmistress was Lattice Vought, in 1890.

First settled in 1884 as a fishing village, and at one time 10 fishing tugs docked here.

In 1893, described as a small hamlet on Lake Michigan. Population 75. Mail, semi-weekly. Hattie C. Vought, Postmistress; Gustafson Brothers (Leander, Charles, and E. G. F.), fishermen; Leander Gustafson, justice; Geo. Hoffey, cooper (barrel maker) and fisherman; Hoffey & Vought (George Hoffey and George Vought), fishermen; George Vought, mason; and W. J. Vought, blacksmith.

1905, population 100. A fishing village in Moran Township. Mail stage, tri-weekly from *St. Ignace.* Hattie C. Vought, Postmistress; Dr. Bennett, physician; Charles Carlson, fisherman; Gustafson Brothers, fishermen, E. G. F. Gustafson, grocery; John Gustafson, fisherman; N. Helber, Chester Keech, Eugene McLaughlyn, Charles Matson, and John Matson were all listed as fishermen.

In 1909, still listed as a fishing village. Only a few changes were made in the business directory. George Haffey, Postmaster, and three new fishermen; Bloom, N. Helber, Axel Movalson, and A. Sunquist. Population 50.

By 1927, the population had increased to 100. Had a Swedish Lutheran Church (still standing on the high bank overlooking the former harbor of the fishing boats); Mrs. Ellen Movalson, Postmistress; Carl E. Carlson, Charles Carlson, Gidion Carlson, John E. Holmberg, and Axel Movalson were listed as fishermen. A new industry had been added, Dovey & Wheeler Lumber Company, planing mills. Other businesses in 1927 were E. G. F. Gustafson, hotel; Elvar Holmberg, general store; Frank Miller, restaurant, general store, and garage; Ellis Movalson, ferns; and Amatus Sundquist, general store.

Today, the former village is a summer resort and tourist area located on US-2 between *St. Ignace* and *Naubinway.* An historical plaque has been placed near the church telling the early history of the site. A motel and one store and gasoline station operate here, and the few homes in the area are new and modern. The fishing and lumbering days are over for *Brevort.*

BRYAN—Was a short-lived sawmill and logging settlement that lasted from about 1907-08 to 1920.

1910, population 200. In Newton Township, 25 miles east of *Manisitique* and 3½ miles from *Pike Lake,* its shipping point on the Soo Line Railroad. C. W. McEwen, Postmaster. Daily mail. The Stack Lumber Company operated a general store and sawmill here.

After 1918, mail to *Pike Lake.*

G. Harold Earle, of the Wisconsin Land & Lumber Company, founders of Blaney Park, said: *"This was a town built by the Stack Lumber Company and named after their Woods Superintendent of that name. The village straddled Highway US-2 just north of Pike Lake, and the old railroad grade leading there from Pike Lake Junction, on the Soo Line, can still be observed.*

"The town had a post office, round house (for repair of train engines, etc.), store, boarding house, and other buildings, including some constructed of logs. It was the headquarters of the Stack logging operation in that area during the first quarter of the century," Earle said. *"It was abandoned about 1925, and there was nothing left there when we were doing some of the initial development work of Blaney Park in the late 1920s and early 1930s. I recall that there were one or two log buildings left which the contractor, who was doing work at Blaney, used as a camp for his crew. I recall that we had a somewhat memorable dinner there in the fall of 1928 at the time the airport at Blaney was dedicated and the contractor entertained some of us, including the six pursuit plane pilots who came from Selfridge Field for the dedication. We were served with a really royal camp-style dinner,"* Earle recalled. He also said that a few years ago (prior to 1971), someone put up a sort of hunting camp north of US-2 in the clearing of the village site, and adjacent, on the south side of the road, there is now a small hotel.

CAFFEY—Was the post office for *Lewis* (see *Lewis*). Was named after its first Postmaster, Wm. N. Caffey, who was Postmaster in 1905. Described as a country post office, on the Soo Line Railroad, in Hendricks Township, 36 miles north of *St. Ignace*.

In 1917, send mail to *Rexton*.

Today there are two houses and a railroad siding.

————

CARRUTHERS—1905 maps, a station between *Huntspur* and *Pike Lake*, on the Soo Line.

————

CHARLES—1910, population 75. On St. Martins Bay, St. Ignace Township, about 12 miles north of *St. Ignace*. Mail stage tri-weekly to *St. Ignace*, fare 50 cents. Telephone. Clarence H. Slocum, Postmaster; Sterling Cedar and Lumber Company, W. C. Sterling, of *Monroe*, Pres., C. H. Slocum, treasurer and manager.

1915, Herman Brooker, Postmaster; Loud Lumber Company, Henry M. Loud (of *Oscoda*) President, Brewster Loud, Vice-President, and H. Kimball Loud, Secretary-Treasurer.

1918, E. Hendrickson, Postmaster; Loud Lumber Company, sawmills and logging.

1927, a discontinued post office, 12 miles north of *St. Ignace*. RFD *St. Ignace*. Smith & Cummins, general store.

————

CORRINE—Had three names. Postal name was *Vine* on maps and called *Viola* in directories. Mrs. H. L. Yale, of *Gould City*, said there are only three or four families living at *Corrine* now (1971). *"It once had a grocery store, post office, saloon, school, depot, and dwellings. One grocery store building is still standing along with several other old buildings,"* she said. Mrs. Yale said there is also an old school building standing, but it may have been moved into later.

Corrine was almost adjacent to, perhaps one-half mile west, of *Gould City*. 1927, 9 miles west of *Engadine*. Mail to *Viola*. Corrine Supply Company, general store.

————

CORYELL—Was located on a long narrow island, a summer resort, on Lake Huron, Clark Township, 16 miles from *Pickford*, 1927, population, 100. Eva D. McBain, Postmistress; Lakeside Hotel, Mrs. E. D. McBain & Son, proprietors.

————

DILLER—Was located at the terminus of a railroad, about 5 miles southeast of *Germfask*. Listed in 1910 as a discontinued post office, mail to *Curtis*. Not listed in 1905.

DONALD—Was located in Garfield Township, about 4 miles due east of Manistique Lake. 1927, RFD *Engadine*.

ELLIOTS—1910, mail *Cedarville*.

EPOUFETTE—(French for "a place of rest"). It is believed that Father Marquette once stopped here to rest on his trip down Lake Michigan from *St. Ignace* as his first stop.

The settlement was established by a French fisherman in 1859 but was founded as a post office only after lumbering operations started in 1881. Cabins of the village stretched for two miles along the harbor. Fishing was the industry until the 1960s.

In 1887, was a post office in Hendricks Township, 33 miles northwest of *St. Ignace. "It is on the shore of Lake Michigan, and on the tri-weekly stage route between Manistique and St. lgnace . . . The chief shipment is fish. Population, 50."* John R. McLeod, Postmaster, fisherman and farmer; Ronald M. Corey Alexander Godreau, Amble Goudreau were all fishermen; Louis Godreau, tug captain; David Miles, engineer; Chas. Tull, shoemaker; M. Belanger (pronounced Bell-on-gay) & Company, Magloire Belanger, F. S. Postal, and D. & B. Wolf, successors to Magloire Belanger, manufacturers of lumbermen's tools; and Cairns E. Smith & Company (Cairns Smith and Chas. L. Gray, successors to Chas. L. Gray & Company), general store.

The lumbering days were apparently over by 1893. Only one general store was listed, that of J. R. McLeod.

1905, tri-weekly mail stage to *St. Ignace*, 11 miles from *Rexton*, the nearest rail approach. L. A. Sweet, Postmaster; Henry Drosha, Geo. Ross, and L. A. Sweet, fishermen; Peter Goudreau, grocer and fisherman; and G. C. Sweet, saw-mill.

In 1909, the settlement took on the look of a mercantile and resort center, although several fishermen remained there. In that year, L. A. Sweet, Postmaster; Jos. Bellant & Son, fishermen; David L. Beveridge, meats; Mrs. Mollie Demsha, dressmaker; W. M. Demsha, justice; Peter Goudreau, grocer; Mrs. Ethel McLeod, milliner; Mrs. J. R. McLeod, hotel; W. M. Ogle, blacksmith; Prout & Shampine, fishermen and lumber; B. V. Weatherwax, lumberman; Mrs. M. Wheelock, teacher. Some of the fishermen were Gustaf Holm, Chas. McPhail, and D. Maugh.

During the years the population remained about the same, averaging about 75 permanent residents. In 1915, Mr. Sweet was still Postmaster and had most of the industry in town, except for fishing, in which he also kept his hand. He ran a saw and shingle mill and a grocery store in addition to the Postmaster. Jos.

Bellant & Son, fishermen; along with Leo Bellant, P. Kewandeway (Indian) and Prout & Shampine; Mrs. J. McLeod still operated the hotel.

1918 saw the first beginnings of the area as a summer resort. In that year C. B. Kinyon & Son are listed as "summer resort" and Mrs. McPhail opened another hotel, in addition to Mrs. Sweet's. A few new fishermen, probably sons of the old-timers, were listed Bellant and Nelson Bellant, Wm. Prout, Fred Shampine, and Heiberg & Griechehammer were additions to the fishermen. L. A. Sweet kept on as Postmaster, lumberman, etc.

Today the area is built up with summer homes; an occasional fish net can be seen in the area, but fishing on the Great Lakes has come to almost a stand still in 1971. There is a post office located in the front part of a house (1971), but there is no lumbering or commercial activity except tourism. There is a motel, restaurant, and another business place that was closed along US-2 in 1971.

FIBORN QUARRY—Compounded from names of W. F. Fitch and Chas. S. Osborne, former Michigan Governor, promoters of the quarry. 1910, on the Duluth, Southshore & Atlantic Railroad, Hendricks Township, 13 miles west of *Trout Lake*.

1927, population 75. Herbert Ames, justice; and The Fiborn Limestone Company, quarry and general store.

GARNET—This was the railroad name for the one-time lumbering center. The postal name was *Welch*. Between 1897 and 1900, the village reached a population of 500, and as late as 1938, a small shingle mill operated here.

1905, population 400. On the Soo Line Railroad, Hendricks Township, 42 miles northwest of *St. Ignace*, and 15 miles east of *Engadine*. G. A. Donaldson, Postmaster and general store; Mrs. John Coleman, dry goods; Andrew Anderson, mill wright; Mrs. John Graham, boarding house; Louise Graunstadt, teacher; John Hanson, harnessmaker; W. R. Hudson, notary; Hudson & Donaldson, saw and planing mill; A. B. Lenhart, railroad agent; D. McInnis, hotel; James Nickel, saloon; Elizabeth Ranson, teacher; R. W. Spring, justice; and W. H. Tucker, physician.

1910, population 350. Wm. R. Hudson, Postmaster; Hudson Lumber Company, saw and planing mills; Wm. R. Hudson, supervisor, and Dr. Tucker.

1915, population 150. Located in Hudson Township. Telephone. W. N. McLeod, Postmaster; H. P. Blair, railroad agent, D. N. McLeod, saw and planing mill.

There was still considerable logging and related industries at *Garnet* at the end of World War II. The McLeod Lumber Company still had their mills here, along with E. C. Stickler & Company, and the Wellman & Aldridge Company manufactured handles for axes, hammers, shovels, etc.

Even today, 1972, *Garnet* has kept on as a community, although it is practically a ghost town compared to the days at the turn-of-the-century. It has a new post office, a small wood frame building, a Baptist church, three or four houses, and a small sawmill operating on Garnet Lake. It is located on H-40, a new designation for primary county routes being tried by the State Highway Department. Perhaps increased traffic on the blacktop road will revive *Garnet* and its future may still lie in the tourist trade. Only time will tell.

GILCHRIST—Walter Burton was the first Postmaster on September 26, 1879. The post office was closed from June, 1883, to June 1888, and again until October, 1891. Reopened on November 26, 1906.

Was named for John Gilchrist, an early land owner.

In 1905, listed as a station on the Minneapolis St. Paul & Sault Ste. Marie Railroad, 18 miles west of *Trout Lake*, mail to *Naubinway*. Located in Garfield Township.

By 1909 the tiny hamlet was being promoted as a future village by F. Lowen, who was then Postmaster, railroad, and express agent. Lowen advertised as *"Agent for the Town Site of Gilchrist."* In that year Charlotte Chambers was school teacher, and Adam Houghton operated the hotel. There were about 50 residents.

By 1915 the struggling village had a stage twice daily to *Naubinway*, a few miles south on Lake Michigan. B. Lowen, Postmaster; A. B. Klice, Lumber Company, sawmill; George Mahn, general store; and A. F. Turner, general store. There were 60 people living here.

In 1917, things remained about the same. E. E. Howe was the new Postmaster. Other listings for that year were W. P. Austin, railroad and express agent; Mrs. A. Houghton, grocer; A. P. Houghton, cigars; and the A. B. Klice Lumber.

By 1927, 10 years later, the population had increased another 10 people, making a total of 70 residents. Now located 10 miles east of *Engadine*, on the Soo Line. Daily stage to *Naubinway*. The post office had been discontinued and the mailing address was *Naubinway*. R. E. Corey, grocery, was the only business listing.

Today the former hamlet is located on H-40 between *Engadine* and *Garnet*. There isn't much left to show it was at one-time a village. There are four or five summer cabins and one tiny store building that looks as though it had been vacant for many years.

GOULD CITY—This village was founded in 1886 by Sam Stiles, who was a lumberman and also opened a grocery store here.

The few remaining residents of *Gould City* probably do not consider their town a ghost town, but compared to the lumbering days of the 1880s it is only a ghost of its former self. By-passed by Highway US-2, which is heavily traveled by tourists during the summer months, a small amount of pulpwood cutting is the only industry.

The post office was established in 1888, when Adolph Highstone became the first Postmaster. It was named after a Gould, said to be the first commercial fisherman on the northern Lake Michigan shore.

In 1893, a post office in Preston Township, on the Soo Line Railroad, 70 miles north of *St. Ignace*. F.W. Robinson, Postmaster; Bovee-Robinson & Company, general store and wholesale cedar; Michael Cassidy, and James Healy, justices; Quirk Brothers & Furman, general store; W. Statts, shingle mill; and Dr. J.W. Summers, druggist.

By 1905 the tiny village was in full swing, with extensive lumbering operations in the area, two churches, Catholic and Presbyterian, two hotels and two saloons, two general stores, sawmills, etc.

Although not a complete ghost town, *Gould City* is only a shadow of what it once was. This picture was taken of the main street in the 1930s. Most of the buildings are gone today.   Photo by Roy L. Dodge (1971)

In that year Frank W. Robinson, Postmaster; Michael Cassidy, barber; Theopilus Grenine, physician; J. C. Helay, notions; A.D. Kell, shingle mill (2 miles east); Roderick Lyman, hotel and saloon; John A. McDonald, blacksmith; A. McEachern, cedar; Charles May, hotel; Mrs. Clara Parker, general store; Robinson & Freeman, general store and sawmill; J. W. Saunders, doctor; Geo. Schram, blacksmith; Simmons Manufacturing Company, hardwood lumber; W. R. Voight, railroad agent; W. F. Wiebel, jeweler; and A. H. Wilson, saloon.

There were only a few changes in business in 1910. F. H. Freeman was Postmaster; other changes were Wm. Lyman, hotel and saloon; Lyman & Ferguson Company, general store; John A. McDonald, blacksmith; and Benjamin Wilson, barber. Others remained the same.

During the years the population hovered at around 200 permanent residents, plus woods workers. 1915, telephone. Wilson Newton, Postmaster; Wm. Bowman, grocery; Eli Cook, jeweler; Peter Cummings, harness maker; J. C. Healy, notions; Wm. Lyman, hotel; Lyman & Ferguson Company, general store; A. McEachern, cedar; Charles May, hotel; Mrs. Clara Parker, general store; and Harry Sotter, sawmill.

Things remained the same in *Gould City* through the 1930s, with hemlock and hardwood timber the main industry of the area.

Today many of the old weathered buildings remain standing and several are occupied by businesses. A Standard gasoline station and an "agate shop" are on US-2 where the gravel road leads south to *Gould City*. The old Presbyterian Church is still in use, but in 1971 the Catholic Church was nearly razed and is being torn down. McNeil's Bar now occupies what looks to be one of the old hotels. Some of the old places were destroyed by fire in 1929, including the old MacBee building, and the business block that contained the J. C. Healy notions, grocery store, the old William Lyman Hotel, and the Lyman & Ferguson Company general store. Today only the post office stands on the site.

Mrs. Parker's old store and dry goods is now the I.O.O.F. Hall, and the Charles May hotel is the McNeil Bar. May was at one time Michigan State Representative from the area.

George Judson, of *Gould City*, said Harry Salter's sawmill was across the tracks from the depot. Only the tracks of the siding remain. The mill was also once operated by a man named Pixley, he said. *"There was a livery stable in town atone time owned by William Bowman,"* Judson said. *"He also ran a sort of taxi service along with it."*

The last street in the village is now vacant and the one-time roadway grown up to weeds. At one time this was lined with houses. One street has eight old houses, and most of them are vacant. (Much of the information for this town was furnished by Mrs. H. L. Yale, of *Gould City*, in 1971).

GREENE—In 1910, a spur or station on the Duluth, South Shore & Atlantic Railroad, a about 1 mile above *Moran*. Mail *Allenville*.

GREYLOCK—1910, mail *Engadine*. On the Soo Line Railroad, about 1½ miles east of *Engadine*.

GROSCAP—pronounced "grow cap," means "great elevation." Originally was called *St. Helena*. An island by this name lies 2 miles off shore in Lake Michigan. The island was used in early days to supply ships with wood fuel and supplies. In 1850, Archie and Wilson Newton set up a shipping and fishing business and the community thrived for more than 30 years. James Blanchard was the first Postmaster in December of 1892.

In 1905, described as population 225. On shore of Lake Michigan, and in Moran Township, 8 miles west of *St. Ignace*. Mail tri-weekly. Alfred A. Corp, Postmaster and fisherman. (The Moran Township Historical Society has erected a memorial plaque near the site on US-2). Some of the fishermen listed in 1905 were John Boleyn, Alfred A. Corp, Ambrose Corp, L. Gustofson, Louis St. Andrew. Other listings were: Joseph Boleyn, constable; John Bourisan, carpenter; William Bryce, cattle and grain; Roy Clay, sawmill; Ed J. Kachapelle, grocery; and John St. Louis, hotel.

1910, population 240. Alfred Corp, Postmaster. Business listings the same.

The only change in the business directory for 1915 was Amelia A. Corp, Postmistress. Tri-weekly mail. 1917, remained the same. No postmaster listed for that year.

HASLEMERE—1910, a station on the Soo Line Railroad, mail *Engadine*. Located about 1 mile west of *Engadine*.

HUNTSPUR—Was located on the Soo Line Railroad, in Newton Township, near the west Mackinac County line.

In 1893, population 100. Postal telegraph. McDonald & Company, lumbermen; George Pankratz, drugs; and Whitney, Tuttle & Smith, sawmill.

1905, population 150. Nineteen miles northeast of *Manistique*, on the Soo Line. Samuel Stites, Postmaster, dry goods and groceries; and J.W. Wilson, saloon.

1910, population 100. W. U. Stites, Postmaster and general store, and Wilson, saloon.

GROS CAP AND ST. HELENA ISLAND

French fishermen who came to Gros Cap (on the shore below) early last century also participated in its offshore settlement. St. Helena Island, where ships obtained wood fuel and other supplies. There in 1850, Archie and Wilson Newton set up a fishing and shipping business. The community thrived for more than 30 years.

MICHIGAN HISTORICAL COMMISSION REGISTERED LOCAL SITE NO. 22

Erected by the Township of Moran, 1962
Approved by the
Michilimackinac Historical Society

This plaque located along US-2 highway tells the story of *Gros Cap*, another ghost town in the Upper Peninsula.   Photo by Roy L. Dodge (1971)

In 1915, the Schoolcraft Land & Improvement Company had taken over operations here. Guy D. Welton was Postmaster, general store, logs, cedar products, etc; Wincell L. Vanatta, mill and box factory, was the only other business listing.

Mrs. H. L. Yale of *Gould City* said, *"All that's left are a few chimneys and two flowing wells and the site is probably now property of the Inland Lime & Stone Company."* H. Rindy was the first Postmaster on October 9, 1889. Post office discontinued in 1937.

––––––––

ISLINGTON—listed as a post office in 1927. Not listed after 1956.

––––––––

JACOB CITY—The original name of *Moran*. (See *Moran*) Named for the president of the German Land Company, of *Detroit*, a colonization scheme made up of 27 investors. Mr. Jacob was accused of fraud and ousted from the company in 1883. The company then borrowed money from W. B. Moran, a member of the company, and renamed the village after him.

––––––––

JOHNSON'S—see *OZARK*

––––––––

KENNEDY—Not a ghost town. Name changed to *Engadine*. Originally platted by the Robert Dollar Lumber Company in 1889. In 1893 name changed to *Engadine* for a province in Switzerland of that name.

––––––––

KENNETH—This was originally named Johnson and was renamed *Kenneth* by William Ross, an early lumberman, to honor his son, Kenneth Ross.

1905, a post office on the D. S. S. & A. Railroad, 22 miles north of *St. Ignace*.

1910, population 40, in Moran Township, 7 miles southeast of *Trout Lake*. J. D. Leonard, Postmaster; W. J. Ross, general store (the William Ross mentioned above); and Leonard & Murray, sawmill.

1915, population listed at 165. J. D. Leonard, Postmaster. There was extensive lumbering activity. Some companies listed that year were: Beveridge Cedar Company, saw and shingle mill; Central Paper Company, sawmill and pulp wood; in addition to the Leonard & Murray mill, and Jerry Taylor, general store.

1917, population dropped to 75. Telephone connection. No Postmaster listed. Same lumber mills listed as 1915, and W. J. Ross & Son, grocers; Jerry Taylor, general store.

––––––––

LAKESIDE—1910, send mail to *Cedarville.*

––––––––

LES CHENAUX—Today is a scenic resort center, pronounced "lay-she-no," meaning the channels. In 1887, a newly established post office in Marquette township, 22 miles northeast of *St. Ignace*. Population 50. Mail by special supply. W. A. Patrick, Postmaster.

1905, population 50. Daily mail. R. S. Melchers, Postmaster, and Islington Hotel. Daily mail.

Not a ghost town. Was and still is a resort on one of 35 islands in Lake Huron off the shore of the county, northeast of *St. Ignace.*

LEWIS—Was first named *Lewis* in 1891. The postal name is *Caffey*. Named for Wm. N. Caffey, first Postmaster in 1899 and the office was closed in 1909. Post office re-opened in June of 1913, with W. N. Caffey as Postmaster. All that remains is the faded railroad sign *CAFFEY* and the old cemetery.

1905, a station on the Soo Line Railroad, 8 miles west of *Trout Lake*, its post office. Located about 1 mile east of *Rexton.*

McKESSON—Was a post office October 14, 1916. Listed as a post office in 1927 but not in 1932.

MEADS QUARRY—1910, on the Soo Line Railroad, about ½ mile due west of *Hendricks Quarry*. Mail to *Garnet.*

MILLECOQUINS—On the Soo Line, about 1½ miles northwest of *Naubinway*. Designated on 1969 highway maps, near *Engadine*, but nothing remains.

MYER—1910, a summer post office (also in 1927), in Cedar Township, RFD *Cedarville.*

MORAN—First named *Jacob City*, settled in 1881. In 1887, located in Brevoort Township, 10 miles north of *St. Ignace*. Postal name is *Moran.*

In 1893, called *Moran*, and still is. Population 100. Andrew Langstaff Postmaster and builder; William J. Albrecht, justice; George Appleford, blacksmith and wagonmaker; Frank Becker, justice; Sam Burton, justice; Charles Cowden, builder; S. Fell, railroad agent; David Harris, justice; J. F. Hess, superintendent of Martel Furnace company, general store and charcoal manufacturers; and Albert A. Smith, coroner and justice.

The 1905 Michigan Gazetteer & Business Directory mistakenly says *"Name changed to Allenville,"* but local historians say this isn't so. It is more likely that the post office was discontinued for some years. The 1905 Michigan Legislative Manual doesn't list *Moran* as a post office for 1905 but it is listed as a railroad station on railroad time tables for that year. The post office was closed from 1904 until 1912, and was a post office in 1970.

Locted near *Moran* is one of few active remaining fire towers in Michigan. The first fire tower was a platform in a pine tree at *Raco* near *Sault Ste. Marie.* Today observation planes have replaced most of the lookout towers for this purpose.   Photo by Roy L. Dodge (1971)

The town revived again, and in 1915 had a population of 200. Telephone. C. P. Becker, Postmaster and railroad agent; S. Christenson, and S. W. Peacock each had general stores; and Charles Sackweh, general store.

In 1917, H. H. Winters, Postmaster; C. P. Becker, railroad agent, F. M. Becker, blacksmith; Christenson and Sackweh still operated general stores. Other new listings were: John E. Lipnitz, hardware; Murray Brothers, sawmill; Standart Post & Tie Company; and R. A. Wartella, general store.

By 1927, 10 years later, the town was booming. A bus ran daily to *St. Ignace* and *Manistique*. Had Catholic, Episcopal and Lutheran churches, hotel, etc. In that year Louise B. Quay was Postmaster; Conrad Becker, dairy farm; Frank Becker, autos and gasoline station; the Burma Mercantile Company, Carl North, manager, general store, and meats; Mrs. Lillian Norway, proprietor of Litzner's Inn Hotel; Frank Luepnitz, garage; Phillip Luepnitz, proprietor; Aloysius J. Roggenbuck, oil station; Charles Sackweh, general store; August Schimmelphfennig, carpenter; Robert Sikerasy, justice; Standard Oil Company; Texaco Oil Company; Quay Brothers, managers; L. E. Topps, barber, billiards and restaurant; Wing & Becker, radio equipment.

Sometime during the 1930s and 1940s the wheels of industry stopped rolling in *Moran*, alias *Jacob City*, and one by one most of the former business building were deserted. Many of the old two-story weathered false-front buildings along the two main streets of town, unpainted and empty. None of the mills remain along the railroad tracks that run parallel with County Road 123, today a short-cut for travelers between M-28 and the new divided US-2 Highway from *St. Ignace* to *Sault Ste. Marie*. The old depot and railroad station has long since disappeared and the buzz of activity of the logging days has come to a dead stop.

One of the few active remaining steel fire towers of the Department of Natural Resources still stands near *Moran* (1970), one for the old buildings on the north side of town had opened a drive-in pasty shop, and some ladies were holding a continuous used clothing and rummage sale in one of the abandoned stores. There are still one or two gasoline stations open, and perhaps one or two stores, but old *Jacob City* is gone, and *Moran*, which folded for 10 years at the turn-of-the-century, is once more a ghost town. Only the post office and a few residents remain to show it was once a town.

———

NERO—1910, a station on the railroad between *St. Ignace* and *Allenville*.

204

NOGI—Founded by W. E. Johnson of the Central Paper Company, of *Muskegon*, in 1905. Was named for Count Maresuke Nogi, a Japanese hero in the Russo-Japanese War. *Nogi* lasted for about 20 years until destroyed by forest fires. Located between *Greene* and *Kenneth* along the railroad.

———

ORVILLE—See *Scott's Point* for history.

———

OZARK—Settled in 1875. From French, Aux Arks, meaning "at the bend." 1887, the post office for a station known as *Johnson's* on the D. M. & M. Railroad, in northern part of Mackinac County, 23 miles from *St. Ignace*. Is a lumbering place only, and 400 men are employed in the woods. Daily mail. James F. Hess, Postmaster and superintendent Martel Furnace Company, Mackinaw Lumber Company, Frederick Mahl, blacksmith; Martel Furnace Company, general store and charcoal kilns; Rady Brothers, lumbermen.

1893, a village on the D. S. S. & A. Railway, in Moran Township, 23 miles northwest of *St. Ignace*. "Ships lumber and charcoal. Population 200. Daily mail. James F. Hess, Postmaster". Other business listings for that year were: J. F. Ames, carpenter; William Butchart, blacksmith; Albert Eckert, clerk; James F. Hess, railroad agent and superintendent Martel Furnace Company (charcoal kilns); Gretta Hoban, music teacher; Martel Furnace Company, general store and charcoal; David Mitchell, charcoal burner; George Moore, blacksmith; Peter Slehuber, stone mason; and Alex Swanson, charcoal burner.

1905—population 60. Telephone. James A. Hough, Postmaster, general store, tan bark (used for tanning hides), ties, posts and shingles.

By 1910 it is listed as a "flag stop" on the railroad. (A flag stop was a station with no scheduled stops for the train. If a passenger wanted to board a train, he stood by the tracks until the train came into sight, then flagged him down). Although the station was inactive, the post office continued with Hough as Postmaster and manager of the Ozark Cedar & Lumber Company as well as his own enterprises of general store, lumber, shingles, etc. In 1910 the Ozark Quarry Company was also doing business in the area.

Things remained about the same, business-wise, in 1915. Hough expanded his enterprise by adding furniture to the line in his general store, and also ran the quarry. J. W. Dell, sawmill; and The Grimmer Land Company was advertised.

A small boom hit the town in the 1920s, and in 1927 the population was listed at 200. Irene A. Dell, Postmaster; John C. Burgess, repair and blacksmith; Clarence B. Dell, general store; Fiborn Limestone Company, Charles B. Mann, superintendent; C. E. Hough, lands and timber; Jackson & Tindle, loggers; Nicholas Koski, produce; Samuel D. Lovegrove, livestock; and Mrs. George Mahl, produce.

To recoin an old phrase, all good things come to an end, as did *Ozark*, which isn't designated on most maps today.

The post office closed on August 12, 1966. Christine E. Clark was Postmistress from 1952 until the last day cover was issued.

———

PALMS—Was named in 1882 for a *Detroit* financier connected with the D. M. & M. Railroad, Francis Palms. When the post office opened in 1884, it was named *Pines*, with Charles E. Switzer the first Postmaster. The post office closed May 17, 1897.

———

PENNSYLVANIA—1910, mail *Cedarville*.

———

PERRONS—Was a flag stop on the Soo Line, ½ mile west of *Engadine*.

———

PIKE LAKE—Often confused with *Pike Lake Junction*, 3½ miles north. The name was first given as *Bryan* (also see *Bryan*). Founded in 1905-06 as the railroad headquarters for the *Escanaba* lumber company and named for Wm. P. Bryan, logging foreman.

C. W. McEwen was the first Postmaster in June of 1906. The post office name was changed to *Pike Lake* on November 17,1914.

In 1915, described as in Newton Township, on the M. & S. Railroad. Richard B. Stack, Postmaster; L. C. Eagle, express and telegraph agent; and Stack Lumber & Land Company. Population 200.

The post office closed in August of 1920, after the timber in the area was exhausted. Mail to *Viola*.

By 1930 most of the buildings had fallen down or been removed. Today the site is overgrown with weeds and brush and nothing remains.

———

PINES—(also known as *Palms*). 1893, a station on the Soo Line, in Moran Township. R. Fischer, Postmaster, and S. Fell, railroad and express agent.

1905, a discontinued post office. Send mail to *Ozark*.

———

POINTE LA BARBE—French for "point of the barber." This was a landing place near the present day Mackinac Bridge adjoining a large Indian and fur-trading center of the 17th century. Here, it is said, traders and trappers were "barbered" before proceeding to trading headquarters after their months or years in the back lands gathering peltries. An ancient Indian cemetery, now called *Gros Cap* or Moran Township cemetery, remains cared for near the highway in this area, and a historical plaque has been erected here by the Moran Township Historical Society.

_____

PRENTIS BAY—Listed in the 1893 Michigan Gazetteer as on the shore of Lake Huron, bordering on Chippewa County. Settled in 1872. Population 50. Mail tri-weekly. William A. Terry, justice of peace.

Apparently never developed as a village. In 1905, mail to *Stalwart*.

_____

RAPINVILLE—1887, a newly established post office in Garfield Township . Ship from *Naubinway*, 10 miles distant. Mail weekly. Edmund A. Rapin (for whom the town was named), Postmaster.

For a short time, about 1905, a weekly mail was received, but the place never developed into a village. In 1906, Rapin "gave up the ghost" and the post office was discontinued.

The settlement is designated on 1905 maps, just south of *Donald* and near *Milakoki Lake*.

_____

REAVIE—Listed in 1910 as on the Soo Line Railroad, mail to *St. Ignace*.

_____

REX—The railroad name for *Rexton*. See *Rexton*.

_____

REXTON—Settled as a lumbering village in 1895 by the D. N. McLeod Lumber Company and is said to have been named by them in honor of the King of England.

In the early 1900s was a booming lumbering town, with a hotel, shingle mill, sawmill, several stores, and three saloons. In 1905, population 200. On the Soo Line, Hendricks Township. George W. Warner, Postmaster, railroad and express agent; J. A. Browning, hotel; Cedar River Land Company, shingle mill; Cross & Cogswell, sawmill; McAuley & Strouble, general store; Ed. Massey, saloon; Jim Nickle, saloon; William Sommerville, general store; G. R. Tucker, saloon.

Additions to the 1909 business listings were: D. McLeod & Company, general store and shingle mill; J. King, hotel; and Fred Wood, saloon. Others remained the same.

Rex, or *Rexton*, which was the postal name, reached its peak in 1915 with 400 population. G. W. Warner, Postmaster and grocery; Dr. Daniel Ammerman; Augulin Brothers, hotel; William Cocian, hotel; Peter Corier, livery; J. W. Gilligan, general store; Dr. Godfrey; Peter Gondreau, general store; H. C. Griffin, restaurant; Christ Hansen, sawmill; Lloyd M. Prentice, optometrist. Samuel King and Charles Maddox were blacksmiths.

In 1927 the business directory listed J. Alfred as Postmaster. Daily bus to *St. Ignace, Manistique* and *Escanaba*. William Augulin, hotel; A. M. Coplan, general store; Dernsha Brothers, garage; Grant Heminger, hotel; Jay Jones, soft drinks; John McCullough, justice; Charles W. Maddox, livery and garage; Fred Miller, general store; E. J. Perreard, express agent; and Daniel Stein, furs and tallow.

A few houses still stand in *Rexton*, formerly on US-2 which is today known as County Highway H-40. It has a church and one gasoline station. The four or five old buildings that were at one time businesses are all closed and boarded up. The post office closed September 7, 1961 and *Rexton* is now RFD *Trout Lake*.

SAND BAY—Listed in 1910. On Bois Blanc island. E. H. Stafford had a sawmill and general store here. Post office opened November 12, 1909 and lasted only a short time.

SCOTTS POINT—Originally named *Orville*. Was located on Lake Michigan, in Newton Township, and was an early fishing village. In 1940 the "Guide to Michigan, The Wolverine State" described the deserted village as, *"Along the smooth sweep of sandy beach are forlorn remainders of another day, dilapidated icehouse, two stripped fishing tugs, broken net reels, and piles that were once foundations for net houses and docks."*

Mrs. H. L. Yale, of *Gould City*, said there are apparent foundations remaining today (1971), and the site is now a township park. At one time the village had wide streets and many buildings, she said.

In 1887 was *Orville*. A settlement and post office on the weekly mail line between *St. Ignace* and *Manistique*, Newton Township, 40 miles by water from *St. Ignace*. *"A new dock has recently been completed and steamboats call here during navigation . . . Population 100. Settled in 1876. Has weekly mail by stage from St. Ignace. Fare $3.00."* John Davenport, Postmaster; Lambert Bunnell, justice; J. Byers, constable; John Cassidy, blacksmith; James C. Healy, A. McEachern, and John McNaugle, justices of peace; Newton Brothers, fish dealers and general store; M. Patoin, blacksmith; and Charles Shaw, constable.

1893, ten miles from *Gould City*. Population 150. Mail tri-weekly. A. J. Freeman, grocer; Newton Brothers, general store and fish; and Charles Tarrien, cooper (barrel maker). (Nearly every fishing village had a cooper, as fish were packed in barrels between layers of salt.)

By 1905 the village was apparently deserted, and only one or two fishermen remained. Post office discontinued October 21, 1897. Send mail to *Gould City*.

SEABROOK—Was a short lived post office in the 1880s, located about 8 miles southeast of *McMillan*, in Portage Township.

1887, a discontinued post office. Mail to *McMillan*. The former site of this place is now in Luce County.

SIMMONS—G. Harold Earle, of the Wisconsin Land and Lumber Company, said that the town of *Simmons* was established in 1902, south of *Gould City*. There was a sawmill there, dry kilns, lumber yard, boarding house for workers, general store, a clubhouse, and quite a number of dwellings, he said. The town was named after Mr. Simmons, the founder of the Simmons Manufacturing Company in *Kenosha*, Wisconsin, and was operated by the Simmons Company under the management of a man named McClellan. Lumber from the mills was used in the manufacture of furniture in *Kenosha* from 1902 until 1907, when the entire property, including the railroad connecting with the Soo Line at *Bovee*, was acquired by the Wisconsin Land & Lumber Comapny.

In 1905, described as a post office in Mackinac County, 8 miles south of *Gould City*. Mail daily.

1910, population 35. In Newton Township, 8 miles from *Bovee*. Stage twice daily to *Gould City*, fare 50 cents. James P. Struble, Postmaster and lumber inspector; and Simmons Lumber Company.

Post office discontinued February 15, 1911.

STATTS SPURR—Shown on 1905 maps on the Soo Line, about one-half mile west of *Haslemere*, and east of *Gould City*.

VINE—Designated on 1905 maps as the post office at *Corrine Village*.

VIOLA—Settled in 1890, also called *Yatton*. (Also see *Corinne*) The post office at *Corrine Village*, Newton Township, on the Soo Line, 8 miles west of *Engadine*. Population 250. H. V. Pierce, Postmaster, general store and shingles; Michael Cassidy, justice; Chicago Lumber Company, general store; A. B. McArthur, constable; McIntyre & Landers, sawmill; D. Potvin, saloon; Lyman Smith, justice; John Stevens, hotel; and Elisha M. White, justice.

1905, population given as 100. W. J. Fessant, Postmaster; Mr. Baker, express agent; Neil Carmichael, land looker; J. H. Collier, livery; William Hearn, boarding house; Lyman-Rod & Company, general store; D. McArthur, saloon; A. McEachern, cedar; George Mauders, general store; Viola Lumber Company, sawmills; Walter S. Wilson, saloon.

In 1910, about the same. W. J. Fessant, Postmaster, Corrine Supply Company, general store; D. McArthur, saloon; Robert Perry, hotel; Viola Lumber Company; and Mrs. Walter S. Wilson, saloon.

1915, population 75. Telephone. Mrs. Minnie Wilson, Postmistress; Corrine Supply Company, general store; L. Engil, express agent; A. J. Strom, hotel; Dr. C. B. Toms, physician; and Viola Lumber Company

1918, population 100. Only three listings for that year: Mrs. M. Wilson, Postmistress; Corrine Supply Company, general store; A. J. Strom, hotel; and Dr. C. B. Toms.

1927, A. J. Strom, Postmaster; Corrine Supply Company, Mrs. Minnie Wilson, proprietor; and Dr. C. B. Toms.

Post office was discontinued between May 1941 and 1947.

WALKER'S POINT—Post office established on February 21, 1899. 1905, population 50. On Bois Blanc Island, 9 miles northeast of *Cheboygan*, from which it receives semi-weekly mail. Fannie K. Hamilton, Postmistress.

1910, population 125. Amelia A. Poiner, Postmistress and Arthur Betts, sawmill.

1915, population 80. Fannie E. Hamilton, Postmistress and Arthur J. Betts, sawmill.

1917, population 80. Silas Miller, sawmill; George M. Nelson, general contractor and real estate; Fred Roberts, boat line; and Richard H. Vosper, lumber.

In 1927 there were no business places listed. Send mail to *Cheboygan*.

WELCH—Located between *Gilchrist* and *Rexton*. *Garnet* was the post office at this settlement or siding in Hendricks Township. 1905, *Welch* listed as population 400. On the Soo Line. G. A. Donaldson, Postmaster; Andrew Anderson, mill wright; Mrs. John Coleman, dry goods; J. G. Donaldson, general store; Mrs. John Graham, boarding house; Louise Graunstadt, teacher; John Hanson, harnessmaker; W. R. Hudson, notary; Hudson & Donaldson, saw and planing mill; A. B. Lenhart, railroad agent; D. Mc Innis, hotel; James Nickel, saloon; Elizabeth Ransom, teacher; R. W. Spring, justice; and W. H. Tucker, physician.

1904, name changed to *Garnet*.

WILMAN—Listed in 1910 Rand-McNally Atlas. Mail to *Curtis*.

WILWIN—Walter Romig, of *Grosse Pointe*, in his book "Michigan Place Names," said Frank Chesbrough built a sawmill here in 1915 and platted the village in 1916. It was named for his two sons, Will and Erwin. Alfred King was appointed Postmaster on October 9, 1916, but declined, so storekeeper Seward M. Shaw took office on July 11, 1917, and operated until 1927. In that year, listed as a discontinued post office, on the Soo Line, Hendricks Township, 6 miles from *Trout Lake*. Send mail to *Trout Lake*, Wilwin Lumber Company and Young Lumber Company, lumber manufacturers. Today it is a ghost town.

───────

YATTON—Was another name for *Viola*, the post office for *Corrine*. Shown on 1905 maps as *"Viola or Yatton."*

Chapter Fifteen

MARQUETTE COUNTY

Marquette County was named in honor of Father Marquette, the Jesuit missionary. The county was laid out in 1843 and attached to Houghton County until 1846. It was reorganized in 1848, and the County Government organized in 1851. The city of *Marquette* is the county seat.

As are most Upper Peninsula counties, Marquette County is made up of many national origins, including French, Finnish, Irish, Canadian, German, Italian, Polish, Swedish and Welsh.

Early history has been amply recorded, and the Peter White Public Library, in *Marquette*, is regarded as the finest library in the Upper Peninsula, with more than 100,000 volumes. The J. M. Longyear Research Library of the Marquette County Historical Society is also the finest library of this type on Lake Superior.

The mining of iron ore has always been the main industry in the county, with lumbering second, but production declined in the 1960s and many people were unemployed. Today more modern methods of mining have been developed and, with the approval of the Tilden Mine project, which includes the construction of a dam about 6 miles up the Middle Branch of the Escanaba River to create a 14,000 acre impoundment, called the Greenwood Reservoir, for use in processing low-grade iron ore, the economy of Marquette County is expecting a boom unheralded in its history from both the $200 million construction cost of the project, with a $38 million payroll, plus the new pelletizing plant of the company, and the benefit to the tourist industry resulting from the attraction of the huge reservoir.

Marquette County is one of only three Upper Peninsula counties with an increase in population, instead of a decrease, in the past decade, 1960-70. The population increased during this period from 56,154 in 1960 to 64,686 in 1970.

In 1867, the Michigan Supreme Court ruled against the legislature and in favor of the citizens of Marquette County after some of the most valuable mining property in the county and the city of *Ishpeming* had been placed in a new county, named Washington. The original Marquette boundaries were re-established and Michigan lost Washington as a county name.

GOLD AND SILVER MINES OF MARQUETTE COUNTY

Gold and silver mines are mentioned in the *Ishpeming* area in 1887, and it was reported that mines were being worked with good prospects of success.

The Ropes Gold Mine, 4 miles from *Deer Lake* (north of *Ishpeming*), was the largest gold mine in the state from 1883 to 1897. The mine produced gold bullion valued at $647,902. In 1940 the buildings and trestle work of the mines were still standing, surrounded by piles of ore-bearing quartz. When the price of gold was increased in the 1930s, many prospectors worked the tailings at the old mine and made good wages.

About 9 miles from the Ropes Mine was the Barnes-Hecker Mine, where the disaster of November, 1926 occurred. Here 52 men were trapped 1,000 feet below the ground. The bodies were never recovered and the company sealed the shaft and moved the machinery to another location, leaving the miners entombed in the mine.

About 1½ miles from this mine was the Michigan Gold Mine, discovered in 1888. This mine produced about $90,000 in gold. After it was abandoned, a stock company organized in 1932 and reopened the mine, producing about $6,000 in gold bullion. This attempt to reopen the mine was abandoned in the fall of 1937.

MARQUETTE COUNTY GHOST TOWNS

ALBION MINES—1878, in Marquette Township, about 5 miles south of *Greenwood*. Mail to *Ishpeming*. Not listed in 1905.

ANDERSON—In 1910, on the Munising, Marquette & Southeastern Railroad.

ARNOLD—This place had two names. The railroad name was *Watson* and the postal name *Arnold*, after Ed Arnold of the Mashek Chemical & Iron Company, of *Escanaba*. Henry Arnold was the first Postmaster, June 21, 1909.

1915, population 50. On the Escanaba and Lake Shore Railroad, 26 miles north of *Escanaba*. In Wells Township. Telephone. Henry Arnold, Postmaster and Supervisor; John Klanski, cattle buyer; George M. Mashek, lumber and general store; and Frank Smith, hotel.

1917, remained about the same. Arnold was Postmaster; John Gignare, hotel; Wm. J. Jaeger, real estate; Larson Brothers, logging contractors; and George Mashek, general store, lumber, etc.

1927, population 50. William J. Jaeger, Postmaster and general store; Joseph L. Beaudreau, village clerk; John Bruce, highway commissioner; Matt Katick, billiards; Oscar Kellomenie, justice; Art McLeod, hotel; Ediore Patient, village supervisor; James Rabitallile, soft drinks; Watson Store Company, George M. Mashek, president; William Jaeger, cattle, loggers, lumber, farm machinery and real estate.

Mrs. B. Johnson, of the *Menominee Herald Leader*, said the old tavern has been turned into a youth center. One old general store is now an I. G. A. market with one section left as it was at the turn of the century. Post office discontinued January 6, 1961. The Watson Store, all that remains in the village, is now RFD *Cornell*.

BAGDAD—1910, a station on the D. S. S. & A. Railroad. Mail *Negaunee*. Became a station about 1890. Another stop 1 mile down the track was named *Bagdad Junction*. Was the site of a stone quarry. Now just a sign along the railroad.

BANCROFT—1887, a station on the Marquette Houghton & Ontonagon Railroad, 2 miles west of *Marquette*. Not listed in 1893. In 1860 was the location of the Bancroft Iron Company furnace on the Dead River.

BARNUM—1910, on the D. S. S. & A. Railroad, mail *Ishpeming*. The old Cliff mine shaft still stands near Cliff Street in *Ishpeming*. It is one of the oldest mines in the area and was formerly the Barnum mine.

BARTLEY—A post office by this name was established on November 27, 1905, with Anthony C. Cafferty as Postmaster.

BASIL—1910, on the Duluth South Shore & Atlantic Railroad, mail *Harvey*.

BEACON—1879, a recently established post office, in Michigamme Township. Is also known as *Champion Mine*. Has Catholic church, primary school, and 700 population, mostly miners. R. T. McKay, Postmaster and drugs; William Andrews, meat market; Bigelow, Dunsmore & Company, general store; I. C. Bray, agent for Champion Iron Company; and James Pascoe, Superintendent, Champion Mine.

1887, the post office at *Champion Mine* village, Champion Township. About 2,000 miners are located here. Catholic, Methodist, and Swedish Lutheran churches, a fine hospital, and a town hall. W. J. Gill, Postmaster. Some businesses for that year were: Ed Derie, saloon; Dr. J. Freund; Joseph H. Gill, librarian; Hart Brothers & Company, general store; A. Longborg, shoemaker; Joseph Mitchell, meats; Clifford, Monroe, hospital steward; Miss Mary Beck, teacher; R. Simmons, blacksmith; John Swartz, shoemaker; T. H. Wallace, express agent; and Rev. A. W. Wilson, Methodist.

1893, population 1,000. Simon Kinsman, Postmaster. Isadore Freund, in charge of hospital; had one saloon and a "temperance saloon"; John B. Montgomery, superintendent of schools; Rev. John H. Reynaert, Catholic; C. A. Monroe, Beacon House hotel; and many other business places.

1905, population 1,500. Elizabeth Kinsman, Postmistress Some changes in business directory were: Abbie Coffey, teacher; Rev. James Elford, Methodist; Rev. Father Gerard, Catholic; Mabel Miles, teacher; Kate Sower, teacher; Alice E. Thurston,teacher; and Paul Van Riper, physician.

1909, about the same. Richard Simmons, Postmaster; Robert Fox, Beacon House hotel; Bessie Beatty, teacher; Oliver Iron Mining Company owned the Champion mine. Teachers were: Nellie Feely, Elizabeth Gill, May LaVigne, Nellie McKinney, and Mabel Record. W. Rees, Principal, and F. S. Monical, Superintendent of Schools. Ministers were Rev. Robert Strike, Methodist, and Rev. A. Hassenburg, Catholic.

The mine closed in 1910 and by 1915, population dropped to 600. A stage ran six times daily to *Champion*. Lillian Fish, Postmaster; Beacon House hotel; Dr. Paul VanRiper, hospital doctor; Gideon Marchaid, livery; H. S. Thompson, Assistant Superintendent for Oliver Iron Mining Company; Michael C. Quinn, general store.

Paul Petosky, of *Ishpeming*, said the *Champion* mine closed about 1968 or 1969. Before that it was closed, reopened, and then closed again. At the time it ceased operations it was owned by the North Range Mining Company.

The name of Champion Beach was changed to "Van Riper State Park" in honor of Dr. Paul VanRiper who served so many years in the *Champion* hospital.

Beacon and *Champion* are both designated on 1972 State Highway maps.

————

BEAVER—1879, a station on the Chicago & Northwestern Railway, 48 miles from *Ishpeming*.

————

BECK—Shown on 1905 maps, near *Beacon*.

————

BIRCH—1909, population 600. On the M. & S. E. Railroad, Powell Township, 15 miles northwest of *Marquette*. Telephone. Frank E. Krieg, Postmaster; Charles N. Bottom, physician; and Northern Lumber Company, sawmill and general store.

In 1915 the only change in the business directory was the Lake Independence Lumber Company started a branch operation here.

1917, population 150. Same business listings as 1915.

In 1927, listed as a discontinued post office, RFD *Big Bay*.

Town practically deserted by 1920. There is one building standing today.

BOSTON JUNCTION—1887, on the Marquette Houghton & Ontonagon Railroad, 9 miles west of *Ishpeming*. Not listed in 1893.

―――――

BROWN—Shown on 1905 maps between *Michigamme* and *Champion*.

―――――

BRUCE—Listed as a station on the Marquette Houghton & Ontonagon Railroad in 1879. Six miles from *Marquette*.

Also listed as a station 1887, not listed in 1893.

―――――

BUCKROE—1910, a station on the Munising Marquette & Southeastern Railway, 12 miles from *Marquette*. Mail to *Birch*. Also listed in 1927. Named for its location in the heart of the deer country.

―――――

BURTIS—1910, on the M. M. & S. E. Railroad. Mail to *Big Bay*.

―――――

CARLSHEND—Settled in 1885. In 1905, population 25. Listed as a country post office, on the Munising Railroad, Skandia Township, 20 miles south of *Marquette*. (Shown on 1969 Michigan Highway map). Erickson & Johnson, general store; C. P. Johnson, general store; James McMaster, blacksmith; Manigold Company, grocery and sawmill; and A. Seeman, blacksmith.

In 1910 the population was 100. One business listing had been added in that year, Alfred Sirman, carpenter. C. P. Johnson was Postmaster.

The post office here was established in December of 1894, and from that time until 1934 there were three Postmasters, all named Johnson, Charles P., Harry D., and Gilbert A. Johnson, according to Ernest Rankin of the Marquette Historical Society.

In 1915, there were only two business listings: C. P. Johnson, general store; and Manigold Company, grocers.

In 1927, located on Highway US-41, 11 miles north of *Gwinn*. Had Swedish Mission, Episcopal and Methodist churches. Harry D. Johnson, Postmaster; C. P. Johnson, livestock; Gilbert A. Johnson, general store; Manigold Company, grocery; and the Standard Oil Company were listed.

Carlshend still had a post office in 1970. Was first *Carlslund*, meaning "Carl's land" for Carl Peter Johnson.

―――――

CARP—Was a station on the eastern division of the Marquette Houghton & Ontonagon Railroad, 11 miles from *Marquette*, in 1879. Not a post office. Listed as a station in 1887, not listed in 1893.

216

CARP FURNACE—Listed in 1910 Rand McNally Atlas, on the Munising, Marquette & Southeastern Railroad, mail *Marquette*. Not a post office.

Nick Ilnicky, of the Marquette Historical Society, said the place was founded in 1847, and Peter White was either the first or second Postmaster. Located in Negaunee Township.

———

CASCADE—Listed in 1910 Rand McNally as a station on the Chicago & Northwestern Railroad, mail *Marquette*. In 1878, the location of the Cascade Iron Company who later developed the iron discovery.

———

CASCADE JUNCTION—1879, located at the intersection of the C. & N. W. and the M. H. & O. Railroads, 10 miles from *Ishpeming*.

———

CEDAR BANK—Listed in 1910 Rand McNally Atlas on the Munising, Marquette & Southeastern Railroad, mail *Forsyth*.

———

CHAMPION—Settled in 1868. In 1873, described as a village of 300 inhabitants on the Marquette, Houghton & Ontonagon Railroad, 32 miles west of *Marquette*. The surrounding country is mountainous, but little cultivated. Immense beds of iron ore exist here, and mining and smelting are extensively carried on. In 1871 the *Champion* mine shipped 67,588 tons of ore and 5,994 tons of pig iron. It is the fifth mine in the state in point of production.

L. H. Doty, Postmaster; Champion Mining Company, iron mines and general store; and Champion Furnace Company, blast furnace and general store.

In 1877 the population increased to 600. The blast furnace, owned by the Morgan Iron Company, burned in 1874, and had not been rebuilt at that time. The Keystone mine, just east of *Champion*, had shipped 19,000 tons of ore in the past three years. A Catholic church had been built, and Rev. J. F. Berube was the minister. Christopher A. McRae was Postmaster in 1877, O. H. Chamberlain was principal of the Union School. Rev. J. J. Hodge was the Methodist minister, and the town had several business places, including a saloon, two general stores, meat markets, hotel, boot and shoe stores, etc.

1887, population 300. M. C. Belhumen was Postmaster.

In 1893, located on the Duluth, South Shore & Atlantic and Chicago & Northwestern Railways. A Lutheran and Finnish church was added, making four churches in town. Thomas H. Wallace, Postmaster. Champion was a full-fledged town, with two hotels, grocery, co-op general store; a milliner and a dress shop; two barbers; two livery stables; a restaurant, bakery, meat market; tailor shop, confectionery, saloon, jewelry store; two shoemakers; a photographer; furniture and undertaker; and a hardware.

217

By 1905 the population had reached a peak of 2,500. Had a doctor, George Beech; wagonmaker, hotels, etc.

In 1910, the railroad station for *Beacon*, ¾ of a mile distant, population 700. Thomas Wallace, Postmaster. Business places remained about the same.

Margaret Cronin was Postmistress in 1915. Daniel Belisle, wagonmaker; Margaret Belhumeur, notions; L. J. Cardinal, express agent; Mae Dishno, restaurant; O. H. and N. J. Huber, meats; Jacob Levine, general store; John Mahoney, livery; G. Marchand, livery; Paul Edwin, express agent; and Ralph R. Thomas, furniture. William Derrie, grocery; Charles Rohl, jewelry.

1927, population 800. Was served by three railroads, the C. M. & St. P.; Chicago & Northwestern; and the Duluth South Shore & Atlantic. A moving picture theater had been added. Other business listings were: Mrs. Kate Baupied, restaurant; Oscar J. Bennon, garage; Louis J. Cardinal, express agent; Champion Gravel Company, Phillip B. Spear, President; George Metherall ran the theater; Rev. W. Dapper, Catholic; Charies A. Herngren, furniture; Gust Kulin, justice; Gideon Marchaud, livery; John Nelson, confectionery; August Oldgren, blacksmith and wagonmaker; Carl H. Rohl, justice; Mrs. Lars Sundlie, grocery; and Joseph Verville, general store.

Champion is still designated on State Highway maps and is still a populated village, located on Highway M-28. There are about 30 old houses here, a large store called the "Village Market"; the old depot, on the Soo Line, is still standing, but doesn't have a need for five stages per day to *Beacon*. Along the highway in the same area is another store, "Northland Food Center," a laundromat, and Ernie's Cafe is near the road and adjacent to the Peshekee River. There are far fewer people here than when 2,000 miners lived in the area and things were booming. *Champion* is a ghost of its former self.

CHAMPION JUNCTION—In 1887, on the west of *Ishpeming*.

CHAMPION MINE—See *Beacon*.

CHESHIRE—See *Forsyth*.

CHESHIRE-JUNCTION—Railroad name for *Swanzy*. See *Sanzy*.

CHOCOLAY—In 1887, a small station on the D. M. & M. Railroad, 4 miles west of *Marquette*. Postal name *Harvey*. (Still shown on 1972 maps. Now a built-up section of suburban *Marquette*, with motels, resort center, etc.)

The settlement was made in 1860 and called *Chocolay* after the creek upon which it was located, near Lake Superior. In 1879 had a population of 75, and was in Chocolay Township, Semi-weekly mail stage to *Marquette* and *Munising*. Had a steam sawmill and an iron furnace. The post office was named *Harvey* after H. W. Harvey, the Postmaster. 1879 business listings included Joseph Barnard, blacksmith; Edward Fraser, steam sawmill; John Gillet, lumberman; Northern Iron Company, pig iron; and Ameda Young, wagonmaker.

1893, population 100. L. D. Harvey, Postmaster; Ed Frazer, sawmill; H. W. Harvey, job printer; H. Receine, dry goods and grocery; Frank W. Sambrook, sawmill. Charles Becker, Bernard Goodman, and F. Sambrook were listed as justices.

By 1905 the population had dropped to 25. William Smith, Postmaster, general store and farm machinery; Carl Baker, farm implements; Clifford Bordeau, justice; William S. Ewing, farm implements; Fred Snyder, shoemaker; and Zephire Tousignant, sawmill.

1910 population given as 130. Two saloons were listed for that year, one run by Sidney Bordeau and one run by Pat Ford. Other listings were John Penney, grocery; Fred Schneider, shoemaker; John Keefe, confectionery; and John Turcott, carpenter.

By 1915, the post office was closed and *Chocolay*, or *Harvey*, was RFD *Marquette*. There were only four listings for that year, a grocery, general store, and two farmers who sold implements. In 1917, only John G. Keopp was listed as a grocer.

———

CLARKSBURGH—In 1872 described as: *"A village of 500, in the town of Ely (Township), it is on the Marquette, Houghton & Ontonagon Railroad, 26 miles from Marquette. A branch of the Escanaba River flows through the village. The country is rough and hilly and only produces iron and lumber. The Michigan Iron Company's furnace is located here, and produced 4,400 tons of pig iron in 1871. First settled in 1862. H. J. Colwell, Postmaster."*

Other listings for 1872 were A. S. Amerman, physician; H. J. Colwell, Iron Company superintendent; E. Dulong, general store; Jno. (John) Forray, drugs; and Jno. Kaiser, jeweler.

In 1877, post office discontinued. Population 500.

The post office was re-established in 1881, and in 1887 had a Catholic church, population 100, Edwin Sterne, Postmaster and daily mail. Other listings were Don C. Barney, railroad agent; Louis Fortier, Andrew Nault, and Louis Nault, justices; Frank Smith, sawmill; A.E. Sterne, teacher; Edwir Sterne, Superintendent of Poor and Collection Agent; and Frank Tourius, supervisor.

1893, population 150. A. S. Sterne, Postmaster, Supervisor and Deputy Town Treasurer; John Crawford, railroad agent; John Herkins, grocery; George Lord and John McGaffin, justices; Frank Smith, sawmill; Frank Tourgus, blacksmith; James Tredeau, saloon; and Albert Verville, constable and saloon.

In 1905, listed as: *"A station on the D. S. S. & A. Railroad, 3 miles from Humbolt, its post office."* The post office was discontinued on May 28,1894.

———

CLEVELAND MINE—1879, 1 mile west of *Ishpeming*. Also listed in 1887 and 1893. Founded by the Cleveland Iron Mining Company in 1866.

———

CLOWRY—Was on the Chicago & Northwestern Railroad, between *Michigamme* and *Ishpeming*, a few miles northeast of *Champion*. Ernest Rankin said it had a post office from May 22, 1892 to May 4, 1894, with William F. Tobin as Postmaster. 1910, listed as a station on the C. & N. W. Railroad, mail to *Ishpeming*. Also listed in 1927, and shown on 1920 railroad maps.

Was located on part of the land of the Clowry homestead, hence the name.

———

COLLINSVILLE—In 1879 described as, *"A small hamlet near the shore of Lake Superior, a short distance above Marquette."*

Never was a village or post office. Listed each year through 1927. Was the site of the Collins Iron Company forge, built about 1856 and named for Edw. K. Collins, company president.

———

CYR—1910, a station on the C. & N. W. Railroad, mail *Turin*. Founded by Dr. Louis D. Cyer, who built a hunting camp here.

———

DALLIBA—Located in Champion Township, was a platted village at one time. Louis Hole, of the firm of Strange & Hole, Attorneys, in *Harrison*, Michigan, said around 1965 the townsite was acquired by the firm in lieu of cash bond for a client. The town was near an abandoned mine location and there was evidence of foundations on the site. No other information is available.

———

DEAD RIVER—Listed as a station on the Lake Superior & Ishpeming Railroad, 1910, mail *Negaunee*. Called *Riviere de Mort* by the French (river of the dead) on which the station was located.

———

DEXTER JUNCTION—Listed in 1887 as a station on the Marquette Houghton & Ontonagon Railroad, 7 miles west of *Ishpeming*.

———

DIORITE—Was settled in 1909, population 150. In 1915, population 650. On the C. & N. W. Railroad, Ely Township, Charles J. Johnson, Postmaster; American Boston Mine; George Argall, livery and sales stable; Dr. Richard A. Burke; Diorite General Store; and Frank Snow, hotel.

1917, John T. Dower, Postmaster. Other business listings remained the same.

1927, population 350. Two miles north of its station on the Duluth South Shore & Atlantic Railroad, 10 miles from *Ishpeming*.

Earl DeMolen, of *Kingsford*, said the company houses at *Diorite* were purchased by Henry Ford and when the new town of *Kingsford* was formed for a Ford plant the houses were moved there and most of them are still in use. Post office closed January 15, 1940. First post office opened October 20, 1908.

DISHNO—1910, a station on the C. & N. W. Railroad. Not a post office. Mail *Michigamme*. Listed in 1894 and as late as 1927.

DODGE CITY—Was a village located in the northwest part of Powell Township, near *Big Bay*.

DORIAS—1910, a station on the D. S. S. & A. Railroad, mail *Sand River*.

DUKES—Is still a farming community. Was first named *Lehotia*. The post office was established June 3, 1929. Axel G. Laxo was Postmaster.

1910, a station on the Munising, Marquette & Southeastern Railroad mail to *Skandia*.

DUNCAN—1910, a station on the M. & S. E. Railroad, mail to *Birch*.

EAGLE MILLS—Settled in 1854, Negaunee Township; in 1879, population 67. A station on the Marquette Houghton & Ontonagon Railroad, 7 miles west of *Marquette*. Had a steam saw and planing mill. Daily mail. F. W. Read, Postmaster and lumber mills.

1887, F. W. Read, Postmaster and lumber mills. Four men listed as justices: Alex Campbell, Thomas Chalkline, Peter Fontaine and John Lay.

1893, population 150. On the D. S. S. & A. Railroad. F. W. Read, Postmaster, general store and lumber; Matthew Cleary, hotel and livery; A. A. Clumpner, railroad agent; James Dunlop, justice; W. K. Dunwoody, township clerk; Marcus Ferguson, justice; George 1. Johns, blacksmith; Peter Peterson, harness; August Sly, justice; and Alex Tremblay, livery.

Apparently the timber ran out in the area and after 1905 *Eagle Mills* is listed through 1927 as a station on the railroad, no population and no post office. There are a few buildings remaining today.

The post office was closed from July, 1908 until June, 1911, and finally closed for good on April 15, 1912.

ERIE MINE—Shown on 1905 maps near the south end of Lake Michigamme.

FORESTVILLE—1910, a station on the Lake Superior and Ishpeming Railroad. (Not a post office. Mail *Marquette*.) Marquette Township. Prior to 1900 was the location of a forge to melt pig iron. At one time had several hundred population. No buildings remain.

FORSYTH—Also known as *Little Lake*. In 1879, population 50. Forsyth Township, a station on the Chicago & Northwestern Railway. Has a primary school, steam sawmill, planing and shingle mill. Daily mail. J. A. Clark, Postmaster, and Isaac Johnson, lumber mills.

In 1887, also known as *Chesire Junction*, 19 miles due south of *Marquette*. Settled in 1863. Population 150. Stage daily to *Chesire Mine*. Fare 50 cents. Daily mail. H. E. Bennett, Postmaster and railroad agent; Chesire Iron Manufacturing Company, lumber manufacturers and general store; Phillip Coombs, justice; Henry Ferguson, justice; Girard & Morristette, lumber mills; McArthur Brothers, lumber; and William G. Wilson and A. P. Wood, justices.

1893, population 200. Also known as *Little Lake*. Daily mail. Martin Ramile, Postmaster, flour and grain; Wilfred Boucher, timber; Louis O. Girard, sawmill; Frank Lavalley, shoemaker; Basil Raby, timber; and William S. Wilson, justice.

1905, Isadore Cyr, general store; L. Girard, sawmill; and Ramile Martin, grocery.

1910, population 200. William S. Wilson, Postmaster; George H. Burque, hotel; Archie Godin, saloon, B. J. Goodman, sawmill; W. J. Murray, railroad agent; and Martin Ramile, grocery.

1915, population 250. Bank at *Gwinn*, 5 miles distant. Telephone. George W. Goodman, Postmaster; Little Lake Lumber Company, saw and planing mill; Henry Ramile, railroad; and M. Ramile, grocery.

1917, population 300. Charles Soderstrom Postmaster; Lumber Company; other same as 1915. Little Lake Lumber Company; other same as 1915.

In 1927 the population had dropped to 150. Mrs. John A. Flahetery, grocery; John Flaherty, Jr., garage; Helena Land & Lumber Company, sawmill; E.W. Hews, general store; Henry Ramile, justice; and Fred Sherbinow, soft drinks.

In 1971, had a gasoline station, garage, a store and a post office. The old depot was still standing. Post office name changed to *Little Lake* in March, 1966.

GENETIAN—1910, on the C. & N. W. Railroad, mail to *Sands.*

———

GIVINA

———

GLEASONS—1879, a station on the Republic Branch of the Marquette Houghton & Ontonagon Railroad, 32 miles from *Marquette.*

This station was not listed again in Michigan Gazetteer, but a *Gleason* is listed as a station on the Escanaba & Lake Superior Railroad in 1910, mail *Northland.*

———

GOODRICH—1879, listed as a station on the Saginaw & Winthrop branch of the M. H. & O. Railroad, 19 miles from *Marquette.*

———

GOOSE LAKE—1887, listed as a station on the C. & N. W. Railroad. Mail to *Negaunee.* Also listed in 1910, Rand McNally Atlas, same description.

———

GRAND VIEW—Listed in 1910 Rand McNally Atlas. Mail *Marquette.*

———

GRANITE—Listed in 1910 Rand McNally Atlas. Mail *Republic.* On the C. & N. W. Railroad, 5 miles north of *Republic.*

———

GREENGARDEN—Ernest Rankin, of the Marquette Historical Society, said the post office was established December, 1894, and was discontinued in September of 1911, and had three Postmasters. *"Very few people know where it was located,"* Rankin said. It is still marked by a church and a graveyard at the top of a steep hill.

This was never an established village, listed as a farmer's post office in Chocolay Township, 11½ miles southeast of *Marquette* and 7½ from *Harvey.* Mail tri-weekly. Wm. F. Koepp was the first Postmaster. Albert Bauer was Postmaster in 1905. In that year only two business places were listed; Albert Bauer, general store, and Charles Wittier, farm implements. All other listings were farmers in the area. They were Robert Barry, William Barry, Frank Basal, George Basal, James Berry, Christ Borchart, Ernest Borchart, William Borchart, John Bucholtz, Peter Buzze, August Dorow, Carl Heldman, Theodore Huebner, Gustave Koepp, Lewis Koepp, William F. Koepp, Carl Kundee, Antoine LaMere, John Lefke, Michael McCarty, August, Fred, Henry and William Priebe, Adam and Casper Reder, Fred Sonnenberg, John Voce, and Carl, Charles and William Zerbel, farmers and justices.

1910, population 30, located 2½ miles from *Magnum.* Daily mail. Augusta B. Bosel, Postmaster; McReavy & Anderson, sawmill; Ernest T. Wattles, grocery; Carl Zerbel, justice; Robert Zerbel, farm implements; and William Zerbel, justice. On the Minneapolis St. Paul & Sault Ste. Marie Railroad.

1915, was RFD *Marquette*. Only one business listing, R. A. Zerbel, farm implements.

_____

GREENWOOD—Also called *Greenwood Furnace*. Had a post office from March, 1867 to October of 1875. When the smelting furnace went out, so did the town.

1873, described as the first station west of *Ishpeming*, on the M. H. & O. Railroad. Ely Township, 9 miles west of *Negaunee*. *"It is the location of the blast furnaces of the Michigan Iron Company, which in 1871 produced about 4,500 tons of pig iron. E. W. Burroughs, Postmaster; Michigan Iron Company, furnaces and general store."*

From 1879 through 1893, listed as a station on the railroad. First called *Greenwood Furnace*, the post office operated from March 8, 1867 until October 27, 1875, the year the furnace closed.

_____

HARLOW'S—Listed in 1879 and through early 1900s as two miles west of *Marquette*, its post office.

_____

HARPERVILLE—Ernest Rankin said this one had him stumped. It is not the town the song "Harperville P. T. A." was written about. Rankin said it was near *Ishpeming* and was a post office from February, 1893, to May 1897. Jacob Harper was Postmaster. Probably never operated as a post office. This sometimes happened, especially in the Upper Peninsula.

_____

HARVEY—See *Chocolay*.

_____

HELENA—In 1879 was a station on the C. & N. W. Railroad, 35 miles above *Escanaba*. Never was a village. Mail to *Turin*. Shown on 1969 Michigan Highway maps on M-35, 6 miles south of *Little Lake*.

_____

HOIST—Listed in 1910 Rand McNally Atlas as a station on the Lake Superior & Ishpeming Railroad, mail *Negaunee*.

_____

HOMIER—1910, a station on the Munising, Marquette & Southeastern Railroad, mail *Big Bay*.

_____

HUFF—Was established as a post office in July, 1894, and discontinued May, 1895. Named after the first Postmaster, James Huff, Ernest Rankin said. Was located near *Carlshend* in Skandia Township. Post office closed on May 23, 1895.

_____

HUMBOLT—This mining village was settled in 1864 and by 1872 had a population of 2,000. In that year was located on the M. H. & O. Railroad, Ely

Township, 28 miles west of *Marquette*. Was the location of the Washington Iron Company mines and in 1871 produced 48,725 tons of iron ore. Also located on the Escanaba River.

J. F. Allen was Postmaster and druggist in 1872. Other listings for that year were: Dr. L. Brodiur; Napoleon LaBarre, barber; F. Larmsere, veterinary; Merryweather & Company, general store; Merryweather & Sanford, meats; E. T. Sherman, silversmith; E. G. St. Clair, banker; John L. Swartz, shoemaker; Miss Trotter, dressmaker; Thomas Wallis, hotel; Washington Iron Company, general store; and William Zeitier, shoemaker.

1879, population 300. Was the location of the Edwards and Humbolt iron mines. In 1877 the Humbolt yielded 17,000 tons of iron ore. Daily mail. Michael B. McGee, Postmaster and station agent; Clarence F. Cochran, doctor; John Maas, agent for the Humbolt Company; John Kaiser, watchmaker; Charles A. Draus, shoemaker; Nicholas Lonstorf, Albert J. and John B. Maas, general store; Amos J. Mead, general store; William Pelmear, saloon; Joseph Schaller, druggist; and Mrs. Elizabeth Wallace, hotel.

In 1887, was located in Humboldt Township. Population 200. Had a Methodist church. Daily mail. James L. Cox, Postmaster and miner; William Becker, shoemaker; Edwin Colenzo, justice; Conrad Boom Company (sorted logs at a "booming" area on the river); Richard Edwards, clothing; J. Gilbert, machinist; Frank Hausmann, wagonmaker; John Mass, manager, Humbolt Iron Company; James Laird, butcher; F. N. Maas, general store; Dr. Rudolph J. Mass, justice; Mass & Sanders, livestock; Alfred Mitchell, justice; William Pelmear, saloon and clothing; James Sanders, blacksmith; Orrin H. Shafer, station agent; Robert Shied, constable; Frank Sparr, justice; Frederick Vogtlin, deputy sheriff; and Mrs. Elizabeth Wallace, hotel.

1893, on the Duluth South Shore & Atlantic Railroad, 12 miles west of *Ishpeming*. Population 500. Some new additions to the business directory for that year were: G. Lobb, manager of Bessie Mining Company; Miss K. Bright, teacher; Robert Maxwell, President of Foxdale Mining Company; William Pelmear, Postmaster and manager of Gertrude Mining Company; R. A. Parker, agent for Sampson Iron Company; and R. S. Walker, physician.

By 1905 the population was down to 200. Bessie T. Pelmear, Postmistress; Matt Autis, general store; Jennie Home, teacher; Mrs. John Julyan, general store; H. P. Smith, station agent; Louis F. Tourville, general store. Others remained about the same.

In 1915, population 275. Only four business listings for that year: Gertrude Champloi, Postmistress; Matt Antio, general store; Paul VanRiper, physician, and Washington Iron Company, of *Marquette*, proprietors of the Barron Mine.

1918, population 150. Had a telephone. About the only change in the business listing was Jacob Wisuri, Postmaster.

The mines closed in 1927. The post office was discontinued in 1936, and had 16 Postmasters during its history. Paul Petoskey, of *Ishpeming*, said there are only two or three people living there today.

———

IRON CITY—First settled in 1872, when the Republic mine was opened and the place was first settled. Located in Republic Township (1873), was officially named *Republic*, after the mine and township. Is still a village today, although a far cry from the one time boom town of more than 2,000 miners who worked in the mines. Many of the old buildings are now vacant, but may well become a boom town again in the future if the new experiments with pelletized ore prove successful, as they have in many areas of the iron country.

———

JOPLING—Listed in 1910 as a station on the Lake Superior & Ishpeming Railroad, mail *Humbolt*.

———

KATES—Was a station in 1905, located at the terminus of a branch of the Escanaba & Lake Superior Railroad that extended from *Northland* about 10 miles. *Kates* was located near the Marquette-Dickinson County line in the extreme south part of the county. 1910, mail *Princeton*. Had a post office for about one year, from April 25, 1908 to 1909.

———

KILNS—In 1887 was listed as a station on the D. M. & M. Railroad, 9 miles east of *Ishpeming*. Not a post office. Not listed in 1893.

———

KLOMAN MINE

———

LAWSON—Listed as a station on the Munising, Marquette & Southeastern Railroad, mail *Carlshend*. Was the first name for *Dukes* which was also called *Lehtola* by Finn settlers.

———

LEHTOLA—Name changed to *Dukes*. See *Dukes*.

———

LITTLE LAKE—Also called *Forsyth*. See *Forsyth*.

———

LOWMOOR—1910, station on Duluth South Shore & Atlantic Railroad. Mail to *Munising*.

———

McFARLANDS—See *Turin*.

———

MAGNETIC MINE—Listed in 1910.

———

MANGUM—In 1905 was a lumbering and sawmill settlement, on the Minneapolis St. Paul & Sault Ste. Marie Railroad, 10 miles southeast of *Marquette*.

Typical living room of company house workers lived in during the late 1800s and at the turn of the century. This is one of the restored houses at the ghost town of *Fayette*. Photo by Roy L. Dodge

Telephone. Lars Olson, Postmaster, and Joseph Dupra & Brothers, sawmill.

1910, listed as a farmer's post office, Chocolay Township. Louis Anderson, Postmaster; Genevieve Devins, teacher; August Keopp, feed and grain; Joseph McKim, saloon; and McReavy & Anderson, sawmill.

1915, population 100. M. Healy, Postmaster; Fred Dorrow, produce; August Keopp, grain; S. T. McReavy, sawmill and general store; James Triggs, grain and potatoes; and E. T. Whittier, produce. (1918, remained the same).

1927, post office discontinued. RFD *Yalmar*.

MARIGOLD—Listed in 1910, on the Munising, Marquette & Southeastern Railroad, mail *Carlshend*.

MARTIN—Shown on 1905 maps between *Forsyth* and *Carlshend* on the railroad.

MASHEK—1910, on the Escanaba & Lake Superior Railroad. Mail to *Northland*.

1927, located in Wells Township, Mashek Store Company, general store. Mail received from *Arnold* post office. Named for George Mashek, of the Mashek Chemical & Iron Company, of *Escanaba* who owned the store.

MASS MINE—1927, a station on the Lake Superior & Ishpeming Railroad. Not a post office.

MICHIGAMME—This once thriving city was settled on the site of an iron ore discovery in 1872. The Michigamme Mine, abandoned in 1905, produced nearly one million tons of ore during its 33 years of operation. Today (1971) only one or two freight trains pass by the nearly deserted town and no passenger trains. None of the mines are operating but a few of the less than 100 residents work in mines at *Negaunee.*

In 1909, population 1,000. *"A mining village on the main line of the Duluth South Shore & Atlantic Railroad and on the Michigamme Branch of the Chicago & North West Railroad. Depots located 350 feet apart."*

"Located in Michigamme Township, 26 miles southeast of L'Anse. It is at the western edge of Michigamme Lake and in the vicinity of the Michigamme iron range, which apparently begins near the head of the lake and extends west some 8 miles. There are several mines located along the range. Has Catholic, Methodist, and Swedish Lutheran churches and a graded public school. Gordon J. Murray, Postmaster." (Michigan Gazetteer & Business Directory)

Some mines operating in the area were the Imperial Mining Company, owned by Cleveland Cliffs, and the Niagara Mining Company.

In 1893, population 1,500. There were several mines located along the range. *Michigamme* also had a steam sawmill, four churches, and a public school. Iron ore, lumber, sash, doors, etc. were shipped by rail. Henry J. Atkinson was Postmaster, justice and ran a drug, wallpaper and sporting goods store. In addition to 25 or 30 business places listed, the village was served by several saloons, two large "first class" hotels, and several boarding houses to accommodate mine workers, railroad workers and lumbermen.

In 1893 the Northwestern Hotel and Michigamme House ran large display ads in the Michigan Gazetteer & Business Directory. Mrs. Duncan McMillan, proprietor of the Northwestern, advertised "New building, new furniture, new management. Steam heat and first class sample rooms for commercial men. Located directly opposite the depots."

After the mines went out, lumbering was a big industry for many years, until the 1920s when this too was exhausted. There were dreams for a while during the 1920s, when Henry Ford was prospecting in the area, that he was about to purchase one of the old mines along with a million acres of land in the area and the town would experience another boom. Although Ford visited the town in person and was given the red-carpet treatment by local businessmen, he established his headquarters at *L'Anse*, and *Michigamme* was left without industry or any inducements to bring business to the fast fading village.

Today the boarded-up stores along the one remaining business block stand empty and weathered on a high hill overlooking M-28 and the lake. *Michigamme* is a ghost town. Someone lives in one of the old 20-room hotels that has withstood the years, and any signs of paint have long since been removed by the weather. A large three-story brick school building stands on the hill overlooking the lake, but this too appears to be vacant and unused for a long time. The village still has many of the original houses and two or three churches.

There is a chance that with the tourism boom, increase in population, and new methods of mining being introduced in the 1970s that *Michigamme* will revive again, but for now it is a ghost town.

MIDWAY—In 1887, a station on the Republic branch of the M. H. & O. Railroad, 5 miles from *Humbolt*.

MILWAUKEE JUNCTION—Listed in 1910 as a station on the C. M. & St. P. Railroad and the D. S. S. & A. Railroad, mail to *Republic*.

MINERAL BRANCH—Listed in 1879 and 1887 as on the C. & N. W. Railroad, 2 miles from *Negaunee*.

MORGAN—1872, located on the railroad, 6½ miles east of *Negaunee*. The seat of the Morgan Iron Company's blast furnace, which in 1871 turned out 4,792 tons of pig iron.

In 1877 described as on the Houghton & Ontonagon Railroad. The Morgan furnace was built in 1863, and paid for itself in the first four months of its run.

Another furnace, the *Champion*, was also built here under the supervision of Cornelius Donkersley, but this furnace burned in 1874. The furnace included a foundry, machine shop, blacksmith shop, and carpenter shops and advertised "Lake Superior Charcoal Iron," manufactured from the best specular, granular and hematite ores.

In 1877, Cornelius Donkersley was Postmaster and ran the furnaces; George W. Beardsley, station agent; Dr. William Bradley; John Downey, founder; P. R. Erickson, superintendent for Donkersley; Mr. Mitchell, contractor; Pioneer Iron Company, pig iron manufacturers; F. W. Read & Company, contractors and lumber mills; and Tessier & Lamere, contractors.

229

In 1877 the post office was discontinued and the population was given as 300, mostly miners.

1887, a former post office, 7 miles west of *Marquette*.

NATIONAL MINE—Was the postal name for *Winthrop*. In 1887, was a post office and mining settlement, in Tilden Township, 18 miles southwest of *Marquette*, and 2 south of *Ishpeming*. Daily mail. James Lucks, Postmaster and general store; Lois Anderson, justice; John Carson, justice; Mauritz, justice; and Olof Sandstrom, justice.

1893, population 700. Mail twice daily by stage from *Ishpeming*, fare 20 cents. M. J. Bell, Postmaster; W. W. Brooks, stationer; Andrew Carlson, Maurice Fitzgerald, Patrick McDonald and John Reilley were justices; Lake Superior Iron Company, miners; James Luck, grocer; and Winthrop Iron Company, iron miners.

1905, listed as a post office and mining settlement of 1,000 population. James Lucks, Postmaster and grocer.

1910, population given as 1,500. James Lucks, Postmaster and general store; August Annala, confection; and Rev. B. C. Moore, Methodist Episcopal.

1915, no change in business directory. Population 700.

1917, population 1,000. Thomas Clayton, Postmaster and general store; The Aetna Powder Company, explosives; and August Annala, grocery.

In 1927, population 30, and name changed to *National City*. Thomas Clayton, Postmaster and store; August Annala, general store; Richard Champion, justice; Ernell & LaPointe, radio supplies; Alex Juntila, shoe repair; Richard Kieliman, justice; and Edith Solka, township clerk.

The town (*National Mine*) is still shown on 1972 Michigan Highway maps, and had a post office in 1970.

NEW DALTON—In 1915, on the M. & S. E. Railway, Skandia Township, 16 miles from *Marquette*. Telephone. Send mail to *Skandia*. The only business listing for that year was the Dalton Lumber Company, lumbermills.

1927, W. H. Acker & Son, general store; and Cleveland Cliffs Iron Company, lumber. Mail to *Skandia*.

Edwin S. Harris was first Postmaster on March 6, 1911.

NEW FURNACE—1910, on the Munising, Marquette & Southeastern Railroad. Mail *Marquette*.

NEW SWANZY—1910, on the Munising, Marquette & Southeastern Railroad. Mail *Gwinn*. Was a village in Forsyth Township, formed by the Swanzy Iron Company in 1883.

———

NEW YORK MINE—Listed in 1879, 1887, and 1910. Located 1 mile north of *Ishpeming*. A station on the C. & N. W. Railroad.

———

NORTHAMPTON JUNCTION—1887, a station on the M. H. & O. Railroad, 7 miles east of *Michigamme*.

1893, listed as *Northampton*, a station on the Houghton division of the D. S. S. & A. Railway. No post office.

———

NORTH LAKE—1910, on the Lake Superior & Ishpeming Railroad, mail *Ishpeming*. A former mine location and suburb of *Ishpeming*.

———

NORTHLAND—Settled in 1897. 1905, population 100. On the Escanaba & Lake Shore Railroad, Wells Township, 39 miles north of *Escanaba*. (Near *Ralph*. Shown on today's State maps). Telephone. J. M. Thompson, Postmaster; Joseph Charlebon, saloon; W. P. Lane, physician; Lillian O'Meara, teacher; Isaac Peppin, saloon; P. A. Shepard, notary; Wolverine Cedar & Lumber Company, general store and ties, posts and poles.

1910, population 300. J. W. Gleason, Postmaster; Don Cameron, barber; Joseph Edwards, barber; Isaac Peppin, saloon; J. I. Peraw, saloon; Isaac Piper, Jr., saloon; Phillipa Treloar, teacher; A. A. Wells, station agent; J. W. Gleason, manager, Wolverine Cedar & Lumber Company, general stores, etc.

1915, population 100. Telephone. Miss M. J. Walker, Postmistress; J. B. Cholette, general store; A. Page, hotel; and J. Pintal, express agent.

In 1918, things remained the same with only two changes—P. D. Ferner, express agent, and Eli Lauzon, hotel.

1927, population 100. Had a Catholic church. Rose Roberts, Postmistress and general store; Mayme Kivisto, station agent; Michigan Bell Telephone Company; Ediore Patient, village supervisor; Vena Roberts, general store; and Oscar Vean, general store. Post office open in 1970.

———

ONTONAGON JUNCTION—In 1879, a station on the M. H. & O. Railroad, 15 miles west of *Marquette*. Also listed in 1887. Not listed in 1893.

———

PASCOE MINE—On 1905 maps, about ½ mile north of *Beacon*.

———

PARTRIDGE—1887, a station on the C. & N. W. Railroad, 59 miles above *Escanaba*. Was 3 miles east of *Negaunee*. Shown on 1905 maps between *Goose*

Lake and *Negaunee*. 1910, listed as a station on the C. & N. W. Railroad, mail *Negaunee*.

————

PICKEREL LAKE—1910, a station on the M. & S. E. Railroad. Not a post office.

————

PLAINS—From 1879 through 1927, listed as a station on the C. & N. W. Railroad, 46 miles north of *Escanaba*. No post office. At one time was a settlement.

————

POWELL—Listed in 1910 as a station on the M. & S. E. Railroad, send mail to *Birch*.

————

PRESQUE ISLE—Listed in 1910 Rand McNally Atlas, population 40. A station on the Minneapolis St. Paul & Sault Ste. Marie Railroad.

————

PRINCETON—Settled in 1871. 1905, population 700. A mining village on the Escanaba River, Forsyth Township, 6 miles from *Swanzy*, to which it has stage connection three times daily. George J. Sarasin, Postmaster (also spelled Sarisin and Sarasen); John F. Crooks, station agent; Charles Johnson, saloon; William Jory, justice; G. E. Lingel, physician; B. A. Middlemiss, civil engineer; Princeton Mining Company, Tod Stambaugh & Company, operators; Richard Quayle, general store; Stegmiller Mine, U.S. Steel Company, proprietors; John Thomas, supervisor.

Ernest Rankin said George Sarisin was appointed Postmaster on December 27, 1898, and served for 43 years. The village was the post office for the *Chesire Mine*, about 5 miles west of *Swanzy*.

1909, population 2,000. At that time had a Methodist Episcopal church and a bank. George Behimer, physician; Cleveland Cliffs Iron Company; a Finnish Cornet Band; George R. Jackson, supervisor; Charles Johnson, saloon; William Jory, justice; Joseph Larochelle, saloon; D. R. Macintyre, physician; R. A. Marsh, station agent; had two telephone companies; Oscar Nyquest, confection; Richard Quayle, general store; Austin & Hoyt Stephenson, miners; A. H. Tilson, civil engineer; and U.S. Steel Corporation, proprietors Stegmiller Mine.

1915, population 3,000. Bank at *Gwinn*, 2 miles distant. Only a few minor changes: A. Mertha, physician; M. Q. Molloy, station agent. Others remained the same.

The population increased and decreased according to the mining activity. In 1917, population 900. Same business listings.

1927, population 450. M. M. Duncan, manager of Princeton Mine; Cleveland

Cliffs Iron Company; Mark Q. Malloy, station agent; Edward Olive, confection; and Charles and Oscar Tapola Brothers, garage.

1970, RFD *Gleasons*. None of the former nine mines are now operating.

———

QUEEN MINE—1910, on the D. S. S. & A. Railroad and Lake Superior & Ishpeming Railroad. Mail *Negaunee*. Located about 10 miles west of *Marquette*.

———

RANSOME—1910, on the Munising, Marquette & Southeastern Railroad, mail to *Big Bay*.

———

READE—Listed in 1910 Rand McNally Atlas, on the Escanaba & Lake Superior Railroad, mail *Northland*.

———

RUSE—Was a post office in 1919 and In 1927. Located in Skandia Township. Sam McFarlane was the first Postmaster, July 12, 1917.

———

SAGINAW MINE—1887, a station on the M. H. & O. Railroad, 18 miles west of *Marquette*. John Perkins, native of *Devonshire*, England, was mine captain here from 1873 to 1879. He was later elected State Representative for 1889-90, and re-elected for 1891-92.

———

SAND RIVER—1887, a small station on the D. M. & M. Railroad, 14 miles east of *Marquette*, on the east county line, Chocolay Township.

1893, population 34. Charles A. Hazen, Postmaster and station agent. Hazen was the first Postmaster on March 14, 1891, and it was located in Alger County until September 12, 1908.

1905, J. D. Albright, Postmaster and section foreman; Alice Dooley, teacher; and J. Gannon, fruit.

1909, remained about the same. 1917, Austin Harmon, Postmaster and grocery; Superior Veneer & Cooperage Company.

In 1927, a discontinued post office. Mail supplied from *Onota*.

———

SANDS—A station on the C. & N. W. Railroad, 9 miles north of *Forsyth*. Chocolay Township. Settled in 1874. The village was a mile back of the station. It was named for Louie Sands of lumbering day fame. Wm. E. Lathrop was the first Postmaster on January 23, 1878. Post office continued until February 1955.

1887, population 200. Thomas O'Connell, Postmaster and section foreman; Barney Goodman, charcoal; James E. Goodman, wagonmaker; and C. W. Taylor, justice and general store.

1893, population given at 100. Mail tri-weekly . . . J. B. Goodman, mining supplies.

1905, located in Sands Township; Ernest Yelle, Postmaster; John Flodin, mason; James Miller, constable; Rasmusus Olsen, carpenter; Louise Paulson, teacher; Adam Saramie, justice.

1910, daily mail. Ernest Yelle, Postmaster; Albert Bauer, general store; Joseph Contoir, constable; John Flodin, mason; Nels Jensen, mail carrier; Hannah Kennedy, teacher; S. H. Winthrop, logger; S. C. Miller, township clerk; Rasmus Olsen, carpenter; Adam Saramle, justice; and C. W. Taylor, creamery.

1915. Same Postmaster and only four business listings: Albert Bauer, store; D. S. Comstock, creamery; and Dennis Jewell, logger.

In 1917, one more store was added, that of Dolph Larmie.

1927, had Catholic and Presbyterian churches. Daily mail. Anne M. Olsen, Postmaster; Adolph Contois, justice; B. J. Goodman, logger; Carl Jansen, justice; Nels Jensen, village supervisor; Dolph Larmie, general store; Loren C. Miller, seeds; and the Sands Lumber Company, sawmill.

SCHOOL STREET MINE

SELMA—Listed in 1910, on the Munising, Marquette & Southeast Railroad, mail *Yalmar.* Shown on present day maps.

SMITH MINE JUNCTION—1879, 43 miles above *Escanaba*, on the C. & N. W. Railroad. Also in 1887. Not listed in 1893.

SPEARS—1910, a station on the Munising, Marquette & Southeastern Railroad. Mail *Harvey.*

ST. LAWRENCE—1910, on the C. & N. W. Railroad. Mail *Ishpeming.*

STIMSON—1887, a station on the D. M. & M Railroad, 7 miles west of *Marquette.* Not a post office.

STONEVILLE—This village was formed around charcoal kilns near the M. H. & O. Railroad, 18 miles west of *Marquette* about 1870. The post office opened on February 10, 1873, with James M. Lawson as Postmaster. The post office was closed then reopened several times until it was finally discontinued permanently on March 28, 1895. It was platted by E. M. Spalding for Robert Nelson in 1876 and named from its being in a stony region. The stone foundations of some of its buildings remain, according to Walter Romig in his book "Michigan Place Names."

1879, a post office about 2 miles from *Ishpeming*, its shipping point, from whence it receives a daily mail. Iron ore is about the only industry. Population about 500. George S. Palmear, Postmaster; Michael Carhan, shoemaker; Peter Deroseau, hotel and saloon; Townsend Heaton, physician; C. Merryweather, general store; and C. Merryweather & Company, meat market.

1887, a discontinued post office.

1927, discontinued post office, on D. S. S. & A. Railroad, 4 miles from *Ishpeming*, to which send mail.

SUGAR LOAF—1910, on the Munising, Marquette & Southeastern Railroad. Mail *Marquette*.

SUOMI—"Suomi" means Finland. 1909, a post office in Richmond Township, 12 miles from *Negaunee*, its shipping point. Clara Anderson and Bessie Berrimen, teachers; Halle Lempen, constable; Oscar Ranta, constable.

1915, post office discontinued. RFD *Palmer*.

This place, now in a resort area, never achieved village status. Today it has the distinction of being located on one of the crookedest roads in Michigan. Located on M-35, a smooth black-top highway which is a very scenic drive, there are two or three houses close to one of the sharp curves in the road, and in front of one of them is a small sign that reads *Suomi*.

Nettie Holmi became first Postmistress on February 1, 1908. The office closed in 1912.

SUPERIOR—1910, on the Munising, Marquette & Southeastern Railroad. Not a post office. Mail to *Marquette*.

SWANZY—The postal name for *Chesire Junction*, about 5 miles above *Forsyth*, on the C. & N. W. Railroad. Located in Forsyth Township. 1905, John F. Crooks, Postmaster, station agent and general store.

Swanzy was a post office in October of 1889 and lasted until 1905. In 1893, population 200. C. Hartho, Postmaster and station agent; Escanaba River Land & Iron Company, iron mines; S. O. Girard, lumber; and Thomas M. Wells, general store.

After 1905, mail RFD *Forsyth*.

SWEITZER—Listed in 1910. Mail to *Harvey (Forsyth)*.

TAYLORS—1910, on the C. & N. W. Railroad. Mail *Sands.*

TILDEN—1877, a post office, 4 miles south of *Negaunee.* Named for Samuel Tilden, president of the Iron Cliffs Company about 1872. The post office operated from March, 1874 to February 12, 1877.

This abandoned mine has made recent headlines in newspapers around Michigan (July, 1972) with the announcement that the Cleveland-Cliffs Iron Company is building a dam to flood the Escanaba River which will enable them to process iron ore that was previously too expensive to take out. The new mine, which is scheduled to begin production in July of 1974, will be called the Tilden Mine and Pellet Plant and is expected to produce 4 million tons of iron pellets annually, and increasing to 12 million tons in two phases by mid-1977, just 100 years after Tilden ceased to be a post office.

The opening of the new mine should have a tremendous effect on the economy of the county, one of two Upper Peninsula counties that showed an appreciable increase in population from 1960 to 1970.

The Cleveland-Cliffs Company has owned the Tilden Mine since 1865, the news article stated, and has been mined by open pit methods on a small scale since 1927.

"The process now takes crude iron which contains 36 per cent iron ore and upgrades it to a product containing 65 per cent iron, making it economically feasible to ship and opening up a vast new economic development in Michigan's Upper Peninsula," the article said.

TURIN—The post office for *McFarlands.* This office operated from February 27, 1883 until May 31, 1954. Named for Walter McFarland born here in 1872, and the log cabin in which he was born was still standing in 1965.

In 1887, a station on the C. & N. W. Railroad, Turin Township, 35 miles southeast of Marquette. Population 150. Daily mail. John T. Brown, Postmaster and farmer; Glynn-Eddy & Company, sawmill; Harry Finney, justice; C. Havens, station agent; Andrew Kleiber, grocery and saloon; John Kleiber, carpenter; John Micks, carpenter; Nicholas Oswald, justice; Robert Postal, farmer; Francis V. Saver, carpenter; and F. V. Sonier, justice.

1893, *"formerly known as McFarland,"* 2 miles from *Lathrop*, its express and telegraph office. Population 50. Daily mail. Fred Guines, justice; and Albert Oswald, justice. (Only business listings for that year. John T. Brown was still Postmaster.)

1905, daily mail. John T. Brown, Postmaster; Andrew Baker, contractor; Jrs. J. C. Findlay, music teacher; A. P. Gogarn, general store; Grimes Brothers, sawmill and railroad ties; Charles Grimes, blacksmith; A. E. Heberman, express agent; F. C. Keupper, sawmill and township supervisor; Matt McFarland, justice; T. J. McManus, township clerk; E. L. Porter, constable; and Thompson & McManus, railroad ties.

1909, only changes in the directory listings were Charles D. Grimes, Postmaster. Others remained the same as 1905. Population 52 (census).

1915, population 30. Henry McFarland, Postmaster. Telephone. Grimes Brothers, threshers; F. C. Keupper, sawmill; and H. McFarland, general store. (Note: If only one or two business places are listed, it doesn't necessarily mean there were not more stores).

1918, population 300. Agnes H. Keupper, Postmistress; John Banks, sawmill; Nicholas Britz, general store; A. P. Gogarn, general store; Charles Grimes, blacksmith; Grimes Brothers, threshers; and Wesley Miller, cattle dealer.

In 1927, population listed as 375. Bus to *Marquette* and *Escanaba* three times daily. Catholic and Methodist churches. Telephone. Joseph J. Kodanko, Postmaster; Carl Brunnegerber, Jr., sawmill and thresher; J. E. Coyne, justice; Sam Hammerburg, well driller; Joseph J. Kodanko, general store; Marcott Brothers, garage; and Wesley Miller, soft drinks.

Although *McFarland (Turin)* is shown on 1972 Michigan State Highway maps, not much remains of the former village. One of the old hotels is now a tavern, one church is about to collapse and appears to be unused, and the old brick school building is empty and neglected.

————

TYLERS—Listed in 1910 Rand McNally Atlas. Mail *Republic*.

WABIK—1910, on the C. M. & St. P. Railroad and C. & N. W. Mail *Champion*. One mile west of *Champion*. Named from "pewabik," Chippewa for any mineralized formation.

————

WATSON—Postal name *Arnold*. Changed because another town was named *Watson*, in Allegan County. See *Arnold* for history.

————

WEST BRANCH—1910, a station on the Escanaba & Lake Superior Railroad, mail *Princeton*.

————

WEST ISHPEMING—1910, on the C. & N. W. Railroad, mail *Ishpeming*.

————

WHITEMAN—1910, a station on the L. S. & I. Railroad, mail *Negaunee*.

————

WINTHROP—This was the railroad name for the location. Postal name was *National Mine*, see for history.

WINTHROP JUNCTION—Listed in 1910, on the D. S. S. & A. Railroad, mail *Ishpeming*.

WINTHROP MINE—1879, on the Saginaw & Winthrop Mine branch of the M. H. & O. Railroad, 18 miles from *Marquette*. Also listed in 1887. Not in 1893. (See *National Mine*.) This mine was opened in 1870 and later became the Winthrop Iron Company.

WITBECK—Post office opened in November, 1888. Listed in 1905 as a discontinued post office. In 1909, had a post office. Located on the C. M. & St. P. Railroad, 29 miles from *Ishpeming*. Population 37, Telephone. Mrs. Agnes Schroeder, Postmaster and boarding house; Louis Adams, summer resort; Cornelius Bornfield, wood; James Campfield, livestock; Charles Doane, lumberman; Mitchell Dykes, livestock; John Peterson, lumbermen; J. F. Viele, summer resort; and Anton Voegtline, sawmill.

On May 28, 1910 name changed to *Witch Lake*. 1927, RFD *Republic*.

Today (1971) is a resort area and has one sawmill in operation.

WOLVERINE—1910, a station on the Escanaba & Lake Superior Railroad, mail *Northland*.

WORCESTER—In the summer of 1849 Robert J. Gravaret, of *Mackinac Island*, began building a village at the mouth of the Carp River and it was named *Worcester* for the Massachusetts home of Amos R. Harlow, leader of a second group that followed. Houses, stores, and a hotel were built. Forges and ore docks were constructed. Many Irish, German and French flocked to the mines and many settled in the town. In 1850 it was renamed *Marquette*, which was incorporated as a village in 1859. In 1868 it was nearly destroyed by fire. The city was quickly rebuilt and in 1871 *Marquette* was incorporated as a city.

William Graveratte, of *Pinconning*, Michigan, claims to be a descendant of Robert Gravaret and thinks there is a high school there named after Robert Gravaret, but isn't sure. During the years, William Graveratte said, the original spelling of the name was changed to the present.

YALMAR—Settled about 1870 and named for Hjalmar Bahrman. The "Hj" is pronounced "Y." Was a post office from February 1895 to February, 1933.

In 1905, located on the M. & S. E. Railroad, Skandia Township; 13 miles southeast of *Marquette*. Daily mail. Telephone. Charles Wilson, Postmaster and general store, station agent, ties, posts, poles, etc.; L. E. Backman, justice; John Bergdahl, meats; August Berglund, shoemaker; Dalton Lumber Company, sawmill; A. P. Johnson and Olof Johnson, carpenters; John Sandberg, musician; A.

Seagreen, flour mill; Joseph Speeker, blacksmith; John V. Stack, blacksmith; Touchette Lumber Company, sawmill; and the Valmar Lumber Company, sawmill.

1910, population 150. Same business listing as 1905.

In 1915, Charles Wilson was still Postmaster, until the 1920s. In 1927, population 150. Was located on Highway US-41. Had Lutheran and Methodist churches. Mrs. Florida Wilson, Postmistress; Mrs. J. C. Johnson & Sons, aplarists (raised bees), poultry and eggs; S. Johnson, station agent; Joseph Specker, blacksmith; and A. P. Wilson, general store.

Chapter Sixteen

MENOMINEE COUNTY

From 1861 to 1863 Menominee was officially named "Bleeker County." The story is told that Anson Bangs, an influential land owner in the lower peninsula, obtained the passage of an act by the State Legislature creating Bleeker County, which was his wife's family name. The residents of the county forced the change to Menominee, which was the name of a tribe of Indians famed for their "good grain" or wild rice. Historians say the Menominee Indian tribe of Wisconsin was a handsome, well-built race, often called the "White Indians." The county government was organized in 1863, and the name changed to Menominee.

Samuel M. Stephenson was an early leader in the development of the county and its timber resources. Stephenson moved from Delta County to Menominee in 1858 and built the second sawmill on the river. In 1881 he had held the office of Supervisor since the county was organized, in 1863. He served as district Congressman in 1877-78 and was elected to the United States Senate in 1879-80 and again in 1885-86. A town in the county was named *Stephenson* in his honor and later his two brothers, Issac and Robert joined him in the lumber business.

Menominee has a well-documented and recorded history, an active historical society, and a historical museum at *Menominee*.

Menominee County borders on Green Bay and Wisconsin and is in the southwestern portion of the Upper Peninsula. The city of *Menominee* is the county seat. The 1880 population was 11,987 (whites only) and in 1960 was 24,685. The decade between 1960 and 1970 showed a decline to 24,587 or loss of 98 population.

MENOMINEE COUNTY GHOST TOWNS

AMES—In 1910 was a station on the Wisconsin-Michigan Railroad (called the "Whisky-Mich"). Mail to *Nathan*.

ARNOLD—1910, a station on the Wisconsin-Michigan, mail to *Nathan*.

ARTHUR BAY—In early days was also called *Hayward Bay*, and was first officially named *Leathern*.

1887, 500 workers in camps, under Jerry Madden, camp boss.

James Borski, of *Menominee*, said Mathias Bailey and other fishermen were the first settlers at *Arthur Bay* long before the locality bore the name *Arthur Bay*. About 1878 this place on the bay shore became a scene of bustling activity when Leathern & Smith set up a lumber and shingle mill and began logging operations. Year by year for over a decade these operations became more extensive until in 1887 there were several hundred men at work in various woods camps and the store near the bay did a heavy business. In that year the mill cut one million shingles.

The main job of logging was soon ended, the mill burned, Borski said, and *Arthur Bay* was once more left to the fishermen. John Leathern sold out his interests, in 1887, to W. S. Horn who renamed the place for his son Arthur and it has since been known as *Arthur Bay*.

In 1890 in Ingallston Township, 18 miles northeast of *Menominee*. Formerly called *Leathern*. Population 100. Stage tri-weekly, with mail, to *Menominee, Cedar River* and *Ingalls*. C. M. Chase, Postmaster; M. Bailey, fisherman. Many other business listings for that year were fishermen, A. G. Johnson, A. Baker, Robert Beattie, G. Ellinger, Owen Gartland, John F. Nelson, Fred VanPatton, and J. W. Williams, were all fishermen.

Postmaster Chase was also township clerk; Samuel Haywood, ties, posts, etc.; D. C. Miller, justice; and H. Sweet Cedar & Lumber Company, general store, saw and shingle mill. The mill was rebuilt by James Crozier, Borski said, and later (1896) was sold to Charles Zeiser.

A news item of September 8, 1888, mentioned the schooners *Hershel, Bates, Australia, Bradley, Mowry, Winsor* and the scow *Success* all cleared *Arthur Bay* with cargoes of lumber during the past week for W. H. Horn.

By 1896 the village was a ghost town. A news item of December 16, 1893 read as follows: *"Arthur Bay is a deserted village, and exists now only in name. Spencer and Riley still continue to run their stage through the place, but only because it is on the way to Cedar River. Timber resources are exhausted."*

The 1905 Michigan Gazetteer had the following description in that year: *"A rural post office . . .8 miles north of Menominee, whence it received a tri-weekly mail by stage. Charles Zeiser, Postmaster, sawmill and general store."*

1910, population 25. Tri-weekly mail stage, fare $1.00. A. C. Schulz, Postmaster, general store, lumbering and telephone company manager; Archie Bailey, sawmill; C. L. Bailey, township treasurer and stage line; Ed Barstow, fisherman; Bertha Duke, teacher; Hayward Brothers, saw and shingle mill; R. F. Kleinke, justice; and M. Golden, manager of saw and shingle mill.

Post office discontinued July 31, 1935.

1915, Edward Barstow, Postmaster and fisherman; and Charles Zeiser, general store and sawmill.

Borski said the mill was torn down in 1918. In 1927 was located on M-35. Triweekly mail by bus from *Menominee*. Hayward Brothers, sawmill and Leota Hayward, Postmistress.

Nothing remains today (1971).

———

BAGLEY—post office established December 3, 1874 and closed August 31, 1933. In 1877 described as a post office and station on the C. & N. W. Railroad, Menominee Township, 32 miles north of *Menominee*. It was settled in 1873, and named in honor of ex-governor John J. Bagley. (Jim Borski said it was named by S. G. Baldwin, at that time superintendent of the railroad), Population 25. Hemlock bark (used in tanning hides), cedar posts and venison are shipped. Daily mail. Henry G. A. Wachter, Postmaster. Unless otherwise noted the following were farmers in the area: Antonia Bauis, R. G. Brown, warehouseman; Wm. Burt; Peter Houle; Orren Johnson; August Mauck, laborer; Jos. Metcalf; B. Nadear; David Nadeau; Louis Nadeau; Geo. R. Paynter; Lucius Russell, justice; John Schroeder, section boss; Wm. H. Stewart; and F.A. Wachter, farmer and jobber.

James Borski, of *Menominee*, said the C. & N. W. Railroad put its rails through the area in 1872, and the following year a large camp was built for the crews of the gravel trains. First mills were built to harvest the lumber. Logs were hauled to neighboring mills or driven down the Little Cedar River to *Ingalls* and *Stephenson*, then later to *Talbot*. Fred Wachter, a veteran woodsman was first on the ground. He was a large scale operator of logging camps. Wachter erected the hotel at *Bagley*, which replaced an earlier company boarding house belonging to Victome and Rice. This firm had a sawmill east of C. & N. W. tracks and Wachter had a large cedar yard on the west side. Consequently there was an *East Bagley* and a *West Bagley*.

By 1887 the population was more than 200. Some of the listings for that year included: S. Erickson, showmaker; J. C. Mc Graw, station agent; J. B. Rose, mill superintendent; E. P. Royce & Company, general store; John Sturrock, notary, express agent and general store; A. Vanderheiden, general store; Chas. Wackenreiter, physician; F. A. Wachter, hotel; and Frank Wagner, blacksmith. A dozen or more are farmers were also listed.

In 1889, Borski said, forest fires burned two lumber camps, barns and the dam on the river. Despite the fires *Bagley* was booming in the 1890s, population 225. Some business listings for 1893 were: E. P. Barrass, general store; Anthony Deckleman, contractor; L. Liebman, general store and music teacher; J. G. Leitch, railroad and express agent; I. B. Longrie, cedar; Oliver Perra, hotel and saloon; E. P. Royce & Company, general store and sawmill; Sandburgh & Lord, posts and pnies; M. A. Sweig, wholesale cedar; Fred Wachter, hotel and lumber.

1905, population 168. Rosina Wachter, Postmistress; Joseph Kell, hotel; Clem Larson, station agent; Louis Liebman, music teacher; Louis Morrison, lumber mill; John Strutz, tailor; Mitchell Sweig, sawmill; and Henry G. A. Wachter, lands and notary.

In 1910, population 78. As more land was cleared more farmers settled in the area and the place took on the air of a permanent village. Rosina Wachter was Postmistress and the Bagley Orchestra, with Louis Liebman as leader had been formed.

Old settlers say that *Bagley* was once the busiest town along the line between *Menominee* and *Escanaba* but by the late 1920s it was only a crossroads town. *Dagett*, 7 miles distance was the nearest bank. Had a Moravian church. Rosina Wachter was still Postmistress; Ray Bardwell , station agent; R. E. Carnegie, gas station; Nure Brothers, potato buyers; and Peterson Brothers, general store.

Today, 1971, no one could guess that this was once a busy town, Borski said. The Bagley Lumber Company is located here and there are a few farms in the area. Nothing like it was in the 1880s and at the turn of the century.

BALLOUS—1910, on the C. & N. W. Railroad. Mail *Bagley*. Named for M. H. Ballous, manager of a mill for making barrel stock (staves and headings) that located here when the station was founded.

BANAT—Some of the earliest Hungarian immigrants into Michigan settled in Menominee County. This article appeared in the November 9, 1909, edition of the *Menominee Herald-Leader* about *Banat*, which was the name of a farming region in Hungary: *"G. H. Hagen, agent for the Menominee Land & Abstract Company, was in the city with a family of immigrants bound for the new settlement of Banat, 36 miles north of Menominee on the Wisconsin & Michigan Railroad. The settlement which already has 37 families is unique in the county, and promises to develop into one of the most prosperous.*

Comprised mainly of Hungarians, the village is laid out in exact reproduction of the method in vogue in the old country. The settlement has one immense building 120 ft x 16 ft. which houses seven families; it is divided into compartments for each family.

The settlers are under the leadership of one of their own race, who keeps a general supply of necessaries and sells them at cost.

The farms vary from 40 to 160 acres and are about 3 miles from the village. The men and women go to the farms each morning and return in the evening. This unusual procedure is patterned after villages of Hungary.

Since the settlement was first formed some months ago, the advancement has been rapid . . . A general store building has been erected and F. J. Schmidt, colonizer, placed in charge . . ."

By 1915 the population had grown to 313, in Holmes Township, about 6 miles northeast of *Daggett*. Frank J. Schmidt, Postmaster, and real estate; Jos. Broenel, station agent; Jos. Orth, hotel and meats; John Roth, general store; and John Signer, creamery.

By 1918 the population was nearly 400. Additional business listings were: Peter Fink, blacksmith; Levy Frock & Son, general store and cheese factory; and Mrs. Albert Winter, hotel.

In 1927 had a Catholic church and grade school. Two power stations costing $3 million were being built on the Menominee River near the town, 3 miles west at the Rosebush Lake Resort with a paved road connecting the site with *Banat*. Business listings for that year show that the settlers were rapidly becoming Americanized and within a few generations lost their original ethnic identity. 1927, John Roth, Postmaster and general store; The Banat Dance Hall, Christ Kausch, prop.; Herman Brensike, meats; the D. N. F. Telephone Company; John Drum, blacksmith; John Klippel, trapper; Paul Merschdorf, harness; Stegan Reisner, cabinet maker; Schmidt & Mathias, threshers; and Ed Vroman, trapper.

The Hungarians soon lost their identity of Magyar origin. Few realize that the Magyar language is very similar to Finnish. The Magyars and Finnish races were originally pushed out of their native homeland at the base of the Ural Mountains, therefore, their languages are very similar. Many immigrants from central Europe were called "Hungarians" even though they were not of true Magyar origin.

BIRCH CREEK—Never was a town. In 1879, Menominee Township, 7 miles north of *Menominee*. Not a post office. Was a station on the C. & N. W. Railroad, founded in 1855 and named for the township.

BIRD—Listed in 1910 as a station on the Wisconsin-Michigan Railroad. Mail *Faithorn*.

BLOUNT—1905, population 40. On the C. & N. W. Railroad, Nadeau Township, 2 miles from *Nadeau*. Named for C. H. Blount, first Postmaster, general store and sawmill. C. March, station agent.

1910, population 45. Same listings as 1905. After 1910, RFD *Nadeau*.

BLUM—1910, on the Wisconsin-Michigan Railroad, mail *Faithorn*.

BROOKS—1910, a station on the Wisconsin & Michigan Railroad, Holmes Township, 46 miles north of *Menominee*. Population 25. Named for Howard S. Brooks, first Postmaster, on January 12, 1900. Discontinued November 30, 1903.

CAMP 6—1910, on the Escanaba & Lake Superior Railroad. Mail *Whitney*.

CARBONDALE—In 1887 described as a recently established settlement on the C. & N. W. Railway, 12 miles north of *Menominee*. Population 50. Daily mail. James W. Osborne, Postmaster, justice, general store, and dealer in cedar.

Was a post office from December, 1881 until April, 1904. Has RFD *Wallace*.

CEDAR FORKS—1872, one of two post offices listed in the county. Described as: *"A post office on the stage route from Menominee to Escanaba, at the point where Cedar River empties into Green Bay. From November to April, daily mail by stage passes through here. During the season of navigation the mail is carried by water. Cedar Fork is 30 miles north of Menominee the terminus of the C. & N. W. Railroad, and 25 miles south of Escanaba."*

The town was settled in 1850, and in 1877 the population had reached 300. The village was also called *Cedarville*. Fish, game, lumber, lath, posts and some farm products were shipped. *Stephenson*, 12 miles west, was its railroad station. A stage ran to *Stephenson* during the winter. Mail delivery twice a week. In that year (1877) Edward P. Wood, Postmaster; Hubbard & Wood sawmill; Nicholas Jerue, hotel; Mrs. McCullough, hotel; John P. Macey, station agent; G. F. Rouele, collection agent; Jesse Spalding, general store and lumber; Wilmot Armstrong, fish dealer and Edward P. Wood, general store.

Only a few changes were made in 1879. John P. Macy, Postmaster and collection agent; and McGillis & Plau, shingle mill.

Between 1879 and 1887 the name of the town was changed to *Cedar River*, which it remains today. In 1887, W. O. Thurston was Postmaster. The population had increased to 400 and many business places had been built, in addition to those mentioned.

In 1910, the population had dropped to 150, and 1927 was given as 200.

Today *Cedar River* is shown on state maps and is now a resort area. Remains of the old lumber mill are on the north side of the river. South of the river is the old lighthouse keeper's house, still standing (1971). Has two churches, one of them, Protestant, has been moved from its former location east of the highway to the west side.

CEDAR—1887, a station on the P. Division of the C. & N. W. Railroad, 31 miles west of *Escanaba*. Also listed as such in 1893. James Borski said the settlement was named for the river upon which it was located. *"Many cedar mills were at this place,"* Borski said. Located northwest of *Hermansville*, nothing remains.

1910, listed in Rand McNally Atlas on the C. & N. W. Railroad—mail to *Vesper*.

In 1927, Charles Johnson, general store. Mail RFD from *Hermansville*.

————

CEDARVILLE—See *Cedar Forks*.

————

CLEAREMANS—(or *Cleeremans*)—1910, on the C. & N. W. Railroad, mail *Eustis*. Was named for Jerry Cleareman, a lumberman who lived here. Never became a town or village. Nothing remains. Was located west of *Perronville*.

————

CLYTIE—1910 Rand McNally Atlas, a station on the C. & N. W. Railroad, mail to *Hermansville*. Another logging settlement lost to the limbo of time. This place, like so many others, was apparently not of enough significance to even appear on maps.

————

COMUS—In 1887 was a station on the Felch Mountain Branch of the C. & N. W. Railroad (tracks removed in 1971), 3 miles west of *Whitney*.

————

CONGO—Another station on the "Wisky-Mich" Railroad lost to memory by all but a few. 1910, mail to *Nathan*.

————

CUNYARD—Was a post office for only a short time, from about 1895 until 1897, after that mail to *Hermansville*. On present day maps, spelled *Cunard*, 4 miles west of *Hermansville*. 1971 had a gasoline station, out of business, on US-2 Highway, and a large sawmill and lumber yard owned by Johnson Lumber Company Named for John Cunyard, lumber camp foreman in 1880. Had four names. First *Cedar*, then *Camp 4*, *Vesper* and *Cunyard*.

————

DeLOUGHRAY—1910, on Chicago & Northwestern Railroad, mail *Harris*. In 1905 was the postal name for *Indiantown*.

1887, a village in Spalding Township, 15 miles west of *Escanaba*. A station on the C. & N. W. Railroad. Population 50. Had a Catholic church. Michael Harris, Postmaster, sawmill, general store and justice of peace.

Other listings for that year were Fred Bessior, barber; Geo. DeLoughary, charcoal kiln; Alphonse Derosher, farmer; John Forest, school moderator; Henry Frank, shoemaker; J. B. Frechette, station agent; David Golder, carpenter; Frank Krouce, farm machinery; W. B. Mallory, railroad agent; Andrew Oasie, blacksmith; Ed Santo, book agent; and Alex Shivrett, blacksmith.

1893, was called *Harris Station*. Population 600. Additional listings for that year were Frank Krutsch, charcoal kilns; and Frank Loeffler, saloon.

September 6, 1900, name changed to *Harris*. Population 50. Telephone. M. B. Harris, Postmaster, general store and cedar products; Frank Kutsch, charcoal kilns; Jos. Laraux, saloon; and Napoleon Nault, carpenter; Jos. Kell, saloon; Laura Hill, teacher; Laura McCarthy, teacher. Within the next few years Ed Tuttle ran a sawmill and the Mashek Lumber Company operated a mill.

Today, 1971, three of the old store buildings remain standing on the north side of the railroad and can be seen from US-2 highway.

DOUGHERTY—1910, a station on the C. & N. W. Railroad. Mail *Spalding*.

DRYADS—1887, a station on the Felch Mountain branch of the C. & N. W. Railroad (tracks removed 1971). 1910, mail *Whitney*.

ENGLISH—In 1877, the post office at *Kloman Station*, on the C. & N. W. Railroad, in Ingallston Township, 26 miles southeast of *Escanaba*. *"The settlement was formed here in May, 1872, and now has a population of 50. Charcoal is the only shipment."* Daily mail. Henry H. Sterling, Postmaster and general store.

1879, population 45. Mary O'Neil, Postmaster; Thomas Kettleson, justice; Robert O'Neil, charcoal; and Anton Sipchen, constable.

1887, shipments should be made to *Powers*, 3 miles north. Population 180. Daily mail. Robert O'Neil, Postmaster; A. A. Archibald, express agent; J. Moore, telegraph agent; and L. Nicholas, general store.

1893, Henry Dishneau, Postmaster and general store; Edw. Dishneau, charcoal kilns; F. C. Huse, station agent; W. H. LaFayette, carpenter; and P. Perry, telegraph agent.

The post office operated from February, 1875 until May 23, 1895. Shown on 1905 maps. After 1905 listed as *Kloman*. Mail *Powers*.

EUSTIS—Settled 1891, a post office and station on the M., St. Ste. M. Railroad, Spalding Township, 13 miles from *Escanaba*. Population 25. G. W. DeLoughary, Postmaster; general store and charcoal kilns; Kate Bacon, school teacher; Daniel Dwyer, dairy; L. J. Esler, carpenter; Mrs. L. J. Esler, physician; and B. F. Ferguson, station agent.

1905, population 50. John W. Henderson, general store.

1910, population 25. Send mail to *Shaffer*.

EVERETT—1910, on the Wisconsin-Michigan Railroad, mail *Nathan.*

FAITHORN—Was first named *Pembina* (see *Pembina* history) named for J. N. Faithorn, one of Wisconsin-Michigan railroad owners. *Faithorn* was the postal name. *Faithorn Junction*, railroad name. 1910, population 175. On the Wisconsin & Michigan and Minneapolis St. Paul & Sault Ste. Marie Railroads. Clarence Harter, Postmaster; C. B. Betts, station agent; A. W. Brandt, log contractor; John J. Dunn, Jr., general store; A. E. Haines, notary; George Harter & Son, sawmill; and Wm. Maxwell, blacksmith.

In 1915, John J. Dunn, Jr., was Postmaster, general store, and cattle and grain dealer; Robert Dunn, fruit trees; Geo. Harter & Son, general store, sawmill and hotel; and A. G. Spiering, station agent.

1918, population 150. Same directory as 1915, with one addition, Clarence Harter had a sawmill, store and hotel, and E. W. Wilson, station agent.

The post office operated from March, 1905 until March 31, 1955.

FARNHAM—1910, a station on the M. St. & Ste. Marie Railroad, mail Spalding. 1927, 7 miles east of *Hermansville*, mail *Spalding*.

FAUNUS—1910, a station on the C. & N. W. Railroad, mail *LaBranche*, Borski said the name was taken from ancient mythology. Nothing remains today. Post office operated from 1896 until 1908. One of several towns along the railroad named from mythology by the railroad company.

FISHER—Postal name *Koss*. 1905, population 150. On the Wisconson-Michigan Railroad, Stephenson Township, 24 miles north of *Menominee*. J. F. Bronoel, Postmaster and station agent; Wm. B. Flynn, hotel and saloon; G. Goldborg, general store; Mrs. M. Leroy, general store; and the Stephenson Land & Lumber Company, logging, etc.

1910, a few additions were made to the business directory, Lizzie Deehr, teacher; G. H. Hagen, land agent; Mrs. Eva Longrie, general store; and C. H. Worcester Company, posts and poles.

1915, population 150. Post office discontinued, mail to *Stephenson*. Listings for that year, G. H. Hagen, land agent; James Johnson, real estate; Kobeson & Solper, sawmill and hotel; and Mrs. LeRoy, general store.

Koss (or *Fisher*) on the "Whisky-Mich" Railroad as it appeared during the boom days of the railroad. The Koss Hotel is in the foreground. Note the handcar or "velocipede" near the crossing sign.   Photo courtesy of James Borski, *Menominee*, Michigan

The story of Fisher, written by James Borski, of *Menominee*, also tells the history of the Wisconsin & Michigan Railroad, called "Wisky-Mich" by old time residents.

In 1867, John Bagley ran his narrow-gauge railroad from *Ingalls*, Michigan, to a point on the Menominee River with the purpose of unloading logs for the mills down river. This landing was called the *Trail Camp* and here was only one little shack to keep out of the weather. In 1893, Bagley sold his narrow-gauge to a group of Chicago businessmen and became a director. Its new owners were J. N. Faithorn, S. M. Fisher, (who the town was named for), a Mr. Kough and Mr. Nathan. These men formed the Wisconsin & Michigan Railroad. The trail camp was renamed *Fisher*. The W. & M. Company built a bridge across the Menominee River at *Fisher* but that spring the high water and floating logs caused it to wash away. Another bridge was built the latter part of 1894. This bridge is still in use and converted for automobile traffic.

During 1895, the W. & M. officials entered the lumbering business to bring business to their railroad. They built a large sawmill, called the Northern Supply Company. This mill was located on the river bank just east of the bridge. The company had over 300 men employed in 1896 and operated several general stores and supply stores along the railroad right-of-way. The huge mill prospered and in 1897 the W. & M. Company moved its general office to Fisher. As there were severa *Fishers* in Michigan, the post office established in 1897, bore the name *Koss* for the auditor of the railroad company until 1898.

Due to financial difficulties, the railroad was forced to sell the mill and stores and move its general office. The C. H. Worcester Company, of *Chicago*, purchased the mill and started into full production. The new company built the Koss Hotel, a 25-room building with a saloon downstairs. It also built a company store for its workers. At this time the company employed 80 men at the mill and cut 70 to 80 thousand feet of lumber per day. The town had four streets and 200 homes.

On the morning of May 14, 1900, disaster struck and the little town of *Koss* was burned by forest fires. Only a few houses, the Wisky-Mich depot and office of the C. H. Worcester Company remained. The fires started the night before and 100 men worked digging ditches to hold it back, but in vain. The losses were the large sawmill, many business places, in addition to the hotel, and nearly all of the homes. The mill also lost all the logs and thousands of feet of lumber piled in their yards.

The Worcester Company rebuilt the mill but lack of timber forced its closing. The Wisconsin-Michigan Railroad ceased its operations on June 30, 1938 and *Koss* was gradually forgotten. Today people drive over the old railroad beds and few know they exist. Only some old foundations and the railroad bridge are left to show the town existed.

In the early days of the Wisky-Mich John Bagley operated three wood burning and two coal burning locomotives, plus 64 freight cars. In 1894 standard gauge tracks replaced the narrow-gauge and in 1902 three passenger trains ran daily, in addition to four freights, two log trains, and a special for cattle, iron ore and miscellaneous freight.

———

FOX—1905, a country post office, located on Green Bay, Cedarville Township. Started as a fishing village. 1910, population 100. Mail tri-weekly. Mrs. Grace M. Zettel, Postmistress. Fishermen listed were: Albert Baker, John Barstow, L. S. Harkins, W. Harkins, C. Henson, Jos. Juneau, C. Paulason, N. Peterson, Alex Savoy and Wilhelm Brothers Kenfield & Zettle and A. C. Shulze were timber dealers.

Business listings remained about the same until the 1920s when timber became the important industry in the area. 1927, population 80. Located on Deer Creek and M-35 highway. Stage tri-weekly to *Cedar River*, Emma Anderson, Postmistress. Listings of timber dealers were: Geo. Anderson, Wm. Edstrom, John Everson, Mark Hall, Jacobson Brothers, O'Day Brothers, N. P. Larson, John Marinson, Sander Olson, Berger Peterson, N. Peterson, Roy Peterson, Alex Savoy, and H. Sundby. Only a few fishermen were listed: Albert Baker and M. Zettel. Was a post office until August 31, 1951.

FUMEE—in 1887, listed as a station on the Peshtigo division of the Chicago & Northwestern Railroad, near the Wisconsin State line. No post office.

———

GARDNER—1910, a station on the Wisconsin-Michigan Railroad. Mail *Nathan*. Was a logging spur about 1894. Named for Auti Gardner, a lumberman, in 1934.

———

GOURLEY—1905, population 100. Cedarville Township, 9 miles from *Harris*. Daily mail. John A. Louderville, Postmaster; Mashek Lumber Company, sawmill and lumber.

Jim Borski, of *Menominee*, said in 1883 three families from Nadeau had settled here and the next year raised cabins. H. Jasper built the first sawmill, which was destroyed by fire in 1904.

In 1905 Arthur Gourley bought the Jasper mill and founded the town of Gourley. At one time there was a general store, post office, saloon, and saw and shingle mill. There were about 18 houses. The mill had all modern equipment, including an electric lighting plant which served the village and private residences.

First camps in the area were built by the Spalding Lumber Company and were later sold to Crawford. Camps "J" and "I" were located near *Gourley*.

The first school was built in 1890 and lasted until 1913, when it too became the victim of a fire. *Gourley* was one of the last villages to be settled in the county, Borski said. Today the mills are gone, along with the railroad, and there is nothing to remind one of the bustling little community.

———

GRAVEL PIT—See *Talbot*.

———

HAMLIN—1910, on the "Wisky-Mich" Railroad, mail *Faithorn*.

———

HAMMOND—1910, another station or flag stop on the Wisconsin-Michigan Railroad. Mail *Nathan*.

———

HANSEN—1910, on the C. & N. W. Railway, mail *Wallace*.

———

HARRIS—See *DeLoughtray* for history.

———

HAYWARD BAY—See *Arthur Bay*.

———

HELPS—1910, on the C. & N. W. Railroad, mail *Labranche*. James Borski said it was named for Arthur Helps, an English writer. Was a logging town at one time. Nothing remains.

HOULES—1910, on the C. & N. W. Railroad, mail *Harris*. This burg was named for A. Houles, an employee of the railroad. Was another logging point on the railroad. Nothing today.

———

HYLAS—In 1887, a station on the Felch Mountain Branch of the C. & N. W. Railroad, 9 miles southeast of *Metropolitan*, nearest post office and 4 miles east of *Hardwood*, now located in Dickinson County.

Borski said the name is taken from a dictionary of mythology.

Nothing remains here. The tracks were removed in 1971.

———

INDIANTOWN—1887, the postal name for *DeLoughray*. 1910, mail *Harris*. Named because of the numerous Indians in the area. Was located about ½ mile west of *Harris* and on the railroad. (See *DeLoughray*) Named for Mrs. Simons, an Indian midwife who served the area in early days.

———

INGALLSTON—1910, population 27. Borski said a sawmill was set up here in 1866, by the Ingalls Brothers from *Menominee*, from whence its name was taken. It was first called *Section 19*.

Robert Beattie, a fisherman, was one of the first to settle here in 1867. Beattie Creek was named for him. Two years later he was joined by his brother. Owen Gartland and Louis Grabowsky settled here about the same time. Gartland was a cooper and made kegs for the fishermen to pack their fish in. Charles and Edwin Quimby along with John Nelson were early fisherman also, he said.

In 1887 the town was listed as *Ingalls*, the "ton" or "town" was added later. In that year described as 19 miles north of *Menominee*. Population 250. Settled in 1868. Daily mail. Louis Dobeas, Postmaster, general store and lumber; J. Bagley, general store; George Carley, boarding house; Carley & Parmenter, lumber and shingle mill; E. Dam, charcoal kiln; Forest Mill lumber Company; C. T. Morbeck, general store; Wm. H. Morris, justice; F. Schafer, saloon; and Josiah Wilson, justice.

1893, remained about the same. John L. Sutherland, Postmaster; Bagley, general store; Geo. Barker, thresher; Ira Caley, lumber; Lewis Dobeas, store; G. Felger, meats; Michael Garragan, charcoal kiln; John Gerondale, meats; Jos. Gravel, saloon; Octave Gravel, charcoal; L. A. Jennings, general store; Jennings & Colburn, shingle mill; Hugh Kerns, blacksmith and saloon; C. T. Morbeck, general store; John Sutherland, station agent; Miss Lizzie Sutherland, music teacher; J. J. Tobin, saloon, John White, hotel; and John Williams, charcoal kiln.

For a time Mr. and Mrs. Edwin Quimby ran the large boarding house, erected by the Ingalls Brothers to accomodate mill workers. At this time there was no road to *Menominee* and the families followed the shoreline to reach the city.

252

The post office was established in 1898 and the mail brought from *Menominee* by horse and buggy. John Renner was the first mail carrier. Mail was delivered three times a week.

Between the lumber and fishing industry the people managed to build up nice homes. In 1900, *Ingallston* produced more herring than any other fishery in the United States. Today, fishermen's boats and nets can still be found in this area, Borski said.

Mrs. Charles R. Stucker, of *Menominee*, is a granddaughter of Robert Beattie, an early settler. She said her Mother lives in what was the old *Ingallston* school in 1890. *"It was moved north of Beattie Creek and used as a town hall until about 1921,"* she said. The roof was raised to make room for the children, Mrs. Stucker said. About 1908, a new house was built for Hugh Beattie, now Margaret Merrimen's place, and has been remodeled several times. The house where Mrs. Orian now lives was the old Frank Ziminski home, built before 1910. The Ray Pawlowski home was moved from *Menominee* about 1900 and the old house by the Golf Course was also built in the 1890s, she said.

INGALSDORF—In 1887, was the name of present day *Norway*.

Charcoal kilns along the C. & N. W. Railroad in Menominee County. Once an important industry in the Upper Peninsula only a few bricks remain today where these charcoal kilns once stood in many areas along a railroad track.
Photo courtesy of James Borski, *Menominee*, Michigan

JOHNSON'S SPUR—1910, on the Minneapolis St. Paul & Sault Ste. Marie Railroad, mail to *Hermansville*.

_____

KELLS (or *Kellsville*)—Jim Borski wrote the story of this one-time settlement. *"In 1893, the Ingalls, White Rapids & Northern Railway, forerunner of the Wisconsin & Michigan, located its headquarters at Kellsville. The place was named after Andrew Kelly, a foreman with the narrow gauge railroad company. At this time the railroad company had a general store and a round-house built of huge logs. The purpose of the line and its spurs was to haul logs to the Menominee River to supply the mills at Menominee."*

Art Cordes, 95-year-old pioneer (1971), remembers the place well. *"On hunting trips we stayed at the narrow-gauge headquarters many times. The main lumber camp was very long. Downstairs was a dining room, wash room, cook shanty and office, all separated by partitions. The upstairs was divided into two sections with stairways at each end. This was the camp sleeping quarters and I slept there among the company men. It was not uncommon to hear the men speak different languages all at one time,"* he said.

During this year (1893) the company built homes for 250 men who worked in the woods and on the railroad. They also built shops for the locomotives and log cars. Five locomotives were used here. The following year the Wisconsin & Michigan bought the line and extended it farther north.

A news item of May 12, 1888 reads: *"Kellsville—There are two cooks here who are jealous of each other. One is called 'The biscuit shooter' and the other 'the hash slinger.' They met in the store one evening this week and started to scrap. The biscuit shooter hit his opponent over the head with a stove cover and the hash slinger countered with a smashing blow that damaged the other's features. The referee decided the fight a draw."*

News item of May 17, 1890: *"Forest fires in the area. An Indian feast, or pow-wow, took place about a mile from Kellsville Sunday night."*

Borski said he talked to an old timer who remembered the pow-wows that took place when he was a boy. Indians had two large dance rings near *Kellsville* and along the river. Rings can be seen today where they were driven into the ground, Borski said.

News item of November 1, 1890: *"By the way we want to protest against the name 'Kellsville' as applied to our lay-out here. From time immemorial these have been the 'Shaky Woods' and have been known as such by every hunter and woodsman since the banks of the Menominee first echoed the ring of the woodsman's axe. Long after the last pine has disappeared from its rugged hills, the Shaky Woods will be remembered as the largest body of solid pine in this* region. Many a mule whacker will have reminiscenses of breakdowns and hard toiling and the amount of profanity it required to persuade a mule team through Shaky Woods in the spring of the year. Because a man named Kelly built a lumber camp here is the old name with all its associations to be laid aside?," The report read. "Not much! Just drop that 'Kellsville' when you mention our forest home and lumberjack's retreat. Speak of it as The Shaky Woods!"

Borski said the plea fell on deaf ears and the area is still called *Kells*, the "ville" having been dropped years ago.

In 1905, many farmers started to clear land in the area, Borski said. News item of April 19, 1910: "*About 50 Menominee people left on the W. & M. Railroad this morning to witness the stump-pulling demonstration at Kells by the Northern Turpentine Company. The company will begin active operations in a short time. The new industry has contracted to clear thousands of acres of pine stumps. There will be four distillation plants and one refinery where the crude products will be separated. The stump puller, operated by steam, is capable of uprooting 10 stumps at one time on its tentacle-like cables. The one to be demonstrated is of smaller size.*"

This marked the end of logging in the area, but there are a lot of nice Norway pine left, Borski said. The Shaky Lakes are in this area also. All that remains near *Kells* are the old Whisky-Mich roadbed, an abandoned school house and a few farms.

KEW—1910, on the C. & N. W. Railway, a short distance north of *Menominee* on present day US-41 highway. This tiny settlement was named by W. B. Linsley, a lover of flowers, from the famous Kew Botanical Gardens near *London*, England. Old-timers in the area said Linsley was interested in the wild cherry that grew here and wild cherry trees still grow in the area today.

Kew's "railroad station" was only a box car on the siding to accommodate farmers who lived south of *Birch Creek*. Was only a flag stop along the line for passengers and picked up cans of milk. James Borski said the faded railroad sign *KEW* still stands alongside the tracks, the lone reminder that this was ever a station.

KILLGOBIN—This ghost town has been so long gone that it has been disregarded by historians. Jim Borski, of *Menominee*, said the site was adjacent to the Riverside Country Club along the Menominee River.

"*It was the first permanent white settlement on the Menominee River,*" Borski said. The sawmill dominated the buildings, which comprised 10 or 12 houses on high ground above the mill. It contained a blacksmith shop and other fixtures of the early sawmill settlements. The population of the community was more than half Irish, thus the name, Killgobin. *"The name is almost entirely forgotten now and is probably the reason it was not written in any of the early history books,"* Borski said.

The houses were of frame construction. One large structure built to house three families was called "The Barracks." A two story boarding house stood on the high bank near the mill and endured after most of the settlement was gone. Some buildings had shaved shingle roofs (shakes) and some had batten roofs.

None were painted. In these houses lived the men who worked in the saw-mill. The Menominee River Boom Company built its scaling gap (sorting bins) at this place and rebuilt the old *Killgobin* dam for their use. Broken pottery lying in some places beneath the sand is all that shows *Killgobin* ever existed.

Borski said there are many flint chips remaining on the site left by Indians that lived here and an Indian war was fought in the same area.

KLOMAN—See *English* for history. Named for Andrew Kloman, of *Pittsburgh*, Pa., owner of charcoal kilns at this place and an iron ore operator. Nothing remains today.

KOSS—Also called *Fisher*. See *Fisher*.

LA BRANCHE—Named for pioneer settler, Israel LaBranche. First post office 1902. 1910 population 100. In Spalding Township, the C. & N. W. Railroad, Felch Mountain Branch, about 10 miles northwest of *Perronville*. Telephone. N. Blaney, Postmaster; George LaBranche, saloon; Wm. Mueller Company, saw, shingle mill and general store; and E. Richer, saloon.

1915, population 50. Louis Belanger, Postmaster, general store and sawmill. The post office operated until May 15, 1948.

All that remains of the one-time village, located 2 miles east of Ten Mile Creek, on M-69, is a tavern in an old building, covered with insulbrick, one house, and an old two-story frame building that may have been the hotel near the C. & N. W. Railroad grade.

LARSONS—1910, on the Minneapolis, St. Paul & Sault Ste. Marie Railroad. Mail *Schaffer*.

LAURIS—1910, a station on the Wisconsin & Michigan Railroad. Mail *Nathan*.

LEAPER—1910, on the C. & N. W. Railroad, mail *Loretto*.

LEATHEM—First name for *Arthur Bay*. See *Arthur Bay*.

―――――――

LITTLE RIVER—John Miller became first Postmaster on March 4, 1884. 1887, located near the Wisconsin State line, Menominee Township, 9 miles north of *Menominee*. Population 80. Semi-weekly mail stage to *Menominee*. Robert Mulholland, Postmaster; Peter Nelson, meat market; and Michael O'Connel, hotel.

1895, population 95. Robert Mulholland, Postmaster; John E. Boland, hotel; and Peter Nelson, meat market.

April 15, 1902, a discontinued post office. Send mail to *Menominee*.

―――――――

LONGRIE—Linda Kruhmin, of *Stephenson*, Mich., said it was located on the old "Wisky-Mich" railroad, 20 miles north of *Menominee*, in Lake Township. *"Longrie was a small village with a mill, cedar yard, school, a combination post office and general store, and a blacksmith shop. Lumber and sugar beets were shipped on the railroad,"* she said. The land is now locally owned and is being farmed. All that remains are a few foundations and the one room school. Listed as a post office in the 1912 Standard Atlas of Menominee County by Geo. A. Ogle & Company

―――――――

MALACCA—Shown on 1905 maps, just west of *Hermansville*. On the Minneapolis St. Paul & Sault Ste. Marie Railroad. Mail *Hermansville*. Named for a species of tree.

―――――――

MENOMINEE RIVER JUNCTION—Settled in 1872. Was original name of *Spalding*. Not a ghost town.

―――――――

MUMFORDS—1910, on the C. & N. W. Railroad. Mail *Bagley*. Named for a man by that name who operated charcoal kilns at this location.

―――――――

NATHAN—In 1894, when the Wisconsin-Michigan (Wisky-Mich) railroad was changed from narrow gauge to standard, the new Board of Directors consisted of a large dry-goods concern of *Chicago* made up of Kuhn, Nathan and Fisher. The name of Nathan was taken from one of the directors, J. Nathan. The post office was called *Wittmund* and opened on March 1, 1895. Renamed *Nathan* April 3, 1895.

The first settlers were Eugene Houte, who built the Nathan Hotel and had a large sawmill here. Others were a Mr. Wittrick, who had a trading post and saloon, and C. W. Wilkins, the first Postmaster. The first post office at the site was named *Wittmund*, later changed to *Nathan*. The first school opened in 1897 and the first church later. In 1896, there was one hotel, a store, the saloon mentioned above and the Wisky-Mich depot. There were also several logging camps in the area. The Menominee Indians, near the White Rapids on the Menominee River, did a lot of trading here. When they rode into town on their ponies to trade furs for staples, children of the village hid under their beds in the safety of their homes.

1905, population 75. On the W. & M. Railroad, Holmes Township. Charles W. Wilkins, Postmaster and general store; Erickson & Adams, saloon; Eugene Houte, cedar posts; Alex LeGrove, blacksmith; and C. W. Wilkins, store, hotel and station agent.

Only one addition was made to the business directory in 1910, that of J. J. Nickolai, meat market, and in 1915, Olive C. Wilkins, Postmaster.

By 1927, the population had dropped to 35. Charles W. Wilkins, Postmaster; C. A. Erickson, justice; and the Nathan Cheese Factory, C. Wilkins, proprietor, and the general store.

After the railroad removed the tracks, the village started to die completely. Today, remains of the old grade can be seen and hunting camps are built on its base. Remains of the Wittrick store and the large Wilkins building are all that is left today. The post office was discontinued December 31, 1940.

ORO—1905, a station on the "Wisky-Mich" Railroad, between *Vega* and *Cleermans*. Named from the Spanish *oro*, meaning "gold" because it was thought the ore had been found here. Rumors of a gold rush were false. Nothing remains of the station.

OSBORN—1905, a station on the C. & N. W. Railroad between *Carbondale* and *Wallace*, north of *Menominee*.

PEMBINA—1887, a settlement and post office 12 miles south of *Waucedah*, its nearest depot. Settled in 1871. Population 50. Semi-weekly mail from *Waucedah*. M. E. Harter, Postmaster and tailor; Albert Brandt, farmer; John Dunn, farmer; Peter Lacroix, and Frank McCamley, Peter Nelson and Frank Parr, all farmers; and Wm. Maxeell, blacksmith and wagonmaker. 1893, in Holmes Township, 1½ miles from *Menominee River Station (Spalding)*. Daily mail. Population 150. A. W. Brandt, Postmaster; Frank Farr, justice; Harter & Lacroix, cedar; Johnson, cedar; Peter Lacroix, justice; Wm. Reippley, constable; J. F. Marsh, township clerk; and A. U. Slaybaugh, justice.

1905, Clarence Harter, Postmaster; George Harter & Son, general store, shingle mill, lumber etc.; C. E. Johnsone, cedar; A. Kunsch, railroad agent; A. F. Stundermeyer, express agent, plus a dozen farmers listed.

1905, name changed to *Faithorn*. (see *Faithorn* for history)

PHEE—1910, a station on the "Wisky-Mich" Railroad. Mail *Nathan*.

RADFORDS—1910, a station on the M. St. P. & S. Ste. Marie Railroad, mail *Harris.*

————

RAPIDS—1887, a post office, in Wallace Township, 21 miles north of *Menominee* within 1 mile of the Wisconsin state line. Its shipping point is *Ingalls (Ingallston).* Population 30. Weekly mail. Julia E. Bigger, Postmistress.

Wm. D. Bigger was first Postmaster on March 4, 1884. Post office discontinued November 5, 1887.

————

RONDA—1910, a station or flag stop on the Wisconsin & Michigan Railroad. Mail *Nathan.*

————

SECTION 19—First name for *Ingalls* or *Ingallston.*

————

SWANSON—1910, a station on the Wisconsin & Michigan Railroad. Holmes Township. Named for Solomon Swanson. Ole Olson was first Postmaster on July 18, 1905.

————

TALBOT—1887, named for Samuel H. Talbot, of a lumbering firm. Also known as *Gravel Pit,* in Nadeau Township, 30 miles north of *Menominee.* Settled in 1879. Population 60. Daily mail. Fred W. Sensiba, Postmaster, notary, general store, and engineer of water works; Ellen G. Benjamin, capitalist; S. A. Benjamin, engineer; B. M. Bodle, jobber; L. W. Burch, jobber; Wm. French, railroad agent; Geo. Lemke, shingle mill; Alex Lozo, jobber; and W. C. Oakes, hotel.

1893, a village in Nadeau Township, population 300. James Bute, Postmaster; Chas. Anderson, engineer; John Anderson, teacher; Conrad Bailey, blacksmith; Henry Dory, millwright; Geo. Hoffman, jobber; Little Lumber Company, Jos. Litile, President, James Bute, Treasurer, and C. J. Huebel, Manager; Theodore Menard, saloon; W. C. Oakes, railroad agent; Fred W. Sensiba, general store and jeweler; John Stehlan, hotel; and Talbot Manufacturing Company, (Samuel and F. J. Pike, general store and sawmill).

1905, population 200. Wm. J. Argabrite, Postmaster and news agent; A. H. Butts, notary; Butts-Lillie & Company, general store; Gardner Brothers, hotel and saloon; Oscar Lamont, railroad agent; Jos. Ruebins, teacher; and Maxmillian Socher, justice.

1909, a discontinued post office. Has RFD from *Daggett.* C. Baumler, saloon; Perrizo & Sonas, saw and planing mills; and the Talbot Lumber Company.

Talbot as told by James Borski: *"In the late 1800s a mill was built by Jubelles on the Little Cedar River. This burned and the holding purchased by the Lilly Company and later by Paul Perrizo. As the forests were depleted it was necessary to make longer and longer hauls of logs. It became necessary to bring timber in from an area 16 miles away. This required three trips a day with a team, but 96 miles a day killed many horses. Mr. Perrizo's interests were bought by Jim and Ray Andrews of Escanaba who shipped in timber from the north. A few years later the mill burned."*

In the 1890s the lumber company had a boarding house and a store. There were homes and saloons, a post office, and a school.

On April 25, 1891, the Talbot Company put two million feet of pine in Little River. The Talbot boiler was enlarged and a lath machine of 20,000 capacity was installed.

On October 21, 1893, three to four hundred canthook and peavy sticks were turned out in a day at the Ira Carley mill. Besides making these sticks, bunks for logging sleighs were manufactured. The mill at this time was also filling an order for narrow gauge cars.

News item of May 19, 1906: *"The peaceful little village of Talbot was practically wiped off the map yesterday. Some 10 dwelling houses, depot, store, warehouse, hotel, post office, blacksmith shop, and other buildings were destroyed together with one million shingles and 15 or 20 thousand cedar posts belonging to small dealers and farmers. The forest fires hit five counties."*

In 1927 there were two general stores, one owned by James Andres, and the other by L. S. Johnson. In 1939, Mrs. Ray Andres had the old dam blown out and the last vestige of *Talbot's* lumbering days disappeared. Today farms are located in the area.

Walter Romig, in his book "Michigan Place Names," said Fred W. Sensiba became its first Postmaster on September 14, 1883 and operated until November 14, 1905.

———

TWENTY ONE (21)—The first name for *Stephenson* in 1872 when the railroad went in. The station was called *Spur 21*.

———

VEGA—1910, on the C. & N. W. Railroad, mail *Loretto*. This name was taken from the Spanish word *"vega,"* meaning a tract of level, fruitful ground . It was supposed to be descriptive of the location. James Borski, of *Menominee*, said nothing remains today.

———

VESPER—Located on the C. & N. W. Railroad, Meyer Township, 12 miles from *Norway*. In 1905, a country post office, Edwin Johnson, Postmaster and general store. The post office opened January 12, 1904 and closed on March 16, 1912. After that RFD *Hermansville*.

VINCENT—Named for Nelson B. Vincent, first Postmaster. The post office operated from June, 1883 to April 8, 1886. In 1887, a discontinued post office, 3 miles east of *Stephenson*, and 23 miles north of *Menominee*. Not on a railroad. Send mail to *Stephenson*.

WHITNEY—Founded about 1878 and named for Charles Whitney, a land surveyor. Became a post office on October 30, 1883 and lasted until June 30, 1939. Located on the C. & N. W. Railroad on what later became known as the Felch Mountain Branch. The tracks were removed in 1971, and if there are any remains of the place today they are difficult to find. One farm house remained in the vicinity, on M-69 highway, in 1971.

1887, John C. Kirkpatrick, Postmaster; Frederick Forrest, proprietor of the Whitney House, hotel; Dr. Geizer, doctor; Allen Kirkpatrick, express agent; Armedes Marcea, blacksmith; L. S. Pitts & Company charcoal kilns and general store.

1893, in Spalding Township. Population 300. J. S. Musson, Postmaster; Neal Livingston, prop. Whitney House; James S. Meussen, justice; Pittsburgh & Lake Superior Iron Company, charcoal and general store; Wm. Russell, contractor.

1905, several farmers listed. F. J. Schweitzer, Postmaster, real estate, cedar and justice; Miss Olive Schweitzer, teacher; David Turpin, barber; and Allan Schweitzer, livestock.

1909, telephone. A. A. Soder, Postmaster; Mary Pryal, teacher and National Pole Company, ties, posts, etc.

1927, population 108. On the C. & N. W. Railroad and M-69 (now County Road 569), R. A. Aldrich, Postmaster, apiarist, poultry, and greenhouses; E. L. Belden, dairy; Emil Dahlstrom, fruit; Axel Johnson, logger; Emil Person, logger; and Thomas Jones, manager of Whitney Farms.

WILSON—Named for Frank D. Wilson, Postmaster in 1881. First named *Myra*. 1887, a new post office on the C. & N. W. Railroad, 18 miles west of *Escanaba*, in Spalding Township. Population 200. Daily mail. Publius Gagnon, Postmaster and general store; W. S. Laing, sawmill and general store; James S. Musson, justice; Geo. M. Smith, shingle mill; and A. Vincent, saloon and hotel.

1893, about the same. Wm. Bellefeuile, hotel and grocery; Rev. Jos. England, Methodist; John Millete, hotel; Frank Pelland, charcoal kilns; R. S. Raymond, blacksmith; and Sanders Brothers, blacksmiths.

By 1905 the population had increased to 425. Located in Harris Township. J. S. Musson, Postmaster and general store; Wm. Bellefeuile, hotel and grocery; Miss Adie Enfield, teacher; Gustav Enfield, general store; Herman Hartwigg, saloon; J. G. Kell, barber; Kellog Switchbord & Supply, of *Chicago*, Emil Hoppe, Manager, cedar yard; May Musson, teacher; F. W. Phillips, railroad agent; R. S. Raymond, blacksmith; U. P. Shannon, Manager of Wilbur Lumber Company of *Milwaukee*, Wisconsin; Alfred Temple, school principal.

1909, only a few changes, Eva Bagley, teacher; Louis Beauchamp, charcoal kilns; Ned Beauchamp, blacksmith; Nicholas Bodette, saloon; Chas. Lewis, school principal; and Martha Tenney, teacher.

1915, population 300. Four miles from *Powers*. Telephone. M. H. Harris, Postmaster and general store; Frank Enfield, general store; Ewert Bros, potatoes; Jos. Kasinski, farm lands; W. Kell, farm machinery; Wm. Kell, Jr., livestock; and A. Transil, cheese factory.

In 1927 Wilson was a flourishing, established village with several cheese factories, restaurants, etc. Population, 400. Now located on US-41. Bus to *Escanaba* and *Menominee* five times daily. Edward J. Hakes, Postmaster, general store and restaurant; R. H. Bagley, potatoes; Wm. Bruchardt, railroad agent; M. & M. B. Eintield, confection; Hans Gudwer, cheese; M. H. Harris, general store; Kampine & Bornhofen, cheese manufacturers; Walter Kell, farm machinery; Anton Marisiecke, cheese; H. H. Nelson, confection; H. O. Olson, cheese; John S. Plausky, blacksmith; C. J. Quade, editor of the *Powers Spalding Tribune*; Frank Raymond, blacksmith; Schoen Brothers, garage; Mose Tanuay, soft drinks; and E. J. Hokes, proprietor of the Willow Tea Room.

Today *Wilson* is a ghost town. The old, two-story brick school house stands empty as do several vacant store buildings along the railroad adjacent to US-2 and US-41 highway. One gas station is open for business along the highway, near Wilson Creek along which the town was built.

James Bush now operates the Wilson Tavern, an early day landmark where all the lumberjacks congregated. It also housed the dance hall where the square dancers enjoyed Saturday night celebrations, Helen Nyland, of *Marinette*, Wisconsin said.

WITTMUND—Name changed to *Nathan*. See *Nathan* for history.

Chapter Seventeen

ONTONAGON COUNTY

Ontonagon County was laid out by the legislature on March 9, 1843 and attached to Houghton County until 1846. The county government was formed in 1848 and legalized in 1852-53. *Ontonagon* is the county seat.

Historians disagree on the origin of the name. One version is that it comes from Ojibwa Indian "onagan" meaning dish or bowl. Another version is that it was taken from the Indian "Nunda-norgan" meaning hunting river.

When the first white men settled here in 1843, the Indians had no knowledge of the ancient copper miners who mined copper from rock ridges and bluffs, using stone hammers, fire and water. Carbon 14 tests have established that this operation occurred here three to five thousand years ago.

James K. Paul, the first white man to settle here, founded the town of *Ontonagon* on May 3, 1843. He died here on May 1, 1881, and is credited with taking out the famous Ontonagon Copper Boulder, which is on display in the Smithsonian Institute, Washington, D. C.

Ontonagon County is the third largest in the Upper Peninsula, with 845,000 acres. Much of the area is untouched wilderness and includes the controversial Porcupine Mountains that is to be designated as a national park.

The American Fur Trading Company established a post at *Iron River (Silver City)* between 1805 and 1820. Beaver, muskrat, mink, otter and other pelts were traded by the Indians for flour, cloth, blankets, trinkets, etc. and, of course, whiskey. Fur trading on a large scale ended in 1880.

During the copper boom, 1845-1870, the population grew from 380 to 5,400. After the big boom, mining was carried on by tributors (individuals) and reorganized companies until 1918 when most operations closed. The activity in copper boomed in spurts of 20 year periods. In 1950, the White Pine Copper Company began development of a new mine at *White Pine*, where one of the largest known deposits of copper in the world has been discovered. A second shaft was begun in 1966 and completed in 1969. This has increased employment from 1,600 in 1966 to about 3,000 by 1971 when it was announced that the Copper Range Mining Company is working to transform the village into a modern community for its workers and their families.

Some of the 3,000 workers at the copper mine near here have to commute up to 90 miles to work each day. Once called a ghost town and nearly deserted, today the village is rapidly becoming a modern city, with $40 million being invested in new housing and related development. *"We needed stability in the community,"* Chester D. Ensign, Jr., said. *"We have had a very high rate of turnover in our work force because of the long daily drive to and from work."*

By September of 1971, 30 new homes had been built, with an additional 170 in the planning stage. A new shopping mail was opened, which will eventually house 15 stores, according to an A. P. news wire story of September 22, 1971.

During the pine timber era, 1880-1900, the Diamond Match Company was the largest operator in the area. During the early 1900s hardwood and hemlock was cut and for some time was a leading industry. As most north Michigan counties, today the harvest of pulpwood is an important industry, along with the rapidly growing tourist industry.

Ontonagon County reached its peak of 12,400 population during the lumbering and farming era in 1920. Today it is one of four counties in the Upper Peninsula with an increase in population between 1960 and 1970. Although a slight one, from 10,584, it shows the population is stable and with the new *White Pine* development and modern methods of mining may increase more in the coming decades.

ONTONAGON COUNTY GHOST TOWNS

ADVENTURE—1910, on the Copper Range and Mineral Range Railroads, mail *Mass*. The old Adventure Mine opened in 1850 and the community was given a post office on September 26, 1851. The post office closed on August 14, 1860.

AGATE—1910, on the D. S. S. & A. Railroad, mail *Trout Creek*. Named by the railroad company, in 1890, for the semi-precious gem stone. 1927, in Interior Township, 3 miles from *Trout Creek*. John Wakevainen, Jr., general store, Postmaster and railroad agent; A. M. Hantamaki Company, filling station; and Andrew Bessen, blacksmith and auto repair. John Wakevainen, Jr. became first Postmaster on May 6, 1926.

AMERICAN LANDING—One of the first settlements in the county and the chief supply point for the early mines. Orin Robinson, in his memoirs, said, *"When I left the country in February, 1856 the mines along the range from the Ontonagon River west to Lake Gogebic, gave great promise for the future but the Forest mine is the only one that has survived as the present Victoria mine, and that was closed for many years."* Robinson said there was no road from *Ontonagon* to any of the mines and all supplies were taken 10 miles up the river, on scows poled by Indians, to the *American Landing*. From here they were teamed along the range to mines 18 to 25 miles distant. *American Landing* was also the shipping point for copper that was mined. This too was floated down the river on scows to *Ontonagon* and shipped to *Detroit* to be smelted. The first road was made through from *Ontonagon* to the range in the summer of 1855, Robinson said, and ran about 20 miles from *Ontonagon* to the *Hudson* mine where it connected with a road running along the range from *American Landing* to *Lake Gogebic*.

BALLENTINE—1893, a post office on Lake Gogebic, Ontonagon Township, 17 miles from *Ewen Station*. Also called *Lake Gogebic*. On the D. S. S. & A. Railroad, population 40. Named after the first Postmaster, H. H. Ballentine. Phillip Bellinger, railroad agent; L. P. Ferguson, hotel and saloon; and A. C. Hargrave, general store.

1905, located in Matchwood Township. Railroad name is *Lake Gogebic*. Population 100. A. C. Hargrave, Postmaster and general store; George Henghens, proprietor of Gogebic Hotel; Daniel Hubbard, saloon; W. E. Johnson, railroad agent; C. Roeske, teacher; and F. Woods, saloon.

Only one addition was made to the 1909 business directory, that of Amy B. Baker, teacher. Others remained the same.

In 1915, no business listings, mail RFD *Korelock*.

BALTIMORE—1910, on the D. S. S. & A. Railroad, mail *Ewen*.

BARCLAY—1893, a special supply post office, 5 miles from *Interior*, nearest rail approach, and 40 miles south of *Ontonagon*. Was a post office intermittently from February, 1892 until July 4, 1901.

1905, a discontinued post office, mail *Watersmeet*.

BASCO—Shown on 1905 maps, near *Paynesville*.

BEASER—1887, first called *Silver City* and also known as *Iron River*, a hamlet on the shore of Lake Superior, at the mouth of Iron River, in Carp Lake Township. Settled in 1850. Population 20. Mail stage from *Ontonagon* weekly. C. L. Pennock, deputy Postmaster; Daniel Beaser, supervisor; Ed Less, fisherman; Charles Oley, justice; C. L. Pennock, clerk, justice and carpenter; L. Terry, fisherman; and Joseph Vasseur, fisherman. Was a post office from December 8, 1875 until September 4, 1889.

See *Iron River* history also.

BELT—1910, mail *Lake Mine*. The post office was renamed *Lake Mine* (formerly *Belt*) on March 15, 1910 until closed on August 31, 1939.

BOHEMIAN—In 1887, a mining village, in Bohemia Township, 15 miles east of *Ontonagon*, and 28 miles west of *L'Anse*, nearest railroad point. Post office discontinued, mail to *Greenland*. Post office operated from March 13, 1893 until December 14, 1885.

———

BRUCE'S CROSSING—Was founded in 1888 by D. M. Bruce, of *Ontonagon*. Originally known as *Military Road*, the name was changed to *Bruce's Crossing* on March 19, 1889 by the D. S. S. & A. Railroad. Is a post office in 1970, located about 1 mile south of the original village named for A. L. Bruce, of *Rockland*.

———

CALDERWOOD—Was named by a group of Minnesota men who organized a logging and sawmill operation in 1880, called the Calderwood Lumber Company.

First settled in 1900, and in 1909 was a recently established post office. By 1915, the population had reached 100. Located in Interior Township, 9 miles from *Trout Creek*. Walter H. Dickinson, Postmaster and justice; and the DeLaittre & Anderson Company, lumber.

In 1927, had a Congregational church and telephone service. George L. Connors, Postmaster; the Calderwood Lumber Company, lumber and sawmill; and Ernest A. Dixon, notary and manager of Michigan Bell Telephone Company office.

The mills shut down about 1930. Not shown on 1972 road map.

———

CHOATE—1905, discontinued post office, mail to *Ewen*. First named *Sucker Creek*, in 1892. Changed to *Choate* in April, 1893 and the post office was discontinued January 14, 1904.

———

CRAIGSMERE—1910, on the C. & N. W. Railroad, mail *Watersmeet*. Named for the Craig Lumber Company about 1885.

———

EAST BRANCH—1927, 4 miles from *Mass*. Send mail to *Mass*. John Niemela was first Postmaster on July 12, 1912 and discontinued about one year later.

———

EVERGREEN—1910, a station on the Mineral Range Railroad, mail *Greenland*.

———

EWEN—Although there are about 150 people left in *Ewen* who do not think *Ewen* is a ghost town, it is a far cry from the booming logging town of 1,000 people it once was in the 1880s and 1890s. Settled in 1889, *Ewen* was named for a W. A. Ewen, treasurer of the railroad in October, 1889.

In 1893, there was a Methodist church, three saw and shingle mills, a planing mill, and a weekly newspaper, *The Ewen Recorder.* Population 800. W. B. Hotfield, Postmaster and general store; Simon Adams, justice; S. D. Burt & Company, planing mill; Clark, Farnum & Company, general store and sawmill; John Connoly, saloon; William Conover, hotel; Louis Danton, clothing; Esh & Conely, hotel; Finch & McLaughlin, saloon; William E. Griffin, land looker; F. J. Hargrave & Company, general store and bankers; Harrison & Lipsette, clothing; H. Hubbell, meat market; Ed Hulick, saloon; John McRae & Company, shingle mill; Robert Morris, shoemaker; Ontonagon River Lumber Company, saw and shingle mill; Charles O'Rourk, brewers agent; F. H. Osborne, drugs; Pursell & Raney, Railroad House hotel; John P. Rossman, meat market; P. Sheeley, manager of Snyder House hotel; John Shilling, saloon; and Simeon A. Snyder, proprietor of Snyder House hotel, were some of the business listings for that year.

Earl DeMolen, now of *Kingsford,* Michigan, and 85 years old, said he moved to *Ewen* with his parents in 1890. *"There was a terrible fire there around 1893, and half the town was burned down,"* DeMalen said. *"My father, Albert DeMolen, bought a team of horses and hauled logs to the McGraw mill in Ewen. We had a very large horse barn and several teamsters kept their horses in my father's barn. We had a large dog called 'Blackeye' and he stole everything he could get his teeth into. Every morning the other teamsters had to come to my father's sleigh and get their sack of straw they used to sit on. By the time they got there old Blackeye had stole the sack and they had to search all over to find it."*

"That winter things were tough," DeMolen recalled. *"There was a big depression and about all you could buy from the company store was flour and potatoes and canned pumpkin in gallon cans. Money was so scarce they had to use coupons and company money and if a person was caught buying anything at another store he was fired from his job. One man on the night shift at the mill disappeared and it was never learned whether he fell into the conveyor and was burned upor just pulled stakes to get away from his wife and get a new start."*

DeMolen's story gives a partial picture of some of the hardships of the early settlers in the logging towns.

The people of *Ewen* made it through the hard winter of '93 and in 1905 the population was about 375. At this time there was a Catholic and Methodist Episcopal church, and John Garvin was Postmaster. Other listings werd Fred Ball, hotel; William H. Brownson, teacher; E. Cole, liquor; Frank Connoly and John Corgorve, liquor dealers; J. F. Fogelsong, hardware; W. B. Hatfield, shingles and lath; Charles Heidman, livery; Northwest Hotel; E. J. Humphrey, logger; Joseph Kostelink, general store, shoes and meats; Dr. W. F. McHugh; M. Meeker, teacher; Dr. J. F. Molly; C. Motron, liquors; Al O'Rourke, livery; J. N. Snits, general store; Mory Sparrey, teacher; Mrs. E. Taylor, proprietor New Home Hotel; Elezear Trombley, blacksmith; George H. Vancor, barber; Ora Wallen and Walter Wallen, teachers; and Robert Trotter, real estate, some of the listings for 1905.

1910, J. A. Waring was Postmaster and general store. The population was listed at 400.

Ewen reached its peak of 1,200 population in 1915 and had three churches and a bank. E. T. Jermain, Postmaster; Lewis Jenson, president of the Ewen State Bank, capital $20,000; E. A. Florentine, physician; Jenson Mercantile Company, general store; M. F. Leach, sawmill and supplies; J. F. O'Malley, physician; and the Ontonagon Valley Creamery Company were some of the new businesses. By that time the saloons were out and pool rooms had taken their place.

FALLS—1910, a station on the D. S. S. & A. Railroad, mail *Painseville*. Post office established December 2, 1895 but never operated.

FLINTSTEEL—1910, about 10 miles east of *Ontonagon*, near the Flint Steel River, was a post office from March 7, 1898 until April 14, 1906 with Peter Hazzy first Postmaster.

FRANCIS—1910, a station on the Mineral Range Railroad, mail *Mass*. Jacob Brown was first Postmaster on March 9, 1906 but closed on May 11, 1907.

GEM—1910, on the D. S. S. & A. Railroad, mail *Painseville*. Was a spur named by the railroad company after precious minerals, in 1890.

GROSBECK—1910, on the D. S. S. & A. Railroad, mail to *Matchwood*, 3 miles east. Was a railroad station in 1894.

HUBBEL'S MILL—See *Rubicon.*

INTERIOR—1893, on the C. & N. W. Railroad, Interior Township, 40 miles southeast of *Ontonagon*. Named for the Interior Lumber Company in 1888 and had 41 buildings. Was a post office from December, 1888 to May 17, 1897. Had saw and planing mills and shipped lumber. Population 1,000. Samuel W. Larsen, Postmaster and justice, J. J. Anderson, supervisor; Frank A. Ansley, justice; Rev. Elford, Methodist; Ferdinand F. Full, constable; I. M. Peason, superintendent of the Interior Lumber Company; Theodore F. Kohl, station agent; Mrs. Irene Shields, teacher and artist; Robert Sturgeon, physician; and G. N. Tibbets, Township Clerk.

Apparently the timber became exhausted, the last log was sawed in 1895 and the town was abandoned. In 1905, post office discontinued, send mail to

Watersmeet. Someone put up a cemetery sign that reads: *Forgotten by everyone but God.* (Walter Romig in "Michigan Place Names")

INTERIOR JUNCTION—Listed in 1910, on the C. & N. W. Railroad, mail *Watersmeet.*

IRON RIVER—This town had the distinction of having had three names during its history. It was first named *Silver City* by Daniel Beaser who platted the village August 24, 1875, after he discovered silver at the location. It was later changed to *Beaser.*

When silver was discovered here in 1872, the territory for 60 miles east and west was staked out in claims, but only sporadic mining followed, ending in 1876. Assays of $1,716 coin silver to the ton of rock showed that the failures were for lack of funds for development. Indians in this district sold pure silver nuggets to the whites, but efforts to locate the source of the nuggets were unrewarded. It is said that one white man learned the secret, but he disappeared and was never heard from again.

From 1873 to 1876, 27 silver mining companies operated here. First assays ranged from $57 per ton and up, but the first silver brick produced at the mill near *Bonaza Falls* yielded $35 per ton.

In 1877, *Iron River* was the postal name for the post office at *Silver City*, in Carp Lake Township, 14 miles southwest of *Ontonagon*. A 20 stamp quartz mill, two hotels and a general store were located here. Including the nearby mine, the population was about 300. Silver and copper were shipped. Daily mail in summer by boat, and in winter tri-weekly by stage (dog sled) from *Ontonagon*. Daniel Beaser, Postmaster and general supply store; H. W. Jones, physician; Edward Lest, proprietor of Pioneer House hotel; Dr. H. D. Pickman, physician for the Superior Mine; Thomas Rexinger, meat market; and D. H. Stoddard, proprietor of the Lake View House.

1879, named for the stream on which it is located. Population of the village, 125. Silver, copper and building stone are the shipments. Same business listings as in 1877.

By 1877 the rush for silver was over and only about 25 people lived here. The stamp mill was closed, along with the two hotels and saloons. Only the founder, Daniel Beaser, and a few fishermen remained. Beaser, the old prospector and Postmaster of the village he had founded, changed the name to *Beaser.* Within the next few years all three names were deleted from directories and maps. Today, *Silver City* is designated on Michigan State Highway maps in approximately the same location of the former town with three names, north of *White Pine.*

JASPER—Shown on 1905 maps near *Trout Creek*.

KORELOCK—1915, population 100. On the D. S. S. & A. Railroad. A. G. Hargraves, Postmaster and general store. *Korelock* was the postal name, railroad name *Lake Gogebic*, not a ghost town.

LAKE GOGEBIC—See *Ballentine*; also *Korelock*.

LAKEMINE—Settled in 1840. 1915, population 150. On the Copper Range Railroad, in Greenland Township, 3 miles from *Greenland*. Telephone. Louise H. Mack, Postmaster; C. H. Mack, Express and telegraph agent.

By 1917 the population had increased to 500. P. J. Harrington, Postmaster and railroad agent; M. Barich, general store; J. Craig, general store; and the Lake Copper Company, C. E. Weed, manager.

1927, population 50. Located on the Copper Range Railroad and on Highway M-26. Bus to *Hancock, Houghton* and *Ontonagon*. J. W. Craig, Postmaster, general store, and also caretaker for the Lake Mine Copper Company.

During the depression years of the 1930s, the post office was discontinued on August 31, 1939 after 31 years in operation.

Also see *Belt* for postal dates and name.

MAPLE GROVE—1893, was another name for *Greenland*. Walter Romig said the first house was built in 1850, and the first store built by J. Budenshaw who platted the village and recorded it in 1858.

MATCHWOOD—In 1888, the Diamond Match Company established their headquarters here to accommodate and supply their numerous logging camps in the area, hence the name. Post office established April 23, 1889.

1893, population 100. On the D. S. S. & A. Railroad; Jerome Brown, Postmaster; Mrs. J. Carpenter, hotel; J. B. Conner, groceries; Daws Brothers, sawmill; Fred W. Kelley, railroad agent; Larsen & Schumaker, general store; and Hugh McQuarie, saloon. A fire in 1893 and another of 1906 destroyed many buildings.

1905, population 200. In Matchwood Township. Jerome Brown, Postmaster, dairy and real estate; E. Brown, real estate; Stanley Brown, teacher; Patrick Connors, pine lands; Currie & Woods, saloon; Nell J. Ferguson, mine superintendent; Charles Gerber, dairy; Patrick Higgins, dairy; J. Hoskins, Township Treasurer; H. G. Lytle, railroad agent; Hugh McQuarrie, grocery; August Nelson, carpenter; Mrs. Anna Stindt, dairy; John Stindt, pine lands; and Rudolph Stindt, dairy.

1910, about the same. Some business changes were: J. Brewer, Postmaster and railroad agent; Gus Bragg, hotel; Coppertown Mining Company, copper mine; William Currie, saloon; and Nellie Reynolds, teacher.

By 1915 the town was surrounded by farms, mostly dairy farms, and the population had dropped to less than 100. Only one or two changes were made in the list of names: J. W. Ferguson ran a hotel and the mine was operated by the Copper Crown Mining Company.

In 1917, population about 40. H. F. Yungbluth, Postmaster. The hotel, one general store, a creamery, and two or three real estate dealers were operating, and the Cass Copper Company was listed.

Only three business listings for 1927: H. F. Yungbluth, Postmaster; H. L. Bittner, general store and station agent; and E. E. Brown, real estate and land.

Post office discontinued between 1956 and 1959.

————

McKEEVER—1910, on the Chicago, Milwaukee & St. Paul Railroad and the Copper Range Railroad, mail *Mass*. Named for R. T. McKeever, general manager of the Copper Range Railroad Company in 1899.

————

MICHIGAN MINE—1910, on the Mineral Range Railroad, mail *Rockland*. The *Michigan Mine* was closed in 1921. It was the site of the largest mass of copper ever found in Michigan, weighing about 420 tons, taken from this mine. In 1937, the New Michigan Mine was opened, about ¾ miles west. The shaft was 1,750 feet deep, with a 48 degree incline. Until 1899 was operated as the Minnesota mine. Was reopened for a short time in the 1940s.

————

MILITARY ROAD—First name for *Bruce's Crossing*. See *Bruce's Crossing*.

————

MINNESOTA MINE—1887 and 1893, listed as south east of *Rockland*. Not a town. Was best producer of copper from 1854 to 1865. Closed in 1870. Platted as *Rosendale*. Post office opened May 7, 1857 and renamed *National* on March 16, 1861. Consolidated into the village of *Rockland* on December 7, 1863 and renamed *Rockland*.

————

MOTELY—1910, a station on the Mineral Range Railroad, mail *Alston*. Located on the Houghton County line.

————

NESTER—Shown on 1905 maps near *Ewen*.

————

NONESUCH—Settled in 1866. Post office established on July 3, 1876. 1879, a recently established post office in Carp Lake Township, on Little Iron River, 21 miles southwest of *Ontonagon*. Named for the mine at which it is located. Copper is the only shipment. Mail stage to *Ontonagon*, semi-weekly. Population 30. Thomas Hooper, Postmaster; James Cash, school teacher; John Dingle, justice and mining captain; Fred Hooper, meat market; Thomas Hooper, miner and lumber manufacturer; Philip Less, justice; Nonesuch Mining Company, Thomas Hooper, lessee; C. Pennock, carpenter; and Austin Stone, shoemaker.

1887, weekly stage to *Ontonagon*. Thomas Hooper, Postmaster, and Joseph C. Thomas, justice. The post office was closed on March 16, 1887. The village site is now part of Porcupine Mountains State Park.

————

O'BRIEN—1893, a lumber camp on the D. S. S. & A. Railroad, in McMillan Township, 24 miles from *Ontonagon*. Population 50. Daily mail. C. J. Boyle, Postmaster; W. A. Andrew, notary; Dennis Carney, county surveyor; Robert Connacher, road commissioner; Thomas Nester (estate), general store and lumber; H. W. Penberthy, overseer of highways; and L. A. Rossman, town clerk.

Name probably was changed to *Nester*, as *O'Brien* was not listed after the 1890s and *Nester* is shown on 1905 maps, near *Ewen*. Post office established October 26, 1888 and until July 10, 1893. This was the site of a Thomas Nester lumber camp.

————

PAULDING—Was a post office and station on the Chicago & Northwestern Railroad, about 5 miles south of *Trout Creek*. The post office lasted from about 1893 to 1904.

In 1927, listed as a discontinued post office, send mail to *Roselawn*. Clyde E. Peck, general store. 1938, population 29. The post office reopened on May 1, 1936 and still in operation.

————

PEPPARD—1910, a station on the Copper Range Railroad, mail *Mass*.

————

PINEX—In 1917, listed as a recently established post office. John Saam was first Postmaster here on May 1, 1916. Named for the pine forest surrounding the area.

————

RADFORD—1910, on the Chicago & Northwestern Railroad, mail *Ewen*.

————

RANGE JUNCTION—On 1905 maps, at the junction of the Chicago Milwaukee & St. Paul and Duluth South Shore & Atlantic Railroads, about 8 miles east of *Rockland*.

————

RIDDLE JUNCTION—A short distance west of *Range Junction*.

————

ROBBINS—In 1893, on the M. L. S. & W. Railroad, Interior Township, 40 miles south of *Ontonagon*. Population 200. Named for the Postmaster, F. S.

Robbins. Settled as a lumbering village and in that year, Brown & Robbins, sawmill ; Fair Lumber Company, planing mill; C. C. Shockley, express agent.

1905, population 40. Located in Haight Township, 10 miles from *Watersmeet*. Fred Jentz, Postmaster and sawmill.

1909, population 30, daily mail stage to *Watersmeet*. C. McLaughlin, Postmaster and sawmill; and Likern-Brown-Phelps Company, sawmill. (These were only places listed, but doesn't mean there were no other business places, such as stores, blacksmith shop, etc., which may have declined to pay for a listing).

1915, no business listings. RFD *Roselawn*.

Was a post office from October, 1891, closed August 3, 1898 but reopened from December 18, 1902 until June 30, 1911.

ROSEDALE—See *Minnesota Mine*.

ROSELAWN—1927, population 15. On the C. & N. W. Railroad, Haight Township, 14 miles southeast of *Ewen*, not on a railroad, and about 2 miles northeast of *Craigsmere*. Bus to *Iron River* and *Ironwood*, Michigan, and *Rhinelander*, Wisconsin. Iness Peck, Postmaster; Edward Johnson, soft drinks; and Clyde E. Peck, general store.

The *Roselawn* post office opened on June 1, 1908 with James Bishop as first Postmaster.

ROUSSEAU—See *Rubicon*.

RUBICON—In 1893 was a newly established post office, originally named *Hubbell's Mills*, and in 1920 was changed to *Rousseau* for Edward Rousseau, Supervisor of Bohemian Township for 27 years.

1927, population 325. Mrs. Leopolding Rousseu, Postmaster; Matt Johnson, logger; Penegor Brothers, loggers; and Edward Rousseau, general store and logger. Was a post office in 1905. Not a ghost town. Shown on 1970 Michigan Highway maps.

RUBY—Shown on 1905 maps, about 2 miles south of *Rapinville*.

SANDHURST—1910, on the C. & N. W. Railroad, about 6 miles south of *Ewen*. Mail *Watersmeet*.

SEAGER—1910, on the Copper Range Railroad, mail to *Wenona*.

SILVER CITY—See *Iron River* for history.

———

SIMER—1910, on the Mineral Range Railroad, mail *Mass*.

———

ST. COLLINS—1910, on the D. S. S. & A. Railroad, 1 mile west of *Bruce's Crossing*. It served as a mail distribution point until the post office opened at *Bruce Crossing* on March 5, 1888.

———

STEVENSON—1910, on the Chicago Milwaukee & St. Paul Railroad, mail *Rockland*.

———

TOPAZ—Named by the D. S. S. & A. Railroad in 1890, after a gem of that name. Rudolph Stindt became the first Postmaster on June 29,1910.

1927, population 100. Settled in 1890, on the D. S. S. & A. Railroad and on Highway M-28, Matchwood Township, 11 miles from *Ewen*. Bus daily to *Ontonagon, Wakefield, Bessemer* and *Ironwood*. Has a Lutheran church and telephone service. Rudolph Stindt, Postmaster, notary, and registered Guernsey cattle, and railroad agent; Charles Grapentine, dairy; S. A. Griewski, poultry; John Kitzman, dairy; Jacob Lata, dairy; Michael Latva, dairy; John Latvala, dairy; John Mattson, general store; Charles Menigoz, live stock; Hans Olsen, dairy; Leon Osier, dairy; Paul Stindt, poultry; and Frank Zemke, fruit grower.

———

VICTORIA—Was named by the Forest Mining Company, in 1858, presumably in honor of Queen Victoria. The first commercial attempt at mining copper in Michigan was begun here in 1770 by Alexander Henry. With the backing of the Duke of Gloucester, he started the mining venture to get out copper and ship it to England. The attempt was unsuccessful. C. R. Everett became first Postmaster September 16, 1899.

In 1905, population 400. On the Ontonagon River, Rockland Township, 4 miles from *Rockland,* daily mail. J. W. Craig, Postmaster and manager of the Victoria Copper Mining Company general store; Dr. W. E. Thompson; and the Victoria Copper Company, sawmill.

1910, daily mail and same Postmaster; De Mar Brothers, saloon; E. W. Knowles, physician; and mining company, general store and mine.

1915, J. H. Kohne, railroad agent; Dr. D. L. Lutes; and J. W. Craig, store manager.

1917, population 750. T. O. Pechauer, Postmaster and store manager. The mine closed in 1921, and the village abandoned.

274

1927, no population given, Post office discontinued, mail to *Rockland*. Nothing remains today except three or four old log cabins that are rapidly deteriorating.

The houses of the former Victoria Mining Company were recently sold (1971) by the current owners, The Upper Peninsula Power Company The old log houses remain under custody of the Copper Range Company. They were used in days gone by workers of the First Victoria and were finished with lath and plaster inside. They may date back to 1858 or earlier.

WAINOLA—Settled by Finns and named for a legendary Finnish name meaning "family." 1915, population 300. In Greenland Township, 4¼ miles south of *Mass*. John Malila, Postmaster and general store; Matt Johnson, feed and grain; and Sam Hautala, meat market.

1927, population 425. Settled in 1887. Had Finnish Evangelical and Lutheran churches. Matt Johnson, Postmaster, logger and general store, farm implements, etc. ; William Heddier, railroad agent; John Kangas, sawmill; John Malila, general store; Penegor Brothers, loggers; John I. Penegor, lawyer. Not shown on present day maps.The post office closed on October 31, 1939.

WEBSTER—1887, see *Rockland*. May have been another name for *Rockland*, or a name of a mine in the area.

WOOD SPUR—In 1910, a station on the Chicago, Milwaukee & St. Paul Railroad, mail *Ontonagon*.

Chapter Eighteen

SCHOOLCRAFT COUNTY

Schoolcraft County was laid out in 1843 and was attached to Houghton County until 1846 and attached to Marquette County until the county government was organized in 1851. The name was taken from Henry R. Schoolcraft, early U. S. Indian Agent in the Upper Peninsula, who served as mediator between the United States and the Indians. He was also a member of the Territorial Council of Michigan and was on the committee that named most of the Michigan counties organized from 1840 to 1846, most of them with names of his own choosing. Schoolcraft became an expert on Indian lore, and had one of the first museums and collections of Indian artifacts in Michigan. Ironically, only Schoolcraft County and a small village in lower Michigan were named in his honor, and most of the first names he selected for counties were changed at a later date by the settlers.

Onota, or *Bay Furnace*, now a ghost town in Alger County, was the first county seat (see *Onota* for history) which was later moved to *Manistique* when Alger County was taken from Schoolcraft County territory and organized about 1882.

The county borders on Lake Michigan, and in 1880 had a population of 1,575. Described in 1887 as: *"The productions are insignificant, and lumbering is the only important industry."* Lumbering was and still is the principal industry, although for some years several stone quarries operated in the county, and today tourism and the resort business is becoming important, especially with the opening of the Mackinac Bridge which allows easier access to the county by motorists from lower Michigan and points south.

Population of the county dropped from 8,953 in 1960 to 8,226 in 1970, a decline of 727 in population. Schoolcraft is one of 11 Upper Peninsula counties that had a decline in population during the last decade.

Schoolcraft County is known as a sportsman's paradise with its many inland lakes, miles of sparkling streams, and beautiful scenery.

SCHOOLCRAFT COUNTY GHOST TOWNS

ACKLEY—1910, mail *Germfask*. Near the Manistique River, on the east side, and was on the old Manistique Logging Railroad.

_____

AMES—1910, on the Soo Line, mail *Wetmore*.

BEESON—or *Beeson's Spur*, was on the Manistique & Lake Superior Railroad, about 1 mile southwest of *Hiawatha*.

CAMP 1—CAMP 14—CAMP 15—CAMP 16—and CAMP 20—Were all on railroad branches or spurs south of *Thompson* on the Soo Line.

CAMP 35—Six miles northwest of *Steuben* on the Manistique and Lake Superior Railroad. See *Steuben*.

CHERRY VALLEY—1910, on the Soo Line, about 2 miles east of *Manistique*, mail *Manistique*. Large limestone kilns were located near here.

COOKS—Originally called *Cook's Mill*, was named after a man named Cooks who built the first mill here after the Soo Line reached the county in 1887. Post office established June 28, 1888 and called *Cooks*, although platted as *Durham* by David Spielmacher.

1893, on the Minneapolis St. Paul & Sault Ste. Marie Railroad, Inwood Township, 12 miles south of *Manistique*. Had a steam sawmill and broom handle factory. Railroad name *Cook's Mills*. Population 200. Henry Delond, Postmaster and general store; Black & Hubschier, saloon; S. W. Crowell, railroad agent; W. T. S. Cornell, barber; James M. Dhumaker, justice; Charles Dockham, justice; E. S. Fuller, mason; George W. Gray, sawmill; Norman McDonald, justice; Daniel McGinnis, justice; J. C. Messinger, blacksmith; M. O. O'Brien, saloon; M. B. Peters, broom handles; E. Tighe, general store and sawmill; and N. Tousegnant, hotel.

1905, population 300. Had Catholic and Congregational churches. Stages daily to *Garden, Vans Harbor* and *Fayette*. John C. Messenger, Postmaster; P. J. Huebscher, proprietor Eagle Hotel; Joseph Gibbs & Sons, general store; George W. Gray, well borer; P. J. Huebscher, sawmill; John Messenger, justice; and E. A. Tighe, general store.

Additional listings for 1910 were: C. W. Banjamin, teacher; Ben Bonno, blacksmith and wagon maker; Rev. W. C. Bowine, Congregational; Nellie Chase, teacher; Eagle Hotel; L. R. Messenger, painter; Jacob Roberts, general store; John Roberts, constable; John E. Wright, saloon and livery barn; and Fred Zurka, meats.

1915, population dropped to about 80. George F. Gray, Postmaster; J. W. Carpenter, railroad agent; Conners & McCafferty, lumber; Neil McClellan, proprietor telephone company; Inwood Creamery Company; William Mannering, tinsmith; E. J. Miller, cigar manufacturer; and John Wright, livery.

1917, population 125. Same Postmaster. Additional listings were: Conners & McCafferty, lumber; Henry Deloria general store; J. J. Griffin, express agent;

Harman & Winkel, livestock; O. J. Levielle, blacksmith; James O'Brien, general store; and M. A. Walter, Confection.

1927, population 100. Bus daily to *Manistique*. Had Adventist, Catholic, and Congregational churches. E. J. Deloria, Postmaster and general store; G. W. Gray, manager Cooks Telephone Company; Eagle Hotel, O. J. Leveille, proprietor; Peter V. Foy, grocery; J. J. Griffin, express agent; Inwood Marketing Association, potatoes; C. B. Jaynes, tinsmith; Standard Oil Company; M. A. Walters, pool, cigars, etc.; Weber & Chenard, gas station.

Cooks is still a small town and on heavily traveled US-2, but today the industry is tourism. Not the booming town of the 1890s when timber was king.

———

CREIGHTON—Was a station on the D. M. & M. Railroad in 1887 and lasted until the late 1930s. Ed Mott, of *Steuben*, said his mother Myrtle (McManus) Mott, taught school here in 1922. *"At that time there were about 30 students in school, there was a general store and quite a few families,"* he said. Today there is nothing. In 1910, mail was sent to *Wetmore*. Named for the Creighton brothers, railroad pioneers, in 1882.

———

CUSINO—In 1909, had a population of nearly 200. Located on the Munising, Marquette & Southeastern Railroad, Cusino Township, 40 miles north of *Manistique*, near the northwest county line. Telephone. John G. Gauthier, Postmaster and general store; William Blom, Township Clerk; W. J. Crego, shingle mill; Mary Fancher, teacher; Dr. S. A. Gates; Arthur Lashbrook, railroad agent; M. A. Nadeu, justice; and C. H. Worcester Company, lumbering.

Cusino had a post office from 1906 until 1912. By that time the lumbering activity ceased and people moved to other areas. In that year there were less than 30 residents. It is designated on 1971 Michigan Highway maps and the old railroad grade is now a road for autos.

———

DELTA JUNCTION—1910, a station on the Minneapolis St. Paul & Sault Ste. Marie Railroad, about ½ mile northwest of *Thompson* on a spur of the railroad.

———

DOGTOWN—See *Thompson*.

———

DOYLE—1910, a station or spur on the Manisitique & Lake Superior Railroad. Mail *Manistique*.

———

DRIGGS—1910, on the D. S. S. & A. Railroad, 8 miles west of *Seney*, its mailing point. Also listed in 1927. Named for Frederick E. Driggs who helped finance the railroad and was manager of the Peninsula Land Company. Was a logging area until 1899. The station operated from 1882 until the turn-of-the-century.

EPSPORT—Was first called *Monistique* and in 1872 had 200 population, *"at the mouth of the Monistique River and is the seat of lumbering operations of the Chicago Lumbering Company, who are proprietors of the village. There has been a settlement here since 1848."* Abilah Weston was the president of the lumber company, address *Painted Post*, New York; E. B. Dean, agent in charge.

In 1877 called *Epsport*, population 500. Stage to *Fayette* semi-weekly. W. M. Colwell, Postmaster. Within a few years it was listed in directories as *Manistique*, which it is today.

FORDVILLE—Shown on 1905 maps on the Blaney & Southern Railroad, west of *Blaney*.

GERMFASK—Not really a ghost town. In the late 1870s, John Grant, the father of 21 children, made the first permanent settlement here, north of *Blaney Park*. The "G" in *Germfask* is taken from Grant, and the name *Germfask* was manufactured by combining the first letters of family names of the eight freeholders who organized Germfask Township. Post office opened February 26, 1890.

In 1893, population 100, a post office on the Manistique Logging Railroad, 7 miles from *Seney*, the nearest bank. Walter Gray, acting Postmaster; Bernard Connoly, justice; Gray Brothers, sawmill; William McPherson, railroad agent; Alex Stewart, justice; and James Welch, justice.

The logging railroad apparently was a narrow-gauge track. There is a story that one of the old narrow-gauge steam engines was found in the 1940s abandoned along the line, and a large white birch tree was growing up through the smokestack.

After the town of *Seney* folded up during the late 1890s, some of the businessmen moved south to *Germfask*. In 1905, John I. Bellaire, formerly of *Seney*, operated a general store here. Other listings were: G. E. LeVeque, general store and shingle mill; Dan McDonald, blacksmith; Angus McDougall, drugs; Ed Menere, hotel; D. F. Morrison, general store; Ostrander Brothers, drugs; A. B. Robbin, sawmill; and Hugh Slay, lumber. Other businesses in the early 1900s, when the town reached a population of 500 or more, were Charles Badegrow, saloon; Dr. N. S. Campbell; C. E. Culver, teacher; John Decker, blacksmith; L. M. French, general store; I. G. Grant, photographer; Dr. S. S. Hackwell; Dr. J. M. Lipson; Florence McKinnon, teacher; D. F. Morrison, general store; J. V. Propst, saloon; Roblin & Hancock, sawmill; William Wickens, hotel; and W. A. Wood, lumber.

Lumbering and tourism are the main industries in *Germfask* today.

––––––––

GRIDLEY—Shown on 1905 maps at the intersection of the Blaney & Southern and Soo Line Railroads.

––––––––

HACO—Shown on 1920 maps, was a station between Cooks and Thompson.

Founded in 1893 by Thomas Mills, an American Socialist, as a cooperative colony. Post office established April 14, 1894.

––––––––

HIAWATHA—Was a post office in 1897. Located 11 miles north of *Manistique*, in Hiawatha Township. Was located on the old Manistique & Northwestern Railroad and in 1900 had a population of 185. Hirsch Byers, who was 70 years old in 1971, said he lived there all his life and recalled when he was a boy there was a railroad station, post office, a store, and 10 or 15 houses. Nothing remains of the original village but it is still shown on some maps and a few people live near the site on the main road. Byers said George Roberts ran a lumber camp here in 1913. Ezra Aldrich was the last Postmaster, in 1941 or 1942. In 1919, Byers said, the Marlin & Drisgram Cattle Company introduced cattle here. In 1920, Byers said, he worked for the Cloverland Cattle Company and they had 1,000 head of beef cattle. There was a hotel here also, he said, and it burned down in the 1930s.

In 1905, F. G. Dodge was Postmaster and J. L. Burnhart was a teacher. Solomon Hutt, stage driver; Hiawatha Manufacturing Company, hardwood lumber; George McCastle, sawmill; and Dodge & Dye, cedar, etc.

By 1910 the population had dropped to 50. Improved farm land ran from $15 to $30 per acre. Business listings were: Solomon Hutt, Postmaster; Wilber Aldrich, supervisor; William Byers, blacksmith; William Conrey, mason; Ralph G. Dodge, justice; James Finn, logger; Joseph F. Hutt, notary; Miss Klugstat, teacher; George McCastle, sawmill; Mrs. Maud McKnight, teacher; and the South Side Lumber Company.

In 1915, Frank Hutt was Postmaster; Joseph F. Hutt, general store; Joseph Snitzler, lumber; Hiawatha Manufacturing Company, hardwood; and the South Side Lumber Company were doing business. The population had dropped to about 20. By 1918, there was only one listing, that of Frank Hutt, Postmaster and general store. The post office was discontinued on January 31, 1941.

––––––––

HIAWATHA MILL—1910, on the Manistique & Lake Superior Railroad, Also called *Hiawatha Station*, 1 mile below *Beesons* and due south of *Hiawatha* Post Office.

INDIAN LAKE—See *South Manistique.*

———

JEROMEVILLE—Listed in 1887 as a station on the D. M. & M. Railroad, 50½ miles from *Marquette.* Walter Romig said it was the first name for *Shingleton,* changed September 20, 1887. Now located in Alger County (not a ghost town).

———

KLONDIKE—Listed in 1910 Rand McNally Atlas. Mail *Steuben.* Was a station on the Manistique & Lake Superior Railroad, about 3 miles north of *Steuben,* in Thompson Township, and near Klondike Lake, a 170-acre lake. The late Ed Mott, of *Steuben,* said one of the old lumberjacks, Charlie Bandue, stayed on after the lumbering days and was the last person to live there, in an old shack by the railroad. He died many years ago at the age of 80, Mott said. Remains of an old lumber camp were evident here in the late 1920s but nothing remains and the railroad has been abandoned.

The last logging camp was run by Guy Burrell in about 1919.

Everyone called Bandue "Klondike Charlie." He lived in the shack alone until 1943, when some of the railroad section gang stopped by his place to say hello and discovered old Charlie had died in his sleep. He had been dead for several days, Mott said. That was the end of *Klondike*, and the last reminder that the place ever existed.

———

LAKEFIELD—Listed in 1927 as a discontinued post office, RFD *Germfask.*

———

LISTON—1910, mail *Seney.*

———

LITTLE HARBOR—1893, population 85. Mail semi-weekly. Thompson Township, 18 miles southwest of *Manistique.*

1905, post office discontinued. Send mail to *Thompson.*

As told by Ernest Williams of *Manistique*, April, 1971:

Many years ago (1887-88) William L. Marble and a man named Alfred A. Tracy built Little Harbor. Marble later moved to Gladstone and founded the Marble Arms Company, who manufactured Marble gun sights, hunting knives, the "Game Getter," and other things. It is still a beautiful harbor, protected on all sides except a very narrow passage on the southeast. It has 20 feet of blue water inside the harbor. Behind it is the townsite along a 90-foot hill that had a road built along the side.

There were two rows of houses three blocks long with what was called "The White House" at the end of the street. This was lived in by Mr. Marble. There was a sawmill and shingle mill combined, a good dock, but the lumber and shingles were piled mostly on shore. There was a store and later a pool hall, which was built just outside of town. Mr. Marble also made hardwood flooring. A Mr. Hectrick, a brother-in-law, was the engineer at the mill. The factory also made lath.

Over the years Little Harbor had two or three owners. Martin Valentine bought the town and ran it for a few years, as he had timber close by. He owned the "Mary Ellen Cook," a two-masted schooner, which he used to deliver his shingles, etc.

Valentine finally sold to Isaac Bonifas who, with his brother, cut timber. His brother was William, or generally called "Bill." Bill later moved to Watersmeet and became a millionaire in the pulpwood and lumbering business.

A Mr. Heffeerman was in charge of the mill for the Bonifas brothers during the last. Heffeerman was shiftless. He drove a driving team and never cleaned the horse stables so the team of horses was nearly standing on their heads.

The town was then sold to Fred Miller, a saloonkeeper from Thompson who had done well at the business. He hired a fairly good mill man by the name of Gazely, who put a new boiler in the mill. He was quite inventive, and made a friction chain drive "nigger" to turn the log on the carriage. It worked well. The only drawback to this investment was that Mr. Miller didn't have much timber, so after he lost about $10,000 he gave up. He sold out to some Jews who dismantled the mill and stored it on the dock for shipment. While the machinery was there awaiting shipment, an old pirate fisherman chiseled all the babbit from the boxes of the machinery and sold it to the junk dealer in Manistique. I don't know what became of the machinery.

There were quite a few families living within a 2-mile radius around Little Harbor. These people always celebrated a circus on the 4th of July. For a few years Shierbecks Circus showed a good one-ring circus in Thompson, and all the local residents took the day off to attend.

Little Harbor residents had to travel to Thompson each year to vote at election time. Many of the people were backwoodsmen without any formal education. One time a father took his son with him and walked the 10 miles into Thompson to vote. The clerk asked the son if he was 21, and the boy answered, "Yup!" He then asked the boy when he became 21 years old. The boy answered, "Back somewheres around rawsberry time."

Long after Martin Valentine sold out at Little Harbor he continued cutting timber in the area and lumbered about 200 thousand feet of hemlock which was hauled by sleigh and dumped over the hill at the harbor to be shipped. During the summer, log skidways were laid end to end to the lake, making a live rollway. A man and team then skidded the logs and two of us worked *rolling the logs which were decked in the water 16 feet high by hand. Valentine also furnished the shingle mill at Thompson with cedar logs in later years.*

Someone bought a clearing on top of the hill and fenced it in. The road has eroded so badly it can't be used, but it is still a beautiful natural harbor. There is no evidence remaining to show that a town ever existed here.

The post office was closed for the last time on May 14, 1910.

McDONALD LAKE—1910, on the Soo Line Railroad, mail *Manistique.*

McINESS—On 1920 maps, about 1 mile north of *Scotts*, on the Manistique & Northern Railroad.

McNEILS—Was located about ½ mile south of *Moran's* at the end of a railroad spur branching off the Manistique & Northern.

MARBLEHEAD SPUR—1910, on the Soo Line Railroad, mail *Manistique.*

MOOREVILLE—1910, on the Blaney & Southern Railroad, mail *Blaney.*

MORAN'S—On 1920 maps located on a spur of the old Manistique & Northern Railroad, about 2 miles west of *Scotts.*

NEW KENTUCKY—1910, on the Blaney & Southern Railroad, mail *Blaney.* This name was from the settlers, called "wood cutters," who moved from Kentucky to northern Michigan during the early teens to harvest hardwood, cedar posts, ties and shingle bolts, etc. after the pine was harvested. There were many such settlements so named in both the Lower and Upper Peninsula during the early 1900s.

NICHOLSVILLE—1910, on the Blaney & Southern Railroad, mail *Huntspur.*

PARKINGTON—1910, population 35. On the Soo Line Railroad, 5 miles east of *Gulliver.* Mail *Huntspur.* A station in 1889, post office opened on November 17, 1898 and lasted until July 15, 1905.

RICHARDSON—1910, on the Manistique & Northern Railroad, mail *Uno.* Located about 2 miles south of *Shingleton.*

ST. THOMAS—1910, mail *Huntspur.*

SCOTTS—1910, on the Manistique & Northern Railroad, about 5 miles north of *Steuben.* Mail *Uno.* The late Ed Mott, of *Steuben,* said there were large lumber camps in the area and it was a station on the railroad. There was a log camp here until 1938 and a few families lived there until the late 1940s. *Scotts* was also called *Sixty Five*, as it was located at the 65 mile marker on the railroad. Nothing remains today.

SENEY—Named for Geo. R. Seney, railroad director of the first railroad between *St. Ignace* and *Marquette*. Post office opened December 28, 1882. This town, which was labeled "Sin Town, U. S. A." and the "Toughest Town in Michigan" during the 1880s, became a ghost town just before the turn of the century, but has revived today as a tourist center and there is much lumbering activity once more as new growths of timber become ready to harvest. The Cleveland-Cliffs Company is active in lumbering and there is a large sawmill operating here. Located on busy Highway M-28, motels, restaurants, gift shops, etc, are prospering here, but very little sign of the "Old Seney" exists today. In 1965 citizens of the village erected white wooden crosses on the graves of unknown lumberjacks, victims of saloon brawls and logging accidents, and erected a sign designating the cemetery as "Seney's Boot Hill."

Seney attracted nationwide attention in the 1880s when the famous news reporter Nellie Bly visited the town and returned to *New York* where her story about the stockades where lumberjacks were held in virtual slavery and houses of prostitution ran wide open was published in the *Police Gazette* and brought about an investigation of the situation by the state. Many of the stories that ensued in newspapers later proved to be untrue, but the sordid reputation of the town was never lived down and the stories exist yet today.

In 1887, described as located in Seney Township, a station on the D. M. & M. Railroad, 45 miles north of *Manistique*. Population 200. Daily mail. J. F. Chislom, Postmaster. Other listings were: John Brian, justice; John R. Conway, hotel and saloon; S. Fell, railroad agent; William A. French, hotel; John Grant and Walter Gray, justices; Phillip Grondine, saloon; Hargrave Brothers & Company, grocers; Thomas Hayes, hotel; James F. Judge, hotel; Robert Lemoine, boots and shoes; John Liston, saloon; Logan Brothers, saloon; Miller & McLeod, hotel and saloon; Leon Mondor, blacksmith; John Nevins, saloon; John D. O'Brien, hotel and saloon; J. W. Pitcher, hotel and saloon; Dominick Potrin, saloon; Joseph A. Sayers, drugs; and James Wheeler, justice.

In 1905, had a Catholic church and a graded school. George M. Falkenhagen, Postmaster; Andrew Daly, restaurant; Edward and Phillip Grondin Brothers, hotel and saloon; Ed Grondin, lumberman; Richard Harcourt, saloon; Fred and Wilkes Hargrave and John W. Thompson, store and Bank; William G. Miller, railroad agent; Charles O'Connor, Michigan Bell Telephone Company; and William Seeley, livestock.

Between 1887 and 1900, the town became noted for the saloon fights, brawls between rivermen and lumberjacks, and houses of prostitution. Two of the most noted of these were Dann Dunn, formerly of *Roscommon*, Michigan, and the

Harcourt Brothers, who also operated a saloon and bawdy house. The feud ended with one of the Harcourts being shot by Dunn, and Dunn in turn shot to death by one of the Harcourts. The Harcourts later became respected citizens of the town and held several township offices during the ensuing years.

John Chisholm, now in his seventies and a reporter for *The Muskegon Chronicle*, of that city, said he lived in *Seney* during the days of the Harcourts. *"A neighbor kid I played with was Hurst Harcourt,"* Chisholm said. *"As you perhaps know, it was said in those days that if a man went into a railroad station anywhere in Michigan and asked for a ticket to hell he got a one-way ticket to Seney. My father had gone there as superintendent of schools,"* Chisholm said. The elder Chisholm took the job in *Seney* because the pay was extra good,

Seney's Boot Hill Cemetary, ½ mile south of *Seney* where unknown lumberjacks were buried during the rough and rowdy logging days of the 1890s.
Photo by Roy L. Dodge (1969)

he said, because the town was so tough and it was difficult to find anyone to take the job. Chisholm said the late Governor Chase S. Osborn once told him that the Cleveland-Cliffs Company added to his father's salary to get him to go there.

"As with all such towns, there were many good families there also," he said. *"General O'Connor, who built the Alcan Highway, was about my age and son of a railroad stationmaster (see 1905, Charles O'Connor). And there was Dr. Bohn, who went on to spend many years in Congress, until the F. D. R. tidal wave of 1932."*

The roaring days of *Seney* have been publicized in many newspaper stories and as the subject of chapters in many books, as well as a complete book by a former resident. Today, the Fox River, once the scene of log drives in the 1880s, is

Logging is still an important industry in the U. P. as shown in this picture taken in *Seney* in 1969.   Photo by Roy L. Dodge

a peaceful stream with a pond set aside for trout fishing where only children up to the age of 14 are allowed to fish. Only one or two of the old buildings remain near the river, where the village was once situated and the plank sidewalks elevated on poles or stilts for protection from the spring floods. Today it lies near the junction of M-77 and M-28, where the old logging railroad once connected with the main line and ran to *Grand Marais*, 25 miles north. Thousands of people travel the road each day during the tourist season, most of them unaware of the town's reputation of nearly a century ago.

SMITH CREEK—1910, mail *Hiawatha*.

SMITH'S—Shown on 1905 maps, on a spur of the Manistique & Northern Railroad, about 1 mile west of *Scotts*, south of *Shingleton*.

SOUTH MANISTIQUE—Locally known as *Southtown*. In 1905, a discontinued post office, send mail to *Manistique*.

As told by Ernest Williams, April 25, 1971:

"South Manistique, or South Town as it was generally called, was two miles south of Manistique. The ground was nothing but sand beach and there was no grass growing there. There were board fences around some homes four feet high to keep the sand from blowing into the yards. The wind had filled some yards nearly full of sand and the streets were all sand, loose sand. I don't know how many houses there had been there, as the town was on its last legs when I was a small boy.

286

Across the Soo Line Railroad, ½ mile west of town, there was a spring house and water was piped into town.

The town was owned by Hall & Buell (in 1887, population 300, Hiawatha Township, 2 miles southwest of Manistique, A. C. Hubbell, Postmaster; Samuel G. Doran, justice; and Hall & Buell, lumber manufacturers). They had a very good sawmill, docks, etc. The company dammed the creek for a log pond with a railroad on each side. One reason the town was short-lived was because enough timber was not available. They lumbered near town, then built a branch railroad to Indian Lake, where they had a "pull up" for logs. They owned some stumpage across the lake and rafted it to the pull up where it was loaded on cars and hauled to the pond.

A friend of my folks had a brother and family living there. We had a bronco, named Maud, and he had a horse named Kit. It was in the winter. We used to put the two horses together to do our light farm work. We drove to Southtown (5 miles) and I remember his brother's house in particular. The floor was laid with pine boards 12 inches wide and was always scrubbed snow white.

Several years later, after the available timber was exhausted, the mill at Nahma burned so they bought the mill and moved it to Nahma by water. Before that the mill stood there but they had a night watchman to protect their property. He was a farmer from Thompson who lived near the railroad there. He had a "pede." (This was a hand operated car called a "velocipede" used by section hands on railroads. It had only three wheels, two on the rear and one on the front.) He used to ride the "pede" up the railroad to the Soo Line, then down to Southtown, which was also on the Soo Line. The section foreman caught him and his pede and told him to keep off the Soo Line, so he wrote to Minneapolis requesting permission to use their road, and they also told him to stay off. Well, he didn't. It was on a foggy morning when the accident happened. There was a log house near the railroad on the southtown road. The family was eating breakfast when the passenger train, called "The Flyer," came along at 7 a.m. and screeched to a halt. After breakfast a boy of the family went out to to the crossing and there laid the pede with the small wheel broken off. He thought he could distinguish someone coming down the track in the fog and upon getting closer recognized the owner of the pede. This man always walked a little stoop-shouldered and bending forward, but what the boy saw nearly made him faint. The man was walking with his hands clasped to his stomach and what appeared to be his intestines in his hands. What the boy thought to be his intestines turned out to be a package of link pork sausage he had been carrying when the accident occurred and the sack had busted, letting the sausage hang out.

287

Well, all the houses were either torn down or moved to Manistique, except one. The man who lived in the house was a fisherman and fished with trap nets on Lake Michigan. (See Little Harbor—pirate fisherman). Indian Lake was 1½ miles west. It is about 5½ by 7½ miles of surface and is not a very deep lake. About the deepest spot is 20 feet. It contained yellow perch, walleyes, blue gill, great northern pike, and also sturgeon, some weighing over 100 pounds.

The old fisherman conceived the idea of trap-netting sturgeon in this lake and he had the help of his two grown sons to trap them. One year they earned $1,800 from this illegal operation. A sturgeon that wasn't quite ready to spawn was tied with hay-wire to a root up Smith Creek until she ripened. At the bank the banker asked him what facilities he had to obtain these large checks. The fisherman said that he had a rich uncle in Canada who sent them to him.

During the winter quite a few families had a fish shanty that they lived in across Indian Lake. Once a week they came to town, or when they had a large enough catch of fish to ship to Chicago.

This old fisherman was smart in legal procedures, as he had studied law. Well, one day the game warden arrested him and told him he had to go into town. The man said he wasn't able to walk that far but he owned an easy running sleigh with four-inch runners so the warden took him to town on the sleigh. The man was brought to trial before a Justice of the Peace, pleaded his own case, and was found not guilty of the charges. After the trial he said to the wardern, "Well, you brought me down here. Now how the hell am I going to get back?" He wound up hauling his own sleigh back to his fish shanty.

This man's oldest son worked for the Coffee Fishing Company of Manistique, who operated three steam tugs, "The Berger," the "Alice C.," and the "Anabel." They paid fishermen $60 per month and paid once a month. Most fishermen were drinkers and when they received their pay most of them got tanked up.

There was a saloon where the Ford Garage is now and most of the fishermen stopped there, probably because it was the first saloon up from the dock. The saloon keeper had a tough reputation and always had a couple of hangers-on who were quite handy at rolling customers. After several drinks on an empty stomach the old fisherman reached into his overall hip pocket to buy a drink and his hand went right on through his pocket. Some scoundrel had cut a hole in it and there was no money. The fisherman's credit was no good in the bar and he couldn't get another drink. He went to the toilet and there sat a Finnlander peacemaker drunk and sound asleep. "One good turn deserves another," the fisherman said as he rolled the Finn and returned to the bar with $40. "Be-jeesus it wasn't a total loss any way!" the fisherman remarked as he ordered the bar a round.

Guess my talk about Southtown has come to a close. As I said before, I didn't know too much about the town. There is no evidence now of a town ever being there. The smelt come up the creek to spawn every spring and are up right now. Many people from Manistique dip them to help defray the high cost of living and also have delicious fish to eat."

There is nothing left of the former town today (1971). For many years the beach along Lake Michigan near the site was covered with driftwood made by the millions of slabs dumped into the lake by the sawmills. The sandy area is overgrown with jackpine, poplar and other scrub growths of trees. Some of an old railroad grade is visible in areas and the hollows of a few basements are evident.

SPRUCEVILLE—Shown on 1905 maps, about 5 miles north of *Manistique*, on the old M. & N. Railroad.

STARR—1910, mail *Seney*.

STATION NINE—1910, on the Manistique & Northern Railroad. Mail *Manistique*.

STEUBEN—In 1896, the Chicago Lumber Company built a railroad from *Manistique* to *Indian River*, 20 miles north, and named it *Steuben*. The company built a dam across the river and the railroad was extended to connect with the Duluth, South Shore & Atlantic at *Shingleton*. The settlement took its name because most of the owners of the Chicago Lumber Company and the Wisconsin Land Company came from Steuben County, New York.

Mrs. Agnes McManus, of *Steuben*, has an abstract dating back to 1853. This abstract shows the first owner as a James Haynes. In 1867, the Chicago Lumber Company bought land here with a contract to cut 200 million feet of pine logs.

In 1902, the Manistique & Northwestern Railroad bought the right-of-way for tracks. In 1912, the Consolidated Lumber Company and the White Marble Lime Company bought land for cedar timber. In 1927, the Weston Lumber Company cut timber in the area, and in 1930 the land was put up for sale for nonpayment of taxes. It was purchased by McManus in 1935.

The late Ed Mott, *Steuben* native and owner of a store and antique shop here for many years until his death in 1971, told much of the history of this area. In 1896, *Steuben* had a recorded population of 450 but it must have taken in an area of several miles and included many logging camps, Mott said. Phil Hermann, an old time native, said when he came here, in 1917, there was a hotel, post office, a few log houses and a large barn where the Chicago Lumber Company kept their horses in winters. Some of the homesteaders close by were Abe Hughes, which

289

is now the Blazed Trail Club, and the Hutts, which later became the North Woods Resort on Murphy Lake, and the Buckleys at Loraine Lake, and the Dickinsons at Uno Lake, and the Blushes, at *Steuben*, on Farm Lake. The first homesteader by the name of Mochesney had gone.

Mott said there were many large logging camps close by run by the Chicago Lumber Company, the Buckeye Lumber Company, Pitts Logging Company, and the Long Ear Logging Company. *"The big 'pull up' for logs was located in Steuben and this was the hub for logging camps,"* Mott said. *"The railroad spur here took all the logs out of the river and the spur went to many camps as far distant as 10 miles through dense swamps,"* he said.

During the 1920s the town revived as many families moved here from Kentucky to cut cord wood, as the pine went first, and then the hemlock and finally the hardwood timber.

"During the 20s there were about 40 families here, the store, a hotel, post office, logging camps, and the section gang and a sawmill," Mott said. *"When all the wood was cut the families left and all that remained were the Parks, as Mr. Parks was a trapper and had cabins to rent, the McManus, Motts, Grays, Ulerys and the Hermanns. Mr. Hermann had the store and post office but today all that remains are the old logging memories as all that is left is the Museum & Antique Shop, and a bait store, grocery and gasoline station for the tourists who might be looking for a lot of woods and a place to get away from the fast world of today,"* Mott said.

The *Steuben* school, with less than 20 students, was operating until 1938. The post office was discontinued in 1958, and the old hotel was destroyed by fire in 1936, Mott said.

Mr. Mott spent most of the winter of 1970-71 researching the history of the settlement and passed away a few months later. In July of 1971 an auction of the contents of the Mott Museum and Antique Shop was held, and hundreds of people came from lower Michigan and other states as well to purchase some of the antique cars, artifacts and antiques Mott had collected over the years. Less than a dozen people live in the immediate area today (1972).

Mott took notes on conversations with some of the old timers in the area. His uncle, Cecil Gonder, moved here in 1919. *"There were so many camps around here then that I have forgotten the names and numbers of most of them,"* Gonder said. *"Mrs. Houghson ran the hotel here and a man by the name of Burrell had the store and another store at 'Camp 35,' about 6 miles northwest of here."* Gonder said. *"Pete Golden had a camp about one mile from Steuben but most of the big camps were coming to an end in the 1920s. Hanneman's came here in 1921 and had a sawmill and logging camp, he recalled. The last river drive through Steuben occurred in 1919 for logs, but pulp wood was floated down the river for many years."*

Some of the people who lived here in 1919 were Burrell, Golden, Sparks, Burlin, Boone, Howard, McManus, Matt, Gonders, Houghson, Phil Hermanns, G. Parks, Williams, Stieguils, Scoggs, Lopers, Fred Dale, who had a camp, John Icen, Dewey, Cottenhams, Mills, J. Habbs, and many more that Gonder couldn't remember.

The last sawmill operated here in 1936 and was owned by Jim Adams. Adams took all of the "dead heads" (sunken logs) from the river and let them dry on the bank for about a year, then refloated them down to the old "pull up" and sawed them into lumber. *"I remember it well,"* Mott said, *"as my grandmother boarded all the mill and river men and the railroad workers boarded here too."*

Ten miles from *Steuben* was a small place called *Ten Mile* where logs were taken from the river during the 1900s. An old man lived here in a tiny log house all his life until about 1966, when he died. His father lived there before him and died in the same cabin in 1924, Mott said. Another man, named Amos Crandel, lived in another shack about 1 mile from *Steuben* until he died, in the 1950s.

"An old man named George Foote died at my grandmother's place in the late 1930s (Mrs. Tom McManus). He came here as a young man and home-steaded near a lake at the bottom of the hill from his old place that is named after him," Mott recalled.

THOMPSON—E. L. Thompson, of *Detroit*, was president of the Delta Lumber Company, and the town was named for him. Reached its peak population in the 1880s and at one time had a population of 500 or more. In 1887, described as a settlement 6½ miles southwest of *Manistique*, on Lake Michigan. Population 325. Telephone connection with *Manistique* and *Seney*. Daily mail. Eugene T. Slayton, Postmaster, secretary of the Delta Lumber Company, and Township Supervisor; A. W. Arms, bookkeeper for Delta Lumber Company; David Bouschor, saloon; George Bouschor, livery; N. Cunningham, blacksmith; S. H. Davis & Company, fish, Malcolm McLean, manager; Millard Duel, justice; James Girvan, poundmaster; J. L. Jewell, hotel; Daniel McGinnis, justice; Joseph T. Mason, manager of Delta Lumber Company store; John Neveux, saloon; Gilbert Olson, constable; J. Patterson, general store; Rice & Bouschor, saloon and livery; Robinson, Arms & Company, poultry; Joseph Severs, justice; John Stark, town clerk; Stark & Duell, fishermen; and E. A. Tighe, sawmill.

In 1893, John A. Robinson was Postmaster. Other new business listings, in addition to 1887, were Frank Colby, blacksmith; Tellus Farley, hotel; Dr. W. W. French; Olsen Gilbert, livery; Christ Johnson, saloon; Joseph Mitchell, barber; Orr Brothers & Company, meats.

The story of *Thompson*, slightly shortened, is best told by Ernest Williams, of *Manistique*, one of the few old-timers left who lived in the area. The following is the story as told by Williams:

E. L. Thompson was associated with the Delta Lumber Company of Chicago who built the town. It was a sawmill town with about 500 population, had three streets four blocks long and four cross streets.

There was a company store, a grocery store, two candy stores, (run by Civil War Veterans who continually quarreled). Their stores were only a block apart. A barber shop, three saloons, three churches and a townhall where a dance was held nearly every Saturday night. One time a fellow who had visited in Rapid River announced that he was giving a dance the following Saturday evening with out-of-town music. Everyone thought that would be fine. Saturday came and a crowd had congregated in the hall when the three-piece orchestra came. It was a man, a chair, and an accordion. Boy, could he play, and we all had a good time!

The sawmill had a band saw, a circular saw, and a gang edger and lath mill. The circular saw squared the logs, then they were transferred to the gang edger where quite a few four-foot saws, spaced one and two inches apart, went up and down at a high rate of speed and produced lumber and plank. The mill ran two eleven hour shifts when we went there. Common labor pay was $1.25 per day. This was during the 1893 panic year.

A 20-foot high tramway led to the docks where the lumber was piled in stacks 30 feet high. The docks were the steam boat docks where the Goodrich Lineand the Hart Line brought freight from Chicago and other ports.

My parents bought a cook stove from Montgomery Ward and it came by boat from Chicago. The freight was $1.28. The two Hart Line boats were named "The Harriet" and "The Eugene."

Pine grew in abundance as pine stumps three and four feet across testify. Now this sandy soil is planted to jackpine and Norway pine and is doing nicely. The new plantings are so thick they hide the stumps.

The railroad here was built before the Soo Line was, so all Soo Line trains had to stop at the diamond in the tracks before crossing. In later years the company had 26 miles of track.

In the early days they had a small locomotive they called "the dinkey" that hauled six and seven linkand pin "russells." The logs were secured with a chain over the load connected by a toggle hook. This logging was done on what we called the Delta plains, which produced many blueberries later on. (I picked over a bushel one day when I was 13 years old and sold them for

$1.25—big money!) This log haul was only 1½ miles from town and up to about 6 or 8 miles out. Then they bought a Baldwin locomotive, called "The One Shot." Later they bought a Michigan Central passenger engine. It had three drive wheels on each side and was quite hard on the light steel rails.

Pine lumber and planks with not a pimple or knot sold for $8 per thousand feet over the rail of a boat bound for Chicago. The "Palorov," a steamship, and her twin, "The Delta," made 28 round trips to Chicago in one season. In later years I have seen as many as 10 boats in the harbor waiting to be loaded. They all happened to arrive at the same time.

The Delta Company finally sold out to Triant & Fuller called "The T. & F Ltd." after they had lumbered the cream of the pine timber. The T. & F. Company operated the mill for quite a few years, then shut down after the last of the pine was nearly gone.

Fred Cooper, with the help of Patsy McNamara and others of Manistique, bought it all. Mr. Cooper didn't operate the mill, but did some logging and shipping by rail.

Finally Paul Johnson, of Cadillac, bought the town. He rebuilt the mill one summer and converted to a hardwood mill, bandsaw and circular and lath mill. There was quite a bit of hemlock, "devil's pine" as it was called, farther north. Mr. Johnson repaired the company houses, painted them, and was thinking about building a flooring plant and other products but his health failed him and he died.

A. M. Chesborough, of Emerson, bought. He had other brothers in the lumber business, but bought alone. He slaughtered the hemlock and hardwood to his heart's content, then closed operations. He still owned quite a large stand of timber but sold it to the Buckeye people.

Thompson had two other communities joining it. Swedetown on the south and Dogtown on the west. Swedetown, or Finntown as it was sometimes called, was owned by their tenants who built their houses with five thicknesses of pine lumber and filled in between with pine sawdust. In the summer, when it was hot outside, it was cool inside. In winter, when it was cold, just a small fire in the kitchen was all that was necessary to keep the houses real comfortable.

Dogtown had eight or nine families and each family had a dog or two. The poorer the family was, the more dogs they had. My farm joined Dogtown and a spring creek flows through it where the State Fish Hatchery is located. It was built in 1919. A larger hatchery was built later, where a creek comes out of a hill. These two hatcheries are supposedly the largest in the world. I have caught as many as 10 brook trout on my own property. Also have pastured and winter fed 17 head of cattle and a team of horses on the 40 acres.

When Thompson was young, people bought 40 acres of land and raised a garden. Eventually they cleared a little more and bought a cow, then a horse or team, but most of them worked in the mill. After the mill went out, most of them moved because they were not real farmers. Those who stayed, or most of them, didn't even bother to raise a garden.

In the spring, yellow perch came into the north slip of the harbor. Fishermen sitting two feet apart all caught fish from eight to twelve inches long. In the south pond, where the creek emptied into the pond carrying silt, there were brook trout. The creek, with no rain, had no hiding places for trout, but when the heavy rains came trout went up the creek. One time my aunt and uncle from Flint visited us. After supper, I caught 22 brook trout nine to 12 inches long. The next day I took my uncle with me and caught 17.

One winter we had good skating on the south pond all winter. When it snowed the creek flooded, but one time the wind blew when it snowed and it froze. We went out on the lake past the north dock. It was glare ice and real cold. We took some driftwood and built a fire and skated around it. The ice gave once in a while, but it does that sometimes and is still safe. I became thirsty and jabbed a hole through the ice with my pocket knife. It was about 1½ inches thick. The next morning when I went to school there was no ice in sight. One featherweight skater had skated way out into the darkness, too.

The charts show a stone shoreline at Thompson, but Manistique's water-powered four band saws let their sawdust go into the river and out into the lake. Lumber boats seeing sawdust on the water knew they were getting close to Manistique. This practice was stopped and a burner was built, but Thompson paid dearly, for they had to dredge the harbor. Even the shore line was covered with sawdust and sand. When I was 16 years old, I fired the tug "J. J. Evans" for the Martin Dredge Company of Marinette, Wisconsin.

An old timer once told me of what a hard time they had getting the harbor started. First they tried to drive piling at the end of the steamboat dock. They drove the piling as much as they could, then used pine slabs and interlaced the cable. Next morning the barrier had broken loose and was way out in the lake.

There was always a light at night on the end of the steamboat dock. I was night watchman at the mill for a short time and took care of the light. After cleaning the mill I walked to the end of all the trams and punched a clock. There were two trams ashore and at one there was a dry shed where they stood the clear hardwood lumber on end to dry. It was birds eye and curley birch.

Herman Shinnerman, the Chicago Christmas Tree man, always docked at Thompson and cut trees of spruce and balsam and bought evergreens for decorations. He had a nearly new two-masted schooner, "The Mary Collins," and was coming up the lake when the pilot said, "There's Thompson. I can see the light on the south dock.' What he really saw was a light in an upstairs log cabin ½ mile east of Little Harbor. They went nearly high and dry on the rocky shore.

Mr. Carrington, the soft drink man of Manistique, nearly went broke trying to float the schooner with rope, blocks and teams. It was a total loss. After that, Mr. Shinnerman rented schooners.

One year he came up with his crew on the "Rause Simmons," a three-sticker owned by Captain Nelson. The schooner showed her age slightly. The sailors were Hogan Hoganson, John Doll, Frank the Liar (who figured a lie was much better than the truth), and two or three others. I worked with these men cutting spruce trees northeast of Thompson on what we called the ridges. Smaller trees were tied in bundles of three or five and the larger trees had their limbs tied close to the trunk. Hogan sang all day long, but only one very short song that went something like this: "Vee vere sailing down de fake. De vind vas flowing free. It was on a trip to Buffalo from Mill-wau-kee."

Mr. Shinnerman always donated the tallest Christmas tree he could find to a certain theater in Chicago, for which he was given a box seat in the show house for the season. My father hauled a 35-foot-high balsam tree to the boat for him. He bought evergreens also, to make Christmas wreaths and decorations. He bought 16 foot boards, 12 inches wide, and housed the deck before sailing home. When he reached the dock in Chicago, he installed stoves and hired women to make up the evergreens.

He generally left Thompson about the middle of November. Father asked him why he didn't go home by rail, and Captain Shinnerman said he wouldn't miss the trip by boat for anything in the world. Hogan told me that he was going by rail because all the rats had left the ship at Chicago. That is a bad omen to sailors.

When they were ready to leave, the weather was unsettled, and the saloon keeper had a barometer that had been his father's, a retired lake captain. He called it his "gee-whall-iker." Once they thought it was out of whack and sent it away to be repaired. The company said they had never seen one like it and knew nothing about it. It was accurate and the saloonkeeper warned Captain Shinnerman about the weather but he only laughed. They set sail in the evening with a stiff breeze blowing, and that was the last anyone saw of them. Fishermen later got their nets tangled in Christmas trees off Wind Point, Wisconsin.

After the boat disappeared, Mrs. Shinnerman came up for a few years and shipped a limited amount of greens and trees by rail. She told me that Hogan had been killed in a barroom brawl after he returned to Chicago.

Thompson's hotel changed hands several times. The last owner was an Irishman. He painted the building and in bold green letters had a sign painted across the front, "The Shamrock Hotel." There was a drilled well in front of the hotel where many got their drinking water and there was a horse trough on the outside.

About a mile toward Manistique was a spring. This was curbed up about five feet high and piped into town. There were three spring houses in town. In the country, any well dug 20 feet deep gave good water, but they all dried up and now a well has to be driven more than 75 feet.

The company boarding house was a place where men congregated nearly every evening until 11 p.m. The yard foreman, a witty Irishman with a haywire mustache, was there when the master mechanic walked in and washed his hands at the sink. In looking over the locomotive he discovered an important inch bolt missing, and had to turn a new one in the lathe. After washing up, he said, "That was the funniest thing I ever saw. The hole was there but the bolt was gone." The yard foreman spoke up and said, "It would have been a damn sight funnier if the bolt had been there and the hole was gone!"

The creek ran past the round house where they kept the locomotives and was joined to the blacksmith shop.

When lumbering in the Thunder Lake country during the summer, they used "high wheels." The two wheels were 10 feet across with an axle and a tongue. That was about all high wheels consisted of. The wheels were six feet apart. From seven to 10 logs were piled upon the axle, a chain was wrapped around them, secured to the axle, and when the tongue was brought down this swung the logs clear of the ground, or almost so, leaving the back of the logs bouncing lightly on the ground after the team was hitched to the tongue to haul them. This swaying contraption was hard on the horses' necks.

The 4th of July was a big day in Thompson for many years. There were bareback horse races, bicycle races, boat races between boys and girls, sack races, three-legged races, egg rolling, and a penny scramble. About the biggest celebration I ever saw there was in 1898 when the storekeeper erected a plank platform and had a piano on the platform, with singing and speeches. The master mechanic's wife recited Abraham Lincoln's Gettysburg Address. Another lady sang, "What did Dewey do to them? Oh, what did Dewey do? He cleaned them up so thoroughly, he only left a f-e-w." Several places sold ice cream and there was a bowery built for the day with little hardwood trees and brush for walls. They danced all afternoon and evening. It was a very hot day, and I gulped so much ice cream I became very sick. This left me with a severe pain and I was sick for about two weeks.

When A. M. Chesborough was going strong, he bought a trim three-masted schooner called "John Mee." The name was later changed to "Edward Skele." He also bought a two-sticker, "The J. V. Taylor," which had a Grand Haven rig to help power the schooner. A Grand Haven rig is a big sheet of canvas that is raised between the two masts to catch the breeze and help propel the boat.

The Skele was piloted by Captain Kittleson, of Milwaukee. The Taylor was skippered by his son, Cpt. Jake Kittleson. The boats hauled lumber to Chicago.

(I made a trip to Chicago once in the month of July. There was no head wind and no wind at all most of the time. One day the sky got black and anything could happen, so they raised the centerboard, but in a short time the skies cleared. On a Sunday we laid near the pier at Milwaukee with all sails up and laid there for four hours. It took five days to make the trip. With a good breeze we would easily make it in 18 hours.)

I told you what a time they had anchoring the first crib on the steam boat dock. The docks and slips, with no lumber to hold them down, were soon no more. The end of the north dock went down and finally, after a few years, the crib at the end of the steamboat dock went out, so now there is no evidence of any docks having been there. The sawdust that had to be dredged is also gone, and the shore line is limestone for ¼ mile, just as the charts said.

There is a nice little park ½ mile north of Thompson with a flowing well, picnic tables, and accommodations along a nice sandy beach where many people swim in the summer.

One-half mile south of Thompson, at the John Starks farm, is Miami Beach, another beautiful spot that has been improved.

Coho salmon were introduced to the Thompson fish hatchery with eggs from the west a few years ago. After they hatched they were planted here and in other streams. They return from Lake Michigan to spawn after two or three years. Now in the fall you can see them jumping off shore. Rainbow, German Browns, steelheads, and brook trout are also caught here. As many as 300 fishermen have been wading there at one time since the Coho were planted. Fishermen come here from all over the world.

Captain Tighe once had a little sawmill on the shore of Lake Michigan, ¼ mile south of Swedetown. There were several houses and a dock. I don't know if this was before the Delta Company arrived or not, but when I was a small boy there were two cribs extending out into the lake. A few years later, Mr. Tighe moved to Cooks, 12 miles southwest, and built another mill on a frog pond lake which bears his name, Tighes Lake. There was a store at Tighes mill on Lake Michigan, owned by John Patterson. Patterson later owned his own store in Thompson, and later took over the company store here.

At the south end of Swedetown, also on the lake, was another lumber and shingle mill owned by Joe Savage. It ran for a few years, then vanished.

The Cheeseborough Company sold the big "Three Spot" engine and tried out a number four, which was also too heavy for the light weight steel rails. They then bought a light two-drive wheel locomotive that had been used on the Manistique and Lake Superior Railroad, called "The Haywire." This locomotive was speedy and that is where it got its power.

Five miles south of Thompson, at Bersaw Creek on the lake, the Bonifas' of Garden owned a sawmill. It was operated by a brother-in-law, Dick Shires. They lumbered timber nearby for a time, then disappeared. The two-masted schooner, "The Arkansas," drug anchor and went ashore there and was a total loss. She was captained by Captain Blake. Another time a sailor who had gone overboard from a boat on Lake Michigan drifted ashore there. The body was badly decomposed.

In 1896 Henry Bradshaw, a photographer at Thompson, took a picture of the town from the top of a balsam tree he had sawed off. The tree stood on top of school house hill. The photo is in the Mincoff studio in Manistique at this time.

The remains of these old lime kilns still stand about two miles east of *Manistique* in Schoolcraft county near the former settlement known as *Cherry Valley*. Lime kilns were important during the early days to supply mortar for building.
Photo by Roy L. Dodge (1971)

A few houses remain along the lake shore in Thompson today and there is a post office, located in one of the old store buildings with a "Beer & Wine Takeout" sign; not much remains. One of the former main streets, now over grown to brush and weeds, is lined with giant poplar trees, and a large school building stands on a hill overlooking the lake, windows boarded, and abandoned.

In recent years there is much activity during the Coho runs, and Thompson may make a revival as a tourist village within the next few years, but the old boom town of yesteryear is no more.

WALSH—The station here opened on the D. M. & M. Railroad in 1886 for loading logs. First called *Eklund*, for the first Postmaster in July of 1927. On August 16, 1927 was renamed *Walsh*, for a local lumberman, and operated until June 30, 1933. After that date mail *Seney*. In 1927 was located on M-28 highway.

WARDS—Shown on 1905 maps, on the old railroad that went from *Seney* to *Grand Marais*, about 5 miles south of *Grand Marais*.

WHITEDALE—Was the name of the railroad station for *Gulliver*, and *Gulliver* was the post office. 1910, population 75, mail *Gulliver*. *Gulliver* was a post office from December, 1889 with Alba Monroe as first Postmistress. Named *Whitedale* for her as *alba* is Latin for white.

1918, population given as 100, on the Soo Line, 1½ miles from *Gulliver*. J. A. Anderson, hotel; T. A. Ghent, general store; A. Gondreu, fisherman; Hawkins Brothers, cranberry growers; Frank House, cranberries; and S. Johnson, fisherman.

Whitedale is shown on 1899 railroad maps, between McDonald Lake and Marblehead Spur and on Lake Michigan.

Other business places in the early 1900s were: Louis Leslie, general store, and Mrs. Mary L. Ghent, general store.

In 1927, William Bowman, general store, and O. O. White, general store. *"Gulliver is its post office."*

BIBLIOGRAPHY

HISTORY OF THE UPPER PENINSULA

"Michigan Fur Trade," by Paul Wesley Ivey, 1919, State Printers, Lansing, Mich.; "Michigan Manual - 1899"; "The People of Michigan," by George P. Graff, State Library Occasional Paper No. 1, 1970; "Michigan - A Guide to The Wolverine State," 1941, published by the Michigan State Administrative Board (W. P. A.); "Early Days of the Lake Superior Copper Country," by Orrin W. Robinson, 1938, 45-page booklet privately printed; "Early Post Offices of Marquette County," unpublished paper by Ernest H. Rankin, former president of the Marquette County Historical Society, 1964; "Michigan and The Old Northwest," by Luke Schreer, 1945.

RAILROADS OF THE UPPER PENINSULA

"Michigan Manual"—1893—1901— 1919; "The People of Michigan," by George P. Graff, 1970; Ernest Rankin, Marquette Historical Society; "Early Days of The Lake Superior Copper Country," by Orrin W. Robinson; "Rand-McNally Shippers Guide of Michigan," 1912.

HISTORY OF ISLE ROYALE

Information by Hugh Beattie, Superintendent, Isle Royal National Park, Houghton, Mich.; "Calling Your Way," July 1971, by Michigan Bell Telephone Company; "Early Days of The Lake Superior Copper Country," "Do You Know," pub. by *Booth Newspapers*, Inc., 1937. "Michigan Gazetteer and Business Directory," pub. by R. L. Polk & Company, Detroit, Mich., 1877—1879—1887, and other years; "Michigan Manual," 1881-1899; and *The Bay City Times*, August 27 and June 6, 1971.

GHOST TOWN AND COUNTY HISTORIES

"Michigan Gazetteer and Business Directory," by R.L. Polk Company, Detroit, Michigan for years 1872 through 1927; "Rand McNally County and Township, Map, Directory and Shippers Guide for 1910, 1912" by Rand, McNally & Company, Chicago, Illinois; "Bark River Centennial," 1972; "Gleason's Michigan Green Guide," by Gleason Map Company of Chicago and Denver, 1916? (undated); "History of Michigan Counties" pamphlet published by Michigan Department of State, September 1968; "Baraga Lumberjack Days—Vol. 1, 1971," booklet published by the *L'Anse Sentinel*; "Michigan Conservation Magazine," issues from 1964 to 1968; "Bay Furnace," published by U. S. Forest Service, Munising, Michigan, undated bulletin; "Michigan Place Names" by Walter Romig of Grosse Pointe, Michigan, 1972? (undated); "The Baraga County Area," Chamber of Commerce information phamplet; *Daily Mining Gazette*, July 19, 1971; "L'Anse Centennial," booklet, 1971; *Evening News*, Sault Ste. Marie, August 23, 1971; "Historical Highlights of Delta County, Michigan," leaflet published by the Delta County Historical Society, January 1958; "The Century Book," Escanaba Centennial Book, 1863-1963; "Michigan's Old Inn," booklet privately printed by John P. Schuch, Saginaw, Mich., President of the Michigan State Historical Society, 1945; "History of Fayette and Fairbanks Township," mimeograph manuscript by Adele Elliott, of Fayette, Mich.; personal correspondence with Calvin J. Ries, Norway, Mich., March 1971; Map and Historical Data of Dickinson County by Dean Turner of N. D. Turner Associates, Inc., Iron Mountain, Mich.; "Ghost Mines of The Gogebic Range," Youngstown Steel Bulletin, by Victor Lemmer, October 1966; "Michigan Postal History of Gogebic County," mimeo of 9 pages by Kenneth Priestly, Vassar, Mich.; "Michigan Natural Resources Magazine," November & December 1969; *Bay City Times*, September 19, 1971; *Detroit Sunday News*, page three, July 18, 1971 (out-state ed.); "Mining in Keweenawland and Treatment of Ores," 12 page mimeo by Calumet Division of Calumet & Hecla, Inc., 1966; "Daily Mining Gazette"—Green sheet, July 10, 1971 and July 17, 1971; "Calumet Township Centennial 1866-1966," souvenir program book; "Schoolcraft Township Centennial," by G. Walton Smith, ed., 1966; *The Herald Leader*, Menominee, Mich., April 5, 1966 and April 13, 1966; *Marquette Centennial 1849-1949*, George N. Skrubb, chairman; "100 Years of History," L'Anse-Skanee Centennial booklet, 1971, by the Baraga County Historical Society; "Fosters Book of Names," 1964, unpublished, bound manuscript by Ted Foster of Lansing, Mich.; "Michigan Flags and History," pub. by J. L. Hudson Company, Detroit, Mich., 1940; "Handy Book for Genealogists, 4th Edition," Everton Publishers, Logan, Utah, 1962; "Before The Bridge," pub. by the Kiwanis Club of St. lgnace, Mich., 1957; "Sault Ste. Marie Tricentennial Program 1668-1968"; "Michigan Conservation Department County Maps, 1953; "The Department of Conservation State of Michigan, 4th Biennial Report, 1927-1928"; "Problems in Lumber Distribution," published in Chicago, 111, 1916; "Primer of Michigan History," by Wm. J. Cox, Lansing, Mich., 1903; "Michigan Pioneers," 1937 Centennial by J. L. Hudson Company, Detroit, Mich.; also personal correspondence and interviews with many Upper Peninsula natives mentioned in various places throughout the book.

The Author
Harrison, Mich.
September 4, 1972

301